A Research Agenda for Environmental Economics

Elgar Research Agendas outline the future of research in a given area. Leading scholars are given the space to explore their subject in provocative ways, and map out the potential directions of travel. They are relevant but also visionary.

Forward-looking and innovative, Elgar Research Agendas are an essential resource for PhD students, scholars and anybody who wants to be at the forefront of research.

Titles in the series include:

A Research Agenda for Global Crime
Edited by Tim Hall and Vincenzo Scalia

A Research Agenda for Transport
Policy
*Edited by John Stanley and David A.
Hensher*

A Research Agenda for Tourism and
Development
*Edited by Richard Sharpley and David
Harrison*

A Research Agenda for Housing
Edited by Markus Moos

A Research Agenda for Economic
Anthropology
Edited by James G. Carrier

A Research Agenda for Sustainable Tourism
*Edited by Stephen F. McCool and Keith
Bosak*

A Research Agenda for New Urbanism
Edited by Emily Talen

A Research Agenda for Creative Industries
*Edited by Stuart Cunningham and Terry
Flew*

A Research Agenda for Military
Geographies
Edited by Rachel Woodward

A Research Agenda for Sustainable
Consumption Governance
Edited by Oksana Mont

A Research Agenda for Migration and
Health
*Edited by K. Bruce Newbold and Kathi
Wilson*

A Research Agenda for Climate Justice
Edited by Paul G. Harris

A Research Agenda for Federalism
Studies
Edited by John Kincaid

A Research Agenda for Media Economics
Edited by Alan B. Albarran

A Research Agenda for Environmental
Geopolitics
Edited by Shannon O'Lear

A Research Agenda for Studies of
Corruption
*Edited by Alina Mungiu-Pippidi and Paul
M. Heywood*

A Research Agenda for Digital Politics
Edited by William H. Dutton

A Research Agenda for Environmental
Economics
Edited by Matthias Ruth

A Research Agenda for Environmental Economics

Edited by

MATTHIAS RUTH

Pro-Vice-Chancellor for Research, University of York, UK

Elgar Research Agendas

Edward Elgar
PUBLISHING

Cheltenham, UK • Northampton, MA, USA

Published by
Edward Elgar Publishing Limited
The Lypiatts
15 Lansdown Road
Cheltenham
Glos GL50 2JA
UK

Edward Elgar Publishing, Inc.
William Pratt House
9 Dewey Court
Northampton
Massachusetts 01060
USA

A catalogue record for this book
is available from the British Library

Library of Congress Control Number: 2020932121

This book is available electronically in the **Elgar**online
Economics subject collection
DOI 10.4337/9781789900057

ISBN 978 1 78990 004 0 (cased)
ISBN 978 1 78990 005 7 (eBook)

Typeset by Servis Filmsetting Ltd, Stockport, Cheshire
Printed and bound by CPI Group (UK) Ltd, Croydon, CR0 4YY

Contents

Contributors

EDITOR

Ruth, Matthias – University of York, UK

CONTRIBUTORS

Andersen, Dana C. – University of Alberta, Edmonton, Canada

Bramoullé, Yann – Aix-Marseille University, Marseille, and Centre national de la recherche scientifique, Paris, France

Breckenridge, Lee P. – Northeastern University, Boston, Massachusetts, USA

Faber, Malte – Heidelberg University, Germany

Frick, Marc – Heidelberg University, Germany

Kander, Astrid – Lund University, Sweden

Kemp, René – UNU-MERIT and MSI, Maastricht University, the Netherlands

Kolbe, Jens – Technische Universität Berlin, Berlin, Germany

Krekel, Christian – London School of Economics, UK

Malghan, Deepak – Indian Institute of Management, Bangalore

Norgaard, Richard B. – University of California, Berkeley, USA

Orset, Caroline – Université Paris-Saclay, AgroParisTech, Paris, France

Ramani, Shyama V. – UNU-MERIT, Maastricht University, the Netherlands

Rubio-Varas, M. d. Mar – Universidad Publica de Navarra, Pamplona, Spain

Sager, Jalel – University of California, Berkeley, USA

Sagoff, Mark – George Mason University, Fairfax, Virginia, USA

Sers, Martin R. – York University, Canada

Stern, David I. – The Australian National University, Canberra

Thampapillai, Dodo J. – National University of Singapore and The Australian National University, Canberra

van Leeuwen, Eveline S. – Wageningen University, the Netherlands

Victor, Peter A. – York University, Canada

1 The roads less traveled

Matthias Ruth

1.1 A call for exploration

Environmental economics has, in principle, invaluable contributions to make to the health and wellbeing of people and the environment within which they live. It is a discipline concerned with the material and energy sources of our lifestyles, and the biophysical implications of our production and consumption choices. The conversion of materials and energy for the creation and delivery of desired goods and services contributes to and enhances livelihoods and standards of living, and also lies at the heart of all environmental problems. One could even argue that, because of the central role the transformation of environmental goods and services plays in fueling our economies and supporting our lifestyles, environmental economics does, and must, lie at the center of any endeavor to sustain the human enterprise; it cannot come as an afterthought, once other economic and policy issues are addressed.

Undoubtedly, though, insights from environmental economics rarely find themselves as preconditions under which other decisions are made. Analysis of and decision making on environmental issues are typically perceived as separable from other issues society needs to tackle. And such separation has not (yet) been perceived as a challenge to the longevity of the economic growth and development agenda that dominates economic policy. Rather, as environmental issues have been relegated to the sidelines of both the worlds of economics and of policy, unprecedented increases in wealth have been observed. Even in societies with much reduced access to that wealth and wealth generation potential, life expectancies, literacy rates and many other indicators of quality of life have, in aggregate, improved. So, why argue for a more central role of environmental economics in economics more generally and, more practically, in investment and policy making?

By most measures, many environmental conditions have worsened – ranging from fundamental disruptions of the global climate and their associated manifestations in the forms of increased frequency and severity of extreme weather conditions, fires, and rising sea levels, to severe reductions in the biodiversity that is so central to maintaining the fabric on which life on Earth, and thus also our food supplies, depends. Many more examples of such backlashes of environmental change on societies and economies could be listed here. The upshot is simple: Environmental degradation, sooner or later, comes back to affect us – be it in the form of direct impacts on our health or the indirect impacts we experience as ever more resources and energy need to be diverted to combat environmental insults, or because the loss of environmental quality deprives us of the joys and wonders that have previously come from living in a world of cleaner air and water for example, friendlier climate conditions, and habitats rich and diverse in the species they harbor.

While it has become clearer for decades that economic decisions must be judged against the backdrop of environmental performance, the implications of that observation for economic analysis and decision making have been less nuanced. For example, in the wake of two world wars, economic policy was largely oriented towards increasing economic output. New and more infrastructure enabled more rapid movement of people, raw materials, energy, water and other essentials for production. Expanded educational and health services improved the productivity of workers. A growing basket of affordable goods and services spread, in tangible ways, wealth into households, whetting their appetite for more.

Growing incomes and an expanding technological base provided households and firms with improved resources and abilities to prepare for, or respond to, undesirable conditions: people buying products that replaced previously available environmental goods and services, such as water filters to make up for a loss of clean water, or insurance against flooding in areas where previously ecosystems provided adequate flood control; or paying for advanced skills and education not just to better their position in an increasingly competitive work environment but to continue to expand their consumption, and thus improve their real or perceived standing in society; firms penetrating new markets locally or globally to diversify their resource base or expand into new areas in which to generate revenue streams; or public, private and non-profit entities providing services to combat droughts, wildfires, rising sea levels, invasive species and other ramifications of human-induced environmental changes. In short, economic growth has largely been perceived as a means to address a multitude of challenges, including the ones caused by economic growth. Such thinking can likely not be carried forward as critical thresholds in environmental performance are reached and surpassed.

The notion of environmental thresholds, and more generally the fact that many environmental systems must be maintained whole in some form, poses challenges for the kind of marginal analysis so common in economics: below a critical size or nutrient loading, a lake ceases to function as a lake; and beyond a level of fragmentation, a wetland stops providing its water purification and flood control functions. The analytical instruments that permeate the discipline do not readily lend themselves to the many real problems environmental economics must address.

In recent years, environmental economics, as an academic discipline, has become increasingly sophisticated in its treatment of environmental issues and the responses to them. One direction for improvement is associated with advanced mathematical prowess and expanded modeling capacities used to explore interactions between the economy and its biophysical environment. Research in this arena largely conforms to the standards and expectations of traditional economics, deploying and refining the tools of the trade that also proliferate other fields of the economics discipline. Computable general equilibrium modeling, behavioral economics, and game theory are just a few examples of such popular approaches. Compiling *A Research Agenda for Environmental Economics* could easily draw on myriad authors engaged in these refinements and help point towards a future that is shaped by the incremental advances along existing trajectories. For this volume, I have chosen a more provocative approach, and instead turned to both experts within environmental economics and experts outside – researchers who are deeply knowledgeable of the challenges associated with conceptualizing, modeling and analyzing human–environment interactions and who understand the implications of such work for decision making at both micro and macro scales. The goal has been twofold – to question basic premises and point towards improvements, and to highlight through select examples the level of logic and analysis that must be brought to bear.

Of course, environmental economics is only one of the academic voices at the table of environmental analysis and decision making. If its point merely is to provide analyses – however sophisticated – within the echo chamber of its own peer group, then connecting with others may indeed be a distraction. In contrast, if there is at least some ambition to bring about solutions to the truly pressing and emerging environmental challenges that have begun to undermine economic prosperity, health and life itself, then an environmental economics that resonates with the theories and constructs of other disciplines may find itself as a valuable ally in problem solving. But, even without that ambition, those in the discipline who have begun to incorporate, for example, more physical or biological reality into their models have also differentiated their research from that of the masses, created a niche for themselves and often found it highly intellectually, if not professionally or socially, rewarding to embrace more of the complexities of human–environment interactions in their analyses than typically done.

1.2 Where to go from here?

One of the challenges for environmental economics stems from the fact that many of the environmental goods and services on which production and consumption depend do not have prices associated with them. Although that challenge has long been recognized – resulting in proposals, for example, to place levies on actions that result in undesirable outcomes or to provide subsidies that help avoid or negate them – the basic instrument set to overcome market failures has largely been market-focused. With markets in place, prices emerge that help reconcile competing interests and shepherd decisions towards Pareto-efficient outcomes. Among the many potential problems associated with this expansion of conventional economics thinking into the realm of environmental decision making, the following two may be worth highlighting.

First, as the Austrian School of Economics repeatedly emphasized, "[b]uyers can see (some of) the prices at which some sellers are willing to sell, and sellers can see (some of) the prices at which buyers are willing to buy, but there is no information available to anyone about an equilibrium price" (Holcombe 2014, p. 12). The absence of global (conceptually, geographically and/or across time periods) equilibrium prices implies that local conditions dominate outcomes. Yet, actions that lead to local optima may not be consistent with actions to be taken when a larger set of buyer and seller interests are to be considered, when consequences are felt across geographies and over (long) periods of time. Yet, these are the very features that plague current environmental decision making.

A second and closely related problem stems from the fact that prices are not just the product of market interactions, but at a deeper level the result of historical and social conditions within which markets operate. Assuming well-functioning markets, rising prices would be associated with increases in the scarcity of a resource and stimulate a decline in demand and a search for alternatives. Where unintended consequences of production and consumption are encountered, externalities may be internalized to adjust prices and the signals they give to change behaviors and technologies. But what if the world is more complex than presumed here? What if prices are not only the product of rational economic decision making and instead reflect deep-seated social tensions and long-overlooked environmental constraints? For example, in societies in which women and children hold limited rights for self-expression and self-determination, the wages paid to them for their labor will be depressed. In places where environmental standards are low, resource extraction and environmental pollution may cause harms that remain unaccounted for in economic decision making. The prices of goods and services in conditions of social and environmental exploitation are then not worth much with respect to their ability to guide economic decisions towards optimal outcomes (Røpke 1999; Ruth 2018). More likely, they will entrench unsustainable practices. Generally, prices may send flawed signals to decision makers, and as a consequence may be inadequate instruments to guide production and consumption choices towards desirable outcomes.

To more satisfactorily tackle, as an academic discipline and as a guide for real-world investment and policy making, the unique challenges that come from reconciling environmental change with economic change, environmental economics will need to simultaneously pursue two agendas. One of these concerns the true integration of insights from the physical and life sciences into models of production, consumption, environmental impact and feedback to the economy. The other must focus on the "human factors" – issues ranging from behaviors of individuals to institutional (including ethical and legal) considerations and the macro contexts from which they stem, such as the historical, cultural and social fabric within which people conceive of and address the challenges to which they must rise.

The first of these concerns, namely how to better integrate biophysical insights within environmental economics, is motivated by a range of observations. For example, if standard models of the conversion of materials and energy violate such fundamentals as the second law of thermodynamics, how can they be meaningful in guiding production or emission reduction decisions? If the conversion of materials and energy generates waste products with adverse impacts on human health and environmental quality, and those externalities manifest themselves over decades, can internalization be done in a timely enough fashion to be meaningful to those affected, not just as a conceptual but as a real solution to the problems at hand? Or shouldn't the models of environmental economics at the outset embed the biophysical information needed to anticipate harm? To pursue such a broader mandate for environmental economics requires much deeper collaboration with other disciplines to assure that the pathways by which economic decisions translate into impact are adequately captured, or that, at a minimum, the uncertainties surrounding such pathways are properly acknowledged.

Similarly, a macroeconomics that is built on the presumption that natural capital (soils, forests and oceans, for example) at best plays a marginal role in the generation of welfare woefully understates humanity's dependence on the environment to assimilate waste, and to provide the diversity and richness of species on which nutrient cycling, primary production and thus food supplies depend. It neglects the importance of stabilizing the climate within ranges to which social and economic processes have been calibrated for centuries. And none of these calls for fundamental reform of the discipline mentioned so far even cover non-utilitarian aspects of the environment, such as the contributions scenic beauty and tranquility may make to people's wellbeing, or the inspiration that may come from being in nature and which has found so many expressions in music and the visual arts, celebrated in concert halls, theaters and museums as cultural milestones of our societies.

1.3 Appreciating the ethical, political and legal landscape

In a diverse set of contributions – from women and men in both the northern and southern hemispheres, the worlds of academics and implementation, the field of economics and beyond – this volume focuses on what environmental economics has been, and must be, as humanity enters a new era of total dominance over all biogeochemical cycles, all species, and at every location on the globe. Mark Sagoff begins, in Chapter 2, by questioning the very tenets of conventional environmental economics: the notion that *utility* or *benefit* can be measured, compared between individuals and aggregated over society as a whole; and that the maximization of *social welfare*, perceived as the collective articulation of the benefits to individuals, is indeed an ethically desirable goal of society. The ability to measure benefit, in turn, is the basis on which to compare alternative actions, such as investment decisions or policy interventions to achieve more efficient outcomes. And the concept of social welfare allows for the identification of actions that would allow it to be optimized, given the very preferences on which welfare is defined. In short, the concepts of utility and benefit, and their measurement, provide the cornerstone for the use of economic analysis in decision making and for policy guidance.

By focusing on markets, and the prices that are determined in them, as the mechanisms with which to promote optimality, environmental economics must treat a wide range of environmental goods and services – from soils and biodiversity to water purification, flood control and climate stability – much like ordinary commodities such as toothpaste, shoe laces, ballistic missiles and insurance schemes. Of course, no real markets exist formally for many of the environmental goods and services over which decisions must be made. However, in their absence, the existence and workings of markets may be inferred through a series of thought experiments in which people would be asked their willingness to pay for a good or service, or their willingness to accept that harm is done to the environment. Aside from the problems associated with the establishment of prices as neutral measures of value, or the fact that many environmental goods and services cannot be parsed into their constituent elements – no flood control of a wetland without adequate species diversity above and below ground, for example – or the presumption that individuals indeed are able to consistently judge the trade-offs they face, estimates of willingness-to-pay and willingness-to-accept have become mainstays in cost-benefit analysis. They enable the discipline to draw from its tool chest the methods and models of market analysis. What it means to arrive in this way at an "optimal outcome", though, likely differs when beginning with a theory of the social good and analyses of what makes investment and policy decisions more effective rather than more efficient.

Beyond a fundamental rethinking of the theoretical foundations of environmental economics, Sagoff offers very practical guidance to those in the field. Understand and embrace the nuances that characterize, for example, the industries converting environmental goods and services, the technologies they use and the regulations that govern them – rather than begin with abstract mathematical constructs that are largely ignorant of those nuances! And attend to the social and technological trends that shape society, and thus the environment, such as the proliferation of artificial intelligence, increasing urbanization, demographic transition and aging, or rapid income redistribution within countries and across the globe, to name just a few. It is these practical, empirical issues that will help assure relevance of the discipline and those practicing it. The call for attention to many of these issues that shape human prosperity also reverberates throughout subsequent chapters of this volume.

Directly connecting with the observation that human–environment interactions manifest themselves in complex ways across time and geographies, and that conventional notions of optimality are flawed, Malte Faber and Marc Frick (Chapter 3) write of the importance of ignorance, responsibility and power of judgment as essential to the analysis of environmental problems. The conceptual and political foundation of environmental economics proposed by them is informed by the biophysical principles mentioned above – specifically the laws of thermodynamics that govern the conversion of materials and energy, and according to which any such conversion inevitably results in the joint production of (undesirable) waste materials and energy, whose recapture requires further resource expenditures.

At a fundamental physical level, the laws of thermodynamics also place economic action along the continuum of time, given the irreversibility associated with the generation of waste from material and energy transformations. But there are other notions of time, such as those associated with evolutionary changes – that are themselves governed, of course, by physical laws – and which explicitly highlight the importance of novelty for any understanding of human–environment interactions, and the admission that surprises may challenge conventional wisdom.

Such a world, characterized by fundamental uncertainty and surprise, is very different from the world of conventional environmental economics where individuals, and the markets in which they act, behave in the fashion of Newtonian mechanics. Instead of maximizing an objective function (social welfare, for example), responsible action, informed by ethical reasoning, must guide the trade-off between desired outcomes on the one hand and, on the other, the many, often diffuse and little-understood, by-products that have impact on environment and society for a potentially long time to come.

Faber and Frick thus contrast the traditional *homo oeconomicus*, who is interested in the short term, with *homo politicus*, who is interested in justice, the common good and the long-term, sustainable state of natural living conditions. Heeding Sagoff's advice, they analyze the performance of the soda-chlorine industry over its roughly 300-year history, with an eye towards the roles individual inventors and institutions have played in not only creating new products and markets but also a host of environmental challenges that, themselves, had to be addressed with new technologies and regulations. All this, of course, has been characterized by considerable uncertainties and surprises along the way, which would have rendered any attempt at formal optimization irrelevant to the individual decisions that needed to be made at any given point in time or any given place. What it calls for, instead, is attention to the condition of the whole, the political community and the common good.

Returning to the recognition that the economy is a thermodynamically open subsystem of the larger ecosystems from which materials and energy are extracted and to which waste and heat are released, Deepak Malghan explores the relationship between the many competing needs of humans and how these may indeed be met (Chapter 4). He emphasizes that the choice between competing ends is inherently a moral exercise, not simply a process by which preferences are satisfied. In contrast, the traditional model of monetary exchanges, which dominates standard economics, emphasizes efficiency and optimality; it perceives social and political processes, as well as the physical environment, as separate and separable from the self-regulating processes of the market place. Malghan argues for a more prominent role of theories and methods from political economy in the treatment of human–environment interaction and the kind of new embedded ethics called for by Peter Brown and Geoffrey Garver (2009) that extends the focus on efficiency to include scale and justice as important determinants for long-term viable activities: the scale of the human enterprise relative to the environment's ability to provide goods and services; and attention to the distribution of the desired and undesired by-products across society.

Emphasizing the interplay of economic decisions, the workings of institutions and changes in the biophysical environment, Chapter 5, by Lee Breckenridge, explores the roles that environmental economics can have in evaluating institutional frameworks, and in particular the governance mechanisms that enable, limit and otherwise configure powers and responsibilities of owners, operators and regulatory authorities in organizing the ownership, management, exploitation and protection of the environment to serve societal goals. Understanding how property rights are formed, articulated and managed is central in this context. Although much of environmental economics presumes market-based exchanges to take place against the backdrop of given property rights, allowing for the appropriation and exchange of environmental goods and services, property rights are far from static and do change as economic growth and development, expectations and environmental change unfold. Property regimes are public goods that require collective action to define and operate, and evolve with their institutional underpinnings. The protocols that are established to monitor and enforce boundaries of property rights, track ownership over time and recognize and implement terms of contracts are key components of a market system, which in turn must evolve as protocols change.

The co-evolution of property rights and markets is essential to the calibration processes by which long-range repercussions in the coupled human–natural system must be addressed. In Breckenridge's words: "By looking closely at how human systems align and coordinate with the functioning of biophysical systems, economic research can illuminate, in effect, the design of institutions that represent successful examples of collective action to organize and control human behavior in interactive relationships with ecosystems." One goal of such alignment is the creation of resilient socio-economic systems, i.e. finding ways in which impacts of adverse environmental conditions and shocks on society can be minimized. Striving for resilience is a particular challenge in light of the considerable uncertainties and surprises that inevitably plague the coupled human–environment system as thresholds are approached and surpassed.

To what extent can markets promote resilience, with their anchor in defined property rights and the biases that come from adjusting to past and current signals on system behavior? To what extent does the pursuit of resilience promote sustainability, given that the material and energy needed to maintain infrastructures (hard and soft) may themselves contribute to the very environmental changes against which society intends to protect itself? How does one go about creating the kind of far-sighted institutions that reconcile historical experiences, and pressing and emerging social needs and interests, with long-term viable outcomes?

Clearly, economics in itself has been ill-suited to promote resilience and sustainability. What will be needed is an infusion of the moral and ethical imperatives of which Sagoff, Faber and Frick have written, and an interplay with the evolution of institutional and legal contexts within which markets must function. Experiences from the United States, for example, clearly illustrate the shortcomings of environmental policies that are, to a considerable extent, shaped by strong concepts of private property and persistent opposition to laws and regulations that challenge the interests of the establishment. As a consequence, the evolution of institutions to mitigate or prepare for environmental changes and shocks has been limited at best. Staggering evidence for deficiencies in policy-driven institutional responses to climate change, for example, can be found both on the mitigation and adaptation side of the problem – there are no federal policies that curb greenhouse gas emissions, and land use laws continue to impede the kind of land management practices needed for effective flood control. However, the United States, unfortunately, is not an outlier. Other countries, especially those with similarly close or closer alignment of economics with the political elites, exhibit similar challenges.

Where the very mechanisms by which markets signal the need for adjustments are in themselves constrained by undesirable social and environmental conditions, little may be expected of economics to help break out of the mold it created for itself. Conversely, where knowledge on how to change that mold can be infused in the models and analyses of environmental economists, the discipline should be able to meaningfully contribute to the solution of increasingly pressing and rapidly emerging social and environmental problems.

1.4   Taking a macro view of economic activity in the environment

Climate change as a fundamental threat to humanity is a recurring theme in this volume: in part because it is what will shape economic decision making for a long time to come; and in part because it poses challenges for the way environmental economics conceptualizes the feedback processes between society and the environment. It highlights some of the existing shortcomings in theory and practice, and it also offers valuable prompts for the discipline to incorporate insights from the biological and physical sciences, as well as ethics, policy and law as described above.

In an effort to describe the interdisciplinary lay of the land, as it were, within which economics must navigate, in Chapter 6 Martin Sers and Peter Victor sketch out how insights from biology and physics must shape development of environmental economics theory. For example, the marginal analysis of conventional integrated assessment models, many of which only capture unidirectional coupling between socio-economic and environmental changes (Motesharrei et al. 2016), is not particularly amenable to the non-linearities, bifurcations and surprises inherent in the real, bidirectionally coupled system. Using a simple arithmetic argument, they state that in macroeconomic models neither growth nor the factors that drive it should be assumed at the outset. Consistent with the arguments presented above, this holds especially in environmental macroeconomics where the physical dimensions of economic growth are of paramount importance.

How then does one go about measuring macroeconomic performance in ways that establish, conceptually and empirically, consistent connections between some forms of environmental changes and changes in the economy? One such measure is the energy return on the energy that the economy uses to explore, extract, process, ship and otherwise make available to producers and consumers in the economy. Declining energy returns suggest that it gets tougher to provide energy, perhaps because technologies have approached performance limits that prevent them from compensating for a more diffuse resource base, or because environmental regulation stipulates the use of technological interventions that themselves require energy, and thus reduce the overall efficiency of the delivery system. Examples of the deployment of such technologies are the scrubbers used to combat sulfur emissions from power generation and the resulting acid rain, or means to capture carbon emissions from fossil fuel burning and subsequent sequestration in geologic formations deep underground. Declining energy returns on energy investment, however, do not only indicate that the material and energy base on which production and consumption depend is eroding; they also do not bode well for long-term prospects of economic growth. The upshot for environmental economics: the discipline must move beyond models of unidirectional coupling between economy and environment; expand its assessment of its resource base beyond simple stock estimates or material and energy balance accounts; and move beyond the naïve capture of global harm in the form of temperature damage formulations.

But even if one sticks to the basic tenets of economic modeling, with its focus on economic growth and its presumed benefits to society, mere modifications to the underlying theory of production alone lead us to question the wisdom of traditional findings. Towards that end, Dodo Thampapillai and Matthias Ruth review in Chapter 7 the contributions by William Nordhaus and Paul Romer, both of whom were awarded the 2018 Nobel Prize in recognition of their contribution to the economics discipline, and whose work epitomizes modern growth theory. Simple expansions of their models to include natural capital alongside labor and human-made capital are presented in which thermodynamic laws constrain resource use and ecosystems provide limited waste assimilation capacities. As a result of these very basic modifications, and otherwise sticking to conventional analysis, the Romer model suggests clear possibilities of the need for de-growth in selected economies. Furthermore, the Nordhausian goals of "optimal pollution" and "optimal climate change" are, at best, analytical artifacts and, at worst, detrimental to the health and wellbeing of society and the biophysical environment on which it depends. If the term "optimality" must be used, then the optimal quantity of pollution would be zero, which is physically impossible, and climate change would not occur, which for biogeophysical reasons cannot be the case either.

Since pollution and climate change occur, in essence, as consequences of energy use, the immediate question arises to what extent technological changes that reduce the need for energy per unit of desirable output can help society stay ahead of generating irreversible damages. How much can technical change run counter to the declining energy returns of investment discussed by Sers and Victor (Chapter

6)? From a theoretical perspective, the laws of thermodynamics constrain material and energy efficiencies of any real-world process. In practical terms, however, a wide range of factors may play a critical role long before maximum thermodynamic efficiency is achieved. The long timeframes required to turn over capital stocks, including the national and global infrastructures on which they rely, also mean that little wiggle room often exists for considerable efficiency improvements, even when new "break-through technologies" are in principle known (Unruh 2000; Ruth et al. 2004). Additionally, there is the interplay of institutional developments with the deployment of technologies, as already explored by Faber and Frick (Chapter 3) and illustrated for the case of the soda-chlorine industry.

Other important drivers behind actual energy use and emissions profiles include international trade, which can help outsource energy- and pollution-intensive processes to other countries, thus reducing national environmental performance measures – though not necessarily benefitting the global system. And to the extent that trade, combined with efficiency improvements, stimulates growth at the sectoral or country level, the net result may be a reduction in the positive effects of efficiency gains on the environment. Improvements in industrial energy efficiency, for example, may make that industry more competitive by helping it drive down production cost and product price, which may increase its markets and thus its output at rates that are higher than the rate of the efficiency gains. Sectoral growth may stimulate demand for more machines and labor, all of which, in turn, will help fuel economic growth. This is precisely where the analysis by Astrid Kander, M. d. Mar Rubio-Varas and David Stern comes in. In their contribution (Chapter 8) they explore determinants for the gap between the rates of efficiency improvement, as measured in terms of energy use per unit of desired output, and observed rates of change in the energy use of the economy.

1.5   Space, perception and behavior

The concept of "environment" can have many different meanings in environmental economics – from a (generic) lake, forest or wetland, for example, whose qualitative features affect enjoyment by those seeking recreation in nature, to the more elusive notion of a stable climate or the more abstract concept of a system that provides materials and energy and receives the waste from their conversion. Rarely, however, are these manifestations of "environment" directly identified in space where they exist. Conversely, the location of people in space has a bearing on how they perceive their environment – not just in an abstract sense (more people, more consumption and thus more impact, for example) but also in the sense that geography matters; as do the associated cultural, social and psychological influences of placement in specific locations on the behaviors of people. It is this interplay of spatial context, values, attitudes and behaviors that lies at the center of Eveline van Leeuwen's chapter on place-based behavior (Chapter 9). Here, she concentrates on the differences in norms and behaviors between rural and urban areas and their implications for policy. To arrive at an understanding of these differences requires knowing the degree to which people "sort" by location as a result of their prefer-ences and constraints – such as the availability of housing and amenities, financial resources, etc. – and how external factors affect behavior.

Drawing on data from the European Social Survey of 2016, van Leeuwen seeks to quantify the importance of the spatial context in values and behavior. Her analysis points towards a research agenda for environmental economics that makes con-tributions at both the micro and macro scale. At the micro scale, consumer choice must be viewed within its spatial context – the proximity to infrastructures such as transport systems and recycling centers, for example – and the opportunities this creates for action, learning and reinforcement of behaviors and norms. At the macro scale, an understanding of the regional dynamics at which externalities are generated, distributed and addressed through investment and policy choices is required to help shepherd development towards sustainable outcomes. And, of course, processes at the micro and macro scale shape each other, which in turn provides fertile ground for research into the relevance of place and space in shaping human–environment interactions.

In Chapter 10, Christian Krekel and Jens Kolbe explore ways to better under-stand and quantify the contributions urban ecosystems make to local economies. Traditional methods focus on monetary estimates based on stated preference meth-ods, such as the contingent valuation approaches criticized by Sagoff in Chapter 2. Hedonic pricing models, in essence, calculate the value of ecosystem services in the vicinity of settlements as a residual of housing prices that cannot be attributed to other aspects. By their very nature, such data deal with aggregate effects and may do little justice to the heterogeneous nature of ecosystems in urban settings. In con-trast, vast amounts of data on human perceptions and actions are available through social media platforms, for example. Similarly, detailed characterizations of the state of ecosystems are becoming available at fine spatial resolution, such as chlo-rophyll and heat maps. The convergence of social and biophysical data then lends itself to quantifications of the contributions of ecosystems to local economies, and, conversely, to assessments of environmental impacts on those ecosystems. Again, as argued by van Leeuwen in the preceding chapter, space matters; and how the norms and behaviors discussed there relate to the changes in environmental values identified with new methods of "big data" analysis and machine learning-driven assessments discussed by Krekel and Kolbe may provide yet another avenue for research in environmental economics. Managing complex issues in a data-rich world is one of the endeavors that economists pride themselves on doing well.

A host of economic factors such as the disposable income of households or the profits of firms influence the level and mix of their production and consump-tion of goods and services, which in turn impact the environment. Furthermore, availability of financial resources of one shapes the performance of the other, for example when household consumption drives firm behavior or when production decisions influence employment, and thus incomes. Drilling down to the interac-tions between firm and household and their implications for environmental impact,

Dana Andersen (Chapter 11) explores the role of credit constraints on composition of output in "clean" and "dirty" industries and the pollution intensity of production.

Firms that face more acute credit constraints tend to invest more in tangible assets such as machines and other forms of productive facilities at the expense of intangible assets such as the abilities and skill levels of their workforce. They do so largely because these tangible assets can serve as collateral against the credits they receive. This preference for tangible assets, in turn, shapes the short-term input mix of firms as well as factor endowments and patterns of production in the long run. The result of both these influences of credit constraints can also be seen in terms of industrial emissions profiles.

With the aid of a two-sector model of households and firms, Andersen illustrates the extent to which increases in human capital can draw resources from pollution-intensive sectors of the economy, leading to a more than proportional expansion of output in clean sectors and an absolute decline in output in dirty sectors. Aside from this direct impact on sector composition of the economy, an increase in human capital may also stimulate policy responses towards tighter environmental regulations whenever environmental quality is a normal good. Thus, credit constraints increase pollution whenever they impinge on investment in human capital. His findings are supported for the cases of sulfur dioxide and lead emissions, using World Health Organization data for about 150 cities in 45 countries, and suggest that policies aimed at promoting human capital or the development of human capital-intensive industries, might be effective at promoting development in a way that is less environmentally damaging than development based on physical capital accumulation.

Indeed, policies of all kinds shape short- and long-run environmental performance, and they also lead to winners and losers within the industrial sector. Given the complexity of economy–environment interactions, the dynamic nature of firm behavior and technology change, the evolution of preferences of people in the context of ever-changing economic and environmental conditions, considerable uncertainties surround, at least *a priori*, the effectiveness of proposed policies. Both the winners and losers may exploit these uncertainties to their benefit, and they may even take an active role not just in identifying uncertainties but by generating doubt and providing misinformation. Even where science shows pretty clear-cut relations between human activity and environmental change, strategies to distort science or poo-poo facts as "fake news" can have far-reaching implications for the support by society for environmental regulation.

In their chapter (Chapter 12) on the manufacture of doubt, Yann Bramoullé and Caroline Orset attend to these unscrupulous practices, which so far have been largely neglected by economists. They develop a simple model composed of four groups of actors. In this model, firms generate emissions and also may decide to produce costly reports that portray their emissions as not being harmful. Scientists carry out research that reduces uncertainty about the impacts of emissions. Citizens receive information from firms and scientists and are unaware when misinformation is presented to them. Governments consider public opinion when determining the degree of regulation of the pollution generated by firms. With this model, Bramoullé and Orset lay out a range of developments that characterize the actions of industry and science, as well as the responses by government. For example, as scientists become increasingly convinced that industrial activity is harmful, industry first devotes more resources to falsely reassure citizens that industrial pollution is benign. When scientific belief reaches a critical threshold, however, firms find it too costly to counter scientific consensus and industry abruptly ends its misinformation. These results are shown to hold whether a command and control approach is used by government to curb emissions or a tax on emissions is chosen. Bramoullé and Orset argue for a wide range of refinements of their model, such as decision making over multiple periods, and the inclusion of multiple lobbies and multiple lobbying strategies. They call for the present specification of belief formation and preferences concerning risk to be refined, and for the representations of the role of science and scientists to be more nuanced. Their detailed exposé of each of these refinements charts the course for an environmental economics that is indeed responsive to the many real and pressing social and political challenges alluded to by Sagoff in Chapter 2, and that occupy the daily headlines of newspapers, TV shows and radio programs of the "post-truth era" in which we currently find ourselves.

And talking of real and pressing problems – there is a big section of human society whose daily challenges have not, by any measure, received the attention they need. These are the large numbers of marginalized people, especially those who live in the global south, the rural areas or city districts with limited access to safe drinking water, clean air, healthy food, and much more. The challenges they face are oftentimes caused, or exacerbated, by the very environmental issues that are core topics in environmental economics. Yet, these are also less glamorous topics. Dealing with the provision of sanitary services in urban slums, where there is no organized voice to speak on behalf of those who have no other option but to defecate in the open, is different from addressing the emissions challenges of the US paper industry, for example, with shareholders, workers and environmentalists organized around the topic, all with resources to fund research and to advice investment and policy making.

René Kemp and Shyama Ramani draw on experiences in India to advocate for a solution design approach that explicitly involves stakeholders to address some of the challenges associated with the transition towards production and consumption processes that are moving society towards sustainability (Chapter 13). They point to the sunk costs associated with existing technologies and infrastructures on the one hand, and institutional rigidities and social structural behaviors on the other that have mutually reinforced each other. At a more fundamental level, though, the solution design approach will require, almost as a prerequisite, environmental economists to embrace as valid and urgent the many messy problems of everyday people in dire situations – the urban and rural poor, young and old, in developing countries. Given the complexities of such situations, all relevant actors at the heart of the problem must be present at all stages of the transition process – from identification of the causes to the design of remedies, the monitoring of implementation efforts and outcomes, and revisions as necessary. This is a fundamentally different approach from the rather prescriptive, historically largely abstract approach of modern environmental economics: an approach that is organic in nature; one that recognizes the co-evolution of social and environmental change; one that gives voice to the voiceless; and one that shares knowledge to achieve sustainability rather than one that prescribes, advises and delegates.

Reinforcing and expanding on the vision articulated by Kemp and Ramani, Jalel Sager and Richard Norgaard (Chapter 14) explore the human dilemma through a co-evolutionary framing and acknowledgment of the interwoven nature of values, knowledge, technology, social organization and the environment. They return to the global challenges posed at the beginning of this volume and found in almost all of its chapters – the immense strides humans have made through the exploitation of fossil fuel reserves to raise standards of living and transform the world around them by building infrastructures and institutions intended to help with the perpetuation of economic growth and prosperity. At the same time, these transformations have also irreversibly altered biogeochemical cycles, undermined the abilities of ecosystems to provide valuable waste assimilation services and habitats for other species, and moved climate dynamics towards tipping points beyond which all bets for future prosperity are off. In the wake of these developments, global and national systems of power and socio-political organization have formed that, so far, have reinforced inequalities and injustices and pitted one part of the globe or one part of society against another in the race for prosperity, as if it all were a zero-sum game.

But are we really playing a zero-sum game? Isn't there a solution in which the abilities of the Earth's ecosystems to provide continued enjoyment and life support are protected, in which those who are worse off will be attended to and those who do the attending benefit as well – in ways other than just cheap profit motives? What are the theories and methods that do justice to the human nature of production and consumption decisions in a finite world? How do we shape our political economy to be in tune with human, social needs rather than the simplistic assumptions of nineteenth-century optimization of individuals' utilities? And yet, what are the insights from prior theories and applications that can and must be salvaged as humanity grapples with the challenges that lie ahead? These are some of the fundamental questions that should shape a research agenda for environmental economics. And these are, indeed, the questions addressed in this volume. Asking them is a first important step. Pointing towards ways to answer them, as the many contributors have done here, helps create momentum for the discipline, and hopefully motivates others to add their intellectual weight, effort and support behind them. This is a call for all hands on deck to shape how the discipline of environmental economics treats the coupled human–environment system and the way it conceives of its role in the discourse about the future of humanity and our environment, before it is truly too late.

References

Brown, P. and Garver, G. 2009. *Right Relationship: Building a Whole Earth Economy*, San Francisco: Berrett-Koehler.

Holcombe, R.G. 2014. *Advanced Introduction to the Austrian School of Economics*, Cheltenham, UK and Northampton, MA, USA: Edward Elgar Publishing.

Motesharrei, S., J. Rivas, E. Kalnay, G. Asrar, A. Busalacchi, R. Cahalan, M. Cane, R. Colwell, K. Feng, R. Franklin, K. Hubacek, F. Miralles-Wilhelm, T. Miyoshi, M. Ruth, R. Sagdeev, A. Shirmohammadi, J. Shukla, J. Srebric, V. Yakovenko and Ning Zeng. 2016. The Essential Need for Bidirectional Coupling of Earth System and Human System Models, *National Science Review*, Vol. 3, pp. 470–494, doi: 10.1093/nsr/nww081.

Røpke, I. 1999. Prices are not worth much, *Ecological Economics*, Vol. 29, No. 1, pp. 45–46.

Ruth, M., B. Davidsdottir and A. Amato. 2004. Climate Change Policies and Capital Vintage Effects: The Cases of US Pulp and Paper, Iron and Steel and Ethylene, *Journal of Environmental Management*, Vol. 7, No. 3, pp. 221–233.

Ruth, M. 2018. Regional Science in a Resource-constrained World, *Annals of Regional Science*, Vol. 62, No. 2, pp. 229–236, https://doi.org/10.1007/s00168-018-0879-0.

Unruh, G.C. 2000. Understanding Carbon Lock-in, *Energy Policy*, Vol. 28, No. 12, pp. 817–830.

2 Environmental economics is dead! Long live environmental economics!

Mark Sagoff

2.1 Introduction

In this chapter, I will opine about the research agenda of environmental economics by praising its future and criticizing its past. In the past, environmental economics has been embedded in welfare economics, and thus committed to the assumptions: 1) that a construct it theorizes, *utility* or *benefit*, can be measured, compared between individuals, and aggregated over society as a whole; and 2) that the maximization of a conceptual substance, *net aggregate benefit*, is an ethically desirable societal goal. These assumptions convinced environmental economists that they could speak truth to power by determining whether Policy A produces greater net benefits and is therefore better than Policy B. In fact, environmental economists spoke only to each other as they disagreed about how to construct and measure "preference," an unobservable theoretical mental state that they construed in terms of behavior which, to be described as making a choice, had itself to be interpreted in terms of the preferences assumed to cause it.

Welfare economics, and thus environmental economics, failed in the attempt to figure out how to identify preference and how to measure, compare, and aggregate the utilities of individuals. Today environmental economists are no longer wedded to this research program. They try not so much to evaluate environmental policies in terms of prior utilities or preferences as to diagnose them in terms of the options they present and the consequences they may create. Economic analysis can help discover how effective a policy may be in serving the ends it seeks. Economic analysis, whatever its presumptions, cannot tell society what its ends should be.

Environmental economists now do what economists do best, which is to map the unintended consequences of decisions that may have the best intentions. They try to understand markets from the inside, that is, from the perspective of those with skin in the game. This is different from looking at markets from the outside: from the perspective of those who apply abstract models to conceptual constructs, such as "preferences," which, with no sense of irony, they call data. To speak truth to power, one must know what power is, who has it, in what legal, political, and social institutions it resides, and what it can do in view of constraints. This kind of knowledge characterizes the future of environmental economics.

2.2   Critiques of welfare economics from the left and right

This chapter is organized in the following way. In the next two sections, I will describe two decades-old critiques of standard environmental economics, one from the left and one from the right. The critique from the left argues that the cost-benefit approach of environmental economics is a trick to slow and stymie environmental regulation by putting it through more bureaucratic wringers, which are likely to favor business interests over the environment. Second, by imputing "shadow" prices to environmental goals – sustainability, biodiversity, ecological integrity, safe and clean water and air, etc. – economists "commoditize" as private preferences what must be treated as public values, legislated ends, and political ideals. The science of welfare economics demonstrates to the satisfaction of its adepts that society has only one collective goal: the maximization of aggregate net preference satisfaction – at least when distributive issues are not pressing. According to this approach, it is essential that economists be paid to determine what "efficiency" in this sense means and how to measure it.

From the perspective of the political right, the cost-benefit or welfare-maximization approach subverts institutions and traditions, such as common law and the balance of powers, in favor of its own collectivist vision, that is, Kaldor-Hicks efficiency, aggregate willingness to pay (WTP), or potential Pareto improvement. To second-guess markets, which notoriously fail to meet this collectivist objective, economists must master continually changing facts of mind-boggling complexity, thus violating the Hayekian maxim that reason must know its limits. Right-wing critics see little need to distinguish this approach from Leninism since it would put a vanguard party of economists in charge of social policy. When they occupy the commanding heights, the welfare-economic vanguard will replace the individual with the collective will, politics with administration, law with science – causing, as Engels said, the withering away of the State.

Critics on the left saw environmental economics and cost-benefit thinking as obstacles to a Progressive agenda because they could be manipulated to belittle as private "preferences" public values they considered to be justified on intrinsic, moral, or political grounds. Critics on the right saw cost-benefit and market-failure thinking as an open door to the Progressive agenda because it could be manipulated to assign stupendous quantities of "contingent" or "hypothetical" WTP to environmental causes and beliefs. As a result, the left and the right in high-profile disputes commissioned "dueling" cost-benefit analyses the primary beneficiaries of which were the economic consultants and expert witnesses hired in the process, which may have been the point. Environmental economists presented a theory according to which they had the competence and expertise to measure WTP (a.k.a. "benefit" or "utility") and thus to determine environmental policy. One could get numbers to favor one's cause by hiring the right economists as consultants and expert witnesses. "You get the WTP you are willing to pay for," one government environmental attorney explained to me.

Both the political left and the political right, however, found the cost-benefit framework useful for two reasons. First, it provided a language, if only a *façon de parler*, in which they could speak to each other. Second, and more important, this language allowed them to tamp down their political fringes. On the left, the radical fringe comprised ecologically minded economists (such as Herman Daly) who opposed economic growth and proposed to "degrow" the economy. On the right, the radical fringe comprised Libertarians (such as Murray Rothbard) who wanted the government to get out of environmental management, except as necessary to privatize everything and then to protect the rights of person and property.

To make things weirder, the radical right and radical left "loopified," that is, they converted the political spectrum into a circle by backing into each other and endorsing the same policy. This was to bring the economy to a screeching halt either (from the left) to protect the integrity, inviolability, and separateness of Nature or (from the right) to protect the integrity, inviolability, and separateness of the Person. Both views evoke Rousseau's State of Nature in which people live solitary simple lives and let each other alone because nature provided for their needs. Only a return to these conditions would satisfy the radical left and radical right. This made cost-benefit analysis (CBA) look good.

2.3   Environmental economics dead or alive?

This chapter then argues that environmental economics as a subdiscipline of welfare economics is dead. By that I mean not simply that it has no influence on environmental policy. That much has been observed again and again: for example, cost-benefit analysis is not used to make decisions but, at most, to justify them *ex post* largely to paper them for review at the Office of Management and Budget. By saying that environmental economics as a branch of welfare economics is dead, I mean more broadly that it does not provide a career path for graduate students who want jobs in academia, think tanks, environmental organizations, or government. A research program that teaches students to "price" market externalities prepares them to wait tables or drive Ubers. There is no market for market failure.

I conclude the chapter by describing four ways I believe the research agenda of environmental economics can revive and prosper. The first I have mentioned. Environmental economics will study what makes policies more *effective* rather than what makes them more *efficient*. Cost-effectiveness has long been mentioned in the literature as a worthy subject; but it has largely been ignored in favor of research on theoretical advances in benefit valuation, in stated and revealed preference assessment, and in modeling compensating and equivalent variations. The path forward has to do with research on the compliance costs of specific policy options and research about the macroeconomic consequences of proposed regulations.

Second, environmental economics will become (and is becoming) an empirical science. By this I mean that its practitioners will know something besides theory.

They will be deeply informed on the ins and outs of some industry that affects the environment; they will know as much about the relevant technology, competition, demand, regulatory burden, and so forth as an investor would learn before taking a position in that industry. For example, if one wants to write about energy issues in the U.S. one must learn all there is to know about the Federal Energy Regulatory Commission, competing technologies, demand, and so on.

An environmental economist who knows, for example, the paper industry through and through could be hired by that industry, by an environmental group, or by a government agency to determine how the industry could improve its environmental performance. He or she might find an academic position in a school of management and public policy. This would not be true, however, of someone who can mathematically model methodological advances in the calculation of non-market benefits, who masters the best ways to elicit stated preference but who knows little about any one industry or technology. A "job" talk on methodological advances in the estimation of non-market costs and benefits is a contradiction in terms.

Third, environmental economists pursue an important research agenda when they address the environmental consequences of large-scale social and technological trends. The population of most industrialized countries is aging; and older people consume differently than younger people. How is that likely to play out for the environment? Similarly, urbanization. Similarly, social media. Similarly, the "gig" economy. It is a worthwhile task to try to predict the environmental consequences of large-scale economic and technological change. It lies beyond the scope of any science, including economics, however, to "valuate" those consequences.

Fourth, environmental economics will see itself more as a branch of macroeconomics than of microeconomics. It will examine the likely effects of policy options on the performance of the overall economy, seeking, for example, to increase employment, control inflation, improve productivity, and in general promote prosperity. Society obviously cares about prosperity, jobs, competitiveness, and inflation. Environmental economists, in contrast, care about Kaldor-Hicks efficiency. There is no known relation between Kaldor-Hicks (microeconomic) efficiency and macroeconomic performance.

I conclude this chapter by summarizing the main point. A successful research agenda in environmental economics will study efficacy not efficiency; it will investigate the likely consequences of policy choices but leave it to others to evaluate them. Environmental economics will succeed as a positive but not as a normative science. There is no such thing as a normative science. No science can tell society what is naughty and nice; no science can define the good (e.g., as "utility" or "preference-satisfaction") and then evaluate social states in terms of it. Because A is preferred to B, whatever that may mean, it does not follow that A is better than B. This is one of the lessons that life constantly presents to us.

There is a practical reason, moreover, that environmental economics must shed the conceptual framework of preference-satisfaction, Pigouvian externalities, market failures, compensating and equivalent variations, potential Pareto improvements, Kaldor-Hicks efficiency, non-market valuation, benefit transfers, and so on. In the last three decades of the twentieth century, the political left and the political right were willing to pay for this research agenda in the belief that it could support their positions. They have by now learned that cost-benefit analysis has had no effect on policy. They are now much less willing to pay for it.

2.4   The critique from the left

Environmental economics as a subdiscipline of welfare economics proposed a Paretian principle to guide social decisions. This is the principle of welfare-maximization, which, in the context of social policy, requires agencies to maximize benefits or well-being across society as a whole, at least when equity issues – matters relating to the distribution of benefits among individuals – are not pressing. As one economist pointed out, the "moral foundation underlying economic analysis, which has as its goal human happiness or utility, is known as utilitarianism."[1] Utilitarianism as in Bentham and Mill had to do with pleasure or happiness. Welfare, and therefore standard environmental economics, however, concerns "utility" – a term that has no known demonstrated empirical relationship to happiness or to any conception of the good not vacuously and trivially defined in terms of "utility."

In opposition to legal, political, and social traditions going back to the sixteenth century, environmental economists by the 1970s had convened on a new basis for environmental law. As environmental economist Robert Stavins wrote, "The fundamental theoretical argument for government activity in the environmental realm is that pollution is an externality – an unintended consequence of market decisions, which affects individuals other than the decision maker."[2] On this basis the field of environmental economics transformed itself from its earlier interest in macroeconomic effects into a study of a myriad of methodological, conceptual, and theoretical problems that arose in choosing which externalities to internalize; measuring WTP; "shadow-pricing" non-market benefits; interpreting revealed, implicit, and stated preference; and modeling concepts such as Kaldor-Hicks efficiency and potential Pareto improvement.

The critique from the left, which was directed against welfare economics generally, held that both individuals and society pursue all kinds of goals – such as a clean, healthful, and natural environment – and respect many kinds of principles other than the maximization of utility. Indeed, a person who respects no principles, pursues no goals, and responds to no ideals other than his or her better-offness – who cares only for Number One – is known as a sociopath. Environmentalists believe

---

1 Goodstein (1995): p. 25.
2 Stavins (2007): p. 1.

they, too, make arguments about the goals society should pursue; and they did not appreciate being told that only welfare economists could think about the common good objectively while everyone else pursued his or her subjective preferences.

During the 1970s and thereafter, critics assailed the welfare-theoretic approach in the context of the problem of pollution. For centuries, common law courts have protected individuals from injuries caused by effluents and emissions. If the waste from a person's privy percolates through his wall and into his neighbor's cellar, for example, common law will require him to cease and repair the nuisance, for, as an English court found in 1705, he is "bound of common right to keep his wall so his filth would not damnify his neighbor."[3]

In thousands of cases, some of which students study in their first year of law school, courts have enjoined and awarded damages for all sorts of nuisances and other torts involving pollution, often treating the violation of regulation as per se negligence. Environmentalists rely on this tradition to argue that industries are similarly bound by common right and by statute to contain their wastes so as not to damnify their neighbors. For these environmentalists, pollution is an invasion of personal and property rights – exactly what Libertarians on the right believe – and should be enjoined or, if that is too disruptive, endured as a necessary evil to be minimized until technology can do better.

In the United States, all (or nearly all) statutes that control pollution are based on and justified by this common law tradition. Plainly, it would be difficult or impossible for each citizen to identify all the sources of pollution that damnify her or him; it would be even more challenging to sue each source in equity, that is, civil law. Therefore, statutes are enacted to protect public safety and health from industrial and municipal pollution. These are often technology-forcing statutes: agencies set incrementally tougher standards over time – air quality standards under the Clean Air Act, for example – to encourage industries and municipalities continually to lessen their emissions per unit of production. These statutes have worked so well that ambient air and water quality has improved immensely since the 1960s while the economy has grown.

During the 1970s and into the 1980s, environmental economists helped inform regulations by estimating the macroeconomic consequences of the environmental statutes enacted during the period. The agencies were particularly concerned that stricter standards would cause unemployment, increase inflation, or limit productivity and competitiveness. I remember that Murray Weidenbaum, first chairman of President Ronald Reagan's Council of Economic Advisors, analyzed the effect of environmental regulation on unemployment and found it was not significant. This may have led the president to invite William Ruckelshaus to return to run the Environmental Protection Agency (EPA). Stricter regulations at other times might

---

3 Elmes (1829): p. 232.

impair employment. This is the reason President Barack Obama refused to allow the EPA to tighten ozone standards in an election year when industries might lay off workers because of new regulations.

Common law traditions and the environmental statutes they justify, while they may be sensitive to macroeconomic considerations, have nothing to do with "internalizing" market externalities, optimizing diseconomies, or balancing social benefits and costs. To interpret the Clean Air Act, for example, as permitting a cost-benefit test is to suggest the possibility that the statute may "really" have called for more rather than less air pollution if that result turned out to pass the Kaldor-Hicks compensation test, according to economists who might be hired for the purpose. Maybe filth was efficient. Environmental economists Maureen Cropper and Wallace Oates wrote in 1992 that "the cornerstones of federal environmental policy in the United States [. . .] *explicitly* prohibited the weighing of benefits against costs in the setting of environmental standards."[4] This is as it should be. Nothing about this has changed.

The standard theory of environmental economics denies that *principles* such as public safety and health, personal and property rights against intrusion, and the responsibility of people to clean up their messes have anything to do with regulation. These are *preferences* people would pay to satisfy. The only principle known to environmental economists is aggregate WTP or Kaldor-Hicks efficiency, at least when distributive effects are not pressing. They ride it like a hobby-horse. In the tradition of naturalist John Muir, conservationists moved by spiritual beliefs successfully pursued a legislative agenda of which the U.S. can be proud. In the tradition of common law, legislatures have enacted statutes to protect personal and property rights against the invasion of pollution. Environmental economists have treated every moral view, argument, belief, or position other than their own welfare-theoretic collectivism as a subjective preference only as good as there is WTP for it. They then set up consulting businesses and offered themselves as expert witnesses to measure the WTP that is not captured by markets.

2.5 The critique from the right

Right-wing critics of the standard approach in environmental economics associated it with the tradition of Progressivism and positivism, following August Comte and Henri de Saint-Simon, who advocated a system of social physics in which experts, primarily economists, managed society from a commanding height secured by their scientific authority. Welfare economics rationalizes the exercise of political and market power by scientizing it. The attempt to rationalize power – rather than to legitimate it – echoes the call of Communism to centralize the management of the economy. It echoes a totalitarian tradition which collectivizes society in terms of a common will or purpose known to the vanguard. Whether the common will

---

4 Cropper and Oates (1992): p. 675; emphasis in original.

consists in a classless society, religious purity, or allocative efficiency is irrelevant; whatever it is, apparatchiks use their science to empower themselves. Aggregate net WTP is not charismatic; it makes a scientized collectivism look innocuous, indeed, ridiculous. But it expresses the same collectivist mentality as Communism, nonetheless.

The idea that welfare economists should rule when markets fail recalls the famous phrase of the political theorist Carl Schmitt (1989): "Sovereign is he who decides on the exception." Market failure is the "exception" or the emergency which empowers environmental economists to exert sovereignty over the allocation of resources. Brown shirts might also help.

Critics on the political right also argued that environmental economists should respect what may be described as the Hayekian sensibility that reason ought to be sensible to its own limitations. According to Hayek,

> The problem of securing an efficient use of our resources is thus very largely one of how the knowledge of the particular circumstances of the moment can be most effectively utilised; and the task which faces the designer of a rational order of society is to find a method whereby this widely dispersed knowledge may best be drawn upon.[5]

Government officials, no matter how many consultants they hire, cannot possibly acquire the information necessary to measure the marginal costs of any pollutant (such as smog in the air) because these will differ from place to place, time to time, circumstance to circumstance, and individual to individual. To measure all the relevant WTP, officials would continually have to engage in surveys of mind-boggling complexity, develop regulations to meet constantly changing circumstances, and then enforce or implement those regulations.[6] The governmental agency responsible for regulating an industry would have to know at least as much as the interested parties about who is willing to pay how much for what – and thus the agency would just step in for those parties in trying to determine the relevant values and take care of the transaction costs that prevented those parties from bargaining in the first place.

The government may be in no better position – it is probably in a worse position – than market players to identify, undertake, and overcome externalities or transaction costs. The same information and transaction costs that prevent individuals from bargaining would have to be borne by the government. According to Ronald Coase, "the costs involved in governmental action make it desirable that the 'externality' should continue to exist and that no government intervention should be undertaken to eliminate it."[7] In the early 1980s, legal commentators cautioned that in the context of the argument Coase presented, regulations were unnecessary in

---

5 Hayek (1944): pp. 27–39.
6 Ruff (1993).
7 Coase (2012b): p. 26.

the absence of market failure, but too complicated and puzzling to be practicable in their presence. Economists commit the "fallacy of disparate comparison" to judge the market with all its warts against an idealized view of the government which they advise or even command.

2.6 Externalities run amok

Right-wing critics of cost-benefit socialism had another reason to worry. As early as the 1960s environmentalists saw that by reinventing their values as WTP or willingness to accept (WTA) they could enlist economic science to their side. Many foundations initiated major programs to fund environmental economists to "green" their science by measuring moral "externalities" such as "existence" and "non-use" values. These foundations encouraged economists to feel the pain of environmentalists and "price" it. A little WTP to protect an endangered lousewort, if multiplied over 100 million households, could represent a lot of economic value. A minnow was worth millions. Anything that might offend the sensibilities of environmentalists could be construed as a third-party cost. In this way CBA, which might have been thought to be a foe of environmental regulation, was transformed into a powerful friend.

Industry groups had to respond when environmental economists appeared in court as expert witnesses to convince juries to give astronomic damage awards to plaintiffs in oil spill and other industrial accidents. The "cost" to be compensated could be billions of dollars once the "existence" value of mucked-up otters was measured and aggregated over 100 million households. (What about the "existence" and other economic value of the sea urchins that flourished in the absence of otter predation?) Exxon Corporation in 1992 commissioned papers from renowned environmental and welfare economists to present "a critical assessment of a survey method known as contingent valuation (CV), a method that attempts to measure individual values for economic goods by asking people hypothetical questions about their willingness to pay for such goods," according to the editor of a volume of essays.[8]

This "critical assessment" set out a portfolio of conceptual, methodological, mathematical, and epistemological problems that complicated the project of measuring the social costs of externalities, for example, in designing surveys meant to determine how much the public was willing to accept in compensation for the otters killed by an oil spill. The myriad technical, conceptual, normative, mathematical, and epistemological problems that beset non-market valuation detailed in the Exxon book published about thirty years ago continues to constitute the agenda of mainstream or standard environmental economics to this day.

Conservatives defend the free market. They agree that having a preference gives the individual a reason to satisfy it. That every individual should be free to try to do

---

8 Hausman (1993): p. vii.

so in ways that are consistent with the like freedom of others is a piety few would deny. What reason has the government or society, however, to seek to satisfy that preference? To be sure, society has a reason to recognize and help satisfy certain kinds of preferences – for example, those related to basic needs (because of a theory of justice), security (because of any political theory), and merit goods (if it wishes). What reason has society to seek the satisfaction of preference per se – not preference related to need, security, or merit but any preference at all – measured by WTP and taken as it comes?

Environmental economists have not answered this question. They rely on the ambiguity of the term "satisfaction." Preferences are satisfied in the same way as conditions or equations, that is, they are met or filled. This has no proven relation with "satisfaction" in any other sense, for example, contentment. Standard environmental economics has been all about the satisfaction of preference. This has no known relation to satisfaction, well-being, or happiness in any definition that can be understood in moral or psychological terms or makes common sense.

2.7   Environmental economics is dead

Four arguments suggest that environmental economics is dead. First, standard environmental economics has not responded to criticisms from the left and the right such as I have described, even though these criticisms have been recited and reiterated for five decades. For example, a paper published by Amartya Sen in 1977, "Rational Fools," which drove a wedge between "welfare" and "preference satisfaction," has been cited in the broader literature 4,690 times (at the time of writing) to rehearse the argument that these terms have no known empirical – only a stipulated – relation to each other. That a person P prefers A to B does not imply that P believes he or she is better off with A than B. There can be other reasons for such a preference. This has been said so many times (as by Sen) that to restate it connives at criminal boredom.

Environmental economists have not responded to the critique of their discipline because they cannot. They cannot say because they do not know why the satisfaction of preferences taken as they come and measured by WTP should be a goal of environmental policy. A reference to economic value, welfare, better-offness, utility, well-being, and so on adds nothing, since none of these concepts have any semblance of a relation with WTP unless they are defined (as they usually are) vacuously, trivially, and tendentiously in terms of it. If there is an empirical relation between WTP and welfare, what is the evidence? For fifty years, critics of standard environmental economics have reiterated that WTP measures nothing but itself and concepts defined in terms of it. If environmental economists have a definition of "welfare" or "utility" other than WTP, what is it? How is the correlation tested?

For fifty years, leading environmental economists have answered these criticisms by ignoring them. Instead, they have refuted two incidental arguments they have found in the literature. They have pointed out correctly that human beings assign all the values, that is, that all values are anthropogenic; but this is irrelevant. Distributional issues and the interests of future generations are also irrelevant to the principal critique of environmental economics, which centers on Paretian concepts of value.

Second, environmental economists over several decades have prepared thousands of analyses of the non-market and especially non-use costs and benefits associated with various policy options – according to some estimates more than 7,500. I do not think that any of these analyses have had any effect on the decisions in question. In other words, analyses prepared by environmental economists that attempt to assign "shadow" prices to market externalities are uniformly academic exercises and have had no influence on environmental law or policy. A good example would be the massive contingent valuation study occasioned by smog that obstructed views in the Grand Canyon. The matter was resolved by a stakeholder negotiation which paid no attention to the study. (Incidentally, the facility in question has closed because natural gas became cheaper than coal, which nobody at the time could have predicted.) I may be wrong; of these more than 7,500 analyses there may be some that did make a difference. If so, a challenge for the research agenda of environmental economics over the next decade might be to track down those few studies.

Third, the theory of non-market valuation and the "best practices" for applying it have become so dense, complicated, difficult, grueling, thorny, and challenging that they defy implementation. As evidence, I point to an article co-authored by 12 environmental economists, "Contemporary Guidance for Stated Preference Studies," which appears in the *Journal of the Association of Environmental and Resource Economists* in the year of grace 2017. The 12 authors – all academics, several of whom have contributed to the literature since the 1980s – have not emerged from the now thirty-year-old debate (since the 1989 *Exxon Valdez* oil spill) "over whether SP [stated preference] methods can provide credible information to inform decision making." In an article with 500 citations, these 12 scholars lay out 23 recommendations, each enormously demanding and each elucidated in terms of many sub-recommendations and stipulations which are themselves intricate and daunting. Here is a paragraph taken at random:

> Comparisons such as these can identify differences between the population and sample in terms of observable characteristics and can be used to re-weight response data to better represent the population (i.e., raking). However, these assessments provide little insight into the representativeness of a sample in terms of unobservable characteristics. To discern whether there is evidence of a correlation between unobservable characteristics and survey responses, a Heckman-type selection model can be estimated. There are various applications in the SP literature. This approach can be applied to continuous and binary response data, but selection models have not been developed for more complex response data and panel data for limited dependent variables. For example, formal sample selection corrections for conditional logit models are not generally

available. In cases where formal methods do not yet exist, approximations may be used to gain insight into possible relationships between response propensities and estimated preferences.[9]

This paragraph does not just bang another nail in the coffin of SP methodology. It is the coffin itself.

The article, which dispenses almost 90 pages of similarly distilled wisdom, sets up a dilemma. Environmental economists will either follow the 23 recommendations or they will not. If they do, they cannot complete an analysis because the "best practices" are too difficult and too costly. If they do not, then the analysis will likely be wrong. Whether it is wrong, however, cannot be known because a non-market valuation is far too expensive to be replicated, and people so constantly change their views that preference, whatever it is, is a river in which one cannot step twice.

Non-market valuation is impossible because market valuation is impossible. Markets reveal prices not preferences. Prices work to convey information and to co-ordinate interests, abilities, and knowledge. It is true that markets fail to maximize aggregate WTP or preference-satisfaction, but this is not what they intend to do or what justifies them. History has shown that open, free, and fair markets do something completely different than satisfy preferences: they promote social prosperity and peace. This is much better than aggregate net WTP.

The problem is not to define and measure value, whether as labor surplus (as Marx believed) or consumer surplus (as welfare economists assume today). According to Hayek, it is:

> to analyze how the spontaneous interaction of a number of people, each possessing only bits of knowledge, brings about a state of affairs in which prices correspond to costs, etc. and which could be brought about by deliberate direction only by someone who possessed the combined knowledge of all those individuals.[10]

Hayek also wrote that "legislation proper [. . .] should not be governed by interests but by opinion, i.e. by views about what kind of action is right or wrong."[11]

Fourth, if the standard theory and its application no longer provide career paths for graduate students, environmental economics is dead. Max Weber, in "Science as a Vocation" (a lecture given in Munich in 1917), argued that the first question one must ask about an academic science is: "What are the prospects of a graduate student who is resolved to dedicate himself professionally to science in university life?" After the Environmental Awakening in 1970, the field of environmental

---

9 Johnston et al. (2017): p. 369; eight citations and two footnotes omitted.
10 Hayek (1948): p. 50.
11 Hayek (1979): p. 112.

economics offered new Ph.Ds in economics many opportunities to make their living by teaching, applying, and advancing the standard theory. MacArthur, Pew, and many other foundations supported environmental economists to elicit WTP for environmental public goods. Do these opportunities and sources of support still exist? If the mountain of non-market valuation has labored to produce not even a policy mouse, this investment is a sunk cost. There is no reason for society to throw good money after bad.

Those who attained professorships in environmental and welfare economics between the 1970s and 1990s, several of whom are co-authors of the "Contemporary Guidance" paper just discussed, will want to teach their science to new genera-tions of economists. Can these professors in good conscience advise and encour-age students to take on the burden, including financial debt, to study and write dissertations in the area of non-market valuation, SP methods and practices, and WTP measurement? If so, I have really missed something. If not environmental economics in its standard form is dead.

2.8   What has environmental economics to do with economics or the environment?

According to Richard Revesz and Robert Stavins, "Most economists would argue that economic efficiency – achieved when the difference between benefits and costs is maximized – ought to be one of the fundamental criteria for evaluating environ-mental protection efforts."[12] The idea that economists can measure (not just define) benefit in terms of preference, which is the essence of the concept of economic efficiency, was by the early 1990s dissolved in sardonic acid.[13] Environmental economists, like whack-a-moles, still pop up to reveal to ignorant laypeople like me the concept of Pigouvian externalities and the importance of paying economists to measure social costs and benefits. They live in the echo-chamber of their fellow environmental economists. No one outside of the circle of welfare economists cares about economic efficiency, or has any reason to care about it, since it seems to be irrelevant to the economic goals people do care about, such as jobs, productivity, and inflation. Nor does anyone other than these economists believe that science can define and measure value.

As William Bromley has written, environmental economists share a "universal conviction that economics is the 'science of choice.'" Choice is defined in terms of preference. Because environmental economists believe they have a science to measure preference, Bromley satirizes:

> There is only one tool that can reveal the "truth" about the socially optimal level of envi-ronmental quality – and that tool happens to be owned by environmental economists. If

---

12 Revesz and Stavins (2007): p. 4.
13 Sagoff (1994).

you want to know what is right (optimal) to do with respect to the environment, then you must ask us – and you must rely on our tool for that answer.[14]

Ronald Coase wrote in the *Harvard Business Review* in December 2012: "The degree to which economics is isolated from the ordinary business of life is extraordinary and unfortunate." He added:

At a time when the modern economy is becoming increasingly institutions-intensive, the reduction of economics to price theory is troubling enough. It is suicidal for the field to slide into a hard science of choice, ignoring the influences of society, history, culture, and politics on the working of the economy.[15]

Economists in the tradition of Adam Smith, in contrast to welfare economists, study how markets work rather than how they fail. These economists recognize that goods do not exist in fixed or static amounts to be allocated and consumed by those who "value" them most. Instead, in the appropriate competitive conditions – conditions in which price signals convey information about such things as scarcity, bring prices down to costs, etc. – economic activity is creative and dynamic. Markets succeed or fail insofar as they encourage innovation; substitute plentiful for scarce goods to serve the same purposes; get more output from less labor, materials, and energy; and promote social prosperity and peace. None of this has any known relation to Static or Sterile-State economics, where preferences and resources are "given" and where environmental economists know or can know enough about them to calculate the collective social interest.

A survey that appeared in the *Journal of Environmental Economics and Management* (*JEEM*) in November 2018, "Research Trends in Environmental and Resource Economics," classified all 1,672 articles published in that journal from 1974 to 2014, along with the 100 most cited articles in four other journals with similar interests. According to this review, "Since the 1990s, there has been increasing interest in general methodological improvements of stated and revealed preference methods."[16] This topic is pursued in hundreds of articles – more than any other. Another survey published in 2017 "made available a unique database comprising 1,657 choice experiment and/or contingent valuation articles published in journals related to agriculture, environment or health between 2004 and 2016."[17]

You might think that environmental economists would look at the compliance costs of regulations as well as their benefits. The MacArthur Foundation, the Pew Charitable Trusts, and other funders, however, wanted to hear about the benefits of regulation – the bigger the better. Likewise, environmental groups wanted big damage estimates; as did plaintiffs. The compliance costs to industry – well that requires a different kind

---

14 Bromley (2004): p. 77.
15 Coase (2012a): p. 36.
16 Kube et al. (2018): p. 435.
17 Mahieu et al. (2017).

of information. The *JEEM* survey comments, "Surprisingly, the journal focuses more on the assessment of environmental damages than on the cost of pollution controls." The authors of the survey add: "To our surprise, studies assessing the costs of pollution control, including estimates of particular abatement cost functions, do not figure at all prominently in the journal (34 articles in all), which focuses more on the assessment of environmental damages rather than on [compliance] costs."[18]

2.9 Long live environmental economics

The authors of "Research Trends in Environmental and Resource Economics" note that in recent years they have seen "a significant shift away from economic theory and towards empirical approaches." They saw a shift away from the estimation of non-market costs and benefits, the valuation of public goods, and the rational construction of abstract theoretical policy instruments, such as "cap-and-trade" regimes. They saw a shift away from statism and scientism toward knowledge about how markets work, how they determine prices for environmental goods, how regulations affect market behavior, and how technological change moves the production frontier. By "knowledge" I mean empirical knowledge; this is positive economics not normative economics. Economists should study facts not values.

There is still enormous work to be done, for example, on the effect of energy markets, including alternative technologies, on the environment especially in view of climate change. The economics of wind and solar generation is so enmeshed in politics and regulation it offers huge research opportunities for environmental economists. Likewise, economists are needed to explore the regulatory context in which nuclear technology can become more relevant as a zero-carbon energy source. This kind of research requires knowledge of a kind not to be obtained by SP surveys even if they meet all 23 criteria for credibility.

Nearly every major industrial investment – for example, in building a pipeline or renovating a dam – goes through a permitting process. How do market players and regulators interact, and what kinds of exchanges do they make? How are projects that affect the environment negotiated? Articles appearing in *Ecological Economics* concerning dam removal permitting at the U.S. Federal Energy Regulatory Commission (FERC) argue that ecosystem valuation studies have had negligible or minimal influence on the agency. "The dominant activity [. . .] was to determine the most feasible and cost-effective way to remove the dams. It was during the resolution phase that an ecosystem valuation study was conducted, primarily to legitimize a decision that had been made earlier."[19]

I looked in recent contents of *JEEM* for evidence of an empirical turn in environmental economics, which is to say a redirection of attention from detecting the

---

18 Kube et al. (2018): p. 446.
19 Gowan et al. (2006): p. 520.

preference schedules inside people's heads toward investigating the economy and the environment. A search revealed that in 2018 alone the term "stated preference" appeared in 137 articles appeared in *JEEM* alone. The word "compliance cost" appeared in four. This is a change. In the previous three years of publication, the term "compliance cost" appeared only once per year.

Environmental economics will make the empirical turn because it must. It cannot continue to be fixated on its theory of valuation; it must be more willing to learn about the economy and the environment. I say this because none of the criticisms of the standard theory I have drawn here is original. I have merely related the views of Amartya Sen, Ronald Dworkin, Guido Calabresi, Duncan Kennedy, and many others I deeply admire. That environmental economists have never responded to this critique should tell you something. Environmental economists have never replied except to point attention to other matters, such as distributional issues, the interests of future generations, and the status of non-anthropocentric values, which are important topics but not relevant.

Mainstream environmental economists play the hurdy-gurdy that sings of Pareto optimality, potential Pareto improvement, Kaldor-Hicks efficiency, compensating and equivalent variations, and WTP, as if their critics have never heard of these things. How ignorant we must be! I believe that younger environmental economists will not be interested in turning the crank on this ancient organ. If they do, when the monkey comes out for funding, its cup will not be filled.

In his essay "What Should Economists Do?" James Buchanan wrote, "The theory of choice must be removed from its position of eminence in the economist's thought processes." He urged: "I want economists to modify their thought processes, to look at the same phenomena through 'another window,' to use Nietzsche's appropriate metaphor. I want them to concentrate on *exchange* rather than on *choice*."[20]

Buchanan continued: "I am simply proposing, in various ways, that economists concentrate attention on the institutions, the relationships, among individuals as they participate in voluntarily organized activity, in trade or exchange, broadly considered." When environmental economists see their task as one of valuation – allocative efficiency – they try to climb into the heads of individuals to view their preferences. They must then remain in their own heads to discuss their methodology. If they look through the empirical window of exchange rather than the hypothetical window of preference – at institutions which enable people to participate in voluntarily organized activity – they still may not be able to solve environmental problems. But at least they will know what the problems are.

---

20 Buchanan (1964): p. 217; emphasis in original.

References

Bromley, Daniel W. "Reconsidering environmental policy: prescriptive consequentialism and volitional pragmatism." *Environmental and Resource Economics* 28, no. 1 (2004): 73–99.

Buchanan, James M. "What should economists do?" *Southern Economic Journal* (1964): 213–222.

Coase, Ronald. "Saving economics from the economists." *Harvard Business Review* 90 (2012a): 36.

Coase, Ronald. *The Firm, the Market, and the Law*. Chicago: University of Chicago Press (2012b).

Cropper, M.L. and W.E. Oates. "Environmental economics: a survey." *Journal of Economic Literature* 30 (1992): 675–740.

Elmes, James. *A Practical Treatise on Ecclesiastical and Civil Dilapidations*. 3rd edn. London: Samuel Brooke (1829).

Goodstein, E.S. *Economics and the Environment*. Englewood Cliffs, NJ: Prentice Hall (1995).

Gowan, Charles, Kurt Stephenson, and Leonard Shabman. "The role of ecosystem valuation in environmental decision making: hydropower relicensing and dam removal on the Elwha River." *Ecological Economics* 56, no. 4 (2006): 508–523.

Hausman, Jerry A., ed. *Contingent Valuation: A Critical Assessment*. Bingley: Emerald (1993).

Hayek, F.A. *Law, Legislation and Liberty*. vol. III, London: Routledge (1979).

Hayek, F.A. *Individualism and Economic Order*. Chicago: University of Chicago Press (1948).

Hayek, F.A. "Scientism and the study of society: part III." *Economica* 11, no. 41 (1944): 27–39.

Johnston, Robert J., Kevin J. Boyle, Wiktor Adamowicz, Jeff Bennett, Roy Brouwer, Trudy Ann Cameron, W. Michael Hanemann et al. "Contemporary guidance for stated preference studies." *Journal of the Association of Environmental and Resource Economists* 4, no. 2 (2017): 319–405.

Kube, Roland, Andreas Löschel, Henrik Mertens, and Till Requate. "Research trends in environmental and resource economics: insights from four decades of JEEM." *Journal of Environmental Economics and Management* 92 (2018): 433–464.

Mahieu, Pierre-Alexandre, Henrik Andersson, Olivier Beaumais, Romain Crastes dit Sourd, Stephane Hess, and François-Charles Wolff. "Stated preferences: a unique database composed of 1657 recent published articles in journals related to agriculture, environment, or health." *Review of Agricultural, Food and Environmental Studies* 98, no. 3 (2017): 201–220.

Revesz, Richard L., and Robert Stavins. *Environmental Law and Policy*. Working Paper No. w13575. National Bureau of Economic Research (2007).

Ruff, Larry. The economic common sense of pollution. *Public Interest* 19 (1993): 69–85.

Sagoff, Mark. "Should preferences count?" *Land Economics* (1994): 127–144.

Schmitt, C. *Die Diktatur: Von den Anfängen des modernen Souveränitätsgedankens bis zum proletarischen Klassenkampf*. Berlin: Duncker & Humblot (1989).

Sen, Amartya K. "Rational fools: a critique of the behavioral foundations of economic theory." *Philosophy and Public Affairs* 6, no. 4 (1977): 317–344.

Stavins, Robert N. *Environmental Economics*. Working Paper No. w13574. National Bureau of Economic Research (2007).

3 Conceptual and political foundations for examining the interaction between nature and economy

Malte Faber and Marc Frick[1]

3.1 Central aspects of environmental problems: nature, justice and time

Rethinking the field of environmental economics in a visionary and perhaps provocative way demands that the research agenda deals with three fields: nature, justice and time. These dimensions are so encompassing that it is necessary to show how they can be approached in an operational way. This chapter attempts to contribute to this task. We shall do this by developing an approach which is based on fundamental concepts such as *absolute and relative scarcity, evolution, ignorance,* and *joint production* based on thermodynamics and responsibility, *power of judgment* and a new understanding of human behaviour – *homo politicus.* This demands *knowledge* from different fields. We note that:

> in modern times, the sciences give us access to all of these fields. No single individual can master all of those sciences at once. Even if there were such a universal genius with outstanding expertise in economics, law, the social sciences and the natural sciences, especially physics, biology and chemistry, that individual still would not possess the skills to bring all of that knowledge together into a comprehensive understanding or help achieve such a comprehensive understanding and its network of concepts. (Faber et al. 2018: 6)

The concepts we propose provide an interdisciplinary approach to environmental problems, and make it possible to identify and systematically organize the knowledge necessary to solve these problems. In doing so, the complexity of environmental–economic interaction can be reduced. The challenge is thereby transformed into concrete questions and made accessible in practical terms for environmental policy measures. We will argue on theoretical, historical, economic, natural scientific, ethical and political levels.

After explaining the six concepts mentioned above in Section 3.2, we will illustrate them in Section 3.3 with a historical example: the development of the soda-chlorine

---

1 We are grateful to Suzanne von Engelhardt for her editorial work, and to Matthias Ruth and Marco Rudolf for helpful comments on this chapter.

industry ranging over a period of 300 years, from 1750 to 2050. In Section 3.4 we show the lessons that can be drawn from the *temporal* structure of the economic environmental interactions, ignorance, the scope of the problems, the actors behind them and their solutions.

In Section 3.5, we apply the concept of *responsibility* to address problems occurring in the interplay between nature and economy. Since the ability of individuals to assume *individual responsibility* is narrowly limited by their ignorance, another dimension of responsibility needs to be employed: *political responsibility*. The latter takes into account a central challenge for effective environmental policy, the occurrence of ignorance and even *irreducible ignorance*. In order to deal with it, the faculty of *power of judgment* is introduced and assigned to the *homo politicus*. The latter does not substitute but rather complements the *homo oeconomicus* model. In our outlook in Section 3.6, we argue that these concepts do not form a hierarchically structured system. Instead they are conceived as a network of interdependent concepts that reference each other but also remain categorically distinct from one another (Faber et al. 2018). From this follows that it is important to find further concepts to reduce the complexity of environmental issues and structure existing knowledge, thus enabling policymakers to be guided by responsibility when taking practical action.

3.2 The concepts

In our past research we have worked with about 15 general concepts that are fundamental to understanding the world (see Faber et al. 2018). They are constitutive concepts of nature, such as *entropy*, and concepts from the social sciences like *homo politicus*. In this section we want to limit ourselves to six of them, and explain their fruitfulness by using them to examine the interaction of nature and economy by the illustration of the soda-chlorine industry.

First, we turn to the notion of absolute and relative scarcity. Thereafter, we explain a central concept in the field of time, that of evolution. In almost all our previous studies on the impact of the economy on the environment, *time* has played a prominent role (e.g. cf. Faber, Proops in cooperation with Manstetten 1998; Faber et al. 1999; Klauer et al. 2017). In doing so, we have repeatedly found that not only are *knowledge* and *novelty* relevant for our research, but above all the explicit consideration of *ignorance* as well.

Two of the six concepts are of particular importance in this chapter: the concepts of production, especially *joint production*, and *responsibility* since they "attempt to capture the physical and the moral side of economic production. Both terms exhibit a structural relatedness, which is why they are especially well suited to more precisely define the requirements of practical politics in their relationship to the environment" (Faber et al. 2018: 6). Finding such concepts or principles is always a matter of *judgment* (Klauer et al. 2017: Chapter 7) because these concepts cannot be deduced from a series of potentially different types of observations. The *power of judgment*, our fifth concept, "has the ability to reflect on such possible principles that may allow us to understand differing fields and how they are interrelated" (Faber et al. 2018: 6f.). Finally, we come to our human actors, *homo oeconomicus* and *homo politicus*.

3.2.1   Absolute and relative scarcity

The concept of absolute scarcity of nature was introduced into classical economic thought by Thomas Robert Malthus. Examples of absolute scarcity are water in a desert or water and food in a besieged castle. Similarly, we experience today that certain environmental goods are becoming scarcer and scarcer, as is the case in the loss of biodiversity (Baumgärtner et al. 2006a).

Economics prominently employs another type of scarcity: the concept *of relative scarcity*, i.e. a good is scarce in relation to other scarce goods. Scarce goods have a positive price. The price of non-scarce goods is zero. The use of relative scarcity implies that each good can be substituted. As the example of the loss of biodiversity shows, this is not always the case. The same holds for the consequences of climate change, such as water scarcity or regular flooding. Here we are talking of absolute scarcity. The longer the time period, the more urgent is the phenomenon of absolute scarcity.

3.2.2   Evolution

While the concept of space is relatively easy to grasp, the concept of time is much more difficult to perceive. The nature of time has been – already in Greek philosophy – a source of contention (Klauer et al. 2017: Chapter 8). To understand and analyse the interplay between nature and the economy we need a broad view of time since we have to consider short-, medium- and in particular long-term repercussions. Hence, we have to structure the flow of time. What then is an appropriate concept of time? A good starting point to get an idea of temporal structures is the concept of evolution. Evolutionary economists (e.g. Nelson and Winter 1982) started their research in the 1960s by following Joseph A. Schumpeter's ideas of evolutionary thought, developed in his seminal work *The Theory of Economic Development* (1934; first published in German in 1912). However, this work had little impact on the research of environmental economists. With the development of ecological economics in the 1980s, evolution became a key concept (e.g. Norgaard 1984; Faber, Proops in cooperation with Manstetten 1998; Schiller 2002).

The concept of evolution is fruitful for the interaction between nature and the economy because it allows us to combine the structure of time with concepts such as ignorance and novelty:[2]

---

2 One must make sure to be careful with analogies from biology for the use in economic theorizing (see for details Ruth 1996).

For instance, the concepts of genotype (the gene structure of a living being) and phenotype (the realization of a living being) can be employed not just in a biological context but also in a physical and economical context. This broad view of evolution is useful for two reasons: (i) Several concepts first introduced in natural science are useful because they provide economics with a physical foundation. (ii) The way natural science has treated time and irreversibility offers important lessons to economics, for many economic actions have irreversible consequences, like the use of groundwater which cannot be replaced if it is extracted too fast. (Faber et al. 2018: 12)

To give an example, the *invention* of a technique can be interpreted as a genotypic change of an economy, while the actual realization, the *innovation*, can be seen as a phenotypic development. As we will see in the following section, the time lag between invention and innovation can be rather long.

Individuals, scientists and politicians who are concerned about the environment are particularly interested in long-term developments during which novelty, in our terminology genotypic change, can unfold; here time, evolution and ignorance are of particular relevance. However,

many branches of science tend to conceive of their objects of study as rather timeless; they tend to represent their findings in "eternal" laws, such as the Law of Classical Mechanics. The application of such kinds of science easily leads to the belief that future events are predictable. This predictability would have been complete for that ideal scientist, Laplace's demon (Prigogine and Stengers 1984). In contrast to this approach, we start from the assumption that the objects and their relationships which science examines are intrinsically characterized by complete or partial emergence of novelty in the course of time. This leads us to develop new concepts to answer this question. A key notion for our approach is evolution. (Faber, Proops in cooperation with Manstetten 1998: 19–20)

We employ a general concept of evolution (developed at length in Faber, Proops in cooperation with Manstetten 1998: Parts II and III) to be able to understand and deal with long-term interactions between economic activity and its impact on the environment, and vice versa. By employing concepts from biology and physics, in addition to economics, we can identify the extent to which we can and cannot predict long-term developments. This enables us to become aware of our ignorance and to incorporate this knowledge explicitly into our theorizing and policies, which is particularly relevant for environmental policy making.

3.2.3 Knowledge, novelty and ignorance

Focusing our attention on our *ignorance* instead of our *knowledge* creates a decisive shift in economic theory and environmental policy. When dealing with an environmental problem, we often notice that we do not know whether we are able to solve it or not. One reason for this state of affairs is that we are not aware of what we can know and what we cannot know. To clarify this important question, an analysis of ignorance is needed. We have dealt with this epistemological question in Faber et al. (1992a, 1992b), where we develop a classification with eight forms of ignorance.[3] A deepened understanding of ignorance yields new attitudes towards environmental problems: attitudes of openness and flexibility instead of control and inflexibility.

Knight (1921) differentiated between "risk" and "uncertainty". Risk occurs when not only all possible outcomes are known, but also their probabilities. In the case of uncertainty, only the outcomes but not their probabilities are known. Ignorance occurs if we do not know the outcomes in advance. To give an example: most people were ignorant about the catastrophe in Fukushima in Japan in 2011. In contrast to risk and uncertainty, ignorance has not yet received the attention it deserves in economics; or, as Hayek put it:

> Perhaps it is only natural that the circumstances which limit our factual knowledge and the ensuing limits to applying our theoretical knowledge go rather unnoticed in the exuberance which has been brought about by the successful progress of science. However, it is high time that we took our ignorance more seriously. (1972: 33; our translation)[4]

In the following sections we shall employ several forms of ignorance from our classification referred to above. Important for our argumentation below are the following:

- *Individual* and *social ignorance*: Ignorance can be ascribed to the individual, a community or even a society. In the first case, we speak of personal or individual ignorance because the required information is generally available within a society but unknown to the individual. The second case falls into the category of social ignorance, i.e. the required information is unavailable not only on an individual level but also to society. These types of ignorance can be reduced by learning on a personal level and by science on a communal level (Faber, Proops in cooperation with Manstetten 1998: 119–120).
- *Closed* and *open ignorance.* We speak of closed ignorance whenever we are unaware of our ignorance. The possibility of risk, uncertainty and surprise remains unexpected in this case. In contrast to closed ignorance, open ignorance occurs when individuals, communities or societies are aware of it and are in a state of openness towards their ignorance (ibid.: 116f.).
- *Reducible* and *irreducible ignorance*: Reducible ignorance can be overcome by learning and by science. In contrast to that, irreducible ignorance cannot be reduced by the accumulation of knowledge (ibid.: 118f.).

---

3 See as well: Faber, Manstetten and Proops (1998: Chapter 11); Faber, Proops in cooperation with Manstetten (1998: Chapter 7); Faber and Manstetten (2010: Chapter 4); also Funtovicz and Ravetz (1991); Smithson (1988). In contrast to these authors, we shall place special emphasis on aspects of time and evolution, for our special interest has been evolutionary problems in a broad sense, including environmental questions as particular cases.

4 Translations from non-English sources are by the authors.

In the following, we link the concept of ignorance with the concepts of joint production and responsibility. The consequences of joint products for the environment need to be taken into account, as does the responsibility of economic and social actors for dealing with those consequences. To be responsible, however, requires the ability to foresee the consequences of one's actions, as we will explain in Section 3.4. Thus, responsibility raises the problem of the limits of knowledge and, in turn, of ignorance.

3.2.4   Joint production

The notion of joint production describes the phenomenon that several outputs *necessarily* emerge from economic activity:[5]

> [It] can capture the essential thermodynamic constraints of production processes, as expressed by the First and Second Laws of thermodynamics, through an easy-to-use and easy-to-understand economic concept. [. . .] This holds for production in both economic systems and ecosystems. Joint production, therefore, is also a fundamental notion in ecology even though it is not often expressed as such in that discipline. Organisms and ecosystems as open, self-organizing systems, necessarily take in several inputs and generate several outputs, just as an economy does. Indeed, such natural systems are the earliest examples of joint production. (Baumgärtner et al. 2006b: 5)

In summary, joint products are essential elements to formulate the biophysical constraints of economic activity. They relate to the repercussions of production and consumption on the environment.

The occurrence of joint production has been well known since the beginnings of agricultural activity; an example is sheep farming: a sheep does not only yield milk, but also wool and finally meat. All sectors of modern economies are characterized by joint production. This is particularly true in the chemical industry, where many of the joint products are useful. But, in the meantime, everyone knows that joint production, as for example the production of steel, yields unwanted goods as well – so-called bads such as dust, waste water, sludge, and CO_2 – which are unwanted because they damage the environment.

"The power and generality of joint production can be demonstrated through the way it embraces four central issues in ecological economics: irreversibility, limits to substitution, the ubiquity of waste, and the limits of growth" (Baumgärtner et al. 2006b: 5).[6] There exists a close relationship between joint production, responsibility and ignorance, as will be shown in Section 3.3.

---

5 Georg Müller-Fürstenberger (1995) conducted a pioneering theoretical and empirical study on joint production in the chemical industry.

6 For more details see Baumgärtner et al. (2006b: 5f.) and Baumgärtner (2000).

3.2.5   Responsibility

Responsibility is a ubiquitous phenomenon. The concept of responsibility broadens the scope of our economic investigation to incorporate an ethical perspective which is based on philosophical reasoning. This is particularly important since

> economic activity generally produces two kinds of output: the intended principal product and unintended by-products. We would expect, and indeed observe, that producers will focus their attention and energies on the former, while the latter will be largely ignored, at least to the extent permitted by legal constraints and social mores. This inattention to the undesired products raises two issues of a philosophical nature, one relating to responsibility, that is ethical, and one relating to knowledge that is epistemological. (Baumgärtner et al. 2006b: 7–8)

What is responsibility? It links the consequences of an action to the actor. There are several forms of responsibility (see Baumgärtner et al. 2006b: Part III). In everyday life, the distinction between moral and legal responsibility is well known. Less familiar is the distinction between individual and collective responsibility. One form of the latter is political responsibility. "Ascribing responsibility in this differentiated way helps reduce complexity, for it shows who is responsible for what and to what extent. This allows us to distinguish between reality and wishful thinking" (Faber et al. 2018: 15).

Responsibility is also an important notion for the understanding of the concepts of *homo oeconomicus* and *homo politicus*, for these two pictures of humankind are characterized by different ranges of responsibility: *Homo oeconomicus* is responsible for his own concerns and his compliance with legal limits. *Homo politicus*, in contrast, assumes responsibility for the good state of the community and its sustainable orientation (Faber et al. 1997).

3.2.6   Power of judgment

Power of judgment is a certain capability which cannot be taught, but can only be learned by experience: "In contrast to the discursive reasoning of mind, the judgments of the power of judgment are not necessarily logically consistent, each time repeatable and necessary (Kant 1960.II: 184). The judgments of the power of judgment do not fulfil the latter three conditions since they have an irrevocable element of freedom and spontaneity and refer strongly to practical knowledge based on everyday experiences" (Petersen et al. 2000: 141–142; our translation).

The concept of power of judgment has a long history in philosophy, and indeed was analysed at length by Aristotle during the fourth century BC. Its revival came with the seminal work of Immanuel Kant in the eighteenth century. As Kant put it, "We need judgment when we wish to make practical use of or follow a theory. [. . .] Thus judgment must 'subsume' specific or practical circumstances under rules and concepts. This is necessary when action needs to occur" (in Klauer et al. 2017: 99).

We illustrate this statement with the famous quote by Martin Luther: "Here I stand, I cannot do otherwise. God help me, Amen!" (Faber and Manstetten 2010: 65; see also 64–67).

Power of judgment was a prominent concept in economics during the eighteenth and nineteenth centuries. However, it fell into oblivion in economics when mathematics started to be increasingly employed over the course of the twentieth century. It had its renaissance in ecological economics at the end of the last century. So what led to this revival? We have explained above with the concept ignorance the important role ignorance plays in the solution of environmental problems. When we are dealing with ignorance, we need power of judgment to make decisions. In addition, the contexts in which environmental problems are solved often require different approaches. As there are no general decision-making rules due to the multitude of contexts, power of judgment is required (Klauer et al. 2017: Chapters 8–10; Petersen et al. 2000). In Section 3.5 we shall give a practical illustration.

3.2.7   *Homo oeconomicus* and *homo politicus*

The concept of the *homo oeconomicus* is perhaps the most central assumption of economics because it is still a central pillar of economic theory. However, it is claimed by behavioural economics as well as by various heterodox economic approaches that this concept of human behaviour in economics is not as relevant empirically as assumed in major economics textbooks. As argued by ecological economists, the major reliance on the *homo oeconomicus* is a hindrance in achieving a sustainable policy, for it undermines individual beliefs in a good society and because the *homo oeconomicus* is solely self-centred (Petersen and Faber 2001).

Nevertheless, this concept captures one important trait of human beings – their self-orientation. For this reason, the concept enables scientists to gain valuable insights into economic behaviour and even to a certain extent into political behaviour, which form the basis for economic policies (Downs 1957). We note in passing: while economics very much emphasizes the competitive nature of humans, and the role of competition in general to achieve desirable (market) outcomes, much of human nature and interactions is based on collaboration, partnerships, etc. (see for e.g. Maturana and Varela 1987: Chapter 8).

Behavioural economics and heterodox approaches hold that the concept of *homo oeconomicus* has not to be substituted but supplemented with other conceptions of humans. In this chapter we propose as an additional dimension of human behaviour the concept of *homo politicus*. The roots of *homo politicus* originate in political philosophy, in particular from Aristotle, Kant and Hegel (see e.g. Faber et al. 1997; Faber et al. 2002; Hottinger 1998; Manstetten et al. 1998).

The *homo politicus* is interested in justice, the common good, and in the sustainability of natural living conditions. A major difference between the *homo oeconomicus* and the *homo politicus* is that the former is limited to a short-term time perspective while the latter has a long-term one too. That perspective enables her/him to care also for long-term interests, in particular for securing the sustainability of natural living conditions. Facing the complexity of *novelty* and *ignorance* linked to a long-term perspective, *homo politicus* requires a particular faculty in order to make good decisions – the faculty of *power of judgment.*[7]

3.3   The case study of the soda-chlorine industry

In this section, we apply the concepts introduced above – absolute and relative scarcity, evolution, ignorance, joint production, responsibility, power of judgment, and *homo oeconomicus* and *homo politicus* – to an example from history, and examine the theoretical and practical insights that can be obtained from them.

Applying the different scientific concepts dealt with in Section 3.2 can be challenging, especially since they originate from very different disciplines. In order to facilitate an understanding, we will illustrate them with a case from industrial history. The history of the soda-chlorine industry exemplarily shows the close connection between the development of an industrial structure, scarcity of natural resources, environmental pollution, and the reactions of economic agents and politics (see Müller-Fürstenberger 1995: 179–221; Baumgärtner et al. 2006b: 292–306). The soda-chlorine industry has been of great economic significance because in the twentieth century it made up about 60 per cent of Germany's chemical industry, and was thus an important driver of economic growth.

We use its history to show the effects of the use of natural resources, of inventions and innovations of new technologies and their repercussions. It can be shown that new techniques were implemented to deal with scarcity of production factors, that environmental pollution was caused by these new technologies, which in turn led to new inventions and innovations in order to avoid pollution. This process, initiated by individuals, institutions and politics, also created new goods which in turn caused new environmental damage and new reactions, both in terms of business and politics. The creativity of scientists and inventors, economic actors and effective regulations by politicians, who assumed responsibility for protecting the public, are the driving forces of this evolution. We note that a key to understanding this development is its long time frame which leads to the occurrence of novelty and ignorance that have to be dealt with by individual and collective economic and political actors over the course of time. The corresponding time frame takes us from the middle of the eighteenth century to the middle of the twenty-first, meaning we shall deal with a time frame of about 300 years.

---

7 We note in passing that the empirical relevance of the concept of *homo politicus* was shown in Petersen and Faber (2000).

3.3.1   From potash to synthetic soda

The textile industry is called the "mother of industry" because it was the first economic activity in history that can be termed an "industry". The most important production factor for bleaching was potash, which was obtained by burning wood. For one ton of potash, for instance, 1400 tons of birch wood had to be burned. This demand quickly led to deforestation. The production factor wood thus became *absolutely scarce*.

For this reason, potash had to be replaced by natural soda, which had to be imported from Egypt or Spain. In Spain it was obtained from Barilla, salt-tolerant plants that became the primary source for soda ash. When soda from Egypt became absolutely scarce and the sea blockade by the British navy stopped the import of Barilla from Spain in the 1760s and 1770s, this led to increasing scarcity of soda on the European continent. Facing this situation of social ignorance concerning the substitution of natural sources of soda, in 1775 the French Academy decided to offer a prize for the invention of the synthetic production of soda. This can be seen as an intervention by a social institution: a collective actor assumed responsibility in order to overcome a situation that was not solved by the market. It took 16 years before this prize was awarded to Nicolas Leblanc in 1791. He had invented the so-called Leblanc process, thus *novelty* had occurred.

Only in 1822, i.e. 31 years after its invention, was the Leblanc process finally innovated in Great Britain in a way that allowed it to be implemented on a large scale in the industry. The scarcity of natural soda was overcome by the manufacturing of synthetic soda. This innovation was triggered by economic actors behaving according to the *homo oeconomicus* model. This development illustrates the importance of the concepts of scarcity, ignorance, *homo oeconomicus*, responsibility, economic evolution, novelty and *homo politicus*, as will be described in more detail in Section 3.4.

3.3.2   Leblanc process, pollution and the Chlorine Alkali Bill

While up to now we have taken an economic and social perspective when talking about scarcity and the way it was overcome, in a next step we turn to an aspect of production that requires the natural sciences. The solution to the situation of scarcity was an economic and social success, but it demanded its price since the production of synthetic soda in the Leblanc process led to the occurrence of joint products. The production of 100kg of soda was accompanied by the production of 69kg of hydrogen chloride (HCL), 68kg of calcium sulphides (CaS) and 83kg of carbon dioxide (CO_2) (see Müller-Fürstenberger 1995: 182; Baumgärtner et al. 2006b: 293–299). The first two joint products, HCL and CaS, created serious social problems and caused damage to the economic system (for details see Baumgärtner et al. 2006b: 294–295). We see that this chemical process necessarily leads not only to unwanted but also to harmful joint products. This illustrates the relevance of natural sciences for an appropriate analysis of economic–environmental interactions.

We observe how, over time, the solution to a problem of economic scarcity generated a new problem: air pollution that endangered humans, animals and plants. The consequences of this pollution became more and more of a problem. This led to public social resistance at the beginning of the 1830s. Here, people stood up and assumed their individual and finally politicians their political responsibility. Again it took a long time before politics reacted and passed legislation in the form of the British Chlorine Alkali Act of 1863. This political intervention, an act of political responsibility, turns out to be a new element within the process of social, economic and environmental evolution.

As a result of the Chlorine Alkali Bill, industrial producers were obliged to convert hydrogen chloride to hydrochloric acid, which they released into rivers and lakes. So instead of polluting the air, water was used as a receptor of pollutants, and was thus itself subsequently polluted. This resulted in the death of fish in lakes and rivers and the corroding of economic assets such as metal boats and sluice gates, consequences people were unaware of – a case of social ignorance. Ten years later, renewed public resistance as a result of individual and social responsibility led to the amendment of the Chlorine Alkali Bill in 1874, which regulated the introduction of fluid waste as well. Politicians had finally assumed their political responsibility.

3.3.3   The Deacon process: a next step in evolution

The pressure exerted by the public initiated intense research, even before the introduction of the legislative amendment of 1874. The result of the research was the so-called Deacon process in 1869, named after its inventor, the British chemist Henry Deacon. Within the Deacon process a new type of novelty occurs: its innovation has made it possible to convert a bad, hydrochloride acid (HCL), into a highly desirable good – pure chlorine. Again, social ignorance evolved into novelty, and thus into knowledge. Henry Deacon, as well as those economic actors who invested in and innovated the new technology, acted as *homines oeconomici*. But they were driven not only by economic motives but also by public demand for solutions to the pollution problem. Individuals and social groups maintained the high pressure over a long period of time, and their success on a legislative level shows that they were driven by social responsibility and power of judgment. Hence, these individuals and social groups acted as *homines politici*. Pure chlorine, produced thanks to the Deacon process, was a good in such high demand that its production became increasingly important. So, ultimately, chlorine turned into the main product and soda the by-product.

At first glance it seems as if the problem of resource scarcity had not only been overcome, but also that a bad (HCL) had even been transformed into a very valuable good. Thus, challenges led to economic progress: an undesired and poisonous joint product led to socio-political and legal demand for change, which in turn led to strong incentives to overcome a technological and environmental status quo. In short, technical progress was able to overcome a severe economic and environmental problem, and at the same time contribute to economic welfare through the production of pure chlorine.

We conclude that the emergence of resource scarcity and pollutants as a result of joint products can be seen as a trigger for inventions and innovations. Ignorance concerning technical progress in terms of novelty had positive and negative effects. While the positive effects were a result of creativity in the market, negative effects could not be solved by the market, but only by politics.

3.3.4   CFCs: the destruction of the ozone layer

The solution to HCL pollution appeared to be a success story for almost a century. One major aspect of it was the development of chlorofluorocarbons (CFCs). Shortly after the invention of the Deacon process, CFCs were created experimentally around 1870. CFCs had many favourable characteristics: for example, they were not poisonous; and they were non-flammable and could be used for very different purposes, in particular for heat insulators and cooling. Therefore, they became an indispensable part of everyday life. Mass production of CFCs started in the 1930s. In 1974, 700,000 tons of CFCs were produced and 350,000 tons were emitted from refrigerators, freezers, cold storage facilities and refrigerator-transportation units and as propellants in spray cans.

In 1985, however, it was discovered that CFCs rise into the stratosphere (12–35km above the earth's surface) and damage or even destroy the ozone layer. This discovery of the amount of destruction came as a complete surprise to scientists and a shock (ignorance) to the general public and to politicians. The shock was even greater since it was forecast that it would take until 2050 for the ozone layer to restore itself to the concentration levels of 1970. The proposed necessary reduction of CFCs in the course of about 65 years was achieved by a worldwide international agreement, the Montreal Protocol on Substances that deplete the Ozone Layer, adopted in 1987. The time span between the invention of CFCs and the elimination of their damaging effects extends over almost two centuries. Once again, political responsibility, this time on a global scale, was needed in order to deal with negative effects caused by polluting joint products.

The phenomenon of CFCs makes evident the long-term time frame which has to be taken into account in such cases. Ignorance and joint production are challenges that require joint action by creative actors: *homo oeconomicus*, scientists and actors with a long-run mindset and a sense of political responsibility, and power of judgment such as *homo politicus*.

3.4   Lessons about the temporal structure of economic environmental interactions, ignorance, scope and actors of the problems and their solutions

In the previous section we illustrated how the concepts explained in Section 3.2 help us to theoretically grasp, systematically investigate and understand an empirical example from the field of complex nature–economy interactions as well as political reactions in reality. We have attempted to explain:

- how the terms and concepts introduced in Section 3.2 capture the emergence and temporal structure of economic and environmental interactions,
- their short-term solutions,
- the ignorance related to them and the repetition of this sequence when further problems arise from these solutions in the long run,
- how in this process, economic as well as social and political actors are involved,
- that these actors can be connected with the various triggers for the economic, social environmental and political evolution we have encountered in our historical example.

For ease of representation, it may be useful to describe this evolution, highlighting not only the corresponding concepts but also the relevant actors, in five consecutive stages:

1. The scarcity of production factor wood leads to substitution efforts (1750–1822, from potash to imported natural soda and Barilla). Here, an economic problem is solved by economic actors via the market system.
2. Renewed scarcity of soda leads to inventions and innovations. The question of how to deal with absolute scarcity of soda in 1775 led to the French Academy's announcement of a prize for producing synthetic soda. The Leblanc process was *invented* in 1791 but not *innovated* until 1822, thus leading to a substitution of imported natural soda and Barilla by synthetic soda. Here an economic problem was solved by economic and scientific actors via a social institution (*homo politicus*) providing the necessary incentive to promote the invention made available by science, and leading to its subsequent innovation via the market by *homo oeconomicus*.
3. However, there existed *social ignorance* concerning the environmental consequences of the Leblanc process. In the course of time, social resistance by *homines politici* arose against the effect of HCL pollution caused by consequences of joint products of the process. They affected people's health and led to a political reaction which initiated a change in the production process over the course of time (1863, Chlorine Alkali Bill).
4. There existed social ignorance concerning the environmental consequences of the Chlorine Alkali Bill. Social resistance by *homines politici* arose against the effect of pollution caused by *joint products* in the water which affected people's health and economic activities. A call for action articulated by society and jointly by consumers and producers (*homines oeconominici*) led to the invention of the Deacon process in 1869 and to the amendment of the Chlorine Alkali Bill in 1874. The innovation of the Deacon process caused a very important novelty: a polluting substance, HCL, became the basis for a completely new and very valuable product, pure chlorine.
5. In the 1970s, CFCs were invented. Again, there was social ignorance

concerning the health effects of the use of CFCs, for their potential health dangers were only recognized in 1974, and the causal relationship between damage to the ozone layer and skin cancer was not discovered until 1985. This came as a great *surprise*, not only to the public but also to science. Due to the great danger, a ban on CFCs was agreed on internationally in the Montreal Protocol. It was predicted that this ban would lead to the reduction of CFC levels in the atmosphere, restoring the levels of 1970 by 2050. This problem was first discovered and articulated by scientists and physicians. Their demand for a solution as well as demands by social actors (*homines politici*) led to international political regulation and the substitution of CFCs.

In four of these five cases, it is not the market (and therefore not *homo oeconomicus*) that provides the impetus for change, but social and political forces (and thus *homo politicus*) that set incentives for evolution in the form of legal regulations. Individuals act collectively (protesters), and politics ultimately assumes responsibility for regulating and changing an economic process with negative joint products.

This call for politicians to assume responsibility and enact appropriate regulations is also a well-known phenomenon in the current debate on the environment. In the following section, we want to use our concepts to show what needs to be known about the problem, and who can and should take responsibility for action in general.

3.5   Approaching the ethical core of environmental problems

The complexity of environmental problems results from the fact that they are multi-layered. At its core, this is an ethical problem, but the natural sciences and economics hold essential restrictions for any solutions. We consider the concept of responsibility to be an operational approach to come to grips with this ethical problem in practice. In the context of environmental problems, the concept of responsibility, though often mentioned, is not often applied in public in an unambiguous manner. Three central questions are:

- Who is responsible for the causation of environmental problems?
- Who is responsible for taking appropriate measures in the future?
- Who are the addressees for these two questions?

Our search for answers to these questions has been inspired by the seminal work *The Imperative of Responsibility: In Search of an Ethics for the Technological Age* by Hans Jonas. He turned to the concept of responsibility because he realized how challenging the various problems of the technological age were for classical ethical approaches (Jonas 1979: 222). The ability of humans to influence and damage the natural foundation of life was unknown in the context of traditional ethics in earlier times. Nature was considered to be outside the realm of human action. Jonas's approach is to reformulate the classical term of responsibility in the context of environmental destruction. He developed an "imperative of responsibility" that basically augments the obligation of humans to preserve the natural environment as it is the foundation of human existence (Jonas 1979: 36; also Baumgärtner et al. 2006b: 226; Becker et al. 2015). The root of this obligation lies in the power given to human beings by technology and the potentially destructive dynamics generated by it. Jonas formulates in the first two sentences of his preface of the German edition:

> When Prometheus was finally unleashed and given unprecedented force by science and relentless momentum by the economy, this called for an ethic by which he voluntarily restrains his power to prevent calamity to mankind. The transformation of the promise of modern technology into a threat, or its inextricable ties to it, form the starting point of this book. (Jonas 1979: 7; our translation)

Jonas sees clearly that freedom and power are linked to responsibility since only a person who acts freely can be called responsible for their actions and their consequences (Jonas 1979: 232; Baumgärtner et al. 2006b: 226).

In the following we want to complement the insights of Jonas by making use of the concepts explained in Section 3.2. We do this by closely connecting the concept of responsibility to the concepts of joint production and ignorance. This helps us to understand how environmental problems emerge, and how the characteristics of their occurrence shape the way they can be addressed in a responsible and sustainable manner. Once we have developed this understanding, we propose the *homo politicus*, characterized by the ability of power of judgment, as the actor who practically assumes this responsibility (see Baumgärtner et al. 2006b).

3.5.1 Individual responsibility

First, we ask what responsibility means beyond its manifold uses in everyday life. Responsibility expresses a causal connection: Whoever is responsible for an act can be ascribed to this act and its consequences. No consequences immediately result from this causal ascription for the actor. Beyond the mere attribution, this "causal power" as Jonas calls it, may have legal consequences and may have moral consequences. An essential precondition for these consequences is the freedom of an individual: "responsibility means that one is the perpetrator of one's deeds. A person can determine his will *freely*; he is free to determine his aim of acting and to do something in order to realize this aim" (Baumgärtner et al. 2006b: 226; emphasis in original). Hence, an individual who acts freely might be held responsible for something legally and morally as well. This means that he can be made "liable" for the action and its consequences on a legal level, and has to accept that his actions and its consequences are judged by others as "morally good" or "morally bad" (Jonas 1979: 172; Baumgärtner et al. 2006b: 226f.).

What does this mean for the responsibility an individual has to assume? This question can be answered by referring to negative and positive responsibility. In terms of negative responsibility, a freely acting individual is obliged to refrain from actions that cause harm to others. Anyone who assumes negative responsibility acts in accordance with this obligation.

Those who assume positive responsibility extend this obligation to refrain from harmful acts, and commit themselves to take care of the good condition of those for whom they declare themselves responsible. Positive responsibility does not only mean the omission of harmful actions but also working actively towards a good condition.

3.5.1.1   Joint production and ignorance as limits of individual responsibility

As noted above, freedom is a necessary condition for responsibility:

> Responsibility is the flip-side to a human being's freedom to act. A person is only the author and master of his actions insofar as he can assume responsibility for his actions and their consequences. That for which someone assumes responsibility can be ascribed to him [. . .] thus, only he who can assume responsibility is actually capable of taking concrete action. This raises the question of the extent of one's responsibility. (Baumgärtner et al. 2006b: 229)

An individual who is not free cannot assume responsibility for his deeds.

A second necessary condition for responsibility is the ability to acquire the available knowledge in society about the consequences of one's actions. Individual ignorance does not necessarily protect an individual against legal punishment. However, whenever this knowledge cannot be acquired, responsibility cannot be assumed (for a detailed analysis see Baumgärtner et al. 2006b: 230f.). Thus, it may occur that joint production is connected with irreducible ignorance. In contexts of high complexity, for example in the case of CFCs explained in Sections 3.3 and 3.4, there was no knowledge of the joint products or their negative consequences. Individuals as well as society were in a state of closed ignorance because no one was aware that possible negative joint products existed concerning the use of CFCs. Hence, neither the individuals nor society can be ascribed moral or legal responsibility (ibid. 229–233). Therefore, the question is: Who assumes responsibility in this case? We will turn to the answer in Section 3.5.4.

3.5.2   The scope of political responsibility

Returning to Hans Jonas, we find that he gives politics a special position in the area of responsibility: He speaks of a duty of power and the associated responsibility for something:

> Yet there is a completely different concept of responsibility which does not concern the *ex post facto* reckoning of what has been done, but rather the determination of what is to be done. Accordingly, I therefore do not feel primarily responsible for my behaviour or its consequences, but instead for the thing that lays claim to my actions. (Jonas 1979: 174; our translation)

Where does this new form of responsibility come from and how is it justified? Jonas argues that the voluntary will to power and its assumption becomes an obligation.

Political power extends the sphere of influence beyond individual borders, and thus also the sphere of responsibility. This extended kind of influence is found in the ability to change the legal framework of action and the incentive structures for individuals, economic actors and communities by means of laws and political measures. This influence of politics has been illustrated in the history of the soda-chlorine industry by the Chlorine Alkali Act, its amendment and the Montreal Protocol (see Sections 3.3 and 3.4).

In contrast to the private individual, politicians have far more access to the available social knowledge since they can rely on science, expert committees and specific studies. Hence, they are not restricted to the same extent as individuals. Nevertheless, politicians are confronted with *irreducible ignorance*. Since political responsibility assumes responsibility for the good state of society, politicians are nevertheless obliged to make good decisions when they are confronted with complexity and irreducible ignorance (Baumgärtner et al. 2006b: Chapter 14).

3.5.3   Power of judgment as a concept of how to deal with political responsibility

How should politicians live up to this responsibility? First of all, political actors must be aware that they are assuming a positive responsibility for something (a department, a ministry, a region or a country and its people). This responsibility means that they are committed to creating and maintaining the good state of this "something". In order to fulfil this obligation, especially in the context of environmental issues, it is essential to develop an understanding of the complexity – a knowledge of the emergence of absolute and relative scarcity as well as evolution, joint products and the three forms of ignorance.

Taking on political responsibility then means acting in the face of these difficulties and being able to make, while not best, good decisions. Since politicians are confronted with different contexts – i.e. every problem they face is different from the one they faced before – they cannot rely on general rules but have to find a new solution for every context. To be able to develop these solutions they have to rely on the faculty of power of judgment – power of judgment understood as knowing how: judgment knows how to deal with concepts such as the ones mentioned above, and how to apply them to specific contexts and cases (see Klauer et al. 2017: 107).

3.5.4   *Homo politicus* as an actor of political responsibility

Unlike *homo oeconomicus*, *homo politicus* is not exclusively interested in his or her own welfare but in the good condition of the whole, the political community (a department, ministry, region or country), and the common good.

Homo politicus looks for solutions that are firstly objectively measured and, secondly, find a consensus in the long term, i.e. the de facto agreement of the actors and interests involved and affected. In pursuit of this goal, homo politicus will not sacrifice his own welfare but will nevertheless put his own interests – including those in the gain of personal power – in the back seat if necessary. [. . .] But in order to achieve this goal – the agreement of actors with often quite different interests – homo politicus must be able to understand these interests or the perspectives of the respective interested actors. This ability is the prerequisite for homo politicus to be able to judge, decide and act in such a way as to meet the approval of these actors who are affected by the decision and action of homo politicus. (Petersen et al. 2000: 141–142; our translation)

"In the power of judgment and the action of *homo politicus* determined by it, we therefore have an element of unpredictability. Because this action can change both laws and institutional framework conditions of the economy as well as norms and preferences, it represents a possible source of evolutionary change" (Petersen et al. 2000: 141–142; our translation), and hence an element of irreducible ignorance. To be able to do this, the *homo politicus* has to find means to achieve his aim and make sure that it is realized. This requires the willingness and courage to do what is recognized as right and to take on personal risks and disadvantages (ibid.).

3.6   Outlook

We owe the essential line of our argumentation in this chapter to decades of interdisciplinary research at Heidelberg University.[8] In our scientific work we repeatedly had the experience that it is not so crucial to simply accumulate knowledge.[9] Rather, we found it to be important to systematically structure the available knowledge by assigning it to more general concepts. For example, economic activity can be described by the concept of joint production and its repercussions on the environment; the behaviour of actors can be categorized by the concepts of *homo oeconomicus* and *homo politicus*. Temporal developments can be described by our concept of evolution, neo-Austrian capital theory (Faber 1979; Stephan 1995; Faber et al. 1999) and a theory of stocks (Faber et al. 2005; Klauer et al. 2017: Parts II–IV).

We also found that concepts like *joint production* and *responsibility* allow us to gain essential insight into the physical, economic and ethical sides of production since they have a structural relatedness (Baumgärtner et al. 2006b: 223–267).

---

8 This research has been published in printed media such as books and journals. Additionally, a summarized and systemized version of this material has been published as a website: www.nature-economy.de. Furthermore, a discussion paper reflecting on the process, methodology and content of this website has been published by Faber et al. (2018).

9 This endeavour was motivated by our advising activities for national and international governmental bodies on environmental policy over the course of four decades. These activities have accompanied our scientific research from 1980 to the present. This engagement has made us aware of scientific gaps.

With this in mind, we have directed our attention once again to the development of such structural relatedness; in this way we have generated new concepts and methods (see e.g. Faber, Manstetten, and Proops 1998). Our overriding question has been: How does the economy interact with nature, and vice versa? This question can be refined and applied as a theoretical perspective to environmental policy areas such as waste, water, CO_2 and biodiversity.[10]

Asking these questions is one way of developing a perspective and approaching the respective fields and concrete cases. It is certainly not the only way. The concrete examples of waste, water, CO_2 and biodiversity, and the corresponding scientific literature, show how many other approaches there are, because each of these areas demands the recognition of its context and the different questions asked. And yet we believe that our conceptual approach with a systematic order of knowledge and the elaboration of relatedness between the individual concepts and areas of knowledge represents a perspective of its own. In practical terms,

> practical in the sense of practical philosophy which concerns itself with human action, this means that these fields can only be understood through science which is accessed through simpler overarching concepts. These concepts do not form a hierarchically structured system within our approach. Instead they are conceived as a network of interdependent concepts that reference each other but also remain categorically distinct from one another. (Faber et al. 2018: 6)

We argue that the systematization of the necessary existing knowledge is an important success factor for environmental policy. This line of argument is reinforced by current digital developments, for an incredible amount of knowledge is readily available in a few clicks. Paradoxically, however, people do not perceive this knowledge as a reduction in complexity, but as an ever-growing overload.[11]

In this chapter, we have employed six general concepts to analyse environmental problems, to reduce complexity, and to offer theoretical and practical considerations to approach them. In addition to these six concepts, our approach includes nine others (Faber et al. 2018). Of course, many more such general concepts exist – like *resilience*,[12] *flexibility, freedom, will*[13] and *consent* – which we consider promising.

---

10 See for waste Faber et al. (1989); for water Faber et al. (1983), Jöst et al. (2006), Niemes and Schirmer (2010); for CO_2 and climate change Proops et al. (1993), Jöst (1994); for biodiversity Baumgärtner (2007); for population Jöst (2002), Quaas (2004); for sustainability Klauer (1998), Klauer et al. (2017).

11 See Faber, Manstetten (2010: 6–8).

12 See for example: Derissen et al. (2011), Baumgärtner and Strunz (2014), Ruth (2018: 78f.).

13 Petersen (1996); Petersen and Faber (2001).

References

Baumgärtner, S. (2000), *Ambivalent Joint Production and the Natural Environment*, Heidelberg: Physica.

Baumgärtner, S. (2007), 'The insurance value of biodiversity in the provision of ecosystem services', *Natural Resource Modelling* 20(1), 87–127.

Baumgärtner, S., Strunz, S. (2014), 'The economic insurance value of ecosystem resilience', *Ecological Economics* 101, 21–31.

Baumgärtner, S., Becker, C., Faber, M., Manstetten, R. (2006a), 'Relative and absolute scarcity of nature: assessing the roles of economics and ecology for biodiversity conservation', *Ecological Economics* 59(4), 487–498.

Baumgärtner, S., Faber, M., Schiller, J. (2006b), *Joint production and Responsibility in Ecological Economics: On the Foundations of Environmental Policy*, Cheltenham, UK and Northampton, MA, USA: Edward Elgar Publishing.

Becker, C., Ewringmann, D., Faber, M., Petersen, T., Zahrnt, A. (2015), 'Endangering the natural basis of life is unjust: on the status and future of the sustainability discourse', *Ethics, Policy and Environment*, 18(1), 60–67.

Derissen, S., Quaas, M.F., Baumgärtner, S. (2011), 'The relationship between resilience and sustainability of ecological-economic systems', *Ecological Economics* 70(6), 1121–1128.

Downs, A. (1957), *An Economic Theory of Democracy*, New York: Harper & Row.

Faber, M. (1979), *Introduction to Modern Austrian Capital Theory*, Heidelberg: Springer.

Faber, M., Frank, K., Klauer, B., Manstetten, M., Schiller, J., Wissel, C. (2005), 'On the foundation of a general theory of stocks', *Ecological Economics* 55, 155–172.

Faber, M., Manstetten, R. (2010), *Philosophical Basics of Ecology and Economy*, Oxford/New York: Routledge.

Faber, M., Manstetten, R., Petersen, T. (1997), 'Homo politicus and homo oeconomicus: political economy, constitutional interest and ecological interest', *Kyklos*, 50, 457–483.

Faber, M., Manstetten, R., Proops, J.L.R. (1992a), 'An anatomy of surprise and ignorance', *Environmental Values* 1, 217–241.

Faber, M., Manstetten, R., Proops, J.L.R. (1992b), 'Towards an open future: Ignorance, novelty and evolution', in: Costanza, R., Norton, B., Haskell, B. (eds), *Ecosystem, Health: New Goals for Environmental Management*, Washington, DC: Island Press: 72–96.

Faber, M., Manstetten, R., Proops, J.L.R. (1998), *Ecological Economics: Concepts and Methods*, Cheltenham, UK and Northampton, MA, USA: Edward Elgar Publishing.

Faber, M., Niemes, H., Stephan, G. (1983), *Umweltschutz und Input-Output-Analyse mit zwei Fallstudien aus der Wassergütewirtschaft*, Tübingen: J.C.B. Mohr (Paul Siebeck).

Faber, M., Petersen, T., Frick, M., Zahrnt, D. (2018), 'MINE – Mapping the Interplay between Nature and Economy: a digital gateway to the foundations of ecological economics', *Discussion Paper Series No. 658*. University of Heidelberg, Department of Economics.

Faber, M., Petersen, T., Schiller, J. (2002), 'Homo oeconomicus and homo politicus in ecological economics', *Ecological Economics* 40, 323–333.

Faber, M., Proops, J.L.R. in cooperation with R. Manstetten (1998), *Evolution, Time, Production and the Environment* (3rd, revised and enlarged edition), Heidelberg: Springer.

Faber, M., Proops, J.L.R., Speck, S. with F. Jöst (1999), *Capital and Time in Ecological Economics: Neo-Austrian Modelling*, Cheltenham, UK and Northampton, MA, USA: Edward Elgar Publishing.

Faber, M., Stephan, G., Michaelis, P. (1989), *Umdenken in der Abfallwirtschaft: Vermeiden, Verwerten, Beseitigen* (2nd revised edition), Heidelberg: Springer.

Funtovicz, S.O., Ravetz, J.E.R. (1991), 'Global environmental issues and the emergence of second order science', in: Costanza, R. (ed.), *Ecological Economics: The Science and Management of Sustainability*, New York: Columbia University Press.

Hayek, F.A. von (1972), *Die Theorie komplexer Phänomene*, Tübingen: Mohr (Paul Siebeck).

Hottinger, O. (1998), *Eigeninteresse und individuelles Nutzenkalkül in der Theorie der Gesellschaft und Ökonomie von Adam Smith, Jeremy Bentham und John Stuart Mill*, Marburg: Metropolis.

Jonas, H. (1979), *Das Prinzip Verantwortung. Versuch einer Ethik für die technologische Zivilisation*, Frankfurt am Main: Insel.

Jöst, F. (1994), *Klimaänderungen, Rohstoffknappheit und wirtschaftliche Entwicklung*, Heidelberg: Physica.

Jöst, F. (2002), *Bevölkerungswachstum und Umweltnutzung. Eine ökonomische Analyse*, Heidelberg: Physica.

Jöst, F., Niemes, H., Faber, M., Roth, K. (2006), 'Beschränken Chinas Wasserreserven seine wirtschaftliche Entwicklung?', *Discussion Paper Series 433*, Department of Economics, Heidelberg University.

Kant, I. (1960), *Werke in sechs Bänden*, Edited by W. Weischedel, Darmstadt: Wissenschaftliche Buchgeselschaft.

Klauer, B. (1998), *Nachhaltigkeit und das Problem der Bewertung von Natur: Welchen Beitrag kann das ökonomische Konzept der Preise zur Operationalisierung von Nachhaltigkeit leisten*. Heidelberg: Physica.

Klauer, B., Manstetten, R., Petersen, T., Schiller, J. (2017), *Sustainability and the Art of Long-Term Thinking*. Oxford/New York: Routledge.

Knight, F. (1921), *Risk, Uncertainty, and Profit*, Boston: Houghton Mifflin.

Manstetten, R., Hottinger, O., Faber, M. (1998), 'Zur Aktualität von Adam Smith: Homo Oeconomicus und ganzheitliches Menschenbild', *Homo Oeconomicus* 15(2), 127–168.

Maturana, H.R., Varela, F.J. (1987), *The Tree of Knowledge: The Biological Root of Human Understanding*, Boston: Shambala.

Müller-Fürstenberger, G. (1995), *Kuppelproduktion: Eine theoretische und empirische Analyse am Beispiel der chemischen Industrie*, Heidelberg: Physica.

Nelson, R.R., Winter, S.G. (1982), *An Evolutionary Theory of Economic Change*, Cambridge, MA: Harvard University Press.

Niemes, H., Schirmer, M. (2010), *Entropy, Water and Resources: An Essay in Natural Sciences-Consistent Economics*, Heidelberg: Physica.

Norgaard, R. (1984), 'Coevolutionary development potential', *Land Economics* 60, 160–173.

Petersen, T. (1996), *Individuelle Freiheit und allgemeiner Wille: James Buchanans Politische Ökonomie und die Politische Philosophie*, Tübingen: J.C.B. Mohr (Paul Siebeck).

Petersen, T., Faber, M. (2000), 'Bedingungen erfolgreicher Umweltpolitik im deutschen Föderalismus: Der Ministerialbeamte als Homo Politicus', *Zeitschrift für Politikwissenschaft* 10(1), 5–41.

Petersen, T., Faber, M. (2001), 'Der Wille zur Nachhaltigkeit: Ist, wo ein Wille ist, auch ein Weg?', in: Birnbacher, D., Bruddenmüller, G. (eds), *Zukunftsverantwortung und Generationensolidarität*, Würzburg: Königshausen & Neumann: 47–71.

Petersen, T., Faber, M., Schiller, J. (2000), *Umweltpolitik in einer evolutionären Wirtschaft und die Bedeutung des Menschenbildes*, in: Bizer, K., Linscheidt, B., Truger, A. (eds), *Staatshandeln im Umweltschutz. Perspektiven einer institutionellen Umweltökonomik*, Berlin: Duncker & Humblot: 135–150.

Prigogine, I., Stengers, I. (1984), *Order out of Chaos*, London: Heinemann.

Proops, J.L.R., Faber, M., Wagenhals, G. (1993), *Reducing CO_2 Emissions: A Comparative Input-Output Study for Germany and the UK*, Heidelberg: Springer.

Quaas, M.F. (2004), *Bevölkerung und Umweltökonomie: Zeitliche und räumliche Perspektiven*. Marburg: Metropolis.

Ruth, M. (1996), Evolutionary economics at the crossroads of biology and physics, *Journal of Social and Evolutionary Systems* 19(2), 125–144.

Ruth, M. (2018), *Advanced Introduction to Ecological Economics*, Cheltenham, UK and Northampton, MA, USA: Edward Elgar Publishing.

Schiller, J. (2002), *Umweltprobleme und Zeit: Bestände als konzeptionelle Grundlage ökologischer Ökonomik*, Marburg: Metropolis.

Schumpeter, J.A. (1934), *The Theory of Economic Development: An Inquiry into Profits, Capital, Credit, Interest and the Business Cycle*, Cambridge, MA: Harvard University Press (first published in German in 1912).

Smithson, M. (1988), *Ignorance and Uncertainty: Emerging Paradigms*, Heidelberg: Springer.

Stephan, G. (1995), *Introduction into Capital Theory: A Neo-Austrian Perspective*, Berlin/Heidelberg: Springer.

4 Ends, means, and the economics of environment

Deepak Malghan

4.1 Introduction

Growing recognition of the fact that standard economics is incapable of explaining certain well-established biophysical facts that have a bearing on the human economic predicament has led to the rise of heterodox schools such as ecological economics (Røpke, 2004, 2005). Schumpeter (1954) introduced the term "preanalytic vision" to refer to the "distinct set of coherent phenomena as a worthwhile object of our analytic effort." The heterodox literature has used the term in an ontological sense to represent a set of axiomatic relationships governing economy–ecosystem interactions. In Kuhnian terms, preanalytic vision, as used by this literature, represents the operating paradigm for a discipline.[1]

In this chapter, we attempt to understand the origins of these varying preanalytic visions of the economy, including ones that posit the economy to be a thermodynamically open subsystem of the larger ecosystem (Ruth, 2018). Given that the revisionist literature emphasizes the need to debate on the preanalytic visions for the economy, we ask the following question: What are the determinants of preanalytic visions in economics? In answering this question, we find that what are considered "preanalytic" visions of economics (the neoclassical as well as the heterodox variants) can in fact be analytically deduced from our beliefs about "ultimate means" and "ultimate ends."

4.2 Ends and means

The most important of the predicaments studied by economics is that of scarcity. Scarcity arises because human wants are not satiable but the means to fulfil these infinite wants are finite. The normative goal of modern economic organization is to maximize the aggregate welfare (as measured by fulfilled wants) in a society, and to this extent economics becomes the study of allocation of scarce means among competing ends (Robbins, 1932). Thus, as Daly (1993) suggests, an understanding of the nature of these "competing ends" and "scarce means" is fundamental to

---

1 See for example Daly (1991) and Costanza et al. (1997). On the connection between ecological economics' use of "preanalytic vision" and the scientific paradigms described by Kuhn (1962) see Røpke (2005).

understanding the human economic predicament. However, contemporary economic discourse seldom tackles the ends part of the ends–means foundation of economics – at least in its formal models.

We have adapted below a scheme for studying ends and means from Daly (1993). The ends and means are represented on an ends–means spectrum in Figure 4.1. At one end of the spectrum we have the *Ultimate End*. For our purposes here we do not need to define Ultimate End in teleological terms. *Telos*, or otherwise the need for an Ultimate End in an ends–means spectrum, is directly related to the human economic predicament of "infinite competing ends". Given that we cannot fulfil all our competing ends (even in principle), the Ultimate End provides, at the very least, a mechanism for ranking our competing ends. Given the scarcity of means relative to the ends, every society has to choose between competing ends. Ultimate End is not contingent on any particular moral principle; but at the same time it cannot be devoid of some moral content. Ultimate End helps us make choices between competing ends, and choosing between ends is inherently a moral exercise, unlike merely satisfying preferences. Choosing between national defence and public education has an irreducible moral element unlike choosing between two similar toothpaste brands. The ends–means spectrum in Figure 4.1 represents the spectrum for society as a whole but can be adapted to individual economic agents. Continuing down the spectrum from Ultimate End, we have Intermediate Ends as shown in Figure 4.1.

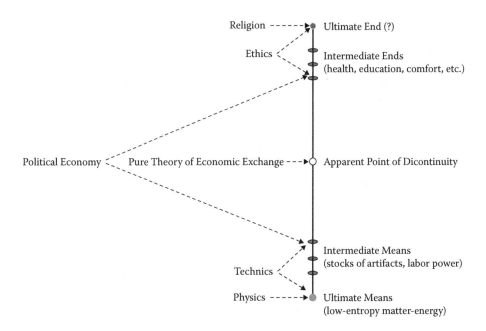

Source: Reproduced with changes from Daly (1993, p. 20).

Figure 4.1   The ends–means spectrum

At the opposite end of the spectrum from the Ultimate End is Ultimate Means. Ultimate Means is the terrestrial stock of low-entropy matter-energy and the incident solar radiation. Human agency (even in theory) cannot alter the nature of Ultimate Means at the global level. As we move up the spectrum from Ultimate Means towards Ultimate End, every point is a means towards achieving ends represented by points above a chosen point, and is also the end achieved by using the means at points below it. Intermediate Means are "ends" achieved using Ultimate Means, and Intermediate Ends are means to achieving the Ultimate End. Thus the ends–means spectrum is a continuum of points that are simultaneously a means for some higher-order end and the end achieved by a lower-order means. The movement along the continuum involves purposeful action of the human agency.

As indicated in Figure 4.1, we consider a portion of this continuum terminated at each end by Ultimate Means and Ultimate End. Ultimate Means cannot be a product of purposeful human agency and is therefore not an end. Ultimate End, by definition, cannot be the means for any higher-order end.[2] In terms of the ends–means spectrum in Figure 4.1, the ultimate goal for economics is to use Ultimate Means in satisfaction of the Ultimate End. The various disciplines that study different parts of the ends–means spectrum are shown on the left of the spectrum. Given that the human economic predicament defined in terms of ends and means intersects a variety of disciplines across the ends–means spectrum, the traditional focus of political economy on the middle portion of the spectrum warrants serious enquiry. One of the most important consequences of the exclusive focus of political economy on the intermediate portion of the ends–means spectrum is that it does not recognize any absolute limits imposed by either Ultimate Means or Ultimate End (Daly, 1993). Indeed, Daly originally developed this spectrum to explain the reasons for, and the consequences of, modern economics' obsession with economic growth by laying out a framework to study the desirability and possibility of continued economic growth.

4.2.1   Apparent point of discontinuity

Unlike traditional political economy, modern economics that focuses on pure theory of exchange does not consider any kind of ends. In what is a significant departure from even its antecedents in utilitarian ethics, contemporary microeconomic theory is built around subjective individual preferences. The utility maximization exercise, that is the bedrock of consumer theory, is reduced to an ordinal preference ranking exercise rather than fulfilment of a set of ends. Preferences and ends belong to distinct axiological categories. In particular, preferences lie outside the realm of moral discourse, while moral disputes are integral to ends. Thus, while the neoclassical price theory is able to resolve the problems associated with classical value theory, it ironically achieves this by seriously limiting moral possibilities

---

2 More formally, we only study the portion of the continuum contained in the open interval (**UM,UE**), where **UM** and **UE** represent respectively Ultimate Means and Ultimate End. If EMS is the ends–means spectrum, then EMS∈ (**UM,UE**).

for the participating economic agents. The success of the "marginal revolution" allowed economics to borrow the mathematical apparatus of classical physics. The diffusion of the mathematical apparatus helped establish economics as a "science". However, this ascendancy of logical positivism required the abandonment of the study of ends. In particular, *homo economicus* as a behavioural abstraction moved from classical utilitarianism's concerns with ends to mere rank ordering of subjective individual preferences (Malghan, 2009). Utility maximization over a preference set is a technical exercise devoid of any moral content. Two individuals can engage in a moral dispute over ordering a set of ends, but such possibilities are exhumed when interpersonal comparison of subjective preferences is disallowed. Thus in Figure 4.1 there is an apparent point of discontinuity in the ends–means continuum, depicted in the figure as a point at the centre of the ends–means spectrum.

We thus have three distinct points on the spectrum representing breaks from the ends–means continuum: Ultimate Means at the bottom of the spectrum; Ultimate End at the top; and the point of discontinuity in the middle. Every other point is part of the continuum (and here shown as shaded ovals). The point in the middle is studied by pure theory of economic exchange. We have labelled this as *apparent* point of discontinuity because it exists only in the idealized theory of pure exchange. One only needs to look at how macroeconomics is organized – modern macroeconomic theory was indeed developed as a means to achieving a very tangible end of pulling the world out of the Great Depression. The next section briefly describes the main features of an "embedded" economy, before illustrating how the embedded economy is directly related to the ends–means spectrum discussed here.

4.3   An embedded economy

The primary normative goal of modern economic organization has been the establishment of a fully autonomous and self-regulating market system (Cleveland, 1987; McNeill, 2001). This goal of economic organization also forms the basis of neoclassical economics, perhaps best captured by the familiar picture of the circular flow of goods and money that is the staple of any introductory macroeconomics textbook. In this circular-flow ontology the economy is unaffected by social, political processes as well as physical environment – the economy is simultaneously disembedded from both the social-political fabric and the larger biophysical environment (Costanza and Daly, 1987; Daly and Farley, 2004). In his seminal work, Polanyi (2001) marshals a large swathe of historical evidence to suggest that a completely disembedded economy is a utopian ideal whose pursuit results in tragic consequences.

The pioneering critique by Polanyi has evolved into two distinct discourses. Historians, sociologists, political scientists, and anthropologists have fleshed out the consequences of the "great transformation", and studied continuing efforts to create large-scale, self-regulating markets. If these various social sciences have studied the disconnect between the economy and the larger social-political fabric, ecologists and other physical scientists have focused on the material foundations of the economy. Prompted initially by the energy and resource crises of the 1970s, and later by the growing problems with finding places to safely dispose of the various waste products of our prodigal resource use, this discourse has tried to anchor the economy to its material foundations. Heterodox approaches to economics of the environment are a direct offshoot of this discourse whose principal precept is that the economy is to be studied as an open subsystem of the larger biophysical system that contains and sustains it.

If an economy that is disembedded from either the physical environment or the larger social fabric is an empirical impossibility, what explains the enduring appeal of an autonomous, self-regulating market as the dominant goal for economic organization, and neoclassical economics as the theory that studies such an economy? Political, sociological, historical, and even cultural explanations are indeed central to a nuanced understanding of our complex economic organization. Our goal here is much more modest – at the expense of a refined understanding that is possible with political or historical studies, we seek a more direct explanation in terms of the fundamental constituents of the human economic predicament. The human economic predicament has been traditionally defined in terms of ends, and the means to satisfy those ends – economics is a study of means to satisfy competing ends. We suggest here that varying assumptions about how the ends and means are related to each other directly lead to the different "preanalytic visions" of the economy. We find that the preanalytic visions of heterodox schools as well as of mainstream environmental economics can be derived from assumptions about means and ends. Thus what are "preanalytic visions" are actually working visions derived from a preanalytic conception of the human economic predicament cast in terms of ends and means.

4.4   Ends, means, and constraints on an embedded economy

The most important feature of any embedded economy is that it is constrained in one or more dimensions. There is a constraint on the physical size of the economy when the economy is embedded within the larger ecosystem – the economy cannot be larger than the ecosystem. Social, political constraints limit both the physical size of the economy and the qualitative structure of the economy. Our goal here is to understand the nature of these constraints in terms of the basic constituents of the human economic predicament – competing ends and scarce means.

The basic model is presented in Figure 4.2. **UM** represents Ultimate Means; **UE** Ultimate End; and **M** and **E** represent intermediate means and ends respectively. **UM**, **UE**, **M**, and **E** are treated as possibility sets. Thus **UM** represents all states of the world that are permitted by known biophysical laws. From an economics perspective, **UM** is only limited by the stock of terrestrial sources of low-entropy matter and energy and the flow of incident solar radiation. In physical terms, **M** is always some subset of **UM**. Among other things, intermediate means (**M**) is a function of extant technology and can expand with technological progress. As discussed in Section 4.2, unlike **UM**, it is not possible to precisely define **UE**. We will use two extreme definitions of **UE** to illustrate the connection between an embedded economy and the ends–means dialectic. First we will consider a minimalist definition of **UE** where the Ultimate End only helps with the ordinal ordering of lower-order ends. At the other extreme, we will consider **UE** with a teleological definition. The arrows in the left-hand panels of Figure 4.2 represent flow of information between the various possibility sets, with the direction of the arrows indicating the direction of the flow of information. When multiple arrows are incident on any set, that set is the intersection of the two sets from which the arrows originate.[3] For example, in the second row of Figure 4.2, E is the intersection of **UE** and **M** (E = UE > M). When a possibility set has only one arrow incident on it, it is a subset of the set from which the arrow originates. Thus in the second row of Figure 4.2, **M** is a subset of **UM** (M ⊂ UM).

Figure 4.2 shows four different ways in which the possibility sets **M** and **E** are related to Ultimate Means and Ultimate End, on one hand, and the economy on the other. These differing relationships between ends and means are shown on the left-hand side, and the resulting constraints (or lack thereof) on the economy are depicted on the right. In the top row, we have the picture of the economy as a stand-alone entity composed of several self-regulating markets. The economy is unaffected by any ends. Preferences are different from ends and are unaffected by any kind of Ultimate End. Ultimate Means has no bearing on the more intermediate means used to satisfy preferences. In terms of the notation introduced here, **M** and **E** are not subsets (of **UM** and **UE** respectively), but derived independently without reference to **UM** and **UE** respectively; E is a null set because there are no ends in this treatment of the economy; and **M** is an infinite set.

In the second row, we have a preanalytic vision where the economy is embedded within the larger ecosystem. This is the principal ontological vision for heterodox schools that start with the economy being contained within the larger biophysical system (Ruth, 2018). Here, both **M** and **E** are subsets of **UM** and **UE** respectively. More importantly, there is an interaction between the means and the ends. While the means are derived independent of any ends, the ends are contingent on means; E is contingent on both **UE** and **M**. Accounting for the fact that **M** is itself derived from **UM**, ends are now directly or indirectly contingent on both Ultimate Ends and Ultimate Means. For example, one can reasonably argue that under a certain specification of **UE** continuous economic growth may not be excluded from **E** but continuous economic growth is not an end in biophysical schools because it is excluded from Ultimate Means; and Ultimate Means contributes to how ends for an economy are determined within these traditions. Thus the ultimate constraint on the economy in biophysical schools such as ecological economics comes from Ultimate Means.

---

3 We use "intersection" in the usual set theoretic sense. Thus if $C = A > B$ then set C contains elements that are common to both sets A and B.

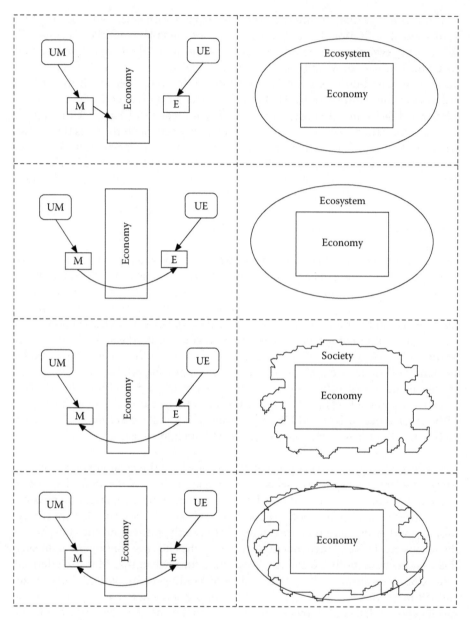

Note: The left column shows the four possible ways in which Ultimate End and Ultimate Means interact. The corresponding columns on the right show the "working vision" for the respective economy that is
derived from the assumptions about the interactions between Ultimate End and Ultimate Means. Arrows in
the left-hand column represent flow of information, a cause–effect relationship in the directions indicated.

Figure 4.2   Ends, means, constraints, and embedded economies

The third row of Figure 4.2 shows an economy embedded within the larger social, political fabric rather than the biophysical environment. This conception of an embedded economy can again be explained in terms of the underlying relationship between means and ends. Unlike the biophysical schools' vision of the economy, **E** is determined only by the Ultimate End. However, **M** is now jointly determined by both Ultimate Means and **E**. Here, the ultimate constraint on the economy is not Ultimate Means but the Ultimate End. Slave labour is a particularly stark example to illustrate how means are constrained by ends. Retooling society in the interest of thermodynamic thrift (which is a major policy prescription that emerges from the vision of various biophysical schools above, especially as we approach limits of terrestrial low entropy stocks like fossil fuels), conflicts with the moral, ethical choices of that society. Slave labour is absent in **M** not because it is not part of Ultimate Means, but because it is not part of any end that the society considers legitimate.

Finally, in the last row of Figure 4.2 we have an economy that is constrained by both Ultimate Means and Ultimate End. Such an economy is simply obtained by combining the biophysical model of the economy and the economy that is embedded within the larger social, political fabric. The nature of the constraint on an economy embedded in the larger social, political fabric is much more complex than the biophysical constraints in the embedded economy of biophysical schools. While the nature of Ultimate Means is clearly discernible (at least in theory), it may well be impossible to completely describe the nature of Ultimate End. The social, political constraint derived from the Ultimate End is therefore depicted in Figure 4.2 as an amoeba shape rather than the regular ellipse that was used for the biophysical constraint.

A philosophical discussion of how the nature of the Ultimate End determines the social, political constraint is beyond the scope of this chapter. However, we will discuss two extreme definitions of the Ultimate End to suggest that a political social constraint is indeed directly related to the constraints imposed on the means available to the economy by the Ultimate End in the same way as the biophysical constraint is directly derived from how Ultimate Means imposes constraints on the possible ends for an economy. When **UE** is defined within a teleological framework, it is straightforward to see why such a definition would place a constraint on the means available. The intermediate ends (**E**) are directly derived from the *telos* underlying the Ultimate End. Since means (**M**) are derived from ends, only those means that are consistent with the ends are permissible. When **UE** is merely an ordering mechanism for ranking intermediate ends, the nature of the constraint imposed on the means needs some explanation. Recall that **UM**, **UE**, **M**, and **E** are all defined as possibility sets. The structure of the economy is constrained by both what is desirable (**E**) and what is possible (**M**). If the intermediate ends (**E**) were not derived from the Ultimate End but were independently determined, the means available to the economy would still be constrained. In other words, we would still have $\mathbf{M} = \mathbf{E} > \mathbf{UM}$, but now **E** is not a straightforward subset of **UE** ($\mathbf{E} \in / \mathbf{UE}$).

4.5   Conclusion

A formal model relating the human economic predicament to the preanalytic visions in economics provides a framework to make a normative assessment of different preanalytic visions. While biophysical schools allude to how the economy is not only embedded within the larger biophysical system but also within the surrounding social, political, and cultural fabric, there is no well-established formal framework within such traditions that can address questions at the intersection of the economy, polity, and society. The ends–means framework presented here suggests that the relative neglect of ends in the formal models of biophysical schools results in a significant lacuna in the understanding of an embedded economy. This is not to suggest that students of biophysical schools are not cognizant of constraints on the economy imposed by Ultimate End rather than Ultimate Means. For example, an early contribution to the literature, Daly (1992), talks about the goal for ecological economics as working out an economic organization that is "efficient, just, and sustainable". The concern with just distribution is directly tied to the economy being embedded within the larger social-cultural fabric.

One of the biggest cleavages that demarcate the boundaries between various schools of environmental economics concerns the desirability of monetary valuation of nature. Is monetary valuation – which relies on economic concepts of natural capital, ecosystem services, etc. – consistent with the preanalytic vision of an embedded economy? Sympathetic philosophers like Brown (2009) have suggested that the value frame that biophysical schools have borrowed from economics and ecology is inadequate to deal with the ethical challenges of an embedded ontology, and have called for the development of a new "embedded ethics". However, there is an increasing recognition within this discourse that a creative middle ground is possible. Such a middle ground would be based on democratic deliberation between multiple stakeholders (see for example the myriad case studies in Zografos and Howarth, 2008). The linkage established here between the preanalytic vision of economics and the ends–means spectrum can help make the normative trade-offs in these deliberations explicit.

Studying the human economic predicament in terms of ends and means helps uncover how the economy is embedded in the larger biophysical environment as well as in the social-political fabric, but does not offer direct clues on how such an embedded economy could be empirically studied. The concept of scale, or the proportional relationship between two entities, holds the key to understanding an embedded economy (Malghan, 2011). In biophysical terms, scale is a measure of the proportional relationship between the physical size of the economy and the ecosystem that contains and sustains it (Malghan, 2010, 2011). Extending the concept of scale to look at other kinds of proportional relationships beyond the physical size of the economy will help various traditions studying the economy–ecosystem interaction problem explicitly incorporate ends in its formal models. The ends–means model presented here suggests that it might be possible to extend the scale methodology beyond biophysical scale.

References

Brown, Peter. The unfinished journey of ecological economics. United States Society for Ecological Economics Meeting, 2009.

Cleveland, Cutler. Biophysical economics: Historical perspective and current research trends. *Ecological Modelling*, 38:47–73, 1987.

Costanza, Robert and Herman Daly. Toward an ecological economics. *Ecological Modelling*, 38:1–7, 1987.

Costanza, Robert, Charles Perrings, and Cutler Cleveland. Historical roots and motivations: Introduction. In Robert Costanza, Charles Perrings, and Cutler Cleveland, eds, *The Development of Ecological Economics*, pp. xiii–xxix. Cheltenham, UK and Lyme, NH, USA: Edward Elgar Publishing, 1997.

Daly, Herman. Towards an environmental macroeconomics. *Land Economics*, 67(2):255–259, May 1991.

Daly, Herman. Allocation, distribution, and scale: towards an economics that is efficient, just, and sustainable. *Ecological Economics*, 6:185–193, 1992.

Daly, Herman. Introduction to essays toward a steady-state economy. In Herman Daly, ed, *Valuing the Earth*. Cambridge, MA: MIT Press, 1993.

Daly, Herman and Joshua Farley. *Ecological Economics: Principles and Applications*. Washington: Island Press, 2004.

Kuhn, Thomas. *The Structure of Scientific Revolutions*. Chicago: University of Chicago Press, 1962.

Malghan, Deepak. Valuing nature: Technocratic governance vs democratic deliberation. *Economic and Political Weekly*, 44(47):34–37, 2009.

Malghan, Deepak. On the relationship between scale, allocation, and distribution. *Ecological Economics*, 69(11):2261–2270, 2010.

Malghan, Deepak. A dimensionally consistent aggregation framework for biophysical metrics. *Ecological Economics*, 70:900–909, 2011.

McNeill, John Robert. *Something New Under the Sun: An Environmental History of the Twentieth-Century World*. New York: Norton, 2001.

Polanyi, Karl. *The Great Transformation: The political and economic origins of our time*. Beacon Press, Boston, 2nd paperback edition, 2001.

Robbins, Lionel. *An Essay on the Nature and Significance of Economic Science*. London: Macmillan, 1932.

Røpke, Inge. The early history of modern ecological economics. *Ecological Economics*, 50:293–314, 2004.

Røpke, Inge. Trends in the development of ecological economic from the late 1980s to the early 2000s. *Ecological Economics*, 55:262–290, 2005.

Ruth, Matthias. *Advanced Introduction to Ecological Economics*. Cheltenham, UK and Northampton, MA, USA: Edward Elgar Publishing, 2018.

Schumpeter, Joseph. *History of Economic Analysis*. New York: Oxford University Press, 1954.

Zografos, Christos and Richard B. Howarth, eds. *Deliberative Ecological Economics*. New Delhi: Oxford University Press, 2008.

5 Ecosystems, legal systems, and governance: an institutional perspective

Lee P. Breckenridge

5.1 Introduction

Scientific reports have reached ever more stark conclusions about anthropogenic destruction of global biophysical systems. Reports of the Intergovernmental Panel on Climate Change point to impending irreversible changes in the earth's climate caused by carbon emissions (IPCC 2014, 2018). The 2019 Global Assessment Report of the Intergovernmental Science-Policy Platform on Biodiversity and Ecosystem Services shows rapidly deteriorating ecosystems around the world (IPBES 2019). Human societies are highly organized to reap economic benefits from resources in the environment, but systematic processes of exploitation undermine the viability of the natural systems on which human societies depend.

In warning about the urgency of transforming human socioeconomic systems, the recent reports vividly capture the extent of the complex interdependence of human and natural systems. At the center of the quandaries they depict lie questions about the adequacy of human institutions and governance. The rules that societies have developed for defining, constraining, and coordinating human activities provide efficient processes for exploiting natural resources but they also offer organized means for paying attention to environmental impacts and transforming current practices.

The scrutiny of institutional arrangements, now given renewed impetus by the latest reports of scientific consensus, is a task that economists are well situated to pursue. As grounds for policy reforms, the tools of economic analysis can offer rigorous insights into the different ways that decision-making frameworks steer environmental and economic outcomes. At the same time, the complexities of the dynamic interactions between human and natural systems that the scientific reports identify, and the recommendations for transformative change that they put forth, pose many research challenges.

5.2   Economic analysis of institutional arrangements for acquiring, considering, and taking action in light of environmental information

The structure and implications of institutions governing human interactions with the environment have been important and expanding areas of research for environmental economics. The discussion presented in this chapter focuses on economists' roles in evaluating institutional frameworks, and in particular on the governance mechanisms that enable, limit, and otherwise configure powers and responsibilities of owners, operators, and regulatory authorities in dealing with property.

The discussion takes a broad functional approach to institutions and governance mechanisms, encompassing the diverse array of systems that societies have developed to channel and coordinate human behavior to enhance collective well-being (Cosens et al. 2018; Vandenbergh 2013). Institutional arrangements include formal requirements adopted in legal proceedings and expressed in writing through constitutional, legislative, and regulatory provisions. Beyond formal legal regimes, relevant societal arrangements also include informal rules or norms that are not written down and codified. While formal laws and informal norms may be legally distinguishable, the observations offered here emphasize, broadly, the importance of discerning the many different kinds of rules by which society through collective action organizes the ownership, management, exploitation, and protection of the environment to serve societal goals (Sills and Jones 2018).

Institutional arrangements include property regimes. In economic analyses of market transactions, the definitions of underlying property rights may lie outside the focus of the inquiry, appearing instead as fixed concepts that provide the modular underpinnings for transfers among market participants. Nevertheless, property rights can vary through time and across different societies and circumstances. Not all property is transferable in markets, and not all property is privately owned. Private, public, or non-governmental entities may hold and manage property under an array of different mandates and constraints, including prohibitions or limits on transfers or changes in uses (Ostrom 1990).

The boundary lines delineating property rights do not exist in a vacuum. Institutional arrangements that define, constrain, and facilitate transactions in property include laws delegating decision-making powers to defined entities for interpreting requirements and settling conflicts, and procedures for implementing and enforcing rights and responsibilities (Alston 2008). Tort laws and criminal laws impose liabilities for spillover effects extending beyond the boundaries of a designated owner's authority. Contract laws governing exchanges of property facilitate creation of complex management regimes embodied in negotiated agreements among parties, and these may provide governance solutions through private action that do not depend on direct government intervention (Vandenbergh and Gilligan 2015; Hadfield 2008).

For property that is transferable, marketability depends on an array of protocols and decision-making forums that follow prescribed procedures to operate effectively. Property regimes with their institutional underpinnings are public goods that require collective action to define and operate. Protocols for monitoring and enforcing the boundaries of property rights, tracking ownership over time, and recognizing and implementing the terms of contracts, are key components of a market system.

Informal norms, if compliance is monitored and enforced through accepted community practices, may function much like, or in lieu of, a formal regime (Ellickson 1991). Norms of behavior that emerge by community consensus and rules promulgated through a formal legal process may be quite similar, and they may converge. Community-based norms may eventually find expression in positive law, or they may appear in private contracts that, themselves, are then enforceable through legal procedures. Especially in common law systems, customs may form the grounds for judicial decisions adjudicating a dispute, with subsequent precedential effect.

The allocation of property rights to designated owners is a foundational process affecting the scope of decentralized authority in society (Merrill 2012). Even in societies that rely extensively on allocations of property to private owners, with powers to make operational commitments through negotiated agreements, governments typically have broad regulatory powers to limit or bypass the autonomy of owners. While the owner of property may exercise decision-making power and control within designated boundaries, government entities may nevertheless hold and exercise significant administrative authority within jurisdictional boundaries (Cosens et al. 2018).

Societies limit the discretion of owners in order to deal with externalities, control monopolistic behavior, ensure public access to resources, and reduce inequality (Merrill 2012). Through government action, societies may grant resource access under specified circumstances to non-owners, and they may impose regulatory constraints limiting resource exploitation. Particularly in industrialized economies with elaborate administrative law systems, regulatory programs run by government agencies effectively limit the autonomy of property rights holders and impose responsibilities to serve particular environmental goals. In pragmatic terms, regulatory programs, subsidy programs, antitrust and public utility laws, taxation programs, and government eminent domain proceedings can all bring government-level coordination and direction to management of property that otherwise lies in the hands of designated owners.

In the environmental arena, economists' growing attention to institutional context and detailed investigation of diverse instruments for government intervention find roots in commentary by Ronald Coase noting the importance of recognizing transaction costs, incomplete information and other causes of market failures, and encouraging empirical investigations of institutional arrangements that address the obstacles (Coase 1960, 1998). Douglass North, Elinor Ostrom and Oliver

Williamson all subsequently contributed influential elaborations on the institutional themes that Coase put forth (see Ménard and Shirley 2008, 2018 and Ménard 2018 for commentary on the emergence of "new institutional economics"). A Coasean perspective accepts the notion that transaction costs and uncertainties will prevent decentralized actors from negotiating to achieve optimal societal outcomes in many situations, and that institutional arrangements can provide beneficial means of coordination outside the operation of markets. Initial allocations of property rights and the configuration of institutions then have real-world environmental and economic effects, with significant implications for achieving social welfare (Lyon 2009).

Economists therefore correctly seek to identify impediments in the property rights system, and to identify government interventions that might alter decentralized decision-making to achieve desired results. Sterner and Robinson (2018) provide an overview and discussion of the justifications for specific types of government interventions to address externalities and correct for market failures.

Institutions generally change slowly; but they may change over time to accommodate altered environmental conditions, newly discovered information, or newly invented technologies (Alston 2008). Institutional arrangements create the context both for market transactions and for regulatory decisions and other government interventions. This institutional context may vary in different locations, cultures, and times in history. The persistence of institutional arrangements over time, the outcomes in environmental and economic terms, the similarities and differences among various systems, and the factors that enable adaptation are all important topics in environmental economics (Libecap 2007).

Economic research brings a systematic approach to identifying the effects of rules, and to evaluating whether those rules advance social welfare. An economic analysis can serve normative as well as purely descriptive functions (Shavell 2004). As economists give renewed attention to the effects of institutional arrangements, they have developed new analytical approaches for tracking and comparing outcomes under differing systems. In the discussion that follows, we consider a few particularly challenging issues for economic research that can influence policy choices and institutional design in the environmental arena.

5.3 Evaluating dynamic interactions and long-range repercussions in coupled human and natural systems

In environmental economics, the attention to existing institutional arrangements – including property rights allocations, liability regimes, and government regulatory interventions – has increasingly tackled evaluations of overall institutional capacity to avoid irreparably disrupting the natural systems on which the socioeconomic system depends. The expanding economics literature on coupled human and natural systems probes the implications of recognizing that human welfare closely depends on protecting the dynamic functioning of biophysical systems (Brock and Xepapadeas 2018). Often this work by economists has entailed collaborations reaching across fields of economics and environmental sciences in interdisciplinary fashion (e.g., Nordhaus 2019; Perrings and Kinzig 2018; Fenichel et al. 2018; Hsiang and Kopp 2018). In natural resource management and social sciences literatures more broadly, socio-ecological scholarship has endeavored to integrate the study of ecological and social systems as a basis for policy-making (Berkes et al. 2002; Delmas and Young 2009).

By looking closely at how human systems align and coordinate with the functioning of biophysical systems, economic research can illuminate, in effect, the design of institutions that represent successful examples of collective action to organize and control human behavior in interactive relationships with ecosystems. Institutional arrangements from this perspective are themselves public goods. The systems may require considerable societal investment to put in place; but, once elaborated, the rules streamline communications and adjustments, orchestrating human activities in ways that pay attention to ecosystem functions and protect environmental dynamics. The analytical scrutiny often puts emphasis on discerning the particular ways that the institutional arrangements coordinate processes for obtaining, understanding, and responding to environmental information about ecological "resilience" (Holling 1973; Gunderson and Pritchard 2002).

The concept of ecosystem resilience as initially advanced by scientists did not carry overt normative implications (Holling 1973; Gunderson and Holling 2002). Researchers have studied the dynamics that enable an ecosystem to absorb or withstand disturbances, returning through self-organization to prior patterns and functions following perturbation. They have also shown that ecosystems may collapse when critical thresholds are crossed, sometimes shifting abruptly in the course of reorganization to new ecological regimes with quite different characteristics. New organisms may thrive, while others may become extinct in the changed circumstances. A later regime may itself be resilient, meaning that a return to earlier conditions might be quite unlikely and indeed infeasible for human agents to engineer. Investigators of complex ecological systems have noted, further, that such phenomena can be studied at multiple scales, that the internal dynamics may differ significantly at the various scales, but that interactions among levels of ecological organization may mean that small perturbations at one scale may have significant and abrupt effects at another.

In the economic analysis of institutions, discussions of ecological resilience often introduce a normative angle. Resilience becomes a shorthand term for an ecosystem's capacity to return dynamically to a desired condition following disruption (Cosens et al. 2018). The suite of desired ecological processes is the perceived pattern that underpins long-term societal welfare. The avoidance of tipping points that might shift the system into some other dynamic equilibrium becomes a societal imperative that can inform institutional design.

Judgments about the implications for societal welfare hinge on judgments about the value to society of ecosystem functions under current and alternative conditions. By asking whether society can ensure a resilient return to desired ecosystem functions after disturbance, commentators implicitly endorse efforts to control disruptive human activities and foster the ecosystem's capacity to recover from perturbation. Conversely, when advocates demand ecological restoration to some earlier ecological regime (by daylighting a sewered stream, for example, or reintroducing an endangered species) they are implicitly faulting the institutional arrangements that allowed degradation or destruction to occur in the first place, and seeking reforms capable of engineering environmental change (Tarlock 2003; Breckenridge 2006).

Researchers ask whether existing systems, ranging from markets through regulatory regimes and taxing and spending powers of government, will be agile and well-informed enough to avoid crossing critical thresholds in the collective control of ecosystem impacts. These topics have garnered particularly urgent attention in recent studies addressing global climate change, where the institutional questions extend on a global scale, beyond domestic legislation to international commitments among sovereign nations (Nordhaus 2019; Perrings and Kinzig 2018). If the goal is to maintain ecosystems that will continue to sustain human society over the long haul, while still reaping benefits that include consumptive uses and destructive exploitation, then the ultimate question is whether society can design institutions and allocate decision-making power in ways that will allow economic development while avoiding detrimental ecosystem tipping points.

How should institutional arrangements be designed to set ecological goals and foster the desired outcomes? In asking such questions, societies are seeking institutions through which people can continually update their knowledge about ecosystem functions, identify biophysical variables, monitor changes closely, pull back from over-exploitation at crucial moments, and invest as necessary to perpetuate ecological functions (Karkkainen 2003). Implicitly, the viewpoint manifests optimism both about societies' capacities to design wise institutions and about the feasibility of far-sighted planning in ecosystem management.

Efforts to prevent ecosystem change in dynamic systems in essence demand considerable flexibility and numerous timely adjustments in human economic activities that otherwise might drive ecosystems to the brink of radical alteration. Since ecosystems are highly complex and evolving, questions about the goals and capacities of governmental or private entities to perceive and act upon information about ecosystem resilience come into focus. From a purely scientific standpoint it is impossible to have definitive and complete information about the relevant phenomena before making decisions. What institutional arrangements can best facilitate continued learning and intelligent response to ecological information? What entities have the best capacities to gather relevant information, consider alternative courses of action, and implement measures? (Cosens et al. 2018; Craig and Ruhl 2014; Karkkainen 2003, 2004).

Researchers working to understand the economic and environmental implications of institutional context have built upon work by Elinor Ostrom and subsequent researchers on community-based management regimes (CBMRs) (Ostrom 1990; Ostrom et al. 2001). These systems sometimes emerge as self-organized property regimes that forego classic individualized property boundaries in favor of communal regimes governing the exploitation and protection of common pool resources. In such systems, communities allocate renewable resource use rights to individuals or households in light of local environmental knowledge. They patrol community-based boundaries drawn to coincide with landscape or watershed features, exclude outsiders, enforce limits on resource exploitation, and sometimes develop complex and adaptive management protocols. Such community-based systems may emerge without necessarily gaining formal expression in national legislation or obtaining explicit central government backing. If a formal legal system recognizes and protects the authority and autonomy of the local community within designated boundaries, then the relevant institutions may be viewed as operating at multiple scales of governance. The local system of control is enabled by, and "nested" within, the larger legal system.

Research into the emergence and survival of community-based management regimes has laid groundwork for empirical efforts to discern successful attributes of local forms of environmental governance, particularly in developing countries that lack strong formal legal systems. Given the often long-lasting and sustainable management of renewable resources in such community-based regimes, these research inquiries have led at times to recommendations for recognizing local norms through formal measures. They call on central authorities to devolve authority to local groups or create co-management regimes in conservation areas where the government formally holds title (Berkes et al. 2002).

While this literature has been especially prominent in international conservation and parks management contexts, analogous questions about institutional design and the nature of property rights extend more broadly to other settings. In industrialized societies with complex written systems of law, researchers can similarly scrutinize the configuration of property regimes and allocation of natural resource management powers among authorities operating at multiple scales (Chaffin and Gunderson 2016). In particular, in multi-layered political systems, where private property owners face various forms of oversight from local, regional, and federal governments, does the resulting resource management system in fact facilitate attention to ecological information and efficiently orchestrate human activities to align with ecosystem dynamics?

Researchers in quite different settings often converge on possibilities for complex hybrid solutions, dividing management and control of resources among multiple entities while encouraging various forms of communication and coordination, as the most effective means of ensuring informed and adaptive decision-making while adhering to long-run assessments of overall societal welfare. Despite significant structural differences among various systems, there are rough analogies among (for example) cap-and-trade pollution control systems, transferable fishing quotas, wetlands and habitat mitigation programs, and co-management systems drawing on the expertise of local communities or individual agents in governing human uses of national conservation areas. Such programs all rely in part on centralized expert authority to discern ecological dynamics and to set limits on exploitation while at the same time respecting local autonomy and innovation by allocating specified powers and participatory rights at the individual or local scale (Rose 2001).

More generally, following rubrics suggested by Elinor Ostrom (2010), researchers look to multi-layered, polycentric governance solutions as means for responding effectively to the multi-scale complexities of ecosystem dynamics. In classic economic models, joint ventures and divided ownership arrangements appear inefficient because of the likely costs of coordination and dispute resolution (Shavell 2004). Nevertheless, in a real-world setting of complex ongoing interactions between human and natural systems at multiple scales, the search for wise solutions often appears to lead, pragmatically, to institutional systems that include multiple layers of authority and control, paralleling multiple complex dynamics and scales of ecological analysis. Incomplete information remains a pervasive issue in reaching collective decisions, but shared "mental models" help members of communities cope with uncertainties (Denzau and North 1994). Incomplete contracts among multiple parties and time-limited authorizations in regulatory regimes can leave future contingencies for further investigation and adjustment.

An extensive legal literature pursues questions about the potential configuration of multi-faceted legal systems capable of fostering adaptive or collaborative governance by participants with various sources of knowledge, leverage and authority. See, for example, Pieraccini (2019), DeCaro et al. (2017), Cosens et al. (2017), Craig and Ruhl (2014), Cosens et al. (2014), Adler (2013), Rosenbloom (2012), Craig (2011), Garmestani et al. (2008), Camacho (2005), Freeman and Farber (2005), Karkkainen (2003, 2004).

New impetus for such inquiries into the effectiveness of institutions arises as global climate change becomes an ever more pressing societal issue (Craig 2010; Gerrard and Kuh 2012; Peel et al. 2012). Global, not just regional, welfare is at stake, potential ecosystem tipping points involve catastrophic and irreversible consequences, and scientific uncertainties about ecosystem dynamics abound. Nevertheless, far from opting for synoptic government ownership or pervasive central oversight, many researchers find promise in diverse forms of private and localized governance, even when non-market values are at stake, and even when the environmental problems under consideration are global in scope (Vandenbergh and Gilligan 2015; Light and Orts 2015; Kennedy 2016; Karkkainen 2004).

Comparative institutional research in environmental economics unfolds in part through microeconomic investigations in an array of different institutional settings. Much recent economic research explores pieces of the puzzle, evaluating regulatory mechanisms already in place and seeking to discern the effects of particular policy instruments in existing laws. Through quasi-experimental approaches, current research seeks to identify specific characteristics of institutional arrangements that successfully coordinate human economic activities with ecosystem functions (Deschenes and Meng 2018; Sills and Jones 2018).

A number of fundamental analytical challenges continue to demand attention. The recognition of reciprocal and ongoing effects between ecosystems and institutions leads to some difficult questions about how to study causation as a central aspect of the economic analysis (Deschenes and Meng 2018; Sills and Jones 2018). For the environmental economist, uncertainties abound, both in the assessment of environmental dynamics and in the investigation of societal responses (Heal and Milner 2018). Moreover, the justifications for recommending particular governance regimes ultimately hinge on discerning the value to society of pursuing specific institutional measures, even as disentangling the effects of multiple overlapping policies may be empirically quite difficult (Holland et al. 2018). Finding analytically rigorous ways to recognize the non-market values to human society of viable, productive ecosystems continues to be an important focus of innovative work in environmental economics underpinning broader efforts at institutional redesign (Fenichel et al. 2018).

Economists have made important progress, often in collaboration with scientific experts, in identifying and measuring values for the "ecosystem services" that ecosystems provide. The analytical task is easiest where the benefits to humans (such as water purification or pollination of crops) have ready examples or analogues in services offered through the market economy (Millennium Ecosystem Assessment 2005). Such endeavors can help in formulating, for example, subsidy programs establishing Payments for Environmental Services (PES) systems (Salzman et al. 2018). Without altering the boundaries of private property rights, these programs incentivize owners to take action that coincides with a defined public interest by paying for prescribed management practices.

Other recent analytical efforts in economics focus on developing new methods for measuring the values of natural resources as capital assets, rather than a source of services. These approaches seek to develop ways of measuring and accounting for the value to society of biophysical systems *in situ*, as perceived within a context of real-world institutions, instead of relying on valuation of ecosystem service flows (Fenichel et al. 2018, 2016).

In summary, research in environmental economics focusing on effects of institutional arrangements must cope with the challenges of tracing interactions between the rules governing socioeconomic systems and the dynamic patterns shaping ecosystems. Each may influence the configuration of the other. Many questions remain to be explored about the effects of particular institutional attributes as these interactions play out.

5.4 Adaptation and resilience in socioeconomic systems

Institutions shape the ecological disruptions that societies cause and the accompanying economic consequences, but they also shape the capacity of human societies themselves to adjust to meet changing environmental circumstances. Studies of the vulnerability of human populations to global climate change have brought new attention to the difficulties that both urban and rural populations will face (Verschuuren 2013a, 2013b). An array of questions about human adaptive capacities in altered environmental circumstances and differing institutional settings have come into sharp new focus (WRI et al. 2011).

Changes in the patterns and severity of extreme weather events are manifestations of broader trends in a changing global climate. Destructive natural events such as hurricanes, wildfires, and floods can serve to highlight societal failures in paying attention and responding to evolving environmental information. Weather-related disasters can offer a window into a society's ability to adapt to environmental changes more broadly, and disaster risk reduction programs can serve as climate change adaptation mechanisms (Van Niekerk 2013). Shocks to environmental and economic circumstances can also illuminate systemic obstacles to safeguarding the well-being of the most vulnerable groups in society (see generally Farber et al. 2015).

References to community resilience have become widespread in assessing potential community responses to climate change. As used by disaster management authorities, resilience may refer to a community's ability to avoid deaths and injuries and to rebuild physical assets or construct new protective structures following an abrupt destructive event, with the goal of approximately reinstating community identity and patterns of life. Although longer-range societal adaptability and changes in surrounding ecosystems may fall outside the scope of the discussion from a bureaucratic standpoint in an emergency management setting, disasters nevertheless present important issues for future planning and institutional reform.

Here, we are concerned broadly with concepts of adaptation and societal resilience that take into account the evolving relationships between human and natural systems. To facilitate successfully human adaptation to changing environmental circumstances, people and their institutions need to be able to perceive and plan for shifts in the environmental conditions that support the socioeconomic system. Retrospective research on previous events may facilitate an effort to identify institutional factors that have prevented society in the past from adequately perceiving risks and planning ahead (Cosens et al. 2018).

In concept, clearly defined property rights and smoothly functioning markets can provide the institutional underpinnings for a socioeconomic system that adapts readily to changing environmental circumstances without significant government regulatory constraints or subsidy programs. If the sea level rises near a coastal property, for example, a private landowner's awareness might lead to adaptive measures, perhaps by changing the uses of the land or moving vulnerable activities elsewhere. The market value of the property could change, and the price signals would communicate perceived risks and knowledge about suitable land uses. Over time, market transactions could lead to changes in the ownership and management of this and similar properties, and real estate development patterns could shift in response to changing environmental patterns. When sufficient information is available, market signals can stimulate adaptation through land markets (Anderson et al. 2018).

Whether and how adaptive measures will be taken in different countries and locations seems to be a complex question, however, and an active area of economic research. Timely responses to new environmental information may be quite difficult when investments are lumpy, assets are immovable, and transaction costs are high. In the context of climate change, the inability to make rapid adjustments in light of new knowledge is a particularly thorny issue for participants in large-scale real estate projects. Another potentially important and persistent issue is whether the people who can best perceive the need to adapt to a changing climate in fact have the authority, motivation, and management control, through secure property rights or otherwise, to make adaptive changes. A lack of secure land tenure or lack of clarity in the definition of property rights in rural areas may hinder adaptation by farmers, for example; but elsewhere, knowledgeable land management decisions by individuals may show promise in changing agricultural practices to adjust to the changing climate (Auffhammer and Kahn 2018). Ambiguities or other inadequacies in the allocation of responsibilities among different levels of governance can also lead to "social-ecological traps" that betray a failure to adapt effectively, giving rise to demands for institutional reform (Baker et al. 2018).

In cities, the population may be so dependent on centrally owned and managed infrastructure that the possibilities for decentralized, autonomous actions may be quite limited. In urban areas, the primary issues may be whether city or utility managers have the necessary funding and motivation to forecast likely events and take adaptive steps on behalf of city residents, and whether those without established property rights in the relevant resources can gain access to what they need.

While in some locations the lack of clear property rights or jurisdictional authority may be an impediment to adaptive measures, in others the configuration of property rights may create obstacles to landscape-level adjustments in land use. Despite the well-documented advantages of secure property rights for enabling market transactions, overly fragmented property rights can become impenetrable obstacles to transactions that would otherwise be to the benefit of society. The issue is especially obvious in situations where "the ecosystem" or "the watershed" – defined at a scale relevant to fostering the sustainability of particular habitats or species – crosses multiple boundaries between property owners and political jurisdictions.

In many rural landscapes, for example, the splitting of land into subdivisions for residential development may raise market values, enhance municipal tax bases, and provide housing for growing populations; and the ensuing urban and suburban development will likely appear beneficial to both owners and municipal authorities. When the property boundaries and zoning controls do not coincide with the patterns of ecological phenomena, however, the resulting land use choices can impose classic negative externalities. Development on one parcel of land can aggravate the downwind wildfire risks on adjoining properties, for example, or the widespread construction of impervious surfaces can cause accumulating stormwater to flood downstream properties and pollute waterways. A "tragedy of fragmentation" or an "anti-commons" may occur (Freyfogle 2002; Heller 1998). Externalities that take the form of incremental impacts from multiple sources may be hard to perceive and document. The barriers to bargained solutions may be so significant that beneficial pooling of resources will not occur without further government intervention to define responsibilities and coordinate adaptive responses.

In a typical urban or suburban landscape in the United States, a zoning code and a building code are likely in place, restricting the uses of different parcels of land and imposing design requirements. The established codes may rest on obsolete and incomplete information about the environmental repercussions of property management decisions, however. Communities often have not developed the institutional capacity to make timely changes to address spillover effects in light of new scientific information (Tarlock 2007; Salkin 2007). Zoning requirements establishing flood plain districts, for example, are typically based on historical records and the frequency of past flood events, not on an understanding of future conditions in a changing climate. Quite often, up-to-date information about trends in precipitation and sea levels and predictions of future floods have not been taken into account. Similarly, new construction permits allowing connections to municipal water infrastructure may be issued based on historically available water supplies rather than on any inquiry into drought conditions likely to occur in the future.

In countries like the United States, with strong concepts of private property and vociferous resistance to laws and regulations that upset investment-backed expectations, authorities at all levels of government have been exceedingly slow to change existing land use rules to incorporate new ecological information and new projections about climate change in particular. By accepted practice, and sometimes through formal grandfathering of existing development projects, land use law in the United States has not proved adept at orchestrating adaptations in land management practices to deal with ecological information (Klein 2019).

Particularly in light of the looming threats of climate change, the demand for more complex institutional arrangements to facilitate societal adaptation is growing (Hirokawa and Rosenbloom 2013). Systemic failures by individual owners to perceive or account for transboundary impacts and long-term repercussions mean that new government interventions and legal reforms will be needed, going beyond current programs for short-term recovery from natural disasters (Sun 2011; Farber 2007; Ruhl 2010, 2011).

Economic researchers can usefully compare available approaches, ranging from changes in liability regimes to regulatory reforms to subsidy programs. They can investigate the approaches to recovery and reconstruction following natural disasters and other environmental changes, looking to see whether government programs to date have built new adaptive capacity in local communities. Careful work in economic history can illuminate the institutional factors that may have helped or hindered adaptation to changed environmental and economic circumstances in the past.

Attention to the disparate impacts of disruptive weather events on vulnerable populations has also brought an expanded awareness of distributional consequences (IPCC 2018). This area invites particular research attention. In classic economic analysis of law, distributional consequences may be set aside for separate consideration, outside of discussions about configurations of property rights and liability schemes, because the tax system is viewed as the best means for directly dealing with the distribution of wealth (Shavell 2004). Nevertheless, as societies turn to potential institutional reforms to facilitate adaptation to a changing climate, it has become clear that some groups are more at risk from the immediate effects of climate change than others under existing allocations of property rights and regulatory regimes. Furthermore, there are dangers that existing institutions may exacerbate disparities and entrench inequalities in society, even if they provide means for returning to established routines following destructive events (Auffhammer and Kahn 2018).

Environmental health economics are an important if complex area for bringing economic analytical tools to bear in scrutinizing salient disparities in environmental consequences for vulnerable populations and investigating the real-world roles of institutions in remedying or aggravating the disparities (Pattanayak et al. 2018; Wiley 2013).

As environmental economists give attention to transaction costs and other justifications for government interventions through regulations and other policy instruments, they should concomitantly give attention to the disparate impacts of environmental change on particular populations, and to the potential distributional consequences of proposed institutional reforms (Lyster 2013; Tsosie 2007; Stephens 2019).

5.5   Sociotechnical advances with transformative institutional effects

Economic historians have long studied the ways that technological change can give rise to new means of delineating property rights, new forms of production, new externalities, and new demands for institutional reform. From power looms to fencing, adoption of new technologies has led to alterations in property regimes and changes in governmental and private roles to coordinate the exploitation and transfer of resources. Changes in water rights and liabilities for water pollution, for example, accommodated new exploitation of water power on many states' rivers in the US during the nineteenth century, but forced landowners to live with changes in the landscape and waterways that they might previously have been able to prohibit under earlier notions of private property and tort law.

Recent rapid developments in digitization and transmission of information have brought a new wave of technological change that promises to transform many aspects of institutional arrangements governing human uses of the environment (Esty 2004). Today, new devices for sensing, transmitting, and understanding information about the environment, and new ways for humans and machines to communicate with each other, both facilitate and challenge the capacity of human institutions to steer environmental exploitation in ways that ultimately serve societal welfare.

Many aspects of existing institutional arrangements originate with efforts to encourage efficient uses of resources while reducing information costs and over-coming challenges posed by scientific uncertainties and gaps in information. Clear boundary lines for land can be justified by concerns for efficiency, as commentators have noted, if the goal is to reduce costs of inquiry and investigation for outsiders and to facilitate rapid transactions. Bright line rules make it easier to know "who is in charge" in a particular location and to streamline the operation of markets (Libecap and Lueck 2011). In effect, they provide heuristics for quick decision-making by market participants (Smith 2012). By contrast, complex management regimes and regulatory requirements, including those imposed by governments in administrative proceedings and those developed in negotiations of shared owner-ship arrangements, may create deliberative processes that slow transactions down and demand ongoing evidentiary attention to ecological context. Nevertheless, the centralization of the decision-making in many areas of government intervention has been justified by the public welfare consequences at stake (Merrill 2012).

Current sociotechnical changes are having dramatic effects on the costs and fea-sibility of obtaining, visualizing, and acting upon real-time information. The new information technologies alter the lines of communication and the interactions of property owners and government regulators. Technological advances are affect-ing all phases of information acquisition, processing, decision-making, and action (Vespignani 2009, 2012).

In recent years it has become technologically feasible to deploy sensors in the envi-ronment and within buildings to obtain and relay information about a wide array of parameters, without costly human labor to conduct sampling by hand. This means, for example, that pollution sensors can automatically obtain and transmit to cor-porate managers and to government regulators information about compliance with permit requirements.

Through automated information processing, regulators may issue notices of non-compliance or penalties in an expedited manner, while managers can readily instigate changes in operations or adjustments to equipment. Through an "internet of things" (IoT) and pre-established algorithmic controls, decisions prescribed in advance can take place without intervening human communications or deliberations. A thermostat or a water level sensor might communicate with a central information-processing platform, for example, triggering changed instructions for fuel use or releases of water through a water control structure, all while taking weather models and conditions predicted by other entities into account. Through iterative processes of monitoring and action, machine learning further offers possibilities for experimentation and updating of algorithms without intermediate human decision-making.

At the same time, the new possibilities for automated information collection and processing present new challenges for ensuring fairness in the distribution of resources and in the control of environmental impacts. If the installation and operation of new technology is affordable only for certain people or organizations, or if the ensuing governmental attention and investments are biased toward particular neighborhoods, for example, then advanced modes of resource management and pollution control may exacerbate rather than remedy inequalities in society.

In short, technological changes in the available means for obtaining, considering, and acting on information are rapidly altering cognitive and transactional possibilities in areas where assumptions about information availability and communication costs have had foundational effects on institutional design in the past. These technological changes could effectively alter institutional arrangements, and they may have significant distributional consequences.

Deployment of "smart grids" for electrical energy generation, distribution, and storage provide one context for considering the potential implications of these technological advances (Binder et al. 2019; Kunneke 2018; Biber et al. 2017; Lyster and Byrne 2013; Kiesling 2008). In industrialized countries, urban populations typically rely on energy generation in centralized plants and distribution through government-authorized entities. Government agencies tightly regulate electric power generation and distribution to ensure safety, reliability, and operations in the public interest. New decentralized technologies for distributed electrical energy generation and storage have given rise to proposals that challenge the centralized paradigm. These proposals include adoption of new digital technologies to coordinate and account for the generation and use of energy by local entities that become both producers and consumers of power (so-called prosumers). The distributed generation and storage agenda has gained momentum as a program for combatting climate change – replacing central fossil-fuel fired plants with solar panels or other renewable energy sources in distributed locations (Jones and Zoppo 2014).

It remains to be seen how institutional structures governing the generation and distribution of energy resources will be reformed in different political and administrative jurisdictions. The available suite of new technologies if fully deployed could enable fine-grained recognition of marketable rights in local entities, automated transactions among vast numbers of market participants, and rapid real-time adjustments in the operation of an extensive network for energy generation, distribution, and storage (Kiesling 2008; Sioshansi 2017). Both private and public property (including factories, houses, schools, shopping malls, and parking lots) could be put into service as parts of a regional infrastructure.

The envisioned coordination among individual owners of assets and providers of services depends on a technology framework or digital match-making platform to gather information and orchestrate actions (see generally, Asadullah et al. 2018). There are analogies to other entrepreneurial initiatives underway in the "platform economy," such as Uber or AirBnB (Cohen 2017).

In a socio-ecological context, the algorithms of the information platforms potentially substitute for other communicative contractual arrangements among individuals and firms and for regulatory programs of government agencies, raising questions both about the configuration of the property regime and about the scope of government interventions (Biber et al. 2017; Cohen 2017). If private entities – even homeowners – can install solar panels on individually owned buildings, will they be able to sell the electricity they generate through the distribution system? Who should own, manage, and operate the equipment? Should governments subsidize the installation of solar panels, or perhaps require their incorporation in new construction as part of a building code? (See De Groote and Verboven 2019 for a recent study of consumer behavior in an incentive program for installing renewable energy technology, finding important budgetary and distributional implications.) Such institutional arrangements must be sorted out through laws and regulations and through contractual negotiations, premised on precise methods for tracking who owns what, allocating benefits, and assigning responsibility for system failures.

Outside the specific context of electric power infrastructure, it seems likely that sociotechnical transformations will bring important changes to existing and envisioned management regimes whenever anthropogenic impacts on ecosystems demand tracking and controlling impacts that cross property or political boundaries. Cap-and-trade regulatory programs, for example, establishing property-like tradable rights within overall limits on resource exploitation, will become easier and less costly to administer. Carbon sequestration to meet climate change goals, with further technological advances and accountability mechanisms, could resemble other types of infrastructure, mobilizing individually owned property in a coordinated way to provide defined public services. Stormwater facilities might be similarly decentralized as "green infrastructure" installations across the landscape, tracked through an intermediary information processing platform (Ashley et al. 2019; Breckenridge 2016). Any habitat providing defined ecosystem services extending across existing property and jurisdictional lines, once coordinated through new forms of communication and automation, could see innovations in institutional arrangements to enable rapid adjustments and more far-sighted planning.

At the same time, reliance on potentially faulty automated devices and processes could trigger a new array of disruptions and catastrophic consequences. The new systems will likely involve increasingly powerful information management platforms serving as intermediaries in gathering and acting upon data. Dependence on such new technologies and management entities to orchestrate environmental exploitation may give rise to new controversies concerning transparency and fairness in resource access and distribution of benefits (Milchram et al. 2018; Brauneis and Goodman 2018). It may also make society vulnerable to new kinds of disruption, ranging from human errors in programming and equipment maintenance to deliberate sabotage of critical infrastructure.

5.6   Conclusion

Economic analysis of law can bring important new insights to institutional design in the environmental arena. New perspectives on interactions between socioeconomic systems and ecosystems have given rise to new questions about how best to characterize and value the benefits to human society of ongoing ecosystem dynamics and how best to trace the causal relationships. Scientific understandings of climate change and the irreversibility of anthropogenic impacts from carbon emissions have brought renewed impetus to inquiries into the potential outcomes of different institutional arrangements. At the same time, technological advances in environmental monitoring, communications, and data processing have opened new possibilities for foreseeing environmental repercussions of human activities and coordinating rapid adjustments through automated but adaptive responses across property and political boundaries.

Economists have important roles to play in assessing the costs, benefits, and distributional consequences of institutional innovations as they emerge. By studying variation in institutional arrangements across locations or over time, paying close attention to the allocation of property rights, the configuration of jurisdictional boundaries, and the implications of externalities, economists can bring important new insights to efforts at institutional design.

References

Adler, R.W. (2013), 'Climate change adaptation and agricultural and forestry law', in J. Verschuuren (ed.), *Research Handbook on Climate Change Adaptation Law*, Cheltenham, UK and Northampton, MA, USA: Edward Elgar Publishing, pp. 214–49.

Alston, L. (2008), 'Property rights and the state', in C. Ménard and M.M. Shirley (eds), *Handbook of New Institutional Economics*, Berlin and Heidelberg: Springer, pp. 573–90.

Anderson, S.E., T.L. Anderson, A.C. Hill, M.E. Kahn, H. Kunreuther, G.D. Libecap, H. Mantripragada, P. Mérel, A. Plantinga, and V.K. Smith (2018), *The Critical Role of Markets in Climate Change Adaptation*, NBER Working Paper No. 24645, May, Cambridge, MA: National Bureau of Economic Research.

Asadullah, A., I. Faik, and A. Kankanhalli (2018), 'Digital platforms: a review and future directions', *PACIS 2018 Proceedings* 248, https://aisel.aisnet.org/pacis2018/248.

Ashley, C., B. Helmuth, and S. Scyphers (2019), 'Ecological design for urban coastal resilience', in M. Ruth and S. Goessling-Reisemann (eds), *Handbook on Resilience of Socio-Technical Systems*, Cheltenham, UK and Northampton, MA, USA: Edward Elgar Publishing, pp. 246–73.

Aufhammer, M. and M.E. Kahn (2018), 'The farmer's climate change adaptation challenge in least developed countries', in P. Dasgupta, S.K. Pattanayak, and V.K. Smith (eds), *Handbook of Environmental Economics, Volume 4*, Amsterdam: Elsevier, pp. 193–229.

Baker, D.M., G. Murray, and A.K. Agyare (2018), 'Governance and the making and breaking of social-ecological traps', *Ecology and Society* 23 (1), 38.

Berkes, F., J. Colding, and C. Folke (2002), *Navigating Social-Ecological Systems: Building Resilience for Complexity and Change*, Cambridge, UK: Cambridge University Press.

Biber, E., S.E. Light, J.B. Ruhl, and J. Salzman (2017), 'Regulating business innovation as policy disruption: from the Model T to AirBnB', *Vanderbilt Law Review* 70, 1561–626.

Binder, C.R., S. Muhlemeier, and R. Wyss (2019), 'Analyzing the resilience of a transition: an indicator-based approach for socio-technical systems', in M. Ruth and S. Goessling-Reisemann (eds), *Handbook on Resilience of Socio-Technical Systems*, Cheltenham, UK and Northampton, MA, USA: Edward Elgar Publishing, pp. 167–95.

Brauneis, R. and E.P. Goodman (2018), 'Algorithmic transparency for the smart city', *Yale Journal of Law and Technology* 20, 103–76.

Breckenridge, L.P. (2006), 'Special challenges of transboundary coordination in restoring freshwater ecosystems', *Pacific McGeorge Global Business & Development Law Journal* 19, 13–32.

Breckenridge, L.P. (2016), 'Water management for smart cities: implications of advances in real-time sensing, information processing, and algorithmic controls', *George Washington Journal of Energy & Environmental Law* 7, 153–63.

Brock, A. and A. Xepapadeas (2018), 'Modeling coupled climate, ecosystems, and economic systems', in P. Dasgupta, S.K. Pattanayak, and V.K. Smith (eds), *Handbook of Environmental Economics, Volume 4*, Amsterdam: Elsevier, pp. 1–60.

Camacho, A.E. (2005), 'Mustering the missing voices: a collaborative model for fostering equality, community involvement and adaptive planning in land use decisions: installment two', *Stanford Environmental Law Journal* 24, 269–330.

Chaffin, B.C. and L.H. Gunderson (2016), 'Emergence, institutionalization and renewal: rhythms of adaptive governance in complex social-ecological systems', *Journal of Environmental Management* 165, 81–7.

Coase, R.N. (1960), 'The problem of social cost', *Journal of Law and Economics* 3 (1), 1–44.

Coase, R.N. (1998), 'The new institutional economics', *American Economic Review* 88 (2), 72–4.

Cohen, J.E. (2017), 'Law for the platform economy', *UC Davis Law Review* 51, 133–204.

Cosens, B.A., L. Gunderson, and B. Chaffin (2014), 'The adaptive water governance project: assessing law, resilience and governance in regional socio-ecological water systems facing a changing climate', *Idaho Law Review* 51, 1–27.

Cosens, B.A., L. Gunderson, and B.C. Chaffin (2018), 'Introduction to the special feature practicing panarchy: assessing legal flexibility, ecological resilience, and adaptive governance in regional water systems experiencing rapid environmental change', *Ecology and Society* 23 (1), 4.

Cosens, B.A., R.K. Craig, S. Hirsch, C.A.(T.) Arnold, M.H. Benson, D.A. DeCaro, A.S. Garmestani, H. Gosnell, J. Ruhl, and E. Schlager (2017), 'The role of law in adaptive governance', *Ecology and Society* 22 (1), 30.

Craig, A.A. (2011), Fourth-generation environmental law: integrationist and multimodal, *William & Mary Environmental Law and Policy Review* 35, 771–884.

Craig, R.K. (2010), '"Stationarity is dead" – long live transformation: five principles for climate change adaptation law', *Harvard Environmental Law Review* 34, 9–73.

Craig, R.K. and J.B. Ruhl (2014), 'Designing administrative law for adaptive management', *Vanderbilt Law Review* 67, 1–87.

De Groote, O. and F. Verboven (2019), 'Subsidies and time discounting in new technology adoption: evidence from solar photovoltaic systems', *American Economic Review* 2019, **109** (6), 2137–72.

DeCaro, D.A., B.C. Chaffin, E. Schlager, A.S. Garmestani, and J.B. Ruhl (2017), 'Legal and institutional foundations of adaptive environmental governance', *Ecology and Society* **22** (1), 32.

Delmas, M.A. and O.R. Young (eds) (2009), *Governance for the Environment: New Perspectives*, Cambridge, UK: Cambridge University Press.

Denzau, A.T. and D.C. North (1994), 'Shared mental models: ideologies and institutions', *Kyklos*, **47** (1), 3–31.

Deschenes, O. and K.C. Meng (2018), 'Quasi-experimental methods in environmental economics: opportunities and challenges', in P. Dasgupta, S.K. Pattanayak, and V.K. Smith (eds), *Handbook of Environmental Economics, Volume 4*, Amsterdam: Elsevier, pp. 286–332.

Esty, D.C. (2004), 'Environmental protection in the information age', *New York University Law Review* **79**, 115–211.

Ellickson, R.C. (1991), *Order Without Law: How Neighbors Settle Disputes*, Cambridge, MA: Harvard University Press.

Farber, D.A. (2007), 'Adapting to climate change: who should pay?', *Journal of Land Use* **23** (1), 1–37.

Farber, D.A., J.M. Chen, R.R.M. Verchick, and L.G. Sun (2015), *Disaster Law and Policy*, New York: Wolters Kluwer.

Fenichel, E.P., J.K. Abbott, and S.D. Yun (2018), 'The nature of natural capital and ecosystem income', in P. Dasgupta, S.K. Pattanayak, and V.K. Smith (eds), *Handbook of Environmental Economics, Volume 4*, Amsterdam: Elsevier, pp. 85–141.

Fenichel, E.P., J.K. Abbott, J. Bayham, W. Boone, E.M.K. Haacker, and L. Pfeiffer (2016), 'Measuring the value of groundwater and other forms of natural capital', *PNAS: Proceedings of the National Academy of Sciences of the United States of America*, **113** (9), 2382–7.

Freeman, J. and D.A. Farber (2005), 'Modular environmental regulation', *Duke Law Journal* **54**, 795–912.

Freyfogle, E.T. (2002), 'The tragedy of fragmentation', *Valparaiso University Law Review* **36**, 307–37.

Garmestani, A.S., Allen, C.R. and Cabezas, H. (2008), 'Panarchy, adaptive management and governance: policy options for building resilience', *Nebraska Law Review*, **87** (4), 1036–54.

Gerrard, M.B. and K.F. Kuh (eds) (2012), *The Law of Adaptation to Climate Change: United States and International Perspectives*, Chicago, IL: ABA Publishing.

Gunderson, L.H. and C.S. Holling (eds) (2002), *Panarchy: Understanding Transformations in Human and Natural Systems*, Washington, DC: Island Press.

Gunderson, L.H. and L. Pritchard (2002), *Resilience and the Behavior of Large Scale Systems*, Washington, DC: Island Press.

Hadfield, G.K. (2008), 'The many legal institutions that support contractual commitments', in C. Ménard and M.M. Shirley (eds), *Handbook of New Institutional Economics*, Berlin and Heidelberg: Springer, pp. 175–204.

Heal, G. and A. Milner (2018), 'Uncertainty and ambiguity in environmental economics: conceptual issues', in P. Dasgupta, S.K. Pattanayak, and V.K. Smith (eds), *Handbook of Environmental Economics, Volume 4*, Amsterdam: Elsevier, pp. 439–68.

Heller, M.A. (1998), 'The tragedy of the anticommons: property in the transition from Marx to markets', *Harvard Law Review* **111**, 621–88.

Hirokawa, K.H. and J. Rosenbloom (2013), 'Climate change adaptation and land use planning law', in J. Verschuuren (ed.), *Research Handbook on Climate Change Adaptation Law*, Cheltenham, UK and Northampton, MA, USA: Edward Elgar Publishing, pp. 325–54.

Holland, S.P., E.T. Mansur, N. Muller, and A.J. Yates (2018), *Decompositions and Policy Consequences of an Extraordinary Decline in Air Pollution from Electricity Generation*, NBER Working Paper No. 25339, December, Cambridge, MA: National Bureau of Economic Research.

Holling, C.S. (1973), 'Resilience and stability of ecological systems', *Annual Review of Ecology and Systematics* **4** (November), 1–23.

Hsiang, S. and R.E. Kopp (2018), *An Economist's Guide to Climate Change Science*, NBER Working Paper No. 25189, October, Cambridge, MA: National Bureau of Economic Research.

IPBES (2019), *Summary for Policymakers of the Global Assessment Report on Biodiversity and Ecosystem Services* (Advance unedited version, May 6), https://www.ipbes.net/global-assessment-report-biodiversity-ecosystem-services.

IPCC (2014), *Fifth Assessment Report of the Intergovernmental Panel on Climate Change*, New York: Cambridge University Press.

IPCC (2018), *Global Warming of 1.5°C: An IPCC Special Report on the Impacts of Global Warming of 1.5°C above Pre-Industrial Levels and Related Global Greenhouse Gas Emission Pathways, in the Context of Strengthening the Global Response to the Threat of Climate Change, Sustainable Development, and Efforts to Eradicate Poverty*, Geneva: Intergovernmental Panel on Climate Change.

Jones, K.B. and D. Zoppo (2014), *A Smarter, Greener Grid: Forging Environmental Progress through Smart Energy Policies and Technologies*, Santa Barbara, CA: Praeger.

Karkkainen, B.C. (2003), 'Adaptive ecosystem management and regulatory penalty defaults', *Minnesota Law Review* **87**, 943–98.

Karkkainen, B.C. (2004), '"New governance" in legal thought and in the world: some splitting as antidote to overzealous lumping', *Minnesota Law Review* **89**, 471–97.

Kennedy, R. (2016), 'Rethinking reflexive law for the information age, hybrid and flexible regulation by disclosure', *Journal of Energy and Environmental Law* **7** (2), 124–38.

Kiesling, L.L. (2008), *Deregulation, Innovation and Market Liberalization: Electricity Regulation in a Continually Evolving Environment*, London and New York: Routledge.

Klein, C. (2019), 'The National Flood Insurance Program at fifty: how the Fifth Amendment takings doctrine skews federal flood policy', *Georgetown Environmental Law Review*, **31**, 285–338.

Kunneke, R. (2018), 'Interrelated technical and institutional coordination: the case of network infrastructures', in C. Ménard and M.M. Shirley (eds), *A Research Agenda for New Institutional Economics*, Cheltenham, UK and Northampton, MA, USA: Edward Elgar Publishing, pp. 72–9.

Libecap, G.D. (2007), 'The assignment of property rights on the western frontier: lesson for contemporary environmental and resource policy', *Journal of Economic History* **67** (2), 227–52.

Libecap, G.D. and D. Lueck (2011), 'The demarcation of land and the role of coordinating property institutions', *Journal of Political Economy* **119** (3), 426–67.

Light, S.E. and E.W. Orts (2015), 'Parallels in public and private environmental governance', *Michigan Journal of Environmental & Administrative Law* **5** (1), 1–72.

Lyon, T.P. (2009), 'Environmental governance: an economic perspective', in M.A. Delmas and O.R. Young (eds), *Governance for the Environment: New Perspectives*, Cambridge, UK: Cambridge University Press, pp. 43–68.

Lyster, R. (2013), 'Adaptation and climate justice', in J. Verschuuren (ed.), *Research Handbook on Climate Change Adaptation Law*, Cheltenham, UK and Northampton, MA, USA: Edward Elgar Publishing, pp. 32–69.

Lyster, R. and R. Byrne (2013), 'Climate change adaptation and electricity infrastructure', in J. Verschuuren (ed.), *Research Handbook on Climate Change Adaptation Law*, Cheltenham, UK and Northampton, MA, USA: Edward Elgar Publishing, pp. 391–420.

Ménard, C. (2018), 'Research frontiers of new institutional economics', *RAUSP Management Journal* **53** (2018), 3–10.

Ménard, C. and M.M. Shirley (eds) (2008), *Handbook of New Institutional Economics*, Berlin and Heidelberg: Springer.

Ménard, C. and M.M. Shirley (eds) (2018), *A Research Agenda for New Institutional Economics*, Cheltenham, UK and Northampton, MA, USA: Edward Elgar Publishing.

Merrill, T.W. (2012), 'The property strategy', *University of Pennsylvania Law Review* **160**, 2061–95.

Milchram, C., R. Hillerbrand, G. van de Kaa, N. Doorn, and R. Künneke (2018), 'Energy justice and smart grid systems: evidence from the Netherlands and the United Kingdom, *Applied Energy* **229**, 1244–59.

Millennium Ecosystem Assessment (2005), *Ecosystems and Human Well-being: Synthesis*, Washington, DC: Island Press.

Nordhaus, W. (2019), 'Climate change: the ultimate challenge for economics', *American Economic Review* **109** (6), 1991–2014.

Ostrom, E. (1990), *Governing the Commons: The Evolution of Institutions for Collective Action*, Cambridge, UK: Cambridge University Press.

Ostrom, E. (2010), 'Beyond markets and states: polycentric governance of complex economic systems', *American Economic Review* **100** (3), 641–72.

Ostrom, E., T. Dietz, N. Dolsak, P.C. Stern, S. Stonich, and E.U. Weber (eds) (2001), *The Drama of the Commons*, Washington, DC: National Academy Press.

Pattanayak, S.K., E.L. Pakhtigian, and E.L. Litzow (2018), 'Through the looking glass: environmental health economics in low and middle income countries', in P. Dasgupta, S.K. Pattanayak, and V.K. Smith (eds), *Handbook of Environmental Economics, Volume 4*, Amsterdam: Elsevier, pp. 143–91.

Peel, J., L. Godden, and R.J. Keenan (2012), 'Climate change law in an era of multi-level governance', *Transnational Environmental Law* **1** (2), 245–80.

Perrings, C. and A. Kinzig (2018), 'Ecology and economics in the science of anthropogenic biosphere change', in P. Dasgupta, S.K. Pattanayak, and V.K. Smith (eds), *Handbook of Environmental Economics, Volume 4*, Amsterdam: Elsevier, pp. 61–84.

Pieraccini, M. (2019), 'Towards just resilience: representing and including new constituencies in adaptive governance and law', *Journal of Environmental Law* **31** (2), 213–34.

Rose, C.M. (2001), 'Common property, regulatory property, and environmental protection: comparing community-based management to tradable environmental allowances', in E. Ostrom, T. Dietz, N. Dolsak, P.C. Stern, S. Stonich, and E.U. Weber (eds), *The Drama of the Commons*, Washington, DC: National Academy Press, pp. 233–57.

Rosenbloom, J. (2012), 'New day at the pool: state preemption, common pool resources, and non-place based municipal collaborations', *Harvard Environmental Law Review* **36**, 446–85.

Ruhl, J.B. (2010), 'Climate change adaptation and the structural transformation of environmental law', *Environmental Law* **40**, 363–432.

Ruhl, J.B. (2011), 'General design principles for resilience and adaptive capacity in legal systems: applications to climate change adaptation law', *North Carolina Law Review* **89**, 1373–401.

Ruth, M. and S. Goessling-Reisemann (eds) (2019), *Handbook on Resilience of Socio-Technical Systems*, Cheltenham, UK and Northampton, MA, USA: Edward Elgar Publishing.

Salkin, P.E. (2007), 'Sustainability at the edge: the opportunity and responsibility of local governments to effectively plan for natural disaster mitigation', in J. Nolon and D. Rodriguez (eds), *Losing Ground: A Nation on Edge*, Washington, DC: ELI Press, pp. 125–62.

Salzman, J., G. Bennett, N. Carroll, A. Goldstein, and M. Jenkins (2018), 'Payments for ecosystem services: past, present and future', *Texas A&M Law Review* **6**, 199–227.

Shavell, S. (2004), *Foundations of Economic Analysis of Law*, Cambridge, MA: Harvard University Press.

Sills, E.O. and K. Jones (2018), 'Causal inference in environmental conservation: the role of institutions', in P. Dasgupta, S.K. Pattanayak, and V.K. Smith (eds), *Handbook of Environmental Economics, Volume 4*, Amsterdam: Elsevier, pp. 395–437.

Sioshansi, F. (ed.) (2017), *Innovation and Disruption at the Grid's Edge: How Distributed Energy Resources are Disrupting the Utility Business Model*, London: Academic Press.

Smith, H.E. (2012), 'Property as the law of things', *Harvard Law Review*, 125, 1691–726.

Stephens, J.C. (2019), 'Assessing resilience in energy system change through an energy democracy lens', in M. Ruth and S. Goessling-Reisemann (eds), *Handbook on Resilience of Socio-Technical Systems*, Cheltenham, UK and Northampton, MA, USA: Edward Elgar Publishing, pp. 340–59.

Sterner, T. and E.J.Z. Robinson (2018), 'Selection and design of environmental policy instruments', in P. Dasgupta, S.K. Pattanayak, and V.K. Smith (eds), *Handbook of Environmental Economics, Volume 4*, Amsterdam: Elsevier, pp. 232–84.

Sun, L.G. (2011), 'Smart growth in dumb places: sustainability, disaster, and the future of the American city', *Brigham Young University Law Review* **2011**, 2157–201.

Tarlock, A.D. (2003), 'Slouching toward Eden: the eco-pragmatic challenges of ecosystem revival', *Minnesota Law Review* **87**, 1173–208.

Tarlock, A.D. (2007), 'Land use regulation: the weak link in environmental protection', *Washington Law Review* **82**, 651–66.

Tsosie, R. (2007), 'Indigenous people and environmental justice: the impact of climate change', *University of Colorado Law Review* **78**, 1625–77.

Vandenbergh, M.P. (2013), 'Private environmental governance', *Cornell Law Review* **99** (1), 129–99.

Vandenbergh, M.P. and J.A. Gilligan (2015), 'Beyond gridlock', *Columbia Journal of Environmental Law* **40**, 217–303.

Van Niekerk, D. (2013), 'Climate change adaptation and disaster law,' in J. Verschuuren (ed.), *Research Handbook on Climate Change Adaptation Law*, Cheltenham, UK and Northampton, MA, USA: Edward Elgar Publishing, pp. 142–70.

Verschuuren, J. (2013a), 'Introduction', in J. Verschuuren (ed.), *Research Handbook on Climate Change Adaptation Law*, Cheltenham, UK and Northampton, MA, USA: Edward Elgar Publishing, pp. 1–15.

Verschuuren, J. (2013b), 'Climate change adaptation and environmental and pollution control law', in J. Verschuuren (ed.), *Research Handbook on Climate Change Adaptation Law*, Cheltenham, UK and Northampton, MA, USA: Edward Elgar Publishing, pp. 383–90.

Vespignani, A. (2012), 'Modelling dynamical processes in complex socio-technical systems', *Nature Physics* **8** (1), 32–9.

Vespignani, A. (2009), 'Predicting the behavior of techno-social systems', *Science* **325** (5939), 425–28.

Wiley, L.F. (2013), 'Climate change adaptation and public health law', in J. Verschuuren (ed.), *Research Handbook on Climate Change Adaptation Law*, Cheltenham, UK and Northampton, MA, USA: Edward Elgar Publishing, pp. 171–213.

WRI in collaboration with United Nations Development Programme, United Nations Environment Programme, and World Bank (2011), *World Resources Report 2010–2011: Decision Making in a Changing Climate – Adaptation Challenges and Choices*, Washington, DC: World Resources Institute.

6   Macroeconomics and the environment

Martin R. Sers and Peter A. Victor

6.1   The context in which environmental economics operates

To understand what type of environmental economic theory to develop, one must begin with a realistic appraisal of the numerous environmental challenges and physical conditions facing economies. The current trajectory of aggregate human impact on the Earth-system may lead, via tipping points in various biogeophysical processes, to the transition of the Earth-system from the current inter-glacial state to a potentially much less hospitable hothouse state (Steffen et al. 2018). Furthermore, as explored in the planetary boundaries literature, anthropogenic impacts operate across a variety of processes, ranging from the perturbation of the cycling of phosphorus and nitrogen to biodiversity loss (Steffen et al. 2015). The complex interactions of numerous biogeophysical processes is a characteristic feature of the Earth-system and presents the principal challenge to any study of the relation of economy and environment. Put simply, failing to understand or incorporate certain processes into models of economy–environment interactions may lead to misleading or simply incorrect analysis.

The above two papers by Steffen and colleagues are mentioned to show that the context in which economies function (i.e. the greater Earth-system) is changing rapidly. Although there is good understanding of how aggregate and cumulative anthropogenic impacts drive many of these changes, there is little consensus on or even understanding of how the economic system will be impacted in turn, and which policies will be successful in adaptation and mitigation. This lack of understanding is a serious obstacle to solutions. There is no real consensus, for example, on how to meet energy needs of societies in a sustainable manner (see Clack et al. 2017 and the response in Jacobson et al. 2017). There is also no deep understanding of how possible rapid changes in energy systems will impact the functioning of economies themselves (Sers and Victor 2018; King and van den Bergh 2018).

In taking the complexity of the Earth-system as a starting point it becomes apparent that some traditional approaches to the study of environmental economics are inadequate. For example, in his recent paper, economist William Nordhaus states that "The most important single economic concept in the economics of climate change is the social cost of carbon (SCC)", which is roughly defined as the economic cost of an additional ton of CO_2 emitted (Nordhaus 2017: 1518). The obvious problem with such a measure is that the "true" value of the SCC is simply incalculable with any useful accuracy due to the non-linear response of the climate system to various anthropogenic perturbations, as well as the hard to predict knock-on effects of such changes on other biogeophysical systems and their associated impacts on the functioning of economies. Added to this is the built-in distributional bias in economic valuation of environmental impacts when concepts like willingness to pay or willingness to accept are used. More generally, conventional tools of microeconomics that focus on changes at the margin are ill-suited to addressing a system characterized by enormous uncertainty whose behaviour may be highly non-linear, irreversible and truly global. Under these circumstances, extrapolation from the micro to the macro is untenable. A system-wide analysis is required, and this is the essence of macroeconomics for the environment.

The purpose of this chapter is not to stress the limitations of current macroeconomic approaches such as integrated assessment models (IAMs); there is already a considerable literature that does that (e.g. Victor 2008, 2019; Ackerman and Munitz 2016; Pindyck 2017). Many of the difficulties that complicate the application of neoclassical methods to studying the environment are the same as must be addressed by any other approach. Instead, we discuss five research areas that represent rich open questions for environmental macroeconomics. First, we examine, in an abstract sense, the manner in which physical laws may aid in the construction of new theory; second, we explore the major open question of the long-term sustainability of growth using relatively simple arithmetic arguments; third, we cover the topic of energy return on investment and the challenge and necessity of constructing macroeconomic models using realistic energetic foundations; fourth, we expand the discussion to the general problem of how to integrate the many and varied physical phenomena of importance; and, fifth, we propose a preliminary approach to understanding how new environmental macroeconomic modelling may be undertaken. This chapter seeks to lay out a series of principles, rather than specific research tasks, that should be considered in the generation of new environmental economic theory.

6.2 Physical foundations for environmental macroeconomics

A macroeconomics that understands the economy as a subsystem of the environment would necessarily develop and apply models that are simultaneously consistent with physical laws as well as the principles guiding changes in output, employment, interest rates and other aggregate variables. This is in contrast to the standard representations of economic activity such as the Solow growth model, which is of a process that is defined without reference to any underlying physical phenomena (energy or material use for example) except for an abstract population growth (Solow 1956). As Ayres and Warr (2010) note, conventional growth models behave as perpetual motion machines as they function without reference to energy (or materials) and can reproduce themselves or grow indefinitely. We therefore propose the broad following principle as the first aspect of a research agenda for environmental macroeconomics:

Principle One: Environmental macroeconomic theory and modelling should be developed so that the consequences computable from the models are comparable with, and do not violate, known physical laws and principles.

This first principle represents an admittedly lofty epistemological goal, which, however, can be understood relatively simply. If new modelling or theory is proposed (a) can it be compared in any fashion to physical principles or quantities, and (b) does it violate these principles? In the following subsection we will examine qualitatively this approach in relation to the first and second laws of thermodynamics.

It should be noted that economics developed its modern mathematical form by borrowing heavily from the methods of physics of the nineteenth century (Miroski 1989). The simple emulation of a very successful physical science is not what is meant in this section when we discuss the relation to physical laws or physical foundations; rather, the question is how to use known scientific knowledge to aid in deriving environmental macroeconomic theory. To understand this premise, we examine in the following subsection the consequences of considering energy and the first two laws of thermodynamics on our formal representations of macroeconomies.

6.2.1   Economics and the laws of thermodynamics

Let us begin by defining a very simple type of economy: a throughput economy, which is a system that takes in some inputs from outside itself (the environment) and expels some by-products back into the environment.[1] It will be shown that any representation of an economic process that involves energy must necessarily, by the first and second laws of thermodynamics, have this throughput characteristic.

First however it is constructive to consider familiar depictions of the macroeconomic process: for example, the traditional circular flow of income and expenditures between households and firms whereby households supply labour in return for wages and make expenditures on goods and services (Figure 6.1). This simple representation is an abstraction that at first does not appear to be a throughput economy.

To understand why the above manner of regarding economies as abstract independent systems is problematic let us consider the following simple thought experiment. Consider the very simple circular flow diagram in Figure 6.1 and assume only a single commodity is produced by firms to be purchased by households. Now, let us make two additional assumptions: the commodity possesses some mass,

---

1 This notion of throughput is used, for example, by ecological economist Herman Daly (2005) to mean the usage and disposal of matter and energy by an economic system.

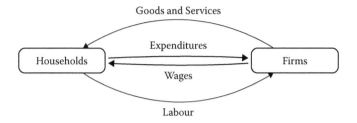

Figure 6.1   Circular flow diagram showing the bidirectional flow of payments between firms and households in order to purchase goods, services and labour

and consumption does not occur at the same location in space as production. The immediate consequence of these assumptions is that some set of forces are necessary to move the commodity from firms to households through a defined distance. However physical work is the product of force acting through a distance; this work is measurable in Joules (a unit of energy). If the only assumptions we make about the circular flow diagram is that output possesses mass and that consumption may take place at a different location in space from production, then the consequence is that energy use is an implicit, albeit hidden, aspect of the model.

Now, let us see an illustration of how physical laws (in this case the first and second laws of thermodynamics) determine the nature of any physically sensible macroeconomic model. The first law of thermodynamics is the statement of the conservation of energy: energy is neither created nor destroyed – only transformed from one form to another Feynman (1963). A conclusion of this law is that the energy necessary to perform the work mentioned above cannot be created in the economic process, and therefore must ultimately enter as an input from the environment.[2]

Now, since this input energy cannot be destroyed, only transformed from one form to another, might it be recycled to run the process again and therefore relieve the economy of the need to take in energy inputs from the environment? That is, if it were possible to isolate the process so that the energy lost as waste heat from friction, for example, were to be recaptured, might the same "energy" be reusable? The answer is no due to the second law of thermodynamics, which states that the entropy of such an isolated system must increase; and, consequently, its ability to do work will decrease. Therefore, the economic process relies on the continual input of energy, which is transformed to provide useful work, and ultimately expelled from the process as waste heat – a throughput system.

The first law, via the famous work of Einstein, may also in ordinary circumstances imply the conservation of mass. This conservation of mass, or the "materials balance principle", has been applied by some economists for some time (see for

---

2 There is some subtlety to this statement involving how we define the boundaries of what is considered the economic process. In this example, coal is viewed as an input taken from the environment and outside the economic system.

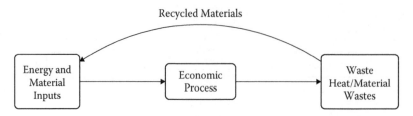

Figure 6.2   The economy as a materials and energy throughput system with some possibility for recycling

example Victor 1972) and is particularly relevant when considering the issue of climate change. That matter is neither created nor destroyed but only transformed implies that material inputs in the form of fossil fuels (coal, oil and natural gas) must be expelled as waste after their combustion; the accumulation of various greenhouse gases (GHGs) in the atmosphere is a result of this. However, unlike energy, there is no law against the complete recycling of material (see Ayres 1999), though in practice this may require prodigious amounts of energy in combination with technologies yet to be invented.

The following important conclusion may be stated: any representation of an economic process that involves energy and materials must be one that takes the form of a throughput system as shown in Figure 6.2. That this can be deduced simply by considering the implications of the first two laws of thermodynamics illustrates the utility of considering the economic process from the basis of known physical law.

In general, the economic system must, by the above logic, be viewed as an open subsystem of the Earth-system: taking in materials and energy and expelling waste (Ruth 2018). If the reader is unimpressed by this seemingly obvious conclusion, it is worth considering that many macroeconomic representations – ranging from the simple circular flow diagram to growth models such as the Solow or Ramsey formulations – are often entirely abstract systems that do not adhere to even these basic conditions. Indeed, failing to account for this throughput nature of the economic system results in macroeconomic models which can, perhaps erroneously, imply the possibility of long-run unbounded or unconstrained economic growth and perpetually increasing social welfare. Economic policies based on such models may therefore be inherently misleading in their prescriptions. Furthermore, this also casts doubt on the association of continual economic growth as a long-term viable societal goal.

In the following section the connection between economic growth and the throughput nature of economies will be made more explicit via the exploration of the concept of growth and intensity reductions.

6.3   Growth and intensity

In the standard IAM formulations the mechanics of the model are such that increased economic growth (and presumably increased utility from consumption) is a benefit which may be decreased by the "damages" and abatement costs associated with accumulation of carbon dioxide (CO_2) in the atmosphere. If, at the outset of such a modelling exercise, it is assumed that the CO_2 intensity (i.e. CO_2 emissions/GDP) declines at some rate, or that total factor productivity (TFP) increases exogenously, then it is entirely possible to generate a scenario in which growth continues indefinitely while emissions are reduced.

In general, for any input M or waste by-product W, for a growing economy to keep constant or even reduce its total throughput requires efficiency gains or intensity declines to occur at the same or greater rate. However, it is insufficient to only consider throughput (flow) as environmental problems are also stock problems. Flows, such as emissions of CO_2, have units of quantity per time interval; stock, such as CO_2 in the atmosphere, is measured simply as a quantity (measured at a specific time). The following mathematical illustrations show that the stock variable is of considerable importance when examining rates of intensity reductions.

Defining GDP at time t as $Y(t)$ and denoting emissions of CO_2 in period t as $E(t)$, the emissions intensity of GDP may be defined as the following ratio:

$$I(t) = \frac{E(t)}{Y(t)} \tag{6.1}$$

Now, assuming some constant rate of economic growth g, what is the requirement for declines in emissions intensity to simply keep emissions at some constant initial level $E(0) = E^c$? Consider the following:

$$Y(0)e^{gt} * I(t) = E^c \tag{6.2}$$

With some algebra the above may be manipulated to obtain the following expression for emissions intensity as a function of time:

$$I(t) = \frac{E^c}{Y(0)}e^{-gt} = I(0)e^{-gt} \tag{6.3}$$

Unsurprisingly, to keep emissions constant with an economy growing at g per cent per year requires emissions intensity to decline at the same rate. To understand the magnitude of this requirement consider the following. An economy growing at 3 per cent per annum will grow by a factor of 10 in approximately 77 years; keeping emissions levels constant requires a decrease of emission intensities by the same factor. Over longer time horizons the emissions intensity must approach zero.

Concerning CO_2 and climate change, the problem is more complex. Climate change is essentially a stock problem, caused by the accumulation of CO_2 (and other greenhouse gases) in the atmosphere. A constant flow of CO_2 emissions will cause the stock to increase. Stabilization of the stock requires a decline in emissions. Importantly, the faster the rate of economic growth, the faster must be the rate of reduction in emissions intensity to achieve any required reduction in emissions if the stock of CO_2 is to be stabilized.[3] To see the basic consequences of this we examine a simplified computation relating emissions to a remaining carbon budget, i.e. future cumulative emissions of consistent CO_2 with a target level of accumulated CO_2 intended to reduce the risk of catastrophic climate change. For a given rate of economic growth g, given initial year emissions given by $Y(0)$ $I(0) = E(0)$, what value r must the emissions intensity decline by per year to cap cumulative emissions at exactly some carbon budget B measured in $GtCO_2$? This can be approximately calculated by solving the following for r:

$$B = \int_0^\infty Y(0)\,e^{gt}\,I(0)\,e^{rt}dt = E(0)\int_0^\infty e^{(g+r)t}dt \tag{6.4}$$

which returns the following formula that approximates the relationship of r and g for given emissions budget B and initial year emissions $E(0)$:

$$r = -\left(g + \frac{E(0)}{B}\right) \tag{6.5}$$

From the 2018 Intergovernmental Panel on Climate Change (IPCC) report it is noted that the remaining carbon budget to obtain a 50 per cent probability of remaining below 1.5 degree C using global mean surface air temperature is estimated at 580 $GtCO_2$, and that this is being reduced by 42 $GtCO_2$ per annum. Taking these emissions as the base year value, we may write E_0 as the product of GDP and the emissions intensity as follows: $E_0 = Y_0 I_0 = 42\ GtCO_2$. Substituting these values into equation (6.6) returns the following value for r:

$$r = -\left(0.03 + \frac{42}{580}\right) = -0.102 \tag{6.6}$$

Therefore, to just cap emissions at the 580 $GtCO_2$ upper bound, a 3 per cent growth rate of the economy implies a value of r of approximately -10.0 per cent. That this value of emissions intensity reduction is much larger than the rate of economic growth is due to the rather severe constraint imposed by the remaining carbon budget, which illustrates a key point: the stock is the critical factor of analysis, and is a major determinant of the magnitude of necessary intensity reductions. Furthermore, attaining such a high value of r would likely imply a major diversion of resources (labour, capital, materials, and energy) away from producing final goods and services, and new capital towards energy efficiency measures and renewable energy infrastructure.

The purpose of this discussion is to make clear that a model or theory built on the assumption of growth and intensity declines, without specifying the actual

---

3 This issue is more complicated than stated here. Emissions reductions arising from the deployment of new technologies as well as the replacement of outdated infrastructure and capital is a source of economic activity itself and, depending on the mixture of energy types utilized, a source of emissions in its own right.

mechanics by which such intensity declines are possible, will lead to misleading results. In particular, the assumption of economic growth rates in models as an assumed long-run property rather than an outcome may be entirely erroneous. Long-term economic growth can, for example, be put synthetically in a model via assumptions such as the continual growth in exogenous parameters like TFP, and just as easily be disallowed by assuming strict resources limitations or limited possibilities for substitution.

Given the importance of the growth in macroeconomics in general, it is essential to treat it as a phenomenon that needs to be explained given other known processes rather than invoked or disallowed by modelling assumptions. This leads us to state the following principle:

Principle Two: Given the existence of a large number of biophysical constraints, long-term economic growth cannot be assumed either explicitly or arise implicitly from modelling assumptions; rather, it must arise as an endogenous element explainable on a physical basis.

The above principle amounts to stating that neither growth nor the factors that drive it should be assumed at the outset, especially in environmental macro-economics where the physical dimensions of economic growth are of paramount importance.

6.4   Energy and EROI

In the previous section it was made apparent that remaining within some given carbon budget requires relatively rapid decarbonization. Whether such decarbonization is possible depends on the physical characteristics of energy systems and cannot be simply assumed. Fossil fuels (coal, oil, natural gas) are useful as energy sources since, among other reasons, they are portable and dispatchable energy sources. Renewable sources such as solar and wind energy are subject to intermittency, require both storage capacity and wide geographic spread to meet demands, and cannot substitute for fossil fuels without extensive changes to the energy using capital stock. Furthermore, given the relatively stringent emission reduction timelines, it is increasingly necessary to build this alternative energy supply and capacity quite rapidly. A fast transition in energy systems is complex and not sufficiently well understood as to simply assume fast and cheap reductions in emissions intensity. To gain some insight into these difficulties we turn to a discussion of the energy related metric EROI.

Energy return on investment (EROI) is the ratio of the energy delivered by some process to the energy invested in capturing and delivering the energy. It may be defined as follows (Hall et al. 1979):

$$EROI = Energy\ Return/Energy\ Invested \qquad (6.7)$$

The lower is the EROI of an energy source, the more energy is needed to obtain some given amount of usable energy. Following a simple calculation, we may derive an expression for net energy available to society. Consider the following definition of net energy:

$$\text{Net Energy} = \text{Energy Return} - \text{Energy Invested} \tag{6.8}$$

Solving the EROI equation for energy invested and substituting this into the net energy equation we have that:

$$\text{Net Energy} = \text{Energy Returned} \cdot \left(1 - \frac{1}{\text{EROI}}\right) \tag{6.9}$$

Using this equation, we can generate the net energy graph shown in Figure 6.3, which displays the percentage or net energy available for use as a declining function of the EROI value.

The meta-analyses undertaken by Hall et al. (2014) indicate generally that the EROI values for fossil fuels are relatively high but declining over time, while the EROI of intermittent renewables such as wind and solar are generally lower or only matching current fossil fuels. They are reduced further when storage is included to overcome intermittency. However, as noted in Bird et al. (2013), the intermittency issue is partly addressed by the smoothing due to the deployment of renewables across large spatial areas, in which case additional transmission facilities may be required. Work by Barnhart et al. (2013), Carbajales-Dale et al. (2014), and Palmer

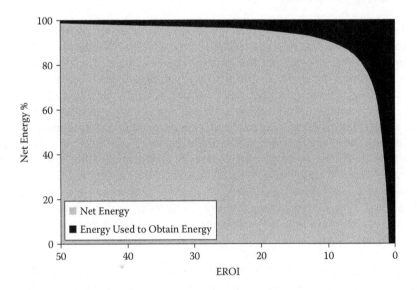

Source: Reproduced from Sers and Victor (2018); concept originally due to Euan Mearns.

Figure 6.3 Net energy cliff

(2017) indicates that renewables at higher market penetration rates may become significantly more energetically expensive, implying lower EROI.

The decline in EROI of fossil fuels is seen by some as limiting future economic growth (Murphy 2014). The possible decline in intermittent renewable EROI may also imply constraints on economic growth. While the first and second sections discussed the plausibility of long-term economic growth by examining thermodynamic and intensity arguments, this section makes a less abstract case. Declining EROIs imply that a greater fraction of energy is spent to obtain energy and therefore is unavailable for other uses, resulting in a shift of resources away from producing final goods and services and towards the primary energy sector. To understand this, it is worth considering the relatively extreme case of EROIs approaching unity. In this case nearly as much energy is expended to obtain a given amount of energy, leaving essentially no surplus energy to power the remainder of the economic process. More generally, declining EROIs imply a reduction in the surplus energy available to society to build new fixed capital, produce goods and services, or be used for consumption – all of these are aspects associated with maintaining steady economic growth. The relationship between energy efficiency and economic growth has been studied in depth by Ayres and Warr (2010).

The possible decline in EROI associated with a shift to renewables presents an especially significant problem if decarbonization of the energy system must occur rapidly. A question of considerable importance is whether the global energy system can manage a transition to less energetically productive technologies while simultaneously remaining within a desired carbon budget. Transitioning too quickly risks a lack of energy available to non-energy sectors. Transitioning too slowly risks failure to meet emission reduction goals. This conundrum is known as the energy-emissions trap (see Sers and Victor 2018). According to Creutzig et al. (2019), it is increasingly unlikely that cumulative emissions targets will be reached without the assistance of largely unproven negative emissions technologies such as bioenergy carbon capture and storage and direct air carbon capture and storage. Understanding further the energetic implications of these technologies is paramount for environmental macroeconomics. There is even the question of whether the decarbonization rates associated with avoiding transgressing carbon budgets with a growing economy are physically possible with the known energy technology. Fundamental upper bounds to the energy conversion efficiencies of technologies may prevent this (see for example the Carnot limit for heat engines, the Shockley–Queisser limit for conventional solar cells, and the Betz limit for wind turbines). It is imperative for environmental macroeconomics to take seriously the task of representing fundamental characteristics of energy systems when theorizing and modelling entire economies; this is presented in the following principle:

Principle Three: Environmental macroeconomics must include energy in ways that are consistent with physical laws and the technical characteristics of different energy systems in order to produce meaningful analyses of the relation between economies and the environment.

6.5   The Earth-system and planetary boundaries

While understanding the role of energy systems should be a fundamental aspect of environmental macroeconomic theory and modelling, it only addresses one of the many biophysical processes that underpin the functioning of the economy. We now turn to a much broader range of phenomena concerning processes at the planetary scale that generally have not been well studied in environmental economics. These are the nine biogeophysical processes underlying the planetary boundaries framework: stratospheric ozone depletion, ocean acidification, nitrogen and phosphorus flow, freshwater use, land-system change, biosphere integrity (functional and genetic diversity), climate change, atmospheric aerosol loading, and the release of novel chemical entities (see Steffen et al. 2015 for details).

At present environmental economics, and more specifically macroeconomics, has very little to say about these processes. For example, the biogeochemical cycling of nitrogen and phosphorus and genetic diversity are not generally phenomena included in the standard suite of macroeconomic concerns. Indeed, historically there is no reason these phenomena would have been of interest to economists beyond perhaps the economic implications of the Haber–Bosch process and the study of the fertilizer industry, and habitat destruction from land conversion. However, the impacts now of potentially large-scale eutrophication and anoxic events as a result of anthropogenic perturbations and the loss of habitat are pressing concerns that have significant macroeconomic causes and implications.

These are formidable problems that do not lend themselves easily to analysis with the concepts and tools of mainstream macroeconomics. For example, the combination of sea-level rise due to ice-sheets melting and the thermal expansion of oceans, along with the slowing of the thermohaline cycle due to the freshening of the surface ocean layer (see Hansen et al. 2015), implies a dangerous combination of increased extreme weather coupled with land loss and flooding. The consequences of rapid sea-level rise on the world's economic systems have already had existential impact on entire nations; yet, the inclusion of ice-sheet and ocean dynamics in macroeconomics is extremely challenging, as is land-use change, habitat and species loss, and increasing exposure to novel chemical entities.

These globally significant environmental issues raise questions about what aspects of the Earth-system should be included in environmental macroeconomics, and how to do so. Going beyond the efforts made so far to include explicitly the carbon cycle and radiative balance models in some IAMs will require considerable imagination and innovation. But it is a challenge to which environmental macroeconomists must rise.

As discussed in Calel and Stainforth (2017), it can be shown that each of the three major IAM models (PAGE, FUND, and DICE) is based on one of two very simple energy-balance models (EBMs). From this starting point environmental macroeconomics must engage with Earth-system models of greater complexity and scope.

Energy balance models, especially the dimensionless ones, exist at the bottom of the hierarchy of climate model complexity, which ranges from EBMs to the enormously complex general circulation models (see Goosse 2015, Chapter 3 for a fuller discussion). In their work Calel and Stainforth note that economists, in seeking to increase the realism of their models, should work with other specialists. Here we fundamentally agree that the study of Earth-system macroeconomic linkages cannot be undertaken solely by economists, but must be truly interdisciplinary. We therefore propose the following principles:

Principle Four: Environmental macroeconomics must move beyond simple energy-balance and temperature damage formulations to encompass a much broader set of phenomena. It is essential for environmental macroeconomists to understand both which processes may be relevant and how to couple these to macroeconomic theory.

Principle Five: Environmental macroeconomics is necessarily an interdisciplinary activity and, as such, new theory and modelling efforts must be undertaken in consultation with and participation from the Earth-system sciences.

6.6   The stock-flow consistent input–output model

In the preceding sections we examined the physical foundations for environmental macroeconomics without specifying how these foundations might be integrated within macroeconomic theory. In this section we outline an approach that may hold some promise for getting started. We begin by separating the problem into four areas. First, it is necessary to be able to track the variety of quite heterogeneous physical flows that constitute the physical throughput of an economy; second, these flows must be related to the real and financial aspects of an economy; third, some rules must be proposed for how these flows impact the greater environment; and, fourth, perhaps the most difficult and poorly understood aspect is how the environment feeds back into the functioning of economies.[4] The last requirement has been addressed most commonly in macroeconomics by the use of damage functions (see Nordhaus 2017 and Burke et al. 2015), which relate temperature increases to losses in economic output. Environmental impacts are much more complicated than just the estimated long-run impacts of temperature changes on total output; environmental macroeconomics requires substantially more research into this aspect.

The first area is arguably the most well understood, and is the domain of environmentally extended input–output analysis which is constructed to map the flows (both physical and monetary) among the sectors of an economy. Modelling linkages between intersectoral flows and the real and financial parts of an economy is less well advanced; however, the following presents one strategy towards improvements. We construct a relatively simple example in order to illustrate how the

---

4 See Motesharrei et al. (2016) for a discussion of this problem and a framework to address it.

approach may work. We begin by defining the following input–output matrices describing an economy with two sectors – an energy sector and a production sector:

$$Z_t = \begin{pmatrix} z_{11,t} & z_{12,t} \\ z_{21,t} & z_{22,t} \end{pmatrix}, F_t = \begin{pmatrix} C_{1,t} + G_{1,t} \\ C_{2,t} + G_{2,t} \end{pmatrix} = \begin{pmatrix} f_{1,t} \\ f_{2,t} \end{pmatrix}, E_t = \begin{pmatrix} e_{11,t} & e_{12,t} \\ z_{21,t} & z_{22,t} \end{pmatrix}, W = \begin{pmatrix} CO2_1 & CO2_2 \\ M_1 & M_2 \end{pmatrix}$$

$$(6.10)$$

where z_{ij} are interindustry transactions in monetary terms; $f_{1,t}$ and $f_{2,t}$ denote the final demand for each industry's output (consumption and government expenditures); E_t is the mixed units version of the Z_t matrix where the first row is replaced with the physical units (Joules) of inputs used by each sector; and the vector W is a matrix of intensities whose components are the emissions of CO_2 per dollar of output and the quantity of fossil fuels (materials) used per dollar of output.

In this simple formulation with only one energy sector the coefficient $e_{11,t}$, the energy input used by the energy sector to produce its output, holds special significance. It is the energy invested portion of the dimensionless EROI ratio. The energy returned in this case is the sum of both interindustry transactions plus that supplied to final demand. Consistent with the discussion in previous sections, we assume this ratio is exogenously determined by the characteristics of the energy technology. Let us also assume there is some price p (more accurately a conversion factor) per Joule of energy such that, for example, $z_{11,t} = p \cdot e_{11,t}$.

To relate this to a larger picture of a macroeconomic system we invoke a transactions flow matrix in keeping with the conventions outlined in Godley and Lavoie (2007). The transactions flow matrix operates under the following principles. First, any financial flow in an economy (wages for example) represents an inflow of funds for one party (the wage earner) and an outflow of funds (a firm paying the wages) by a second party. Second, the sum of all inflows and outflows for a given sector must sum to zero. In writing the sectors of an economy as the columns of a matrix and the various flow types as the rows, it must be the case that all rows and columns sum to zero in a properly specified model where nothing "is left out".

A very simple transactions flow matrix is presented in Figure 6.4 which completes our simple economic model; all rows and columns, by construction, sum to zero.[5]

We see that the elements of the input–output matrices (the entries in bold) are contained within Figure 6.4. In this setup, firms purchase inputs from each other, from themselves, pay wages to the household sector, and supply goods to the government sector. Now, the purpose in establishing this set of interconnections

---

5 The entries in the interindustry transactions row represent the net purchases and sales of a firm of its own and the others firms' output. For the energy firm the interindustry transaction row records the receipts from sales $z_{11,t} + z_{12,t}$ minus purchases $z_{21,t} + z_{11,t}$, which is represented more concisely using summation notation. In this simple formulation $z_{11,t}$ is a sale (to itself) and a purchase from itself which nets to zero.

	Household	Energy	Production	Government	Σ
Consumption	$-C_t$	$+C_t^1$	$+C_t^2$	0	0
Government Expenditure	0	$+G_t^1$	$+G_t^2$	$+G_t$	0
Wage Bill	W_t	$-W_t^1$	$-W_t^2$	0	0
Taxes	$-T_t$	0	0	T_t	0
Interindustry Transactions	0	$\Sigma_j z_{ij,t} - \Sigma_j z_{1j,t}$	$\Sigma_j z_{ij,t} - \Sigma_j z_{1j,t}$	0	0
Change in Money	$-\Delta H$	0	0	ΔH	0
Σ	0	0	0	0	

Figure 6.4 Transactions flow matrix

is as follows: recalling that $z_{11,t}$ and $z_{12,t}$ are the energy purchases (and therefore correspond to some quantity of Joules), we have by the logic of the matrix connected physical energy use (in a simple way) to all other aspects of the economy. An increase in government expenditure or a decrease in consumption demand by households changes the quantity of energy goods required. Furthermore, if the exogenously determined EROI changes in response to a change in the underlying technology, for example, then the flows will change to reflect this.

The total emissions and materials use associated with meeting final demand in this model is given in the standard way from environmentally extended input–output analysis (see Miller and Blair 2009, Chapter 10), which we can write as follows:

$$W_t^T = (WL_t)F_t \tag{6.11}$$

where L_t is the Leontief inverse.[6] If we understand the energy flows as originating from some exogenous stock of fossil fuels and the emissions as being released into the environment we have a throughput model as described in the first section. Furthermore, in a very simple way, we have related energy, macroeconomic phenomena, and waste outputs in a single framework. The above approach may be called a stock-flow consistent input–output (SFCIO) model. In general, a model constructed along the above lines would be much more complicated – involving more financial flows and entities (government bonds, equities, private and central banks, etc.) – and would include a more disaggregated and well-defined energy sector. However, it is the principles we wish to describe here, as the approach itself is very new (see Berg et al. 2015 for one example).

In keeping with the above example, the third area (impact of emissions on the environment) might be represented in the following manner. We introduce two more physical equations (see Myhre et al. 1998 for background):

---

6 The Leontief inverse is calculated as $(1-A)^{-1}$. This A matrix is termed the technical coefficients or direct requirements matrix, where the entries a_{ij} are the ratio of some input bought by the sector to its total output. They are calculated as $a_{ij} = \frac{z_{ij}}{x_j}$ where x_j is the total output of the sector (the sum of intermediate and final demand).

$$RF = 5.35 \ln\left(\frac{[CO_2]}{[CO_2]_r}\right), \Delta T_s = \lambda \cdot RF \tag{6.12}$$

The first is a rough estimate of how the radiative forcing (RF) is related to the ratio of atmospheric concentration of CO_2 to its historical pre-industrial concentration. The second equation relates the radiative forcing to changes in surface temperature via a climate sensitivity parameter. If we include additionally a rule for how emissions increase atmospheric concentration, then our framework has neatly coupled the macroeconomic with the greater environment with respect to climate change.

Aside from introducing a new framework for understanding environmental macroeconomics, the above discussion serves the further purpose of setting up the main problem of this section – how to relate temperature increases to the functioning of the economic system. It works reasonably well because the climatological effects of CO_2 emissions are independent of the geographic location of emission. The same cannot be said of most other environmental problems where locational differences are crucial. A surplus of fresh water in parts of Canada does nothing to alleviate shortages in parts of Africa and the Middle East. The integration of planetary boundaries, where the spatial dimension is critical, must be taken into account; and macroeconomics requires that the macroeconomy be specified in spatial terms as well.

The fourth area, relating the Earth-system to economic functioning, introduces a new difficulty. We might specify a damage function that impacts output, or perhaps one that causes depreciation in some underlying physical capital stock. However, the impacts on other variables in the macroeconomy would only be second order effects. For example, what of government purchases that are in response to, or in anticipation of, climate change? In attempting to introduce some realism to environmental macroeconomic models by including a variety of institutions (private banks, heterogeneous firm types, central banks, etc.) and proposing a variety of interactions it becomes clear that there is no systematic or obvious way in which to introduce Earth-system feedbacks.

This problem is only made more complicated when other possible environmental damages are considered, as they must be when the full set of planetary boundaries is brought into the picture. In short, there is no real understanding of how the environment actually feeds back into the numerous processes that make up the economic system. For example, the alarming declines in insect populations due in large part to habitat destruction documented in a recent study (Sánchez-Bayo et al. (2019) are indicative of the problem; the impacts of these declines may eventually be catastrophic, but there is currently no known way to relate them to macroeconomic variables. This issue of understanding the feedback of the Earth-system on the functioning of economies represents the greatest unknown in generating useful environmental macroeconomic theory and applications.

In this section we have invoked the concept of stock-flow consistency, and shown its implementation in the transactions flow matrix in order to situate the input–

output transactions in a larger conceptual framework as one feature of environmental macroeconomics. It has larger beneficial consequences in that it compels the modeller or theorist to take seriously the nature and logic of the financial sector, which should be a part of environmental macroeconomics – indeed, of all macroeconomics. Among other issues of interest, this is useful for understanding how investment in new technologies (renewable energy systems for example) and mitigation expenses are funded and accounted for, which is a critical part of any environmental transition model.

6.7   Conclusion

In this chapter we have explored several topics and open questions that have generally fallen outside the purview of environmental macroeconomics and, more broadly, environmental economics in general. Many issues – such as the incorporation of realistic energy systems in macroeconomic theory and modelling, the trajectories of growth and decoupling, and, most complicatedly, the impact of Earth-system feedbacks on economic processes – are enormously important both for the scientific understanding of the subject and for the generation of new policies. The current severe and continuously mounting environmental problems demand a more sophisticated approach to the understanding of how economies interact with the greater Earth-system in which they are embedded. The great task for environmental macroeconomists is to understand how the macroeconomic system they study is based upon these processes, and how they influence its trajectories.

References

Ackerman, F., & Munitz, C. (2016). A critique of climate damage modeling: carbon fertilization, adaptation, and the limits of FUND. *Energy Research & Social Science*, 12, 62–67. https://doi.org/10.1016/j.erss.2015.11.008.

Ayres, R. U. (1999). The second law, the fourth law, recycling and limits to growth. *Ecological Economics*, 29(3), 473–483. https://doi.org/10.1016/S0921-8009(98)00098-6.

Ayres, R. U., & Warr, B. (2010). *The Economic Growth Engine: How Energy and Work Drive Material Prosperity*. Cheltenham, UK and Northampton, MA, USA: Edward Elgar Publishing.

Barnhart, C. J., Dale, M., Brandt, A. R., & Benson, S. M. (2013). The energetic implications of curtailing versus storing solar- and wind-generated electricity. *Energy & Environmental Science*, 6(10), 2804–2810. https://doi.org/10.1039/C3EE41973H.

Berg, M., Hartley, B., & Richters, O. (2015). A stock-flow consistent input–output model with applications to energy price shocks, interest rates, and heat emissions. *New Journal of Physics*, 17(1), 015011. https://doi.org/10.1088/1367-2630/17/1/015011.

Bird, L., Milligan, M., & Lew, D. (2013). *Integrating Variable Renewable Energy: Challenges and Solutions*. Technical Report NREL/TP-6A20-60451, September. https://www.nrel.gov/docs/fy13osti/60451.pdf.

Burke, M., Hsiang, S. M., & Miguel, E. (2015). Global non-linear effect of temperature on economic production. *Nature*, 527(7577), 235–239. https://doi.org/10.1038/nature15725.

Calel, R., & Stainforth, D. A. (2017). On the physics of three integrated assessment models. *Bulletin of the American Meteorological Society*, 98(6), 1199–1216. https://doi.org/10.1175/BAMS-D-16-0034.1.

Carbajales-Dale, M., Barnhart, C. J., & Benson, S. M. (2014). Can we afford storage? A dynamic net energy analysis of renewable electricity generation supported by energy storage. *Energy & Environmental Science*, 7(5), 1538–1544. https://doi.org/10.1039/C3EE42125B.

Clack, C. T. M., Qvist, S. A., Apt, J., Bazilian, M., Brandt, A. R., Caldeira, K., & Whitacre, J. F. (2017). Evaluation of a proposal for reliable low-cost grid power with 100% wind, water, and solar. *Proceedings of the National Academy of Sciences*, 114(26), 6722–6727. https://doi.org/10.1073/pnas.1610381114.

Creutzig, F., Breyer, C., Hilaire, J., Minx, J., Peters, G., & Socolow, R. H. (2019). The mutual dependence of negative emission technologies and energy systems. *Energy & Environmental Science*, 12(6), 1805–1817. https://doi.org/10.1039/C8EE03682A.

Daly, H. E. (2005). Economics in a full world. *Scientific American*, 293(3), 100–107. https://doi.org/10.1038/scienti camerican0905-100.

Feynman, R. P., Leighton, R. B., & Sands, M. L. (1963). *The Feynman Lectures on Physics*. Reading, MA: Addison-Wesley.

Godley, W., & Lavoie, M. (2007). *Monetary Economics: An Integrated Approach to Credit, Money, Income, Production and Wealth*. London: Palgrave Macmillan.

Goosse, H. (2015). *Climate System Dynamics and Modelling*. New York: Cambridge University Press.

Hall, C. A. S., Lambert, J. G., & Balogh, S. B. (2014). EROI of different fuels and the implications for society. *Energy Policy*, 64, 141–152. https://doi.org/10.1016/j.enpol.2013.05.049.

Hall, C. A. S., Lavine, M., & Sloane, J. (1979). Efficiency of energy delivery systems: I. An economic and energy analysis. *Environmental Management*, 3(6), 493–504.

Hansen, J., Sato, M., Hearty, P., Ruedy, R., Kelley, M., Masson-Delmotte, V., & Lo, K.-W. (2016). Ice melt, sea level rise and superstorms: evidence from paleoclimate data, climate modeling, and modern observations that 2°C global warming could be dangerous. *Atmospheric Chemistry and Physics*, 16(6), 3761–3812. https://doi.org/10.5194/acp-16-3761-2016.

Intergovernmental Panel on Climate Change. (2018). *Global Warming of 1.5°C*. Retrieved from http://www.ipcc.ch/report/sr15/.

Jacobson, M. Z., Delucchi, M. A., Cameron, M. A., & Frew, B. A. (2017). The United States can keep the grid stable at low cost with 100% clean, renewable energy in all sectors despite inaccurate claims. *Proceedings of the National Academy of Sciences*, 114(26), E5021–5023. https://doi.org/10.1073/pnas.1708069114.

King, L. C., & van den Bergh, J. C. J. M. (2018). Implications of net energy-return-on-investment for a low-carbon energy transition. *Nature Energy*, 3(4), 334. https://doi.org/10.1038/s41560-018-0116-1.

Miller, R. E., & Blair, P. D. (2009). *Input–Output Analysis: Foundations and Extensions*. Cambridge: Cambridge University Press.

Mirowski, P. (1989). *More Heat than Light: Economics as Social Physics, Physics as Nature's Economics*. Cambridge: Cambridge University Press.

Motesharrei, S., Rivas, J., Kalnay, E., Asrar, G., Busalacchi, A., Cahalan, R., Cane, M., Colwell, R., Feng, K., Franklin, R., Hubacek, K., Miralles-Wilhelm, F., Miyoshi, T., Ruth, M., Sagdeev, R., Shirmohammadi, A., Shukla, J., Srebric, J., Yakovenko, V., & Zeng, N. 2016. Modeling sustainability: population, inequality, consumption, and bidirectional coupling of the Earth and Human Systems. *National Science Review*, 3(4), 470–494. doi: 10.1093/nsr/nww081.

Murphy, D. J. (2014). The implications of the declining energy return on investment of oil production. *Philosophical Transactions of the Royal Society A*, 372(2006), 20130126. https://doi.org/10.1098/rsta.2013.0126.

Myhre, G., Highwood, E. J., Shine, K. P., & Stordal, F. (1998). New estimates of radiative forcing due to well mixed greenhouse gases. *Geophysical Research Letters*, 25(14), 2715–2718. https://doi.org/10.1029/98GL01908.

Nordhaus, W. D. (2017). Revisiting the social cost of carbon. *Proceedings of the National Academy of Sciences*, 114(7), 1518–1523. https://doi.org/10.1073/pnas.1609244114.

Palmer, G. (2017). A framework for incorporating EROI into electrical storage. *BioPhysical Economics and Resource Quality*, 2(2), 6. https://doi.org/10.1007/s41247-017-0022-3.

Pindyck, R. S. (2017). The use and misuse of models for climate policy. *Review of Environmental Economics and Policy*, 11(1), 100–114. https://doi.org/10.1093/reep/rew012.

Ruth, M. (2018). *Advanced Introduction to Ecological Economics*. Cheltenham, UK and Northampton, MA, USA: Edward Elgar Publishing.

Sánchez-Bayo, F., & Wyckhuys, K. A. G. (2019). Worldwide decline of the entomofauna: a review of its drivers. Biological Conservation, 232, 8–27. https://doi.org/10.1016/j.biocon.2019.01.020.

Sers, M. R., & Victor, P. A. (2018). The energy-emissions trap. *Ecological Economics*, 151, 10–21. https://doi.org/10.1016/j.ecolecon.2018.04.004.

Solow, R. M. (1956). A contribution to the theory of economic growth. *Quarterly Journal of Economics*, 70(1), 65. https://doi.org/10.2307/1884513.

Steffen, W., Richardson, K., Rockström, J., Cornell, S. E., Fetzer, I., Bennett, E. M., . . . Sörlin, S. (2015). Planetary boundaries: Guiding human development on a changing planet. *Science*, 347(6223), 1259855. https://doi.org/10.1126/science.1259855.

Steffen, W., Rockström, J., Richardson, K., Lenton, T. M., Folke, C., Liverman, D., & Schellnhuber, H. J. (2018). Trajectories of the Earth system in the Anthropocene. *Proceedings of the National Academy of Sciences*, 115(33), 8252–8259. https://doi.org/10.1073/pnas.1810141115.

Victor, P. A. (1972). *Pollution: Economy and Environment*. London: Allen & Unwin.

Victor, P. A. (2008). *Managing without Growth* (2nd edn). Cheltenham, UK and Northampton, MA, USA: Edward Elgar Publishing.

7 Contemporary economics and contraindications for climate maladies: lessons from environmental macroeconomics

Dodo J. Thampapillai and Matthias Ruth[1]

7.1 Introduction

No policy that emanates from economics – whether contemporary or otherwise, whether integrated with scientific knowledge or not – could resolve the climate maladies that confront the planet. The reason has very little to do with the lack of academic rigour of the studies that pre-empt these policies. The reason rests on two main shortcomings. First, whatever knowledge we possess always falls far short of what we do not know. We humbly acknowledge that any suggestion that stems from this chapter will endure the same fate. A second challenge has to do with the fact that even though we do know an awful lot about the technologies and institutional changes needed to slow, if not reverse, anthropogenic causes of climate change, actual implementation of solutions falls far short of what is required at the global scale. No matter how much more we invest in ever-more climate change modelling, and thus gain an ever-more refined picture of the ramifications of human actions, such efforts seem misplaced given the urgency of the problem.

The two shortcomings, of course, are closely related. For example, a lack of knowledge may be politically exploited to delay climate action – a method deployed by some who benefit from the status quo allocation of resources and its associated generation of economic wealth. To the extent that dominant models used in economic decision making contribute to the generation of wealth and accumulation of power among select members of society, use of these models may well be amoral, beyond simply violating physical reality and ecological imperatives.

Against this backdrop, this chapter has a modest goal. We simply modify existing macroeconomic conceptualizations of production, from which we then derive strategies that contrast conventional insights, such as those generated from the works of William Nordhaus and Paul Romer, both of whom were awarded the 2018 Nobel Prize in recognition of their contribution to the economics discipline – one

---

1 With the usual disclaimers, we remain grateful to Thomas Hahn, Geoffrey Harcourt and Krishnan Chandramohan for thoughtful comments and suggestions.

of the most regarded honours bestowed on economists. Their contributions are no doubt worthy of merit for their high level of academic scholarship, rigorous refinements and extensions of worldviews and models developed over decades, if not centuries, by academic economists, and perceived relevance to contemporary issues – especially social welfare, as traditionally defined (see Sagoff, Chapter 2 of this volume), and climate change.

The analytic frameworks of Nordhaus and Romer, though rooted in the neoclassical tradition of a two-factor – labour (L) and manufactured capital (KM) – production function, provide the flexibility for embracing a broader range of pertinent factors in the exposition of economic growth. The alternative framework presented here rests on a three-factor production function that includes environmental capital (KN) alongside KM and L, and rests on premises that acknowledge the laws of thermodynamics and the importance of ecological resilience. In essence, all other foundational elements of the traditional economics approach remain untouched here, such as the notion of a production function that only traces explicitly the desirable outputs from the economy and not unwanted by-products (see Faber and Frick, Chapter 3 of this volume), and one that allows for near infinite substitutability among its inputs (Ruth 2018a, 2018b).

The chapter is structured as follows. The next section provides a brief synopsis of the Nordhaus-Romer contribution. This is followed by a description of the three-factor production function and application towards resolving three questions, namely:

1. How much KN gets utilized (depleted) during economic growth?
2. How much KN remains after a period of growth?
3. Is economic growth really necessary for maintaining and/or improving society's welfare?

As indicated below, the responses to these questions, especially the last one, deviate from the main premises advanced by Nordhaus and Romer.

7.2   The Nordhaus-Romer contribution

The contributions by both Nordhaus and Romer are far too many to present here. The few listed are those that bear direct reference to climate change. Even these few represent a very small subset of a very large array of publications by the two authors, not to mention the papers and books produced by hordes of others emulating, refining and embellishing those works.

7.2.1   William Nordhaus

Nordhaus's work on economic growth and climate change spans more than four decades. Nordhaus (1973) is perhaps one of his earliest contributions to the climate change literature. There he provides a detailed critique of Meadows et al.'s (1972) narrative on limits to growth, which is based on a world model of climate–ecological–economic systems and the feedback processes that connect them. But Nordhaus goes beyond the critique by offering his own assessments of growth, resource constraints and climate effects (for examples see Nordhaus 1974, 1977 and 1982). When Meadows et al. (1992) revisit their scarcity theme with revised models of the global system, Nordhaus (1992) responds with a critique and an argument that the rate of growth of technological change would exceed that of the severity of resource constraints. In fact, one of his key contributions has been combining technology with resource constraints – a theme which perhaps commenced in his 1974 work. It includes the possibility of the table being empty when poor countries get there (Nordhaus 1986).

The pinnacle of Nordhaus's work occurred perhaps with his development, in the 1990s, of the Dynamic Integrated Climate and Economics (DICE) models (Nordhaus 2013, 2018). These models were subsequently extended to include abatement structures in specific regions as Regional Integrated Climate and Economics (RICE) models. The underlying premise of these integrated assessment models is that economic activity results in emissions, which in turn, impact climate variables, most notably temperature; and that the altered climate variables, in turn, affect socio-economic variables of performance. Aside from dealing with environmental issues in a highly aggregate way that lacks biophysical grounding, these models also assume technological improvements to have no bounds. Furthermore, DICE and its cousins are globally aggregated models, and hence run somewhat parallel to the models of Meadows et al. (2004). The major difference to the work by Meadows et al. (2004) is that the biophysical limits to economic growth are not explicit in the DICE/RICE models. Nordhaus and these models have not been immune to such criticism. For example, the critique by Pindyck (2017) echoes the tones of the language Nordhaus (1973, 1992) himself unleashed on Meadows et al. (1972, 1992). Nevertheless, the DICE/RICE models have a substantial following. The aim of these models is to perform policy optimization with reference to an inter-temporal consumption path. Such optimization prompts Nordhaus and his followers to identify, and advocate for, an optimal trajectory of pollution, and hence optimal climate change. This conclusion is tenuous for some because pollution also accumulates – the question remains as to whether the cumulative loads are accounted for – which is a particular challenge for the case of greenhouse gases (GHGs) in the atmosphere, many of which have mean residence times of a century and more.

As indicated, the purpose of this chapter is not to critique Nordhaus, but to suggest a simpler alternative framework. The basis for this simpler alternative framework stems from the fact the underlying production in the economy segment of DICE/RICE models is a Cobb-Douglas production function (involving KM and L) that displays constant returns to scale and Hicks-neutral technological change.

7.2.2   Paul Romer

The basic starting point of Romer's significant contribution also goes back to a Cobb-Douglas production function. In the early 1980s, most macroeconomists continued to be preoccupied with the 1956 Swan and Solow models of steady state equilibrium and its ramifications. Note that Swan's and Solow's models rested essentially on a two-factor Cobb-Douglas production function based on KM and L with constant returns to scale, and aggregate output (Y) was explained on the basis of per unit of population (N) – that is, (Y/N). Further, growth due to technology had to be an exogenous effect. Romer (1986, 1990) revolutionized production theory by rendering technology to be endogenous and demonstrating the presence of increasing returns to scale in the employment of factors KM and L. Romer's initial version (1986) was based on simplifying assumptions of symmetry between individual firms and the existence of a nationwide stock of KM that displayed knowledge externalities. These externalities constituted the basis for increasing returns to scale.

Romer's work led to a range of further analyses involving human capital (Mankiw et al. 1992) as well as social capital and social infrastructure (Hall and Jones 1999). Further generalization of Romer's original work led to the description of economic growth as product of the average productivity of labour (Y/L) and the employment rate (L/N). For examples see Frank et al. (2015) and Hall and Jones (1999). A wide variety of socio-economic factors that could explain (Y/L) and (L/N) became endogenized in the exposition of economic growth. For example, institutional factors that enabled efficient organization factors and resources became important arguments of economic growth. It is possible to argue that the discipline of institutional economics as such receives its validation from Romer's (1986) contribution.

7.3   An alternative framework for production

As indicated in the previous section, the works of both Nordhaus and Romer have their origins in a Cobb-Douglas production function (CD):

$$Y = \alpha \, KM^{\theta} \, L^{\lambda} \tag{7.1}$$

where α denotes a measure of total factor productivity, whilst θ and λ represent the factor shares of national income (Y) accruing respectively to KM and L and owing to constant returns to scale ($\theta + \lambda = 1$).

Critiques of using Cobb-Douglas production functions in the context of economic decision making that affects resource use or environmental impact abound (see, for example, Ruth 2018a). Nevertheless, the production function in Nordhaus' (2013) DICE/RICE models conforms to that given in (7.1) with the exception that it includes a damage coefficient (Λ) that is drawn from the climate impact component of the models:

$$Y = (1-\Lambda)\, \alpha\, KM^{\theta}\, L^{\lambda} \qquad (7.2)$$

The definition in (7.2) does in fact abide by the principles of environmental accounting as given in Ahmad et al. (1989) and Thampapillai and Ruth (2019). That is, the macro-economic equilibrium is defined as $(GDP \equiv Y - D_{KN})$ with D_{KN} being the depreciation of KN instead of $(GDP \equiv Y)$. The difference between the two accounting statements is that aggregate expenditure, namely GDP, must not exhaust all of aggregate income, namely Y. Instead, a certain portion of Y, namely D_{KN}, must be set aside to safeguard KN. Nevertheless, despite Nordhaus' claims of treating the climate system as something analogous to capital, KN remains exogenous to the production function. As indicated below, it is possible to render KN to be endogenous and, in principle, even express it in the same metric as KM is specified in the national accounts.

However, prior to a demonstration of making KN endogenous within the production function, it is pertinent to revisit Romer's original (1986) formulation as well. That is, given the existence of symmetric firms, each displaying constant returns to scale, alongside an economy-wide stock of KM displaying positive knowledge externalities, the amended Cobb-Douglas function would be:

$$Y = \alpha\, KM^{(\theta+\beta)}\, L^{\lambda} \qquad (7.3)$$

In (7.3), β is the knowledge externality coefficient. It is the expansion and generalization of the various sources of this coefficient that enabled a generalized endogenous growth model, as indicated above, namely:

$$\{(Y/N) \equiv (Y/L) * (L/N)\} \qquad (7.4)$$

Because KN bears direct influence on both (Y/L) and (L/N), one could argue that KN is endogenized in (7.4). For example, (Y/L) increases when the quality of KN increases, and so will (L/N) because employers, apart from hiring productive units of L, will be willing to expand operations in places where KN is of high quality. Nevertheless, it is pertinent to endogenize KN within (7.1) and in turn within (7.3) given that, as illustrated below, quantitative appreciation of KN with the same metric as used for KM could be done in principle.

In short, we hold on here to just enough of the standard macroeconomic model of production to outline a parallel to it that, nevertheless, vastly contrasts in spirit and results the models of production, economic growth and climate policy that have for so long dominated contemporary debate. That alternative approach is described in the next section.

7.4   An alternative framework for production

The framework proposed here rests on the premise that one can conceptualize a stock of KN in much the same way as macroeconomists conceptualize the stock of KM. That is, in principle, in the same way that various items of KM (such as buildings, machinery and infrastructure) are aggregated in the national accounts, various natural endowments of a country could be aggregated into a single numerical figure. Of course, at least the following two issues arise when doing so. The first issue is of an empirical nature: a suitable metric to measure KN must exist. The narrative below is based on Thampapillai (2014) and Thampapillai and Ruth (2019). As indicated, the conceptualization and the method developed enable KN to be defined in the same metric as KM. The second issue is more difficult, and pertains to the fact that the items of KN are not easily delineated to fall within the same geographic or accounting systems as those associated with the measurements of KM and GDP, for example. Rather, each economy draws not only on such localized resources as soil or clean air, but also on components of a global ecosystem that provides waste assimilation services, biodiversity and climate stability enjoyed across boundaries. The very notion of sovereign states, within and for which much of macroeconomics has been developed, defies this basic fact. Nevertheless, the method presented here enables policy makers – at least in the first instance – to become cognizant of the extent and roles of KN within the realm of their responsibility.

The main argument here is that an appreciation of the quantum of KN withdrawn is possible when a three-factor function – namely $\{Y = f(KM, L, KN)\}$ – is developed, where the role of KN is explicit. The production function used here can explain the role of KN in determining the level of Y; that is:

$$\{Y = g(KN, KM_F, L_F)\} \tag{7.5}$$

In this function KM and L are fixed at some given level denoted by KM_F and L_F, and changes in Y can be explained by only changes in KN. Consider first Figure 7.1. Here there are two horizontal axes for describing changes in KN. The axis that runs from the origin to the right describes the build-up of KN, whilst the axis that runs from right towards the origin describes the depletion of KN. Figure 7.1 describes a specific production function, namely $\{Y = g(KN, KM_{F1}, L_{F1})\}$, to denote that KM and L are held constant at (KM_{F1}, L_{F1}).

Further, KN has a finite upper limit, namely KN_1. This upper limit is based on the attributes of the ecosystem, specifically the ability and capacity to assimilate wastes. The principles dictate that when KN gets depleted from some upper level KN_1, the output level could remain fixed at Y_1 until KN gets depleted to some threshold level KN_T (see, for example, Carpenter and Cottingham, 1997; Landis, 2008). When depletion exceeds this threshold by letting the stock of KN fall below KN_T, then Y begins to fall. That is, the domain $(KN_T \leftrightarrow KN_1)$ represents the region of assimilative ability, in which KN_1 denotes the limit of this ability, namely assimilative capacity.

The reverse argument can be made with reference to the accumulation of KN whilst holding KM and L fixed at KM_{F1} and L_{F1}. However, accumulation will have limited impacts in the short run because of the time involved for KN to accumulate. That is,

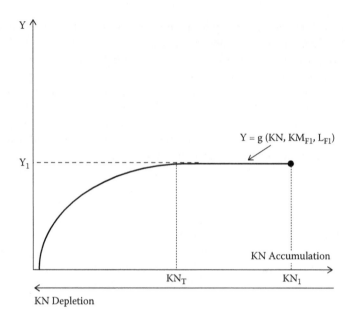

Figure 7.1   Production function and domain of assimilative ability of KN

whilst depletion can be described with reference to activities in the present, accumulation could be the result of activities that had commenced in past time periods. A comparative-static analysis may mask the relevant dynamics. Nevertheless, it is possible for a steady state to prevail. For example, if the rate of accumulation stemming from past and present activities were to balance the rate of depletion owing to current activities and the stock of KN is maintained at a specific level, say KN_1, then this level would depict the steady state. To illustrate, suppose that KN is represented by the air shed within the sovereign borders of a nation. Emission of GHGs is tantamount to the depletion of this air shed. However, activities resulting in the build-up of inland forests and phytoplankton in the oceans can negate the depletion by GHGs. Similar examples, such as abstraction of water from lakes and rivers compensated by conservation activities in catchment areas to increase surface and ground water recharge, could help with conceptualization in this vein.

Reality, however, is one where economic growth – the attainment of higher levels of Y – unfolds with the depletion of KN alongside the accumulation of higher levels of KM and L. This is illustrated in Figure 7.2, which displays two functions: namely one with $(KN_1, KM_{F1}, L_{F1}, Y_1)$, as in Figure 7.1, and the other with $(KN_2, KM_{F2}, L_{F2}, Y_2)$. The increase in Y, namely $(\Delta Y_1 = Y_2 - Y_1)$, is due not only to the increase in (KM, L) but also to the depletion of KN by $(\Delta KN = KN_1 - KN_2)$. That is, three observations can be made as Y increases, and these are:

- The upper limit of KN has receded from KN_1 to KN_2.
- The domain of assimilative ability has shrunk to $(KN_T \leftrightarrow KN_2)$.

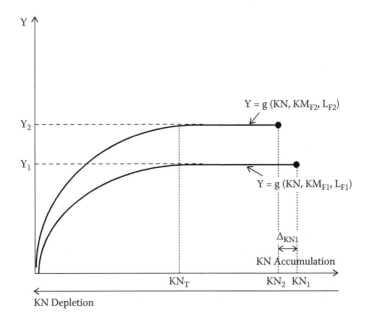

Figure 7.2   KN depletion and economic growth

- The rate at which Y will reduce when depletion exceeds KN_T has increased from δ_1 to δ_2.

Further, following the narrative listed in the publications cited above, the domain of assimilative ability is an indicator of the destruction and diffusion of the KN stock that remains after depletion. For example, ecologists studying the thermodynamic gradients of different ecosystems have confirmed that some ecosystems, such as old growth forests, have much lower rates of entropy generation than cleared land-scapes (Schneider and Kay 1994). Such observations validate the conceptualization given here to indicate that reduced domains of assimilative ability are associated with high levels of entropy production, and indeed fragility as portrayed by the gradient δ.

Figure 7.3 portrays how the production functions described in Figures 7.1 and 7.2 could lead to the display of production that excludes as well as includes KN. The left-hand panel of Figure 7.3 displays a family of production functions for [Y = F(KN, KM_F, L_F)], where KM and L remain fixed – but at different levels. For example, {(KM_{F1}, L_{F1}) < (KM_{F2}, L_{F2}) < (KM_{F3}, L_{F3}) < (KM_{F4}, L_{F4})} and, accordingly, {Y_4 > Y_3 > Y_2 > Y_1}. That is, as the level of (KM, L) gets higher, the size of Y becomes larger, and, following the discussion above, the entropy of the remaining stock of KN increases. It is now possible to articulate the quantity of KN depleted with every increase of Y. For example, in the left-hand panel of Figure 7.3, the quantity of KN is depleted when Y increases from Y_3 to Y_4, that is {KN_3 – KN_4} = ΔKN_3. The premise advanced here is that the utilization ΔKN_3 raises the entropy of the

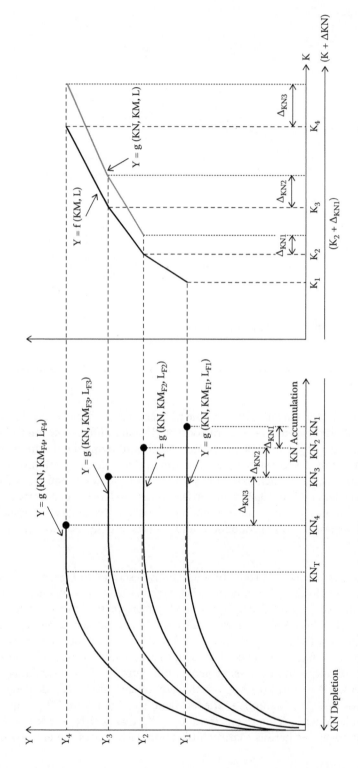

Figure 7.3 Deriving the standard and revised production functions

remaining stock of KN, namely KN_3. Hence, further increase in Y, such as $(Y_4 - Y_3)$ in the context of (KN Stock $= KN_3$), would result in the amount of KN utilized, namely ΔKN_4 to be greater than ΔKN_3.

Based on the information displayed in the left-hand panel of Figure 7.3, two distinct production functions emerge in the right-hand panel. Both functions display diminishing marginal returns. Importantly, the driver of such returns is in fact the increasing entropy of KN. This is because each successive increase in Y entails the utilization of greater quantities of KN compared to the previous utilization. In the right-hand panel of Figure 7.3, {Y = f[KM, L]} is obtained when the quantity of KN utilized (depleted) is ignored. The production function that includes KN, namely {Y = g[KM, L, KN]}, will be always below {Y = f[KM, L,]}, implying that ignoring KN overstates economic performance of (KM, L). Note that the right-hand panel of Figure 7.3 displays two horizontal axes, namely one for KM and the other for (KM+KN), based on the assumption that KM and KN can be measured on the same metric. Following the illustration in Figure 7.3, the basis for the three-factor production function {Y = g[KM, L, KN]} would be {Y = g_1[(KM+KN), L]}. This is illustrated in the next section by recourse to a standard Cobb-Douglas function, which we will use to contrast dominant economic models of resource use and emissions and the implications they suggest.

7.5   The revised Cobb-Douglas function and analytics

7.5.1   KN utilization

The Cobb-Douglas function that excludes KN, namely that given in (7.1) above, will generally conform to the standard identity that underlies national income accounting – that is, (GDP $\equiv$ Y). In this vein, the adaptation of {Y = g_1[(KM+KN), L]} in the form of the Cobb-Douglas function must conform to the basic definition that underlies environmental accounting, namely (GDP $\equiv$ Y $- D_{KN}$). As indicated above, D_{KN} is the depreciation of KN and is usually represented by expenditures such as costs of pollution abatement and water treatment so that KN endowments could continue to provide their services.

Suppose that η represents the share of D_{KN} in GDP. Then multiplying {Y = g_1[(KM+KN), L]} by $(1 - \eta)$ would conform to (GDP $\equiv$ Y $- D_{KN}$) and be tantamount to resolving for $(Y - D_{KN})$. Hence, a revised Cobb-Douglas function that captures the contribution of KN would read as follows:

$$Y = (1-\eta) \, \alpha \, (KM + KN)^\theta \, L^\lambda \qquad (7.6)$$

Note that (7.6) differs from that of Nordhaus (2013) given in (7.2) by the inclusion of KN. Further, the right-hand panel of Figure 7.3 provides a basis for estimating the size of KN that is being utilized (withdrawn). This can be achieved by making the following assumptions:

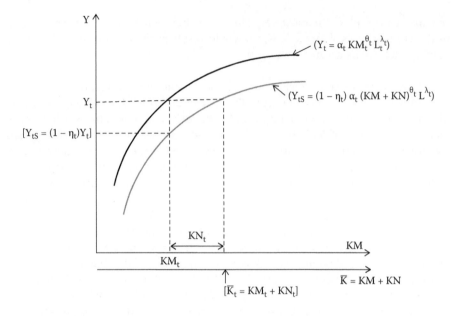

Figure 7.4   Conceptual basis for the estimation of KN utilization

- The function that excludes KN takes the form of the standard Cobb-Douglas function, namely that defined in (7.1);
- The function that includes KN takes the form given in (7.6); and
- Because the two functions differ on the premises of income accounting, namely (GDP ≡ Y) and (GDP ≡ Y − D_{KN}), the vertical distance between the two functions is D_{KN}.

These features are illustrated in Figure 7.4. As shown, the same value of Y is defined by two functions, namely the standard Cobb-Douglas function as in (7.1) and the revised Cobb-Douglas as given in (7.6). A definition for the amount of KN that is utilized (depleted) can be obtained when (7.1) is divided by (7.6); that is:

$$KN = \{[[1/(1-\eta)]^{(1/\theta)}] - 1\} \, KM \tag{7.7}$$

Thampapillai (2016) and Thampapillai and Ruth (2019) illustrate the estimation of KN utilization (withdrawal) as point estimates over a 30-year period from 1970 to 2009 for Australia and South Korea. In this illustration, KN was conceptualized as the air shed of the respective economies, and D_{KN} was estimated as the cost of abating total GHG emissions. The important observations from these studies are that:

- South Korea's and Australia's GDP grew at average annual rates of 7.4 and 3 per cent respectively over the 30-year period;
- KN withdrawal in South Korea and Australia grew at average annual rates of 8.8 and 5 per cent over the same time period.

Given the earlier argument that KN withdrawal causes the entropy of the remaining stocks of KN to increase, economic growth is clearly an entropic process. The notion of a steady state as a smooth upward trajectory of GDP growth, without any oscillation, as espoused by most economists, is clearly a misnomer and a contraindication with reference to welfare. One could argue that the increase in both the frequency and intensity of natural hazards such as hurricanes, droughts, flooding and other extreme weather events – many of which have increased in frequency and severity in recent history – could be the result of the increasing entropy of KN stocks that remain. As indicated below, quantifying the withdrawal of KN in the same metric as KM (in the national accounts) also enables the estimation of KN stocks that remain in terms of a reference estimate in a past period.

7.5.2   KN stocks remaining

In standard macroeconomics, the simplest method to measure the changing size of KM is the perpetual inventory method (PIM). The size of a capital stock at the start of a given period, say (KM_t), is defined in terms of the following items that existed in the previous period: KM stock (KM_{t-1}), gross investment (I_{t-1}) and depreciation (D_{KMt}). That is, $\{KM_t = KM_{t-1} + I_{t-1} - D_{KMt}\}$. Further, the method also involves a proxy approach, based on the average annual rates of investment and depreciation, to estimate the initial stock size in a reference year, such as the start of a time series. The underlying premise in this method is that KM stock will grow as long as investment exceeds depreciation. Thampapillai (2018) and Thampapillai and Ruth (2019) show how this method could be adapted to the context of KN where the net effect is depletion. Denoting the annual withdrawal of KN as defined in (7.7) above, for a given year as $KN_{W(t)}$, the stock size (KN_S) that could have existed in the initial year is defined as:

$$KN_{S0} = \left[\frac{\sum_{t=0}^{T} KN_{W(t)}}{T\delta_{KN}} \right]$$

(7.8)

In (7.8), T represents the length of time considered and δ_{KN} is the average annual rate of KN depreciation. Changes in KN stock are then identified with reference to a modified PM equation as:

$$KN_{St} = KN_{S(t-1)} - (1 - \rho) KN_{W(t-1)}$$

(7.9)

In (7.9), ρ represents a resilience coefficient for KN; that is the ability of KN to regain its attributes when damage is inflicted through depletion. Here ($\rho = 1$) represents complete resilience, whilst ($\rho = 0$) represents complete non-resilience. So, when ($r = 1$), ($KN_{St} = KN_{S(t-1)}$) and when ($\rho = 0$), ($KN_{St} = KN_{S(t-1)} - KN_{W(t-1)}$). The elicitation of r requires scientific information with reference to the KN sink in question (for example see Carpenter et al. 2001, and Brand and Jax 2007). For the application of (7.8) and (7.9) with reference to Australia's air shed, ρ was estimated as indices in terms of the policy dialogue in Australia for tightening GHG emission standards (Thampapillai 2018). For example, a simple index was to compare the actual emission (E_A) with the desired target emission (E_T). If ($E_A = E_T$), then $\rho = 1$; and if ($E_A \to \infty$) then ($\rho \to 0$). On this basis the macroeconomic stock estimate of Australia's air shed in 1970 would have been equivalent to approximately \$38 trillion in constant 2014 Australian Dollars. The average annual depreciation over the period 1970–2015 was equivalent to roughly \$620 billion, leaving behind a KN stock of nearly \$10 trillion. Clearly the stock estimates that remain would depend very much on the validity of the estimate for ρ. Nevertheless, the three-factor production function developed here and the estimation of both the utilization and the stock size of KN should dispel the mistaken notion that KN sinks such as air sheds and oceans are infinite.

7.5.3   Reassessment of economic growth

The importance of economic growth is often validated by the need for the rate of increase of real per capita national product to exceed the rate of population growth. This requirement has become reinforced in contemporary societies, both developed and developing, because of the spread of ageing populations. Given this context, Nordhaus' analyses that dictate optimal rates of emissions would appear justifiable because emissions are inevitable outcomes of economic growth. Further, the analytics of Romer's frameworks give room for significant optimism because of the knowledge externality as shown in (7.3). However, the discussion presented above requires a reformulation of the basic Romer model, and this is as follows:

$$Y = \alpha \, (KM + KN)^{(\theta + \beta - \gamma)} \, L^\lambda \qquad\qquad (7.10)$$

In (7.10), the justification for (KM+KN) follows the discussion presented above with reference to the role of KN depletion in providing the basis for economic growth. Further, following the analysis in Thampapillai and Chen (2018), the same way as the coefficient β captures Romer's (1986) positive knowledge externality, the coefficient γ displays the collective of negative externalities that stem from the depletion of KN. The analysis of the South Korean economy over the period 2010 to 2016 revealed that whilst the application of standard macroeconomic frameworks displayed annual growth rates ranging between 6 and 7 per cent, the application of (7.10) above revealed a much reduced growth rate of about 1.5 per cent. Further, because in Thampapillai and Chen KN was confined to the air shed and did not have other KN endowments such as water and soil considered, the prospect of negative growth could not have been ruled out.

7.6   Conclusion

"Contraindication" is a medical term for treatments that are clinically ineffective, and hence deemed failures. The term is indeed appropriate for proposals to limit pollution to supposedly optimal levels so that optimal amounts of climate change could unfold. This chapter refutes this conclusion by recourse to the content of environmental macroeconomics – where the analytic tools are developed on the premises of the laws of thermodynamics and the notion that ecosystems provide (geographically and temporally wide-ranging yet ultimately limited) waste assimilation services.

As indicated, the production function developed here with KN as an explicit endogenous argument draws on the entropy law of thermodynamics and the principle of ecological resilience as drivers of the law of diminishing marginal returns. This function, in turn, permits the estimation of the amount of nature that gets utilized (withdrawn) as capital each year, and further illustrates that economic growth is an entropic process. The ability to measure the utilization of KN also permits an appreciation of estimating the amount of KN that remains as stock after utilization. The illustration made with reference to Australia highlights the urgency with which measures to mitigate climate change must be adopted. Further, the inclusion of KN as an argument in growth models shows the presence of negative externalities that must be reckoned with. If all aspects of KN depreciation are considered, then the need for de-growth would be inevitable. Hence, it is pertinent to direct Romer's positive knowledge externality towards mitigating the negative externality stemming from the depletion of KN and limiting pollution such that ecological waste assimilation processes are not overwhelmed.

Our arguments above are based on straightforward modifications of existing macroeconomic frameworks and, for illustrative purposes, make use of the standard Cobb-Douglas production function. In essence, we are merely showcasing how the conclusions from mainstream economics are readily undermined with its own constructs when these constructs reflect the contributions natural capital stocks make to the production process. However, we did not formally distinguish here, for example, between different ways in which KN contributes to economic output, such as a stock from which resources are withdrawn or a stock that provides services that can be maintained, at least in principle, ad infinitum (Costanza and Daly 1992). We also did not resort to more meaningful representations of the production process by recourse to alternative forms of production functions (see for example, Ruth 2018a) or question the role of the market place to reconcile decisions of producers and consumers, and thus help establish the prices by which some of the inputs into and outputs of the economy are valued individually and for aggregation (see Chapter 1). Moreover, we did not question the social welfare mindset to which traditional macroeconomic caters. Rather, our goal was a modest one, as discussed above, and we intend it as a motivation, if nothing else, for others to attend to the remaining issues in turn, as we will endeavour, too.

References

Ahmad, Y. J., El Serafy, S. and Lutz, E. (eds), *Environmental Accounting for Sustainable Development*, World Bank, Washington DC, 1989.

Carpenter, S. R. and Cottingham, K. L., "Resilience and Restoration of Lakes", *Ecology and Society*, 1(1): 1–10, 1997.

Costanza, R. and Daly, H. E., "Natural Capital and Sustainable Development", *Conservation Biology*, 6: 37–46, 1992.

Frank, R. H., Bernanke, B. S. and Lui, H.-K., *Principles of Economics* (Asia Global Edition), McGraw-Hill Education, New York, 2015.

Hall, R. E. and Jones, C. I., "Why Do Some Countries Produce So Much More Output Per Worker than Others?", *Quarterly Journal of Economics*, 114(1): 83–116, 1999.

Landis, W. G. "Assimilative Capacity", in Jorgensen, S. E. (ed.), *Encyclopaedia of Ecology*, Elsevier, Oxford, 2008.

Mankiw, N. G., Romer, D. and Weil, D., "A Contribution to the Empirics of Economic Growth", *Quarterly Journal of Economics*, 107(2): 407–437, 1992.

Meadows, D. H., Meadows, D. L. and Randers, J., *Beyond the Limits*, Chelsea Green, London, 1992.

Meadows, D. H., Meadows, D. L., and Randers, J., *The Limits to Growth: The 30-Year Update*, Chelsea Green, London, 2004.

Meadows, D. H., Meadows, D. L., Randers, J. and Behrens III, W. W., *The Limits to Growth: A Report of Club of Rome's Project on the Predicament of Mankind*, Universe Books, New York, 1972.

Nordhaus, W., "World Dynamics: Measurement without Data", *Economic Journal*, 83(332): 1156–1183, 1973.

Nordhaus, W., "Resources as a Constraint on Growth", *American Economic Review*, 64(2): 22–26, 1974.

Nordhaus, W., "Economic Growth and Climate: The Case of Carbon Dioxide", *American Economic Review*, 67(1): 341–346, 1977.

Nordhaus, W., "How Fast Should we Graze the Global Commons?", *American Economic Review*, 62(2): 242–246, 1982.

Nordhaus, W., "Resources, Technology and Development: Will the Table Be Bare When Poor Countries Get There?", *Indian Economic Review*, 21(2): 81–94, 1986.

Nordhaus, W., "Lethal Model 2: The Limits to Growth Revisited, *Brookings Papers on Economic Activity*, 23(2): 1–60, 1992.

Nordhaus, W. (with Sztorc, P.), *DICE 2013R: Introduction and User's Manual*, Yale Economics Department, Yale University, 2013.

Nordhaus, W., "Evolution of Modelling of the Economics of Global Warming: Changes in the DICE Model, 1992–2017", Climatic Change, 148(4): 623–640, 2018.

Pindyck, R. S., "The Use and Misuse of Models for Climate Policy", *Review of Environmental Economics and Policy*, 11(1): 100–114, 2017.

Romer, P., "Increasing Returns and Long-Run Growth", *Journal of Political Economy*, 94(5): 1002–1037, 1986.

Romer, P., "Endogenous Technological Change", *Journal of Political Economy*, 98(5): 71–102, 1990.

Ruth, M., *Advanced Introduction to Ecological Economics*, Edward Elgar Publishing, Cheltenham, UK and Northampton, MA, USA, 2018a.

Ruth, M., "Regional Science in a Resource-Constrained World", *Annals of Regional Science*, 61(2): 229–236, 2018b.

Solow, R. M., "A Contribution to the Theory of Economic Growth", *Quarterly Journal of Economics*, 70(1): 65–94, 1956.

Schneider, E. D. and Kay, J. J., "Life as a Manifestation of the Second Law of Thermodynamics", *Mathematical and Computer Modelling*, 19(6–8): 25–48, 1994.

Swan, T. W., "Economic Growth and Capital Accumulation", *Economic Record*, 32(2): 334–361, 1956.

Thampapillai, D. J., "Lessons from Science: Need for a Rethink of Concepts in Economics", *Economic and Political Weekly*, 49(37): 79–83, 2014.

Thampapillai, D. J., "Ezra Mishan's Cost of Economic Growth: Evidence from the Entropy of Environmental Capital", *Singapore Economic Review*, 61(3): 1640018, 2016.

Thampapillai, D. J., "The Size of an Air Shed: A Macroeconomic Stock Estimate", *Singapore Economic Review*, May, 2018.

Thampapillai, D. J. and Chen, J., "Environmental Macroeconomics: A Neglected Theme in Environmental Economics – Leave Alone Economics", *Singapore Economic Review*, October, 2018.

Thampapillai, D. J. and Ruth, M., *Environmental Economics: Concepts, Methods and Policies*, Routledge, London, 2019.

8 Energy intensity: the roles of rebound, capital stocks, and trade

Astrid Kander, M. d. Mar Rubio-Varas and David I. Stern

8.1 Introduction

Two somewhat contradictory ideas constitute the conventional wisdom on energy intensity and climate change. The first is that declining energy intensity will contribute significantly to mitigating climate change and that energy efficiency policies can contribute to this reduction in energy intensity. For example, the International Energy Agency expects that energy efficiency improvements will contribute about half of the reduction in greenhouse gas emissions required to achieve the goal of limiting climate change to a 2°C increase in temperature (IEA, 2014, 279). Similarly, the IPCC *Fifth Assessment Report* integrates projections from many different models (Clarke et al., 2014, Figure 6.1), finding that 95 percent of models predict that global energy intensity will decline more rapidly than in the past. This idea is technologically optimistic and suggests that more efficient use of energy will contribute significantly to combatting climate change.

The second idea is that historical reductions in energy-related emissions in the developed economies were in large part achieved by offshoring emissions to developing economies (Peters et al., 2011; Steinberger et al., 2012). For example, the IPCC *Fifth Assessment Report* shows that while territorial or production-based emissions fell in the Organization for Economic Co-operation and Development (OECD) countries from 1990 to 2010, consumption-based emissions rose (Blanco et al., 2014, Figure 5.14). This idea is technologically pessimistic, suggesting that, as countries move up the development ladder, they will no longer produce their own industrial goods; they will transition to a service economy and consume industrial goods manufactured in less developed countries. This means that greenhouse gas emissions are not reduced by increasing energy efficiency but are only moved to other parts of the world.

In this chapter, we assess the validity of these ideas and lay out an agenda for future research. Energy efficiency improvements do not necessarily translate directly into reductions in the energy use of the economy. The gap between the two is known as the economy-wide rebound effect. We review the literature on the size of this effect, and briefly present some new empirical evidence. This shows that the economy-wide rebound effect is likely to be large. However, energy intensity declined over the last two centuries in the U.S. and some other developed economies. In many others, it declined rapidly since at least the 1970s. So, this raises the question for future research of what has driven this decline in energy intensity and whether it will continue into the future.

As it is machines, appliances, and structures that actually use energy, the relationship between capital and energy is crucial to understanding how energy intensity evolves. Strong inertia permeates energy systems that have well-established infrastructures on both the supply and demand sides, making it difficult to change course. This inertia seems to be proportional to the scale of the energy system undergoing transition. Future research should investigate how capital stocks affect the pace of change towards a less energy-intensive and less polluting energy system, and how the composition of capital affects this.

While these factors suggest that energy intensity might decline more slowly than the consensus view, our research on trade and energy intensity points in the opposite direction. We show that when technology differences between countries are accounted for, offshoring of energy use through trade specialization is not as important as commonly believed, and cannot explain the entire decline in energy intensity in developed economies after 1970. But there are differences among the developed countries. Anglophone countries seem more prone to outsource than Nordic countries for some reason. In addition, even in countries like Sweden – which is generally seen as a leader in climate ambition, with the world's highest carbon tax and a strong historical dependence on natural resource intensive exports – there was a shift in the period 1995–2009, where the balance of energy embodied in trade went from a large net surplus of exported embodied energy to fairly balanced trade. This still suggests that countries at a certain level of income (or with high carbon taxes) may in fact eventually become service economies while their industrial goods are produced elsewhere, confirming the conventional view. This calls for additional research and the need for continuing the work on environmentally extended multiregional input–output tables on the global scale.

To properly discuss these issues, we need to introduce some conceptual definitions. *Energy intensity* is the physical quantity of energy required per unit of output or activity, so that using less energy to produce a product reduces intensity. It is measured at the national level in joules per dollar produced or equivalent units. Economic *energy efficiency* improves when a given level of energy service is provided with reduced amounts of energy inputs while controlling for other factors. These may include, among others, the price of energy relative to other inputs (labor, capital, etc.), the mix of energy carriers (coal, oil, etc.), and the structure of economic activity (e.g., agriculture, manufacturing etc.).[1]

---

1 A more precise definition is to equate energy-efficiency improvements to energy-augmenting technical change and reductions in technical inefficiency. An energy-augmenting technical change occurs when the same amount of energy produces more output than previously, with the quantities of all other inputs and their own "technologies" held constant. Technical inefficiency refers in economics to production that uses more inputs to produce a given

In physics, *thermodynamic efficiency* is defined in ways that somewhat parallel these economic definitions. 1st law efficiency is defined by the ratio of useful energy output to energy input; 2nd law efficiency compares the input energy for a given useful output to the theoretical minimum energy input required. For example, an electrical resistance heater might have a high 1st law efficiency but poor 2nd law efficiency compared to a heat pump. While an increase in thermodynamic efficiency may often increase energy efficiency or productivity in an economic sense, there are two main differences between this physics-based definition and economic energy efficiency. First, improved thermodynamic efficiency might be achieved by using more of other inputs, such as insulation instead of energy. Economic energy efficiency tries to control for this by valuing those other inputs. Second, economics might place a different value on different sorts of work outputs. In the following, when we refer to "energy efficiency" we mean economic *energy efficiency* unless we specifically refer to *thermodynamic efficiency*.

The last two concepts that we will use are *energy mix* and *energy quality*. The energy mix is the shares of the different primary energy sources – such as coal, oil, hydro-electricity, solar energy, etc. – in total energy use. The different energy sources have a complex set of attributes unique to each of them, such as physical scarcity, capacity to do useful work, energy density, cleanliness, amenability to storage, safety, flexibility of use, cost of conversion, and so on (Cleveland et al., 2008). No single metric can capture all those attributes. However, there are various approaches to measuring energy quality that attempt to capture some aspects of these. One such measure for the quality of aggregate energy divides an index of economic energy volume by total joules of energy. The volume index accounts for shifts towards (or away from) higher-priced fuels. For example, a shift towards primary electricity from coal will usually increase energy quality measured in this way.

8.2   The economy-wide rebound effect and the trend in energy intensity

Already in the nineteenth century William Stanley Jevons claimed that: "[It] is wholly a confusion of ideas to suppose that the economical use of fuel is equivalent to a diminished consumption. The very contrary is true" (1866, 123). Jevons lived in a time when the thermodynamic efficiency of steam engines significantly improved, but coal use also increased dramatically. Jevons drew attention to the fact that if the thermodynamic efficiency of a machine is improved and it consumes less energy for a certain work task, the costs of producing this work task goes down, and so consumption of this work is likely to go up. This is the direct rebound effect. Existing users of the machines may use them more; but, more importantly, the machines will be diffused more generally in society and energy consumption will increase. This was clearly the case for steam engines. The early steam engines had

---

output than the current best practice technology requires.

thermodynamic efficiency of only 0.7 percent and could only be used in the coal mines themselves, where coal was abundant and cheap. During the course of the nineteenth century the efficiency of steam engines rose several-fold, and technical improvements enabled a smooth rotating movement rather than just reciprocating action. This enabled their diffusion to the textile industry, where workers were augmented with steam engines which increased productivity enormously. When steam engines were used as part of the transport revolution in steamships and trains, countries without domestic sources could also access coal at an affordable cost and coal use expanded enormously – not just for steam engines but also for high-temperature industrial processes and cooking, and for low-temperature household heating. When coal was used to transport itself to customers, an enormous expansion in the use of coal took place globally. But does this Jevons' paradox also hold true today?

Most empirical research on the rebound effect focuses on the direct rebound effect (Sorrell et al., 2009) where households and firms consume more energy services, such as heating or lighting, in response to energy-efficiency improvements that reduce the energy required to provide the same level of service and, therefore, its cost. In addition to this direct rebound effect there are indirect rebound effects, which include the energy use effects of: the increase in demand for complementary energy services (and reduction in demand for substitutes); the increase in the use of energy to produce other complementary goods and services; the effect of reduced energy prices due to the fall in energy demand (Borenstein, 2015); and a long-run increase in total factor productivity, which increases capital accumulation and economic growth and, as a result, energy use (Saunders, 1992). These direct and indirect effects sum to the economy-wide rebound effect. With such economy-wide effects taken into account, energy savings due to energy-efficiency improvements may eventually be cancelled out, and energy consumption may not go down.

The size of the economy-wide rebound effect is controversial (Gillingham et al., 2013). Existing estimates vary widely. Some studies confirm Jevons' paradox, where energy use increases following an energy-efficiency improvement, while at the other extreme some find "super-conservation", where energy use falls by more than the efficiency improvement (Saunders, 2013; Turner, 2013). Previous research mostly uses either computable general equilibrium (CGE) models or partial equilibrium econometric models to assess the size of the economy-wide effect. CGE models depend on many a priori assumptions and the parameter values adopted; and partial equilibrium models do not include all mechanisms that might increase or reduce the rebound, and mostly do not credibly identify the rebound effect.

Estimates of the size of the direct rebound effect tend to be fairly modest positive numbers (Sorrell et al., 2009). For example, a household will not drive twice as many miles if it buys a car with an engine twice as efficient as their old car's.[2] It is usually

---

2 On the other hand, in recent decades there has been a trend towards larger vehicles such as SUVs and pickup trucks and faster-accelerating vehicles. This may be partly a response to increased engine thermodynamic efficiency.

assumed that the indirect rebound is positive, so that the economy-wide rebound is greater than the direct rebound effect, and that the economy-wide rebound will be larger in the long run than in the short run (Saunders, 2008), as Jevons also suggested. Turner (2013) argues, instead, that because the energy used to produce a dollar's worth of energy is higher than the embodied energy in most other goods, the effect of consumers shifting spending to goods other than energy will mean that the indirect rebound could be negative and the economy-wide rebound might also be negative in the long run.[3]

There have been limited attempts to determine the economy-wide rebound in a consistent theoretical framework. Assuming a highly aggregated economy with energy- and labor-augmenting technical change, and that the prices of energy and capital are constant (partial equilibrium), Saunders (1992) showed that the easier it is to substitute capital for energy – the higher the elasticity of substitution – the higher the rebound will be.[4] Lemoine (2019) conducts a general equilibrium (all prices variable) analysis of the rebound effect with a large number of consumption goods sectors each with a different constant elasticity of substitution (CES) production technology. He also assumes that overall consumption preferences are CES with a common elasticity of substitution for all goods. Rebound is increasing in both the elasticity of substitution in production between energy and labor and the elasticity of substitution in consumption. General equilibrium effects tend to increase (decrease) rebound beyond the partial equilibrium effect in energy- (labor-) intensive sectors. Reduced (increased) energy use in the energy-intensive energy supply sector, as a result of the fall (increase) in energy use elsewhere in the economy, is important in reducing (magnifying) rebound when rebound is less (greater) than 100 percent. Both backfire and super-conservation are possible, though Lemoine (2019) estimates that economy-wide rebound to innovation across all sectors in the US is 38 percent. This number is quite low because the values of the elasticity of substitution between energy and labor that Lemoine (2019) uses are low.

Existing evidence on the size of the economy-wide rebound effect depends on simulation models (e.g. Turner, 2009; Barker et al., 2009; Koesler et al., 2016; Lu et al., 2017; Rausch and Schwerin, 2018), partial equilibrium econometric estimates (e.g. Adetutu et al., 2016; Orea et al., 2015), or accounting approaches (e.g., Galvin, 2014; Shao et al., 2014; Lin and Du, 2015). Turner (2009) finds that, depending on the assumed values of the parameters in a CGE model, the rebound effect for the UK can range from negative to more than 100 percent. Therefore, CGE models do not provide strong evidence on the size of the economy-wide rebound effect. Rausch and Schwerin (2018) build a small general equilibrium growth model that

---

Similarly, in Austria, the weight and engine capacity of cars increased from 1990 to 2007 as fuel efficiency increased (Meyer and Wessely, 2009).

3 See Borenstein (2015) for further arguments for negative rebound.

4 If the elasticity of substitution is zero, then, irrespective of the price of energy or other inputs, the same amount of energy is always used with given amounts of other inputs. If the elasticity of substitution is generally greater than one, then, if energy became expensive enough it would no longer be used – which is clearly impossible.

they calibrate on US annual data from 1960 to 2011 and so is better empirically validated than CGE models. Rebound to energy efficiency improvements depends on the contributions of energy and capital prices to realized energy efficiency and on parameter values. Super-conservation is possible if energy efficiency improvements are driven by rising energy prices. They find that historically rebound has been 102 percent. This is because the declining cost of capital has dominated increasing energy prices.

There are problems with most of the methods that have been proposed to empirically estimate the rebound effect. For example, the economic accounting approach (e.g., Lin and Du, 2015) assumes that economic energy efficiency can be measured using energy intensity. As explained above, energy intensity does not control for many relevant factors. Actually, changes in energy intensity already incorporate the majority of the rebound effect to changes in energy efficiency because energy intensity reflects changes in other inputs, the structure of production etc., that occur in response to the change in energy efficiency. Adetutu et al. (2016) use a stochastic frontier model to estimate economic energy efficiency, and then a dynamic panel model to estimate the effect of energy efficiency on energy use. As they control for energy prices and output, this is also a partial equilibrium estimate. They estimate that in the short run rebound is 90 percent, while in the long run super-conservation occurs with a negative rebound of 36 percent. This unexpected result is due to the simple dynamic specification that they use, which requires that if some energy is saved in the short run, more will be saved in the long run.

Historical research can also provide evidence on the size of the economy-wide rebound. Taking a century-long perspective, Kander et al. (2013) and Henriques and Kander (2010) make evident that there has been both a fall and a convergence in energy intensity over the twentieth century. Csereklyei et al. (2016) show that developing countries are converging from below towards the average historical level of energy intensity for countries at their income level. Van Benthem (2015) argues that the energy efficiency of many products currently sold in developing countries today is much better than that of comparable products sold in developed countries when they were at the same income level. Energy savings from access to more efficient technologies must have been offset by other trends, including a shift toward more energy-intensive consumption bundles. Though such studies cannot identify causal effects, they suggest that the economy-wide rebound effect is close to 100 percent.

There is, therefore, a gap in the literature. No previous study is at the same time empirical, allows for general equilibrium effects, and explicitly identifies exogenous changes in energy efficiency. In a recent working paper, Bruns et al. (2019) lay out an approach to estimating the economy-wide rebound using structural vector autoregression models that has all these characteristics.

Thinking of energy use as the equilibrium outcome of the demand and supply of energy, the major factors driving changes in energy use will be changes in the price of energy and in income – at the macroeconomic level, gross domestic product (GDP). We can represent this vector of three variables as the outcome of cumulative shocks to GDP, the price of energy, and a residual energy-specific shock:

$$x_t = \mu + \sum_{i=1}^{p} \Pi_i x_{t-i} + B\varepsilon_t \# \tag{8.1}$$

where $x_t = [e_t, p_t, y_t]'$ is the vector of the logs of energy use, the price of energy, and GDP, respectively, observed in period t; $\varepsilon_t = [\varepsilon_{et}, \varepsilon_{pt}, \varepsilon_{yt}]'$ is the vector of exogenous shocks with $\text{var}(\varepsilon_t) = I$; μ is a vector of constants; and B and the Π_i are matrices of parameters to be estimated. We interpret ε_{et} as an energy efficiency shock, as it represents the exogenous reduction in energy use that is not due to exogenous shocks to GDP or energy prices and previous changes in those variables themselves. These shocks do not necessarily imply large changes in energy efficiency; they simply are how exogenous energy efficiency changes are measured using this model. The mixing matrix, B, transmits the effect of the shocks to the dependent variables. Therefore, each of the shocks can have immediate effects on each of the variables. The matrix B is estimated, and the shocks are identified using independent component analysis based on the distance covariance criterion (Matteson and Tsay, 2017). This is an unsupervised statistical learning approach that maximizes the independence of the shocks.

Bruns et al. (2019) then use the impulse response function of energy with respect to the energy efficiency shock to measure the rebound effect. Using the subscript i to denote the number of periods since the energy efficiency improvement, the rebound effect is given by:

$$R_i = 1 - \frac{\Delta\hat{e}_i}{\varepsilon_{e1}} = 1 - \frac{Actual}{Potential} \tag{8.2}$$

where ε_{e1} is the energy efficiency shock in the initial period that represents the potential change in log energy use, e, and $\Delta\hat{e}_i$ is the actual change in log energy use due to the shock as given by the impulse response function. As an example, if in response to a 1 percent improvement in energy efficiency actual energy use declines by 0.5 percent, the rebound effect is 50 percent. On the other hand, if energy use actually increased by 0.2 percent, rebound would be 120 percent.

Figure 8.1 shows the impulse response functions for a structural vector autoregression (SVAR) identified using the distance covariance method and estimated using U.S. monthly data from 1992 to 2016. The first column shows the effect of the energy efficiency shock on energy use, GDP, and the energy price. The effects on GDP and the energy price are generally not statistically significant. The energy efficiency shock results in a strong decrease in energy use initially, but this effect is eliminated over time, resulting in backfire.

We also see that though the initial effect of the price shock on energy use and GDP is positive (but not statistically significant), in the longer run it has the expected negative and statistically significant effects on both variables. In contrast, the price

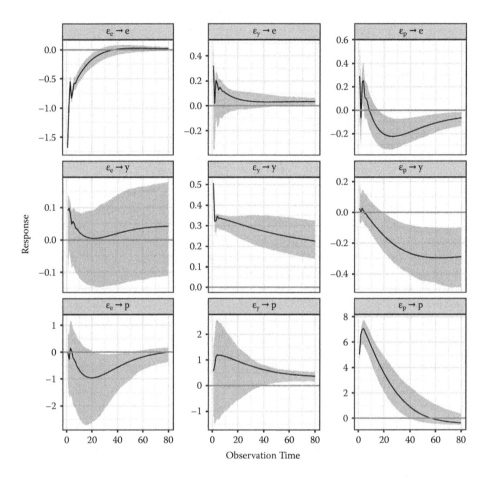

Notes: Grey shading is a 90 percent confidence interval computed using the wild bootstrap with 1000 iterations. ε_e, ε_y; and ε_p are the energy, GDP, and energy price shocks, respectively that drive changes in energy use, e, GDP, y, and the price of energy, p. All variables are in natural logarithms.

Figure 8.1   Impulse response functions for U.S. monthly data

shock appears to have transitory effects on the price of energy but what look like permanent effects on at least GDP. The GDP shock has positive long-run effects on all three variables. The long-run effects, therefore, conform to standard economic theory.

This implies that policies to encourage costless energy efficiency innovation are not likely to significantly reduce energy use and, therefore, greenhouse gas emissions. On the other hand, energy efficiency policies that increase costs – by, for example, mandating equipment that is more expensive despite being more energy efficient – are likely to reduce energy use by more than the thermodynamic efficiency effect. One example of such policies could be to ban the selling of fossil fuel cars after a certain year, and only allow electric cars, which are more expensive. Better options for climate policy are carbon taxes, caps on carbon emissions, funding for research into low-carbon energy and storage, or even subsidizing installation of low-carbon energy technologies or paying for emissions reductions.

We can also use the Bruns et al. model to understand the drivers of energy use in the U.S. Energy intensity has declined over time in the United States (Stern, 2011b). Even if changes in energy efficiency do not reduce energy use in the long run, they may increase GDP by more than they increase energy use because they increase the productivity of the economy. In Figure 8.1 this seems to be the case if we ignore the very wide confidence interval around the impulse response function for the effect of an energy efficiency shock on GDP. Second, as shown in Figure 8.1, exogenous changes in GDP – such as changes in population and technology – tend to increase GDP by proportionally much more than they increase energy use. This may be because, as we can see, GDP shocks also increase the price of energy, which then restricts the increase in energy use. But the fact that energy intensity has declined over time whether energy prices have been rising or falling suggests that energy price shocks do not play a large role. In Figure 8.1, we see that energy price shocks in fact reduce GDP by more than they reduce energy use in the long run. Csereklyei et al. (2016) similarly found that energy intensity only tends to decline if an economy is growing.

The key research challenge emerging from the latter findings is understanding what exactly drives declining energy intensity when rebound to energy efficiency improvements is very large.

8.3   Energy efficiency, capital stocks, and the transition to a low carbon economy

The most important solution for achieving carbon emission reductions is not to reduce energy consumption *per se*, even though it would help, but to switch to non-carbon emitting energy carriers like wind and solar. If this is done on a large scale, this will require large investments in the grid and storage capacity for electricity because the wind does not always blow, and the sun does not always shine in all localities. If savings from thermodynamic efficiency increases could be invested in speeding up the transition to renewables, this could in fact lead to a large reduction in greenhouse gases.

Changing the mix of energy carriers towards higher-quality fuels will achieve both energy efficiency gains and a reduction in greenhouse gas emissions. For instance, while the Chinese economy grew nearly 7 percent in 2017, greenhouse gas emissions increased by just 1.7 percent (or 150 Mt) thanks to continued renewables deployment and faster coal-to-gas switching (IEA, 2018). The energy mix crucially affects energy efficiency, energy intensity, energy security, and carbon intensity of a country, thus also impacting climate change policies. So, the characteristics of the energy we use become as important as to how much energy we use.

Imagine if we could obtain ubiquitous, unlimited, and free energy from our environment as envisaged by Nikola Tesla. Then, it would make sense to switch to it, giving up lower quality, limited, and more expensive energies as quickly as possible, and concentrating as much as possible on this new free, renewable, safe, and clean energy. The limiting factor will no longer be the amount of energy required for production, but how fast we could switch to this new form of energy.

The introduction and use of new energy sources requires the construction of new infrastructure, machinery, and equipment suitable for it. These new capital flows will add up and eventually replace the existing ones, upgrading the capital stock. Theoretical models of the relationship between energy and investment include the so-called putty-putty and putty-clay models. The putty-putty model developed by Pindyck and Rotemberg (1983) assumed that capital and energy are highly complementary both in the short and in the long run, but that capital is subject to adjustment costs. Because of these, the capital stock changes slowly over time in response to changes in energy prices. Since energy and capital are highly complementary in production, energy use changes slowly as well. In the long run, the capital stock adjusts to permanent differences in energy prices, and so does energy use. Since capital and energy are made to be so complementary, energy use responds to prices only if the capital stock does as well. In the alternative putty-clay model, proposed by Atkeson and Kehoe (1999), a large variety of types of capital goods are combined with energy in different fixed proportions. Energy and capital are made to be complementary in the short run, but are substitutes in the long run. Thus, in the short run, energy use does not adjust to changes in the price of energy. In the long run, however, in response to permanent changes in the price of energy, agents invest in different capital with different energy intensities. As a result, in the long run, energy use is responsive to differences in energy prices, and the capital-to-energy ratio changes as agents invest in new types of capital with different energy intensities. Thus, in the long run, composition changes in the capital stock will affect energy use even if the capital stock remains constant. By contrast, in the putty-putty model the quantity of capital must increase (decrease) for energy use to increase (decrease).

Empirical studies of the long-run evolution of the energy–capital ratio produce different results for different periods, types of countries, and industries (Ruth et al., 2004). As the energy–capital ratio captures the consumption of energy relative to the accumulation of capital, a decreasing energy–capital ratio signals economic progress through investment in higher-quality capital. Both Csereklyei et al. (2016) and Kander et al. (2013, 338) show the decreasing trend of the energy–capital ratio over the past 150 years or more for a number of Western countries. This claim finds support in existing data for the more recent period: countries with lower energy–capital ratios tend to be richer than countries with a high energy–capital ratio for the period 1971–2010 (Ducoing et al., 2018, 4). Making use of a slightly different dataset and a shorter period (1890–1970), these authors find that while most European countries show decreasing E/K ratios in the twentieth century, these declines in E/K were less pronounced in the developing region of Latin America.

The concern of both theoretical and empirical studies, however, remains the relationship of energy and capital at the aggregate level. Interfuel substitution (its causes and effects) has tended to be analyzed at the sectoral level. In the electric power market interfuel substitution has been examined in multiple studies during the last three decades (Petterson et al., 2012); similarly in the industrial sector, particularly around the impact of the oil crises (Pindyck, 1979). In a meta-analysis of 47 studies of interfuel substitution, Stern (2012) finds macro-level studies for only six countries (China, Italy, Japan, Korea, the UK, and the US), some of which excluded one or more fuels from the analysis. Stern explains that most interfuel substitution studies only estimate equations for fuel cost shares with the quantity of energy implicitly held constant, and do not consider the effect of changes in output. This seems to be at odds with the empirical observation of how energy systems evolve over time: typically, fuels do not substitute each other, but tend to be added to the mix over time. In order for an energy transition to occur, the old energy carrier, in absolute terms, may remain relatively stable while the new technology expands faster.

Experts in energy transition refer to the "inertia of energy systems" when trying to explain how difficult, painful, and slow it is to alter a given course (Fouquet, 2016; Grübler, 2004; Smil, 2017). Others refer to it as "path dependence," which has become a sort of umbrella category for all theories that explain why institutions, technological standards, or firm capabilities tend to persist. Rubio-Varas (2019) contends that these are two different concepts. While path dependence concerns the weight that past choices have in limiting present and future decision making, the inertia of the energy system embodies a scale or size effect not necessarily present in the former. Path dependency can help us understand lock-in, but it is less helpful to understand "lock-out" or predict the pace of change of the energy system in the future. In that sense, "inertia" may be a more useful concept to investigate pace of change as it provides an upfront, clear hypothesis: changes in the energy system occur faster in systems with lower inertia.

The inertia of energy systems does not have, to our knowledge, a literature grounding the concept theoretically. There exists a literature on the inertia of organizations initiated by Hannan and Freeman (1984). Applied to the energy system, this implies that large organizations are less likely than small ones to initiate radical structural change. This is equivalent to the physics definition of inertia: the tendency of an object to resist changes in its state of motion (including speed and direction). A more massive object has a greater tendency to resist change in its state of motion.

From a different angle, the size of the energy system will also affect decisions over which technologies to invest in (thus its capacity to change over time). Power scaling is well known in the energy sector (Roulstone, 2015). While some technologies perform best at small scale and have difficulties scaling up to massive deployment (solar PV), others are best suited for very large systems. For example, only a few Asian, African, and Latin American countries have ever had power grids large enough to distribute electricity produced by even the smallest commercially available nuclear reactor (Fischer, 1997, 160).

A growing body of evidence suggests that countries consuming large amounts of energy have behaved differently from small energy consumers in the process of altering their energy mixes, that is, in their energy transitions (Marcotullio and Schulz, 2007). Rubio and Folchi (2012), using Latin American data over the twentieth century, show that smaller countries had earlier and faster transitions than larger energy consuming countries did. Henriques and Sharp (2016) find a quick transition from firewood to coal in Denmark, a small energy consuming country too. Rubio-Varas and Muñoz-Delgado (2019) provide evidence for eight European countries over the past 150 years that points to different behavior of large and small energy consumers, indicating that it was more difficult for large consumers than for small consumers to achieve a diversified energy basket.

Plausible candidates for proxies of the inertia of an energy system are the size of the capital stock or total energy consumption. Figure 8.2 plots the level of the capital stock against primary energy consumption for the quartile of countries with the smallest capital stocks and smallest energy consumption versus the quartile of countries with the largest capital stocks and highest energy consumption from 1951 to 2014. Figure 8.2 heuristically shows how the countries with larger capital stock seem to have a more predictable motion (including speed and direction) regarding their energy consumption than the countries with smaller capital stocks in the

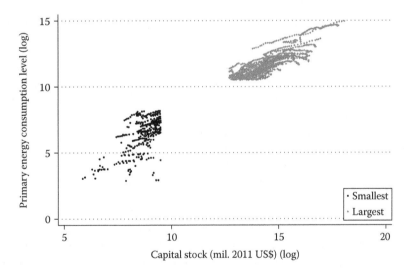

Note: Here and in Figure 8.3 "small" refers to countries pertaining to the bottom quartile of the distribution of both variables; "large" refers to the upper quartile of the distribution of both variables. See Appendix for specific countries/years included and cut-off points.

Source: Here and in Figure 8.3 primary energy consumption from the World Bank-IEA Database; capital stock from the Penn World Tables (Feenstra et al., 2015).

Figure 8.2 Primary energy consumption vs. capital stock (logs of totals by country) of small vs. large countries, 1951–2014

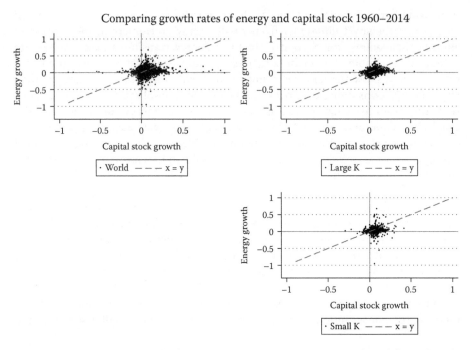

Figure 8.3   Year on year growth of primary energy consumption vs. capital stock (logs of totals by country)

bottom left. It also makes evident that the relationship between the energy consumption and capital stock differs once the size of the capital stock is considered.

Figure 8.3 presents the annual growth rates of energy consumption and capital stock for the whole database (over 150 countries for the period 1951–2014) in the first panel, and those for the large and small quartiles in the second and third panels. In all three panels, observations below the diagonal-dashed line would result in declines in the E/K ratio (since the rate of growth of energy use would be below the growth rate of the capital stock), and most likely to a decline in energy intensity too. The literature cited in the preceding paragraphs in general neglects the bottom-right quadrant, where the capital stock grows but energy consumption declines – which seems to be more prevalent precisely in the countries with smaller capital stocks.

Given that modifying the energy mix and the underlying stock of capital are crucial for the challenges ahead, we need a better understanding of how they change over time, allowing for variations in the size of energy systems. By understanding the inertia of energy systems better, it will become possible to overcome their resistance to change. How much of the investment is determined by energy price signals? How much of the investment decision is determined by the relative price of the machinery/infrastructure? Do agents perceive the price signals combined? We also need a better understanding of the non-negligible number of occurrences where an increasing capital stock is paired with decreasing energy consumption. Such a combination – if not contingent on underutilization of the capital stock, economic crisis, or the shifting of production elsewhere (see below) – would be preferred.

8.4   Energy intensity and trade

Energy intensity reductions are good because they mean that less energy is used to produce a certain value of economic output. In Western Europe energy intensity declined over much of the twentieth century, and most impressively after 1970 (Kander et al., 2013). A simple decomposition analysis shows that in the period 1970–2005 energy consumption in Western Europe did not grow much at all, by 0.7 percent per year, and that the main driver behind the relative stabilization of energy consumption was the drastic decline in energy intensity of −1.6 percent per year (see Table 8.1), which was more than in any period before.

This remarkable trend break in energy consumption, which shifts from very high growth rates in 1950–1970 to low growth rates from 1970 onwards, calls for analysis of what drove this historical shift. Several propositions have been put forward, including: general savings of energy as a response to the oil price shocks; a natural development of societies moving from an industrial phase to a post-industrial society, with the majority of the GDP being produced in the service sector, which requires less energy for its production than manufacturers; the third industrial revolution, which meant a shift of what is being produced in the manufacturing industry (more pills and less steel for example) and stimulated energy savings in old traditional industries too when integrated circuits are used to fine-tune the material and energy use of production. Structural analyses have shown that most of the reductions in energy intensity after 1970 took place in the household sector, as a consequence of the oil crises that prompted better insulation of house roofs and walls, double or triple glazed windows, and more energy-efficient cars, and

Table 8.1   Decomposition analysis of energy consumption in Western Europe 1820–2008, annual growth rates

Period	Energy consumption (%)	Population	Income per capita	Energy intensity (%)
1820–2008	1.86	0.71	0.83	0.32
1870–1913	2.20	0.79	1.16	0.26
1913–1950	0.51	0.45	0.85	−0.79
1950–1970	3.45	0.72	4.10	−1.39
1970–2008	0.53	0.33	1.98	−1.77
1820–2008	1.54	0.60	1.48	−0.53

Source: Kander et al. (2013, 369).

within the manufacturing industry itself, moving it in an energy lighter direction (Henriques and Kander 2010). Only a modest energy intensity effect was achieved from a transition to the service economy because most of the apparent transition is actually the result of Baumol's cost disease rather than changes in actual production (Kander, 2005). What we can consume a lot of is what we as a society are efficient in producing, and that is manufactured products and not services. Still, some expansion of service production has taken place, most of which is also related to the ICT revolution.

These structural changes in a less energy-intensive direction – be it inside the manufacturing sector or as a shift to a higher share of service production in GDP – still begs the question of what the ultimate reason for these changes is. There are two contrasting views here. One is optimistic: that it is the natural course of development for a country that, once it has industrialized and built up long-lasting, energy-intensive infrastructures (such as buildings and household electric appliances, factories, cars, and roads etc.), it will move over to a less energy-demanding phase, when growth takes place in entertainment streaming services like Netflix and Spotify, and in ICT equipment like computers, cell-phones, tablets and smartphones, health care, and consumption of luxury brands of clothes. All these are expensive things that do not require so much energy to be produced and maintained as the typical goods of the previous expansion, such as cars, washing machines, dishwashers, and tumble dryers, etc. On the pessimistic side is the counterargument that ICT gadgets actually require much energy and material for their production, even though the final consumption of them does not. Furthermore, these devices become obsolete very fast so that there is a high turnover rate, which implies wasting of natural resources. Another pessimistic argument is that, even though it may be true that production has shifted to a less energy-intensive direction in some more developed parts of the world, resulting in reduced energy intensity there, this may entirely be a consequence of shifting the problem to other parts of the world. While people in the rich Global North live in the service economy, their manufactured goods are produced elsewhere in the Global South. Production in the North by no means reflects consumption in the North.

The issue of outsourcing or displacing environmental stress to other parts of the world has triggered a lot of research in recent decades, which has been enabled by the emergence of global input–output databases like the World Input–Output Database (WIOD), Eora, and Exiobase. Such databases can be used to assess the energy and CO_2 embodied in international trade. Much of this research shows large embodied flows of energy and CO_2 from the South to the North in traded commodities, and so seems to support the pessimistic view that most if not all of the energy-intensity decline in the North could be caused by outsourcing of heavy polluting industries to the Global South. It has even been suggested that all of the achievements accomplished by the developed countries in relation to the Kyoto Protocol were due to outsourcing (Peters et al., 2011). This suggests that even when the rebound effects in the national economy are not 100 percent, the global rebounds may be of that size.

So, is the pessimistic view correct? Fortunately, it is not when it comes to answering the ultimate development question of whether countries change the structure of consumption patterns in a less energy-intensive direction higher up the development ladder. In fact, they do. This question has mostly been addressed by comparing consumption-based emissions and production-based emissions. The latter is the traditional view of energy use and emissions. Energy use and emissions are attributed to the country where the energy is burnt, or the electricity used. Consumption-based accounting attributes this energy use and emissions to the country where the products that they produce are used. If the energy or emissions embodied in consumption are greater than those determined using the production-based approach a country is said to offshore energy or emissions. Most studies of this question that use a consumption-based approach just account for actual energy use and emissions. But the South tends to use less energy-efficient technologies than the North, and often has a higher carbon intensity of energy use because of a large share of coal in the energy mix (for example in China). So, even when the same commodity (say, 1 ton of steel) is traded between North and South and an equivalent commodity goes in the other direction, this will show up as outsourcing in the conventional consumption-based accounts because of inferior technology in the South. But, in fact, global emissions have not changed due to this exchange of 2 tons of steel (transportation excluded), and it does seem odd to hold the North responsible for poor technologies used in the South.

What we really want to know is whether the North avoids energy use and emissions at home because it imports commodities from the South that are globally more energy intensive. Does the North export pills and software and import steel and paper from the South? One method of circumventing this illusory outsourcing and to find out if the structure of trade has changed is to hold technologies constant for a particular kind of output, and simply investigate the change in the compositional structure of the trade (Kander et al., 2015; Jiborn et al., 2018; Baumert et al., 2019). Technology-adjusted accounts offer several interesting insights. First of all, the net amount of energy and emissions embodied in such global trade is not as large as commonly believed because several inputs move over many national borders back and forth, so that the net flows are drastically smaller than the gross flows. Second, there is no clear North–South divide between who is an insourcer and who is an outsourcer of energy and emissions. If anything, there seems to be a greater tendency for Anglophone countries to be outsourcers than other developed countries, for example the Nordic countries. Third, more careful analyses investigating the structure of both imports and exports for Sweden and the UK demonstrate that even in Sweden there is a tendency of change in international trade towards the end of the WIOD extended environmental accounts period (1995–2009), so that imports become heavier and exports lighter in energy use.

There is also a need for new global energy and CO_2 extended input–output tables going back further in time than 1995 and continuing up until the present time (rather than 2009) in order to monitor the balance of energy and emissions embodied in trade from a technology-adjusted perspective. It is also important that the sector disaggregation is suitable for this purpose. The chemical sector should clearly be separated into pharmaceuticals and heavy chemicals, for instance, because of the large differences in energy intensity between the two. But the electricity sector should not be so disaggregated that hydroelectricity is only traded against hydroelectricity and not against coal-generated electricity. This does not make sense from an energy account perspective, since electricity is the same end product regardless of how it has been produced. Nations with heavy carbon taxes and ambitious, nationally determined contributions according to the Paris Agreement from 2015 must ensure that their accomplishments are not achieved through outsourcing, and carefully monitor their trade patterns.

8.5   Conclusions

A policy of saving energy by energy efficiency improvements runs the obvious risk of not leading to savings of energy on the global scale in the long run. So, to rely on this as one of the most important strategies to reduce climate change, as most nationally determined contribution plans after the Paris Treaty do, seems risky. This does not mean that energy efficiency improvements should not be encouraged and pushed for in the energy policy agenda. A more efficient use of energy is good; but more than that is needed. If we want to reduce carbon emissions, then policy should address this directly by pricing or restricting carbon and encouraging innovation and adoption of low carbon energy and electricity storage.

In a global world, it is mandatory that nations monitor what happens to their international trade so that outsourcing does not undermine national accomplishments. This monitoring should focus on the structure of international trade rather than mixing technology and structure in one measure, like the conventional carbon footprint; the latter can lead to globally inefficient policies as acknowledged by Sachs et al. (2017).

Finally, we summarize the main items of the research agenda that emerges from our discussion:

1.   Empirical measurement of the economy-wide rebound effect is only in its earliest stages. Research should be extended to countries across the development spectrum and the drivers of high rebound understood.
2.   Understanding the drivers of declining energy intensity if Jevons' paradox holds, is also important.
3.   We need to understand how capital and energy use evolves over time, and to what degree, and how the size of energy systems influences this.
4.   We also need a better understanding of the cases where an increasing capital stock is paired with decreasing energy consumption.
5.   There is a need for new global energy and CO_2 extended input–output tables going back further in time than 1995 and continuing to the present (rather

than 2009) in order to monitor the balance of energy and emissions embodied in trade from a technology-adjusted perspective.

6. In the years leading up to 2009, the export portfolios of some developed countries have become less energy intensive while their imports have become more so. This trend towards outsourcing calls for more research.

References

Adetutu, M. O., A. J. Glass, and T. G. Weyman-Jones (2016), 'Economy-wide estimates of rebound effects: Evidence from panel data', *Energy Journal*, **37**(3), 251–269.

Atkeson, A. and P. J. Kehoe (1999), 'Models of energy use: putty-putty vs putty-clay', *American Economic Review*, **89**, 1028–1043.

Barker, T., A. Dagoumas, and J. Rubin (2009), 'The macroeconomic rebound effect and the world economy', *Energy Efficiency*, **2**, 411–427.

Baumert, N., A. Kander, M. Jiborn, V. Kulionis, and T. Nielsen (2019), 'Global outsourcing of carbon emissions 1995–2009: A reassessment', *Environmental Science & Policy*, **92**, 228–236.

Blanco, G., R. Gerlagh, S. Suh, J. Barrett, H. de Coninck, C. F. Diaz Morejon, R. Mathur, N. Nakicenovic, A. O. Ahenkorah, J. Pan, H. Pathak, J. Rice, R. Richels, S. J. Smith, D. I. Stern, F. L. Toth, and P. Zhou (2014) Drivers, trends and mitigation, in O. Edenhofer et al. (eds.) *Climate Change 2014: Mitigation of Climate Change. Contribution of Working Group III to the Fifth Assessment Report of the Intergovernmental Panel on Climate Change*, Cambridge: Cambridge University Press, pp. 317–378.

Borenstein, S. (2015), 'A microeconomic framework for evaluating energy efficiency rebound and some implications', *Energy Journal*, **36**(1), 1–21.

Bruns, S. B., A. Moneta, and D. I. Stern (2019), 'Macroeconomic time-series evidence that energy efficiency improvements do not save energy', *CAMA Working Papers* 21/2019.

Clarke, L. et al. (2014), 'Assessing transformation pathways', in O. Edenhofer et al. (eds), *Climate Change 2014: Mitigation of Climate Change. Contribution of Working Group III to the IPCC Fifth Assessment Report*, Cambridge: Cambridge University Press, pp. 413–510.

Cleveland, C. (Lead Author); D. Budikova (Topic Editor) (2008), 'Energy quality', in C. J. Cleveland (ed.), *Encyclopedia of Earth*, Washington, D.C.: Environmental Information Coalition, National Council for Science and the Environment. [First published in the *Encyclopedia of Earth* February 22, 2007; Last revised November 18, 2008; Retrieved September 18, 2009]. http://www.eoearth.org/article/ Energy_quality.

Csereklyei, Z., M. d. M. Rubio-Varas, and D. I. Stern (2016), 'Energy and economic growth: The stylized facts', *Energy Journal*, **37**(2), 223–255.

Ducoing, C., B. Gales, B. Hölsgens, and M. Rubio-Varas (2018), 'Energy and machines. Energy capital ratios in Europe and Latin America. 1875–1970', *Scandinavian Economic History Review*, **67**, 31–46.

Feenstra, R. C., R. Inklaar, and M. P. Timmer (2015), 'The next generation of the Penn World Table', *American Economic Review*, **105**(10), 3150–3182. Data available at www.ggdc.net/pwt.

Fischer, D. (1997), *History of the International Atomic Energy Agency: The First Forty Years*, Vienna: International Atomic Energy Agency.

Fouquet, R. (2016), 'Lessons from energy history for climate policy: Technological change, demand and economic development', *Energy Research and Social Sciences*, **22**, 79–93. doi: 10.1016/j. erss.2016.09.001.

Galvin, R. (2014), 'Estimating broad-brush rebound effects for household energy consumption in the EU 28 countries and Norway: Some policy implications of Odyssee data', *Energy Policy*, **73**, 323–332.

Gillingham, K., M. J. Kotchen, D. S. Rapson, and G. Wagner (2013), 'Energy policy: The rebound effect is overplayed', *Nature*, **493**(7433), 475–476.

Grübler, A. (2004), 'Transitions in energy use', *Encyclopedia of Energy*, **6**, 163–177. doi: 10.1016/B0-12-176480-X/00023-1.

Hannan, M. T. and J. Freeman (1984), 'Structural inertia and organizational change', *American Sociological Review*, **49**, 149–164. doi: 10.2307/2095567.

Henriques, S. T. and A. Kander (2010), 'The modest environmental relief resulting from the transition to a service economy', *Ecological Economics*, 70, 271–282.

Henriques, S. T. and P. Sharp (2016), 'The Danish agricultural revolution in an energy perspective: A case of development with few domestic energy sources', *Economic History Review*, **69**(3), 844–869. doi: 10.1111/ehr.12236.

IEA (2014), *World Energy Outlook 2014*, Paris: International Energy Agency.

IEA (2018), *Global Energy and CO_2 Status Report: The Latest Trends in Energy and Emissions in 2017.* Available at https://www.iea.org/geco/emissions.

Jevons, W. S. (1866), *The Coal Question* (2nd edition), London: Macmillan.

Jiborn, M., A. Kander, V. Kulionis, H. Nielsen, and D. D. Moran (2018), 'Decoupling or delusion? Measuring emissions displacement in foreign trade', *Global Environmental Change*, **49**, 27–34.

Kander, A. (2005), 'Baumol's disease and dematerialization of the economy', *Ecological Economics*, **55**, 119–130.

Kander, A., P. Malanima, and P. Warde (2013), *Power to the People: Energy in Europe Over the Last Five Centuries*, Princeton, NJ: Princeton University Press.

Kander, A., M. Jiborn, D. Moran, and T. Wiedmann (2015), 'National greenhouse-gas accounting for effective climate policy on international trade', *Nature Climate Change*, **5**(5), 431–435.

Koesler, S., K. Swales, and K. Turner (2016), 'International spillover and rebound effects from increased energy efficiency in Germany', *Energy Economics*, **54**, 444–452.

Lemoine, D. (2019), General equilibrium rebound from improved energy efficiency. *NBER Working Paper* 25172. Revised September 2019.

Lin, B. and K. Du (2015), 'Measuring energy rebound effect in the Chinese economy: An economic accounting approach', *Energy Economics*, **50**, 96–104.

Lu, Y., Y. Liu, and M. Zhou (2017), 'Rebound effect of improved energy efficiency for different energy types: A general equilibrium analysis for China', *Energy Economics*, **62**, 248–256.

Marcotullio, P. J. and N. B. Schulz (2007), 'Comparison of energy transitions in the United States and developing and industrializing economies', *World Development*, **35**(10), 1650–1683.

Matteson, D. S. and R. S. Tsay (2017), 'Independent component analysis via distance covariance', *Journal of the American Statistical Association*, **112**(518), 623–637.

Meyer, I. and S. Wessely (2009), 'Fuel efficiency of the Austrian passenger vehicle fleet: Analysis of trends in the technological profile and related impacts on CO_2 emissions', *Energy Policy*, **37**, 3779–3789.

Orea, L., M. Llorca, and M. Filippini (2015), 'A new approach to measuring the rebound effect associated to energy efficiency improvements: An application to the US residential energy demand', *Energy Economics*, **49**, 599–609.

Peters, G. P., J. C. Minx, C. L. Weber, and O. Edenhofer (2011), 'Growth in emission transfers via international trade from 1990 to 2008', *Proceedings of the National Academy of Sciences of the United States of America*, **108**, 8903–8908.

Pettersson, P., P. Söderholm, and M. Lundmark (2012), 'Fuel switching and climate and energy policies in the European power generation sector: A generalized Leontief model', *Energy Economics*, **34**(4), 1064–1073.

Pindyck, R. (1979), 'Interfuel substitution and the industrial demand for energy: An international comparison', *Review of Economics and Statistics*, **61**(2), 169–179.

Pindyck, R. and J. Rotemberg (1983), 'Dynamic factor demands and the effects of energy price shocks', *American Economic Review*, **73**(5), 1066–1079.

Rausch, S. and H. Schwerin (2018), 'Does higher energy efficiency lower economy-wide energy use?', *Center of Economic Research at ETH Zurich, Economics Working Paper* 18/299.

Roulstone, T. (2015), 'Economies of scale vs. economies of volume', *Nuclear Engineering International*, August. Available at https://www.neimagazine.com/features/featureeconomies-of-scale-vs-economies-of-volume-4639914/.

Rubio, M. d. M. and M. Folchi (2012), 'Will small energy consumers be faster in transition? Evidence from the early shift from coal to oil in Latin America', *Energy Policy*, **50**, 50–61.

Rubio-Varas, M. (2019), 'The First World War and the Latin American transition from coal to petroleum', *Environmental Innovation and Societal Transitions*, **32**, 45–54. https://doi.org/10.1016/j.eist.2018.03.002.

Rubio-Varas, M. and B. Muñoz-Delgado (2019), 'Long term diversification paths and energy transitions in Europe', *Ecological Economics*, **163**(C), 158–168. https://ideas.repec.org/a/eee/ecolec/v163y2019icp158-168.html.

Ruth, M., B. Davidsdottir, and A. Amato (2004), 'Climate change policies and capital vintage effects: the cases of US pulp and paper, iron and steel and ethylene', *Journal of Environmental Management*, 7(3), 221–233.

Sachs, J., G. Schmidt-Traub, C. Kroll, D. Durand-Delacre, and K. Teksoz (2017), *SDG Index and Dashboards Report 2017*. New York: Bertelsmann Stiftung and Sustainable Development Solutions Network (SDSN).

Saunders, H. D. (1992), 'The Khazzoom-Brookes postulate and neoclassical growth', *Energy Journal*, **13**(4), 131–148.

Saunders, H. D. (2008), 'Fuel conserving (and using) production functions', *Energy Economics*, **30**, 2184–2235.

Saunders, H. D. (2013), 'Historical evidence for energy efficiency rebound in 30 US sectors and a toolkit for rebound analysts', *Technological Forecasting and Social Change*, **80**(7), 1317–1330.

Shao, S., T. Huang, and L. Yang (2014), 'Using latent variable approach to estimate China's economy-wide energy rebound effect over 1954–2010', *Energy Policy*, **72**, 235–248.

Smil, V. (2017), *Energy and Civilization: A History*, Cambridge, MA: MIT Press.

Sorrell, S., J. Dimitropoulos, and M. Sommerville (2009), 'Empirical estimates of the direct rebound effect: A review', *Energy Policy* **37**, 1356–1371.

Steinberger, J. K., J. T. Roberts, G. P. Peters, and G. Baiocchi (2012), 'Pathways of human development and carbon emissions embodied in trade', *Nature Climate Change*, **2**, 81–85.

Stern, D. I. (2011a), 'Elasticities of substitution and complementarity', *Journal of Productivity Analysis*, **36**(1), 79–89.

Stern, D. I. (2011b), 'The role of energy in economic growth', *Annals of the New York Academy of Sciences*, **1219**, 26–51.

Stern, D. I. (2012), 'Interfuel substitution: a meta-analysis', *Journal of Economic Surveys*, **26**(2), 307–331.

Turner, K. (2009), 'Negative rebound and disinvestment effects in response to an improvement in energy efficiency in the UK economy', *Energy Economics*, **31**, 648–666.

Turner, K. (2013), '"Rebound" effects from increased energy efficiency: A time to pause and reflect', *Energy Journal*, **34**(4), 25–43.

van Benthem, A. A. (2015), 'Energy leapfrogging', *Journal of the Association of Environmental and Resource Economists*, **2**(1), 93–132.

Appendix: Small and large countries for categories in Figures 8.2 and 8.3

Small (country and years)	Large (country and years)
Albania 1971–1975	Argentina 1987–2014
Antigua and Barbuda 1990–2007	Australia 1958–2014
Bahrain 1971–1980	Belarus 1991–1992
Barbados 1990–2007	Belgium 1969–2014
Belize 1990–2007	Brazil 1962–2014
Benin 1971–1991	Canada 1952–2014
Botswana 1981–1992	Chile 2012–2014
Cabo Verde 1990–2007	China 1953–2014
Comoros 1990–2007	Czech Republic 1991–2014
Congo 1971–1998	Egypt 1999–2014
Côte d'Ivoire 1971–1976	Finland 2003–2010
Djibouti 1990–2007	France 1951–2014
Dominica 1990–2007	Germany 1951–2014
El Salvador 1971–1997	India 1951–2014
Fiji 1990–2007	Indonesia 1976–2014
Gabon 1971–1998	Iran 1979–2014
Gambia 1990–2007	Iraq 2010–2014
Grenada 1990–2007	Italy 1951–2014
Guinea-Bissau 1990–2007	Japan 1951–2014
Haiti 1971–1973	Kazakhstan 1992–2014
Honduras 1972–1977	Malaysia 1996–2014
Iceland 1960–1972	Mexico 1955–2014
Jordan 1971–1979	Netherlands 1968–2014
Lesotho 2004–2007	Nigeria 1977–2014
Maldives 1990–2007	Pakistan 1993–2014
Malta 1971–1993	Philippines 1998–2014
Mauritius 1971–1990	Poland 1971–2014
Mongolia 1985–1987	Republic of Korea 1979–2014
Namibia 1991–1994	Romania 1986–2014
Paraguay 1971–1980	Russia 1991–2014
Saint Kitts and Nevis 1990–2007	Saudi Arabia 1981–2014
Saint Lucia 1990–2007	South Africa 1974–2014
São Tomé and Príncipe 1990–2007	Spain 1970–2014
Seychelles 1990–2007	Sweden 1970–2014
St. Vincent and the Grenadines 1990–2007	Taiwan 1984–2014
Togo 1971–2004	Thailand 1989–2014
Trinidad and Tobago 1971–1975	Turkey 1984–2014
Yemen 1990–1996	Ukraine 1991–2014
	United Arab Emirates 2001–2014
	United Kingdom 1951–2014
	United States 1951–2014
	Venezuela 1983–2014

9 Place-based behavior and environmental policies

Eveline S. van Leeuwen

9.1 Introduction

The world is spiky. Population is far from homogenously distributed over the world, as are economic activities. Notwithstanding the expectation that distance will lose its relevance because of advanced communication technologies, as well as much faster transportation options, the geographical concentration of people and (economic) activities will only increase. In the developing world, the concentration of people and their demand for goods and services are most visible in megacities, which are growing at faster rates than the rest of the countries where they are situated, leaving the rural areas behind in terms of both social and economic capital. In the developed world, urbanization levels are relatively high and seem to have reached a stable state. However, with the growth of elderly populations in rural areas, population decline is generally more prevalent in the countryside, thus creating important discrepancies between urban and rural areas as well (Franklin and van Leeuwen, 2018).

An interesting question is to what extent geography and space matter with respect to the environmental challenges that have different causes and effects in urban and rural areas, and how should these inform environmental economics? First of all, space matters on the 'cause' side. Places with a high concentration of people and economic activities also pose a heavy burden on the local environment in terms of land use and (point-source) pollution. And their relatively higher standards of living – at least on aggregate – also mean that they disproportionately draw on resources (materials, energy, environmental waste absorption capacities) outside their jurisdictions. In addition, space matters on the 'effect' side. In environmental economics there is a significant strand of literature on environmental justice: the notion that environmental burdens are significantly more often imposed on those with lower incomes who cannot protect themselves by lawyering up or moving away (Mohai et al., 2009; Haughton, 1999). In the context of the current challenges surrounding energy transitions, for example, it is the rural population that will be mostly affected by investment in wind/solar and biomass energy that arise from urban energy demand. This development can be unjust if the rural population is not sufficiently compensated, for example by jobs or income redistribution through (energy) taxes.

Apart from mitigation, citizens themselves, in both urban and rural areas, need to adapt as well. They need to change their behavior. But what if the different causes and effects of environmental challenges in urban and rural areas result in different values, norms and behavior of the people living in these areas? Several studies do indeed report differences between city and country dwellers in terms of environmental values and behavior. But it is not clear whether these are caused by personal differences or by their different spatial circumstances.

Therefore, we need better insights into the values, norms and behavior of urban and rural citizens and their development through time and space. As such, the broader and deeper social and historical contexts of values and attitudes that guide our behavior are very much left out of environmental economics. Consequently, the discipline can only offer generic insights and, as a result, may provide guidance for investment and policy making that is blind to the conditions under which such guidance may result in desirable outcomes. In some cases the advice even exacerbates the situation, for the very reason that it is not tied to place, space and culture.

If indeed spatial differences result in different environmental behaviors of people, it calls for more place-based, or at least place-sensitive, research and ultimately place-sensitive policies. This implies that spatial variation in environmental values, norms, and behavior is a very important topic. However, little is known about the relevance of the spatial context of the people who are supposed to be influenced by the policies. What is the geographical difference in trust, where is local participation more prevalent, where are people more exposed to (visible) effects of climate change and measures to address it? Answers to these questions can help us sort out relevant policy questions on how we can motivate urban and rural populations towards improved environmental behaviors. How can we 'nudge' them to actively participate in energy saving, recycling, etc. to accept developments that will be located in their backyard? And how can we avoid sentiments of inequality that increasingly result in protest voices and destabilized societies because certain groups of people feel they are not represented or not heard by (national) policy makers, as we see happening in the UK, the US and, to some extent, also in various European countries (see e.g. Rodriquez-Pose, 2018)?

Although environmental economists often focus on distinct spatial processes, such as harvesting and pollution, on differences between institutional (and geographical) units, such as countries or even regions, or on distinct objects such as households and their decisions, there (still) tends to be a limited focus on the explicit spatial context of these topics. The focus of this chapter is how space and geography matter in environmental concerns and behavior, with a specific emphasis on regional urban–rural differences.

In Section 9.2, I will highlight the mechanisms for differences between urban and rural populations and their behavior. Section 9.3 will focus on the spatial context of values and behavior from a theoretical perspective, while Section 9.4 takes an empirical focus by analyzing urban–rural differences in values, concerns and behavior of European Union (EU) citizens based on the European Social Value Survey of 2016 (ESS, 2016). Section 9.5 looks at the role of cities to sustain our future, while the final section closes with a call to arms.

9.2   Urban–rural differences in population and/or behavior

We all have our own connotations about the differences between urban and rural areas. These are based on our personal experiences, on what we see in the media and read in the newspapers or (academic) literature. Often, this information is biased. In fact, many people have no direct experience of rural people and communities, but encounter rural images, themes and/or stereotypes mostly through the arts, media, and literature (de Souza, 2017; Lichter and Brown, 2011). This means that our image of 'the rural' is often not in line with reality. Similar observations may be made about the perceptions about urban living by people in rural areas.

When not only students but also academics are asked about their image of *the* urban and *the* rural, urban areas are associated with economic growth, (agglomeration), advantages and buzz, as well as with pollution and congestion. In contrast, rural areas are associated with agriculture, nature and quietness (or dullness according to students). However, when we look at the facts we see that regions that have lower economic growth patterns are found in both urban and rural areas, at the core and the periphery (Dijkstra et al., 2013); or that, at larger geographic scales, most gross value added in the agricultural sector comes from areas with intermediate population densities (Spain, Italy, Hungary, Belgium), or even from urban areas, as is the case with the Netherlands. When it comes to the livability of different places, e.g. in terms of life-satisfaction and health, it appears that in the economically developed EU countries differences are smaller and often in favor of rural areas (see e.g. Easterlin et al., 2011; Koster et al., 2017). In less developed countries, it is the cities where welfare improvements started, and where living circumstances are often better compared to rural areas.

Can we then say that people in urban and rural areas are different, or is it mainly the circumstances that are different?

In several countries, cultural differences are declining. Innovations such as telecommunications, internet and high-speed transport have brought the urban into the rural, and vice versa. However, certain differences remain, resulting from: (1) sorting of people due to constraints and preferences; and (2) different external factors affecting behavior.

Sorting involves the (non-random) clustering of similar people into areas where their (similar) preferences are best met. Some people prefer liveliness and a high density of amenities, such as shops and bars, while others prefer open, green spaces and quietness. Another reason for urban–rural sorting is related to jobs and wages: in cities there are generally more job opportunities for highly educated people with higher wages compared to rural areas, while for lower-educated people the wage differences are much smaller and do not outweigh the (social and economic) costs of moving. However, sorting does not always happen on a voluntary basis; it is not only related to preferences. Some people stay behind, are locked in, and cannot relocate even though they would like to migrate to a different place. Not only in Africa or Asia, but also in Eastern Europe, it is mainly the vulnerable (in terms of health or income) and older people who have no option of moving to a better future in the city. In Europe and the USA we can think of people who would like to move out of areas of decline (rural or urban) but who are locked in because of the inability to sell their house or find an affordable place to rent (Molloy et al., 2011). Or of powerless residents who are faced with environmental inequality when undesirable land use (e.g. landfills, prisons) is developed in their neighborhood. Both voluntary and involuntary sorting leads to socio-economic differences between urban and rural populations.

External factors like local environmental differences also result in different behavior of otherwise similar people (through different reference points, attitudes, social norms). This is also stressed by Stern and colleagues in their attitude–behavior–context (ABC) model. As shown in Figure 9.1, depending on personal attitudes (often referred to as preferences in the economic literature) and external (physical and/or social) conditions, an individual will exhibit certain behavior – for example, recycling or not recycling. When access to recycling facilities is either very limited or very good, it almost does not matter whether or not people hold pro-recycling attitudes; they always find a corner solution: either no one recycles or most people recycle. In a situation, however, in which it is possible but not necessarily easy to recycle, the correlation between pro-environmental attitude and recycling behavior is strongest (Stern, 2000; Jackson, 2005). In itself, the ABC model is a valuable framework; however, it is also criticized. As Elizabeth Shove points out, potential drivers and barriers are interchangeable, and little research has been done to dis-

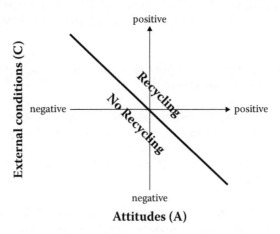

Source: Jackson (2005), based on Stern (2000).

Figure 9.1   The attitude–behavior–context model applied to recycling

tinguish main drivers and barriers. And, indeed, we need to put more emphasis on 'how needs and aspirations come to be as they are' (2010, p. 1277) and why they differ between countries and regions and between urban and rural areas. We need to see the spatial context of a person as an important determinant of consumer choice – i.e. the system of provision of food, water or energy – and the social environment within which that person operates.

9.3   The spatial context of values and behavior

Behavior can be seen as an outcome of many factors. In their seminal paper, Kollmuss and Agyeman describe the concept of *pro-environmental consciousness* which emerges from 'environmental knowledge, values, and attitudes, together with emotional involvement'. According to them, 'This complex, in turn, is embedded in broader personal values and shaped by personality traits and other internal as well as external factors' (2002, p. 256).

An important quest of behavioral scientists is to explain the so-called value–action gap and ask: Why do people's values or attitudes often not match their choices and behavior (Blake, 2001)? One explanation can be found in the spatial context in which these values are shaped and the behavior is facilitated (or not). The spatial context can inscribe certain forms of demand, for example, in transportation modes, in the design and operation of electricity and water infrastructures, and in the architecture of a home itself (Moss, 2000; van Vliet et al., 2005). It can also facilitate or hamper environmental behavior such as recycling, carpooling, or cycling.

Furthermore, the spatial context actively affects personal values and attitudes. Blake (2001), in a study on the Canadian province of British Columbia, shows that concern about extractive industry is higher in places where these industries are prevalent. Another important factor in environmental concern and even environmental behavior is 'place attachment', or emotional attitude towards a place (see e.g. Jorgensen and Stedman, 2006). A study of rural communities in Kansas and Iowa in the USA found that environmental attitudes and place attachment were the strongest predictors of self-reported pro-environmental behaviors (Takahashi and Selfa, 2015). However, the impact of place attachment is not always straightforward. When studying the difference in preferences of urban and rural residents for renewable energy investments such as wind farms and solar panels in Scotland, Bergmann et al. (2008) found urban residents to be more concerned about landscape impacts in the rural areas than the rural residents themselves. Instead, the rural people put more emphasis on the potential of new jobs. Here we see a difference between subjective perceptions, i.e. fed by a personal (emotional) experiences or images, and more objective perceptions (i.e. fed by reality and everyday life) of environmental challenges and solutions.

Although in (micro-)economics preferences are generally treated as exogenous and seen as something that is fixed, in reality they are dynamic and related to the social, physical, and geographical context. Preferences, or attitudes for that matter, can change because of new insights, new experiences, or new role-models. This is confirmed by the (limited) number of studies that focus on urban–rural differences and find that both pro-environmental attitudes and behavior differ between urban and rural residents. Huddart-Kennedy et al. (2009), for example, found that urban residents score higher on pro-environmental behavior and rural residents more on environmental concern. However, they also indicated that some of the rural environmental attitudes and behaviors (such as growing your own food) are not part of most measurement methods (often composed by urban academics), which potentially leads to biased results. Sarvilinna et al. (2018) found that urban residents are more willing to pay for social services, while rural people are more willing to volunteer. According to Burbank (1995, p. 169), 'contextual effects do not come about as the result of social composition alone, but result from individuals learning and acting in an environment with an informational bias.'

9.4   Regional differences in values, concerns and behavior in the EU

If we think about the successfulness of climate change policy interventions, it is well known that political trust is important, as is local participation (Konisky et al., 2008). Personal norms, values and perceptions are also important. Semenza et al. (2011) found that motivation for voluntary climate mitigation is mostly dependent on perceived susceptibility to threats and severity of climate change or climate variability impacts. In this section, the focus is on differences between urban and rural EU residents in terms of political trust, perceptions of the relevance of climate change, and the (stated) acceptance of certain policy measures.

As described in the previous section, environmental behavior is shaped by (among other things) personal values, environmental concerns, and the (local) spatial context within which people grow up, live, produce goods and services, and consume them. To illustrate this on a large scale, i.e. the EU, I use the European Social Survey of 2016, which consists of over 30,000 observations of people who self-reported their values and concerns as well as the regional context within which they operate. In addition, they also reported their type of domicile: 1) big city; 2) suburb or outskirts of a big city; 3) town or small city; 4) country village; 5) farm or home in countryside. I recoded these five categories into three, namely urban (1), intermediate (2 and 3) and rural (4 and 5).

To better understand the importance of the spatial context in values and behavior I ran several linear regression models in which the differences between the three types of living environments are explored, while controlling for the characteristics of individuals – such as age, gender, marital status, household income, un(employment), education level, experienced health, and being an immigrant. I controlled for this large set of characteristics for two reasons: first, the literature shows these are important factors to explain (social) trust, voting behavior, and also environmental concern; and, second, population characteristics of urban and rural areas differ because of sorting – cities are inhabited by more young and higher-educated people, for example. By controlling for these characteristics, I aim to understand to what extent, *ceteris paribus*, urban and rural residents have different values, concerns and/or behaviors.

In addition, I also controlled for the density level of the larger region to account for more and less remote characteristics. Rural communities near larger urban centers are often influenced by access to urban facilities, jobs and culture, and urban areas benefit from nearby rural areas in terms of access to green spaces (see e.g. Henry et al., 1997; van Leeuwen and Nijkamp, 2006; van Leeuwen, 2015). For this, I used the EU NUTS2 classification, which divides the 27 European Union countries into 281 smaller regions based on official administrative units. Germany, for example, is divided into 38 *Regierungsbezirke*, the Netherlands into 12 provinces, and France into 27 *Régions*. In addition, I applied clustered standard errors at the NUTS2 level to account for (unobserved) interdependence of respondents living in the same region.

9.4.1   Personal values

Although personal values only explain a small fraction of the variation in observed pro-environmental behavior, there are consistent patterns of relationships between values and a person's engagement with environmental issues. People who hold altruistic, or self-transcendent, values are, for example, more likely to engage in sustainable behavior such as recycling, have more environmental concerns, and are more likely to be politically engaged (Evans et al., 2013; Slimak and Dietz, 2006).

Within the European Social Survey, a set of 22 questions deal with general personal values, such as whether it is important to an individual to be rich, to have a good time, to get respect, or to be loyal. If we perform a factor analysis with a varimax rotation to summarize these 22 variables into grouped factors, the results point at three main factors that explain 44 percent of the variance in total. The Kaiser-Meyer-Olkin (KMO) value is 0.865, indicating a high consistency and thus a good sampling adequacy for factor-analytic correlation.

1. The first factor (explaining 16 percent) can be labelled as *self-focused*. Values such as important to 'be rich', 'show abilities and be admired', 'try new things', 'have a good time', 'be successful', 'have an exciting life' and 'seek fun' all show high loadings.
2. The second factor (explaining 14 percent) can be labelled as *people-focused*. Here, values as important to 'understand people', 'help people', 'to be loyal', to 'treat people equally' and to 'care for nature and the environment' show the highest factor loadings.
3. The third factor (explaining 14 percent) can be labelled as more *rules-focused*. High loadings are found for important to 'live in safe and secure surroundings', 'do what told and follow rules', 'that the government is strong and ensures safety', 'to behave properly', 'to get respect from others' and to 'follow traditions'.

Table 9.1   Linear regression of personal values factor scores

	Self-focused	People-focused	Rules-focused
Urban area	ref.	ref.	ref.
Intermediate area	−0.086***	0.035	−0.033
Rural area	−0.156***	0.024	−0.018
Density	0.000	0.000	0.000
Household income	0.05***	−0.006**	−0.003
Paid work	−0.014	−0.026	−0.014
Years of full-time education completed	0.012***	0.019***	−0.028***
Not married/relationship	0.146***	0.034**	−0.125***
Age	−0.017***	0.005***	0.006***
Subjective health	−0.100***	−0.027**	0.021**
Female	−0.222***	0.275***	0.026
No immigrant	0.117***	0.053*	0.278***
Country fixed effects	yes	yes	yes
Constant	1.041***	−0.549***	0.440***
Observations	18975	18975	18975
Adjusted R^2	0.230	0.152	0.172

Note: Standard errors in parentheses; $^*p < 0.1,$ $^{**}p < 0.05,$ $^{***}p < 0.01.$

Do people with different 'types' of values sort in different areas? Table 9.1 shows a linear regression of the factor scores at the individual level, taking into account (additional) individual characteristics such as education level and age, and applying clustered standard errors at the NUTS2 level. The independent variables of interest are the types of living environment (with urban areas as the reference category). It shows one important difference: being self-focused is mostly an urban value. No significant differences appear in terms of people-focused or rules-focused personal values across the urban–rural divide.

Many environmental issues, including climate change, can be labeled social dilemmas in which the interests of the individual can be at odds with the interests of society as a whole (Ostrom, 2010). It might come as no surprise that several studies indicated a negative relationship between being self-focused (i.e. self-enhancement) and environmental concern (Schultz, 2001). Based on this, we might expect lower environmental concerns of people living in urban areas. However, this analysis also shows no significant difference between people from different living environments in the level of being people-focused, something that is positively associated with environmental concern. So, instead of differences in personal values, differences in environmental concern might be the explanation for the differences in behavior of urban and rural residents.

9.4.2   Concerns and behavior

In this section, the focus is on trust, political participation, and environmental concern and behavior in urban and rural areas. Figures 9.2–4 show to what extent the type of living environment plays a significant role. Similar to the regression shown in Table 9.1, I controlled for individual and regional characteristics as well as for country fixed effects.

Figure 9.2 shows the significant differences between intermediate and rural areas compared to urban areas in terms of social and political trust. When exploring social and political trust, there appears to be no difference in the level of social trust (in other people), but rural people show much less trust in national political systems and parliaments, and in particular the EU parliament. This is in line with the findings of Kenneth Newton, who concludes that there are only weak associations between social and political trust at the individual level. In addition, he found that political trust, unlike social trust, can be better explained by national-level variables such as unemployment, inflation, economic growth and political corruption: 'different sorts of people express social and political trust, for different reasons. It follows that social and political trust do not have common origins in the same set of social conditions; they are different things with different causes' (Newton, 2001, p. 201). And, as Figure 9.2 shows, the causes might also differ between regions, and in this case between levels of urbanity. A relevant question is whether this difference in trust levels between urban and rural areas calls for the use of different types of policy instruments to achieve desired environmental outcomes. Possibly top-down policies are less likely to be successful in rural areas, and bottom-up projects might be more successful. When lower levels of trust are present, this means more effort is needed by the lead partner, i.e. the government, to create a cooperative relationship.

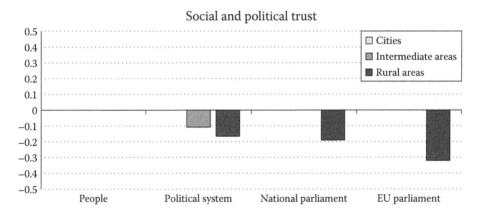

Source: ESS (2016).

Figure 9.2   Urban–rural differences in social and political trust while controlling for individual, regional and country characteristics (cities are the benchmark)

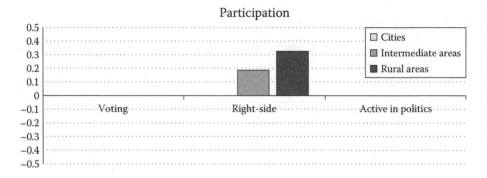

Source: ESS (2016).

Figure 9.3   Urban–rural differences in political participation while controlling for individual, regional and country characteristics (cities are the benchmark)

Unexpectedly perhaps, the lower levels of trust do not result in less participation in terms of voting or being active in politics (Figure 9.3). However, they do result in more votes for right-wing parties. If we interpret these right-wing votes as protest votes, it shows significant worries of people in rural areas. Nevertheless, in terms of satisfaction, it appears that people in rural areas are significantly more satisfied with life as a whole compared to urban people, while there are no differences found in terms of satisfaction with the national economy, health services or national government.

When moving to actual environmental concerns, Figure 9.4 shows that, compared to urbanites, people in rural areas are more aware of climate change (they agree more that it is actually happening and that it is an adverse development). As such there is a difference in perception of the (direct) impact of climate change; but rural people also are less worried and feel less responsibility to reduce climate change. This could be explained by a more anthropocentric orientation of rural dwellers, as reported by Gifford and Nilsson (2014). On the one hand they are more aware of natural processes, climatic cycles and disturbances; but on the other hand they also feel that humans have a unique position as the most important species.

This is in line with Figure 9.5 on climate change actions: people in urban areas are more likely to reduce their energy use compared to their rural counterparts. However, rural people are relatively more in favor of increased taxes on fossil fuels. No differences appear in the acceptance of renewable energy subsidies. Perhaps, rural residents are in favor of taxes on fossil fuels and subsidies on renewables because most renewable energy will likely be generated in their territory.

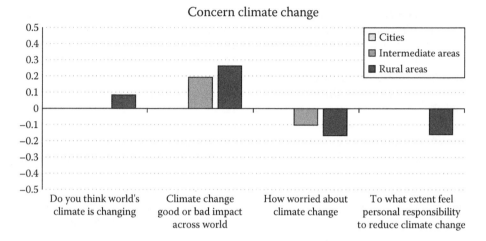

Source: ESS (2016).

Figure 9.4   Urban–rural differences in climate change concerns while controlling for individual, regional and country characteristics (cities are the benchmark)

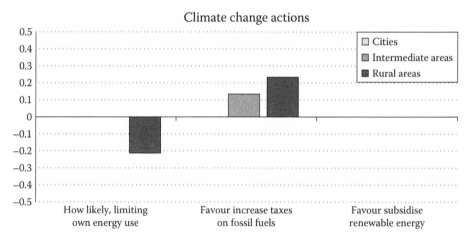

Source: ESS (2016).

Figure 9.5   Urban–rural differences in climate change actions while controlling for individual, regional and country characteristics (cities are the benchmark)

9.5   Urban futures?

Urban areas could very well be *the* places to stimulate pro-environmental behavior of households. If we assume that, in the future, rural areas will face aging and declining populations, with on average lower education levels than urban areas, we can expect more environmental concern and action from the urban popula-tion. In addition, the higher trust of urbanites in the government and the lower share of right-wing votes indicate that cities might be the places for more success-ful environmental and climate-related policies. To the extent that experiences in developed nations translate globally over time, and with more than 50 percent of the world population already living in cities, this could mean that environmental policies and investments reach more people, and, as a consequence, generate mul-tiplier effects that could extend well into the future and further across space. Also, policy makers see urban residents as important stakeholders, in particular because of their voting power (Bergmann et al., 2008). However, rural areas are also needed to combat environmental challenges such as climate change.

Renewable energy has become an essential part of the solution to a number of issues – from addressing climate change and air pollution to reducing geopolitical risks and fostering local and regional economic development. For many renewable energy sources we need space: space for wind farms, solar panels, bio refineries and the pro-duction of biomass; space that rural areas *can* offer but might be reluctant to provide.

The spatial consequence of the energy transition to CO_2-free sources is a major challenge in the western world where public consultancies have a strong impact on implementation processes. The transition from fossil fuels to sustainable (renew-able) sources of energy not only results in a much more decentralized character of energy production, but also in more visible items/activities in everybody's living environment: 'Energy sources that have long remained "underground" will, literally and figuratively speaking, emerge to the surface' (Sijmons and van Dorst, 2012, p. 46). Undoubtedly, the spatial advantages of rural areas will need to be explored to their full extent. But as long as this is not done in collaboration with important local stakeholders it will be perceived as something that is *imposed* on them, e.g. from the central government or from urbanites, likely triggering obstruction. According to Bell et al. (2005), this increasingly results in a 'social gap' between those in favor of renewable energy to preserve the environment (in general) and those that want to protect the local environment they feel attached to.

A second important transition is the circular economy: going from linear to cir-cular supply chains to improve waste management, resource recovery and energy efficiency. The conventional linear economic model starts with the extraction of natural resources, which are then transformed into products, which are bought and used by consumers who, sooner or later, throw them away. This model results in high economic, environmental and social costs related to the extraction, transformation and disposal of resources, and is therefore unsustainable in the long term (Bačová et al., 2016). It also results in spatial disequilibria in terms of stocks and flows of nutrients, ores, or synthetic materials in nature (Ruth and Davidsdottir, 2008).

Instead, a circular model aims at 'closing the loops', for using and re-using materi-als as long as possible. However, this requires collaboration between many different stakeholders across many different territories. As such, a circular economy needs to be tailored to the local and regional context (Bačová et al., 2016). An example is the circular food system, which requires collaborations between farmers, urban and rural citizens, businesses, policy makers and researchers. An important component in this system is of course the agricultural sector. In 2018, the Dutch Ministry of Agriculture, Nature and Food Quality launched its vision of the Netherlands as 'a leader in circular agriculture'. Circular agriculture aims to keep residuals of agricultural biomass and food processing within the food system as renewable resources (Van Berkum and Dengerink, 2019). In circular agriculture, the cycles are closed: as near as possible and as distant as necessary. It, in principle, involves the entire world, both urban and rural areas. This requires optimal use of waste streams.

To enable more circularity we need more insights into the 'geography of waste' – where is it generated and where is it treated? Are these locations most optimal from an economic, social and environmental perspective, and are the costs and gains equally distributed over countries, regions and urban and rural areas? By realizing and highlighting potential local benefits to different stakeholders, such as jobs, tax redistribution or lower energy prices, a more equal playing field is created between different government levels, between urban and rural areas.

9.6   Call to arms

Behavior is at the core of a wide range of disciplines, ranging from psychology to sociology to behavioral economics to other types of economics, such as environmental economics. When going beyond the neoclassical 'rational agent' approach, it is generally accepted that behavior is based on internal factors, such as 'worldviews, values, personal norms, beliefs and attitudes, as well as external forces, for example, social norms, financial incentives and infrastructural constraints' (Jackson, 2005; Shogren and Taylor, 2008). However, it is also noticed that (pro-environmental) values or attitudes do not always result in the expected pro-environmental behavior; this is referred to as the value–behavior or value–action gap (Kennedy et al., 2009). One explanation of this gap is the presence of spatial mediators such as trust in the (local) government; being exposed to positive or negative environmental processes, such as natural landscapes or sources of (point) pollution; or even spatial constraints, such as limited access to recycling facilities. All of the above require more insight into the causes and consequences of spatial heterogeneous values and behaviors. In other words, there is a great need for more spatially focused research.

This chapter calls for unraveling the relative impacts of compositional and spatial contextual factors on the behavior of citizens in both urban and rural areas. How does sorting of similar people in certain areas play a role, and how do social and environmental factors play a role? What happens if people move, or their environment changes? How does this impact their pro-environmental behavior and how can we use these insights to develop optimal policies? For this, it is important to minimize regional, urban-rural biases in our assumptions, surveys and modelling.

At the macro, i.e. regional, level we need to better understand where negative environmental externalities are caused and how the effects are distributed over space. If we think of renewable energy sources or waste handling and recycling, who is benefitting from the activities and who pays the price? If we need tax payers' money to set up climate adaptation projects, which regions should be the net payers and which the net recipients? This is important not only in the context of equality and fairness, but also in the context of perception and imaging. In particular the latter is very important for the cooperation of firms, (local) residents and voters, and as such for the success of policy interventions. For this, spatial models and approaches such as spatial explicit life-cycle assessments and environmental extended regional input–output models will be key.

At the micro level we need to see the spatial context of a person as an important determinant of consumer choice – i.e. the system of provision of food, water or energy – and the social environment within which that person operates. In different socio-spatial contexts, people experience different drivers as well as barriers to pro-environmental behavior. The meaning of distance, for example, to wind farms, train stations or recycling points is different for otherwise similar people in an urban or rural context. As such, distance is far less objective than we often think. This is an interesting research gap which calls for more comparative research between urban and rural areas. This can be done by surveys, asking people to report their (perceived) distances to different destinations, or by making use of stated and revealed behavioral experiments.

Another important research topic is the regional differentiation of actual and perceived environmental risks. Section 9.4 showed significant differences between urban and rural respondents in assessing the actual appearance of climate change. How does the subjective versus objective perception of environmental problems differ between different regions, or urban and rural areas? How does this translate into actual behavior?

In most studies environmentally significant behavior is usually measured via self-reported pro-environmental behavior. But what if people in certain regions, without acting in a conscious pro-environmental way, use far less energy and waste less food, for example, because of more traditional thrifty values? An objective and systematic evaluation of both pro-environmental behavior and the impact of different types of policy interventions in different areas is highly relevant for the development of interventions and policies, and to understand what works where.

Finally, since both environmental concerns and environmental actions are shaped by local context an interesting field of research is the consequence of interaction effects. For example, what does it mean for depopulating areas, for so-called places that don't matter, for areas that are prone to environmental injustice? According to Rodriquez-Pose (2018, p. 189), we should 'focus on tapping into untapped potential and on providing opportunities to those people living in the places that 'don't matter''. This requires both insights into the disappointments and expectations of those people, a redistribution of regional (environmental) costs and benefits, as well as insights into the local spatial opportunities of new activities.

References

Bačová, M., Böhme, K., Guitton, M., van Herwijnen, M., Kállay, T., Koutsomarkou, J., Magazzù, I., O'Loughlin., E., & Rok, A. (2016). Pathways to a circular economy in cities and regions. Policy brief. Available at https://urbact.eu/sites/default/files/policy_brief_on_circular_economy.pdf.

Bell, D., Gray, T., & Haggett, C. (2005). The 'social gap' in wind farm siting decisions: explanations and policy responses. *Environmental Politics*, 14(4), 460–477.

Bergmann, A., Colombo, S., & Hanley, N. (2008). Rural versus urban preferences for renewable energy developments. *Ecological Economics*, 65(3), 616–625.

Blake, D. E. (2001). Contextual effects on environmental attitudes and behavior. *Environment and Behavior*, 33(5), 708–725.

Burbank, M. (1995). How do contextual effects work? Developing a theoretical model. In M. Eagles (Ed.), *Spatial and Contextual Models in Political Research* (pp. 165–178). London: Taylor & Francis.

De Souza, P. (2017). *The Rural and Peripheral in Regional Development: An Alternative Perspective*. London: Routledge.

Dijkstra, L., Garcilazo, E., & McCann, P. (2013). The economic performance of European cities and city regions: Myths and realities. *European Planning Studies*, 21(3), 334–354.

Easterlin, R. A., Angelescu, L., & Zweig, J. S. (2011). The impact of modern economic growth on urban–rural differences in subjective well-being. *World Development*, 39(12), 2187–2198.

European Social Survey (ESS) (2016). *European Social Survey Round 8 Data*. Retrieved from https://www.europeansocialsurvey.org/data/round-index.html.

Evans, L., Maio, G. R., Corner, A., Hodgetts, C. J., Ahmed, S., & Hahn, U. (2013). Self-interest and pro-environmental behaviour. *Nature Climate Change*, 3(2), 122.

Franklin, R. S., & van Leeuwen, E. S. (2018). For whom the bells toll: Alonso and a regional science of decline. *International Regional Science Review*, 41(2), 134–151.

Gifford, R., & Nilsson, A. (2014). Personal and social factors that influence pro-environmental concern and behaviour: A review. *International Journal of Psychology*, 49(3), 141–157.

Haughton, G. (1999). Environmental justice and the sustainable city. *Journal of Planning Education and Research*, 18(3), 233–243.

Henry, M. S., Barkley, D. L., & Bao, S. (1997). The hinterland's stake in metropolitan growth: evidence from selected southern regions. *Journal of Regional Science*, 37(3), 479–501.

Huddart-Kennedy, E., Beckley, T. M., McFarlane, B. L., & Nadeau, S. (2009). Rural–urban differences in environmental concern in Canada. *Rural Sociology*, 74(3), 309–329.

Jackson, T. (2005). Motivating sustainable consumption: A review of evidence on consumer behaviour and behavioural change. *Sustainable Development Research Network*, 29, 30.

Jorgensen, B. S., & Stedman, R. C. (2006). A comparative analysis of predictors of sense of place dimensions: Attachment to, dependence on, and identification with lakeshore properties. *Journal of Environmental Management*, 79(3), 316–327.

Kennedy, E. H., Beckley, T. M., McFarlane, B. L., & Nadeau, S. (2009). Why we don't 'walk the talk': Understanding the environmental values/behaviour gap in Canada. *Human Ecology Review*, 16(2), 151–160.

Kollmuss, A., & Agyeman, J. (2002). Mind the gap: Why do people act environmentally and what are the barriers to pro-environmental behavior? *Environmental Education Research*, 8(3), 239–260.

Konisky, D. M., Milyo, J., & Richardson, L. E. (2008). Environmental policy attitudes: Issues, geographical scale, and political trust. *Social Science Quarterly*, 89(5), 1066–1085.

Koster, E. M., de Gelder, R., Di Nardo, F., Williams, G., Harrison, A., van Buren, L. P., . . . & Achterberg, P. W. (2017). Health status in Europe: Comparison of 24 urban areas to the corresponding 10 countries (EURO URHIS 2). *European Journal of Public Health*, 27, 62–67.

Lichter, D. T., & Brown, D. L. (2011). Rural America in an urban society: Changing spatial and social boundaries. *Annual Review of Sociology*, 37, 565–592.

Mohai, P., Pellow, D., & Roberts, J. T. (2009). Environmental justice. *Annual Review of Environment and Resources*, 34, 405–430.

Molloy, R., Smith, C. L., & Wozniak, A. (2011). Internal migration in the United States. *Journal of Economic Perspectives*, 25(3), 173–196.

Moss, T. (2000). Unearthing water flows, uncovering social relations: Introducing new waste water technologies in Berlin. *Journal of Urban Technology*, 7, 63–84.

Newton, K. (2001). Trust, social capital, civil society, and democracy. *International Political Science Review*, 22(2), 201–214.

Ostrom, E. (2010). Polycentric systems for coping with collective action and global environmental change. *Global Environmental Change*, 20(4), 550–557.

Rodríguez-Pose, A. (2018). The revenge of the places that don't matter (and what to do about it). *Cambridge Journal of Regions, Economy and Society*, 11(1), 189–209.

Ruth, M., & Davidsdottir, B. (Eds.). (2008). *Changing Stocks, Flows and Behaviors in Industrial Ecosystems*. Cheltenham, UK and Northampton, MA, USA: Edward Elgar Publishing.

Sarvilinna, A., Lehtoranta, V., & Hjerppe, T. (2018). Willingness to participate in the restoration of waters in an urban–rural setting: Local drivers and motivations behind environmental behavior. *Environmental Science & Policy*, 85, 11–18.

Schultz, P. W. (2001). The structure of environmental concern: Concern for self, other people, and the biosphere. *Journal of Environmental Psychology*, 21(4), 327–339.

Semenza, J. C., Ploubidis, G. B., & George, L. A. (2011). Climate change and climate variability: Personal motivation for adaptation and mitigation. *Environmental Health*, 10, 46.

Shogren, J. F., & Taylor, L. O. (2008). On behavioral-environmental economics. *Review of Environmental Economics and Policy*, 2(1), 26–44.

Shove, E. (2010). Beyond the ABC: climate change policy and theories of social change. *Environment and Planning A*, 42(6), 1273–1285.

Sijmons, D., & Van Dorst, M. (2012). Strong feelings: Emotional landscape of wind turbines. In S. Stremke & A. van Dobbelsteen (Eds.), *Sustainable Energy Landscapes: Designing, Planning, and Development* (pp. 45–67). Boca Raton, FL: Taylor & Francis.

Slimak, M. W., & Dietz, T. (2006). Personal values, beliefs, and ecological risk perception. *Risk Analysis*, 26(6), 1689–1705.

Stern, P. (2000). Toward a coherent theory of environmentally significant behavior. *Journal of Social Issues*, 56, 407–424.

Takahashi, B., & Selfa, T. (2015). Predictors of pro-environmental behavior in rural American communities. *Environment and Behavior*, 47(8), 856–876.

van Berkum, S., & Dengerink, J. (2019). Transition to sustainable food systems: The Dutch circular approach providing solutions to global challenges. Wageningen Economic Research Report No. 2019-082.

van Leeuwen, E. S. (2015). Urban–rural synergies: An explorative study at the NUTS3 level. *Applied Spatial Analysis and Policy*, 8(3), 273–289.

van Leeuwen, E. S., & Nijkamp, P. (2006). The urban–rural nexus: A study on extended urbanization and the hinterland. *Studies in Regional Science*, 36(2), 283–303.

van Vliet, B., Chappells, H., & Shove, E. (2005). *Infrastructures of Consumption: Environmental Innovation in the Utility Industries*. London: Earthscan.

10 New ways of valuing ecosystem services: big data, machine learning, and the value of urban green spaces

Christian Krekel and Jens Kolbe

10.1 Introduction

There is considerable interest on the side of policy to integrate public goods such as ecosystem services into systems of national accounts. Urban green spaces have gained particular attention in recent years due to rapid urbanisation and rising pressure on open space within cities. There exist no market prices for the value associated with urban green spaces, which is why alternative methods such as stated-preference or revealed-preference approaches are typically used to infer a monetary valuation.

Stated-preference approaches include, for example, contingent valuation, in which respondents are asked to directly place a monetary value on a public good under various hypothetical scenarios; and, in particular, discrete choice experiments, in which they are presented a series of alternative scenarios to choose from (Carson and Louviere, 2011). Despite recent advances such as, for example, virtual reality augmentation, stated-preference approaches often suffer from bias due to strategic, socially desirable, or symbolic answers.[1] This has led many researchers to adopt revealed-preference approaches and, in particular, hedonic pricing: here, changes in real estate prices around a public good are used to infer a monetary valuation. Examples for urban green spaces include Morancho (2003), Kong et al. (2007), Gibbons et al. (2014), and Czembrowski and Kronenberg (2016). The so-called *life-satisfaction approach* (sometimes also referred to as *experienced-preference approach* to keep consistency with stated-preference and revealed-preference approaches) uses data on subjective wellbeing (hereafter referred to as *wellbeing* for short) and, in particular, data on self-reported life satisfaction instead of prices, specifying a life-satisfaction rather than hedonic-pricing regression (Welsch, 2007; Welsch and Kühling, 2009). The impact of the public good on life satisfaction is then traded off against that of income, yielding a monetary value. Examples of research on the value of urban green spaces

---

1 For examples of virtual reality augmentation, see Bateman et al. (2009) on land use change and Patterson et al. (2017) on neighbourhood choice.

include Ambrey and Fleming (2014), Bertram and Rehdanz (2015), and Krekel et al. (2016).[2]

While revealed-preference approaches and the life-satisfaction approach overcome some of the issues associated with stated preferences, they are not entirely free of issues themselves. Hedonic pricing, for example, relies on the assumption that real estate markets are in equilibrium, which is easily violated in case of transaction costs (especially direct and indirect moving costs), incomplete information, or systematic misprediction of future utility associated with moving (see Krekel and Odermatt (2019) for evidence). Life-satisfaction regressions have been shown to yield relatively low coefficient estimates for income (see Clark et al. (2018), for example) which, when trading off the impact of the public good on life satisfaction with that of income, yields a relatively large (and often seemingly implausible) willingness-to-pay. Most importantly, hedonic pricing and life-satisfaction approaches may need to be used complementarily, depending on the degree of real estate market perfection: to the extent that positive externalities of public goods such as urban green spaces have already been internalised into real estate prices, any remaining impact on life satisfaction that comes out of a life-satisfaction regression (controlling for prices) is a residual, the total effect of the externality being the sum of the change in real estate prices and the change in the (monetised) wellbeing impact (Welsch and Ferreira, 2013).[3]

Recognising complementarity between the hedonic pricing and life-satisfaction approach when monetarily valuing public goods, this chapter goes beyond describing issues pertaining to each method (which have already been discussed extensively elsewhere), but instead looks ahead by describing *issues common to both methods* and *future trends in data and methods that have the potential to solve them*. It does so with the example of urban green spaces, focusing in particular on issues pertaining to the measurement of outcomes, large heterogeneity in the quality of urban green spaces, and reverse causality. Novel data to overcome some of these issues can be broadly categorised into: (i) innovations in measuring wellbeing, in particular the use of big data from high-frequency experience-sampling methods, brain imagery, or biomarkers; (ii) innovations in measuring prices, in particular the use of big data from web-scraping; and (iii) innovations in measuring quality of urban green spaces, in particular the use of hitherto unexploited fragmentation measures, big data from crowdsourced imagery combined with novel machine learning algorithms, or satellite imagery of chlorophyll activity. Novel methods pertain mainly to inference, including the use of field experiments and quasi-experiments to overcome issues of reverse causality as well as collaborating with local policy to design, implement, and evaluate interventions on urban greening.

---

2 Another example is White et al. (2013), who study the relationship between mental wellbeing and urban green spaces without inferring a monetary valuation.

3 See Luechinger (2009) for complementarity between hedonic pricing and the life-satisfaction approach in the case of air pollution or Krekel and Zerrahn (2017) in the case of wind turbine externalities.

In what follows, we illustrate these points in detail for the example of our own study – Krekel et al. (2016) – which valued urban green spaces monetarily using wellbeing data. That study is highly representative not only of the current generation of studies using wellbeing data to value the environment, but also when it comes to studies valuing urban green spaces. This pertains, in particular, to the use of panel data on residential wellbeing merged with cross-section, administrative data on urban green spaces; the use of Geographical Information Systems (GIS) to calculate variables of interest (such as coverage of green spaces around households); and the use of fixed-effects estimators. In fact, a similar study (White et al., 2013) obtained very similar coefficient estimates for the UK. We therefore consider our study a good example to benchmark future developments against, and to highlight where improvements are necessary.

In Box 10.1, we summarise, in a simplified manner, the data and basic empirical strategy of our 2016 study, and present its main findings. The rest of this chapter then focuses on how novel data and methods could have overcome some of the shortcomings present in our study. Finally, lessons learnt from the case of urban green spaces can easily be transferred to other topics in environmental, urban, and regional economics.

BOX 10.1   VALUING URBAN GREEN SPACES MONETARILY USING WELLBEING DATA: THE CASE OF KREKEL ET AL. (2016)

In Krekel et al. (2016), we estimate the effect of urban green spaces on residential wellbeing to value urban green spaces monetarily, for the example of 32 major German cities with inhabitants equal to or greater than 100,000. To do so, we obtain panel data on residential wellbeing from the German Socio-Economic Panel (SOEP) for the years 2000 to 2012 and merge it, based on exact geographical coordinates, with a cross-section from the European Urban Atlas (EUA) in the year 2006. We then calculate the coverage in hectares of urban green spaces in a 1-kilometre radius around households. To estimate the effect of urban green spaces on residential wellbeing, we run the following linear regression equation:

$$y_{it} = \beta_0 + MIC_{it}'\beta_1 + MAC_{it}'\beta_2 + GEO_{it}'\beta_3 + LUC_i'\delta_1 + LUC^2{}_i'\delta_2 + \eta_c + \mu_i + \varepsilon_{it} \qquad (10.1)$$

where y_{it} is the life satisfaction of resident i at time t, MIC and MAC are vectors of controls at the individual, household, and city level, including demographic characteristics, human capital characteristics, and economic conditions (for example, income) at the individual level; household characteristics and housing conditions (for example, rental prices) at the household level; and neighbourhood characteristics at the city level. GEO is a vector of geographical controls, including the distance from households to the city centre and from households to the city periphery. LUC is a vector containing the variable of interest, which is the coverage of urban green spaces (alongside coverages of vacant land, forests, and water bodies as other types of land use that are routinely controlled for). η_c and μ_i are city and individual fixed effects. Robust standard errors are clustered at the city level.

Including both city and individual fixed effects, and merging repeated observations on residential wellbeing with only one observation on urban green spaces, implies that variation in our variable of interest comes from within individuals and cities, or, in other words, from respondents who move. The SOEP includes an item that asks respondents for their primary moving reason, and about 79 per cent state that they are moving for reasons not directly related to their surroundings (such as, for example, job changes or family reasons). We thus argue that our estimates are, although not causal, near-causal as moving reasons are unrelated to urban land use in the respondents' surroundings.

Table 10.1   Main Result

| | Life Satisfaction | |
| | Not Controlling for Rental Prices | Controlling for Rental Prices |
	(1)	(2)
LUC_i	0.0066***	0.0059***
	(0.0025)	(0.0021)
LUC_i^2	−0.0001***	−0.0001***
	(0.0000)	(0.0000)
Controls		
Individual	Yes	Yes
Household	Yes	Yes
City	Yes	Yes
City Fixed Effects	Yes	Yes
Individual Fixed Effects	Yes	Yes
Adjusted R²	0.0557	0.0565
Number of Observations	33,782	29,729
Number of Individuals	6,959	6,959

Note: * $p<0.1$, ** $p<0.05$, *** $p<0.01$; robust standard errors clustered at the city level in parentheses. LUC_i is the coverage in hectares of urban green spaces (and other types of urban land use, oppressed for brevity) in a 1-kilometre radius around households. The dependent variable is life satisfaction on a zero-to-ten scale. All figures are rounded to four decimal places.

Source: SOEP v29 (2013), 2000–2012, individuals aged 17 or above, EUA 2006, own calculations. Adapted from Krekel et al. (2016).

Table 10.1 Column 1 shows our main result: we find that increasing the coverage of urban green spaces in a 1-kilometre radius around households by 1 hectare, given a mean coverage of about 23 hectares, significantly increases the life satisfaction of household members by about 0.007 points (0.4 per cent of a standard deviation). Column 2 shows that including rental prices as control attenuates coefficient estimates slightly but leaves overall findings unchanged. Note that, although individual effect sizes are relatively small, urban green spaces affect many residents at the same time: in fact, within major cities, about 6,000 residents, on average, have 1 hectare of urban green space in a 1-kilometre radius to their places of residence.

Trading off the impact of urban green spaces on life satisfaction with that of income, we find that residents would be willing to pay, on average, about 23 Euro of monthly net individual income in order to increase the coverage of urban green spaces in their surroundings by 1 hectare.

10.2   Data

The data used in our study consists of two elements: the first is geo-referenced longitudinal household data that includes wellbeing as the outcome as well as real estate prices and income as controls, alongside a rich set of other covariates. The second element is geo-referenced cross-sectional administrative data on urban land use. Both are merged based on exact geographical coordinates of households and urban green spaces using a Geographical Information System (GIS).

10.2.1   Data on wellbeing and real estate prices

Data on wellbeing and real estate prices in our study come from the German Socio-Economic Panel Study (SOEP), a nationally representative household panel covering almost 30,000 individuals in 11,000 private households in its latest wave (Wagner et al., 2007, 2008). The panel has been conducted annually since 1984, and has been asking household members about their wellbeing from the very beginning. Moreover, since 2000 it has recorded, in every survey year, the exact geographical coordinates of each household at the street-block level (which is very precise in urban areas). As stated in Box 10.1, we restricted our analysis to the years 2000–2012, focusing only on households in the 32 major German cities with inhabitants of 100,000 or more in order to not confound the impacts of urban green spaces on wellbeing with those of urbanisation.

Our outcome is the self-reported *life satisfaction* of household members. The survey asks respondents: "How satisfied are you with your life, all things considered?" Answer possibilities range from zero ("completely dissatisfied") to ten ("completely satisfied"). Besides life satisfaction, we obtained data on rental prices (which we selectively control for in our regressions) and household income (which we need in order to translate wellbeing impacts into a monetary equivalent). To account for self-selection of residents into areas with higher amounts of urban green spaces based on observables, we obtained data on demographic characteristics, human capital characteristics, and economic conditions at the individual level; household characteristics and housing conditions at the household level; and neighbourhood characteristics at the city level. We control for these observables throughout our regressions.

Life satisfaction is a global, evaluative measure of subjective wellbeing. It can be defined as the cognitive evaluation of current life circumstances relative to an ideal life (Diener et al., 1999), and, as such, has a present, backward-looking, and forward-looking component. By and large, people have been shown to make current and future life choices that are consistent with maximising their overall satisfaction with life (Kahneman et al., 1997; Adler et al., 2017). Although it has become the primary outcome for evaluating the impacts of policies and programmes in recent years – the UK Office for National Statistics (ONS), for example, is mandated to collect data on life satisfaction in all its surveys (cf. Dolan and Metcalfe, 2012) – life satisfaction is not entirely without issues.

Issues can be broadly categorised into: (i) conceptual issues pertaining to what life satisfaction actually captures and how survey design, contextual factors, and interview mode can influence self-reports; and (ii) practical issues pertaining to measurement, including the frequency of measurement and location of interview. We discuss each of these points in turn.

Note that there is an ongoing discussion in the economics literature about whether life satisfaction (often referred to as *experienced utility*) can be interpreted as a direct measure of utility itself or only as part of an individual's utility function (see Benjamin et al. (2012, 2014), for example). To be clear, for environmental valuation purposes, we only require life satisfaction to be a valid approximation of utility, and there is an established evidence base that it is (see Adler et al. (2017), for example).

10.2.2   Innovations in measuring wellbeing

Using life satisfaction from household panels entails several disadvantages, all of which are inherent in our study. Amongst the conceptual issues surrounding the use of life satisfaction is the fact that the outcome is prone to bias resulting from survey design, in particular from its positioning within the survey and framing due to preceding items (Schwartz et al., 1987). Answer behaviour may thus be shaped by what is currently salient in memory (primed by preceding items) and towards what attention is directed. Moreover, people tend to neglect the duration of their experiences when evaluating their lives (so-called *duration neglect*) and, instead, focus on experiences at the peak or towards the end of an experiential episode (so-called *peak-end bias*) (Kahneman et al., 1993, 1997). When sampled, life satisfaction has been shown to be prone to contextual effects (for example, whether other individuals are present during the interview, cf. Kavetsos et al., 2014) and survey mode (for example, whether the interview is conducted in person or on the phone, cf. Dolan and Kavetsos, 2016). Although issues pertaining to the left-hand-side variable do not result in endogeneity, they do, nevertheless, result in measurement error. This has led some authors to argue in favour of more instantaneous ways of measuring wellbeing (see Dolan (2014), for example).

There are also practical issues surrounding the use of the concept of life satisfaction: typically, the outcome is sampled once a year, when respondents are in their private homes. Leaving aside infrequency of data collection, interviewing respondents in their private homes neglects the fact that individuals spend considerable amounts of time outside, for example, at work or on the way to or from work. Likewise, temporary visitors are neglected. This implies that the current measurement paradigm is likely to capture only lower-bound estimates of the true effects.

Experience-sampling methods

Novel data can overcome some of these issues. Innovations in measuring wellbeing – in particular the use of big data from high-frequency experience-sampling methods (ESM) such as, for example, *Mappiness* (Mappiness, 2019a, 2019b) – can reduce concerns about survey design coming from the positioning of items within surveys and framing due to preceding items. Mappiness, which was originally developed by George MacKerron at the London School of Economics, is a downloadable app that, after initial registration, asks users – at random times during the day – to first report on feelings of happiness, relaxation, and alertness as experiential measures of wellbeing, and then on a set of contextual covariates that best describe the situation users are currently in, including the type of people they are currently with (for example, family members, friends, or colleagues); the place they are currently in (for example, at home or at work); and the type of activities they are currently engaging in (for example, working, commuting, or leisure activities).[4] Importantly, besides outcomes and covariates, the app samples the exact timestamp and current geographical coordinates of users, allowing researchers to relate experiential measures of wellbeing such as feelings of happiness (which are, by their very nature, much less prone to duration-neglect and peak-end bias than global, evaluative measures such as life satisfaction) to the immediate surroundings of users (for example, urban green spaces). In the field of environmental economics, Mappiness has already been applied to, amongst others, associations of natural land covers and weather conditions with happiness when app users are outdoors (MacKerron and Mourato, 2013). There are now various apps with a similar focus, including the *Happiness by Design* app by Paul Dolan of the London School of Economics.[5]

Experience-sampling methods can help overcome dimensionality issues of traditional, survey-based methods: rather than asking respondents once a year, they sample outcomes and contextual covariates in a random, high-frequency fashion, thus (cost-effectively) providing many more data points for analysis than traditional methods. They can also help overcome lower-bound issues: traditional, survey-based methods typically ask respondents about outcomes and covariates in their private homes, neglecting the fact that people spend considerable amounts of time outside. Experience-sampling methods, in contrast, capture emotional sentiments of respondents (including temporary visitors to sites) where they currently are, thus providing more accurate estimates of the true effects.

Note, however, that experience-sampling methods *per se* do not solve issues of reverse causality and still require a causal-design framework: although they sample outcomes and contextual covariates at random times during the day, the location of respondents may be less random. Taking the example of urban green spaces, it is quite imaginable that respondents with a higher preference for green (which may be correlated with happiness) are more likely to be permanently located or temporarily bypass (for example, by systematically altering their daily way to work) urban green areas, and *vice versa*. Rather than estimating the average causal effect

---

4 Note that, at the point of registration, the app also asks users about their overall life satisfaction (the traditional measure for valuation) as well as relevant controls, including age, gender, relationship status, health, work status, household composition, and income.

5 For an application of expressed happiness on social media and its relation to air pollution, see Zheng et al. (2019). For the validity of happiness measures obtained from big data sources such as social media, see Bellet and Frijters (2019).

of urban green spaces on happiness, one then obtains, instead, an upward-biased estimate.[6] The same logic, however, applies to traditional methods just as well: respondents with a higher preference for green are more likely to be permanently settled around urban green areas, and *vice versa*, yielding a similar upward bias *in addition to* downward bias resulting from interviewing respondents exclusively in their private homes. Although the direction of bias (not necessarily its strength) is clearer in the case of experience-sampling methods, both approaches, nevertheless, require a causal-design framework to arrive at the causal effect of urban green spaces on happiness.

Finally, besides issues of internal validity, issues of external validity when using experience-sampling methods pertain to self-selection of respondents: while household panels such as the SOEP are nationally representative, app users in the case of Mappiness, for example, are a non-representative sub-group – typically being younger, more technologically affine, and more open to experience, which requires additional checks about the generalisability of findings to the broader population.

Given these considerations, experience-sampling methods are, therefore, rather a complement than a substitute for self-reported life satisfaction used by traditional methods so far. However, as experience-sampling becomes – with advancements in mobile technology and user acceptance – more common over time, it is likely to pose a promising alternative at some point.

Brain imagery and biomarkers

Using brain imagery and biomarkers to measure wellbeing is, in a way, the complete opposite of using big data from experience-sampling methods. Due to complexity of (highly costly) data collection, including relative effort and invasiveness as well as data protection and ethical considerations, observations typically come in much smaller numbers. Moreover, due to their complex nature, with many variables (and interactions among variables) in the human system still unknown, interpretations of outcomes are often ambiguous. Finally, brain imagery and, in particular, biomarkers are sensitive to context during measurement, rendering outcomes relatively noisy.

Nevertheless, there have been studies relating brain imagery to urban land use. The study by Kuehn et al. (2017) employs the same data source on urban land use as our study: the authors used magnetic-resonance imaging (MRI) of 341 older adults from the Berlin Aging Study II (BASE-II) and structural-equation modelling to infer three latent factors of brain integrity (amygdala, perigenual anterior cingular cortex, and dorsolateral prefrontal cortex) from three different neuro-imaging sequences (grey matter volume derived from voxel-based morphometry, mean diffusivity derived from a diffusion tensor-imaging sequence, and the magnetisation-

---

6 Experience-sampling methods are, therefore, potentially more suitable for externalities that are exogenously fluctuating such as, for example, air or noise pollution.

transfer ratio). The authors then related these three latent factors of brain integrity to the amounts of different types of urban land use, including urban green spaces, vacant land, forests, and water bodies. They find a significant, positive association between amygdala activity and coverage of *forests* in a radius of up to 2 kilometres around households, suggesting that urban forests (rather than urban green spaces) have salutogenic effects on the integrity of the amygdala, a part of the limbic system that is responsible for coping with stress. This does not imply that urban green spaces have no wellbeing impacts at all: such impacts may, however, not be detectable in this area of the brain. So far, this is the only study using brain imagery to explore the wellbeing impacts of urban greenery. Studies investigating urban upbringing more generally include, for example, Lederbogen et al. (2011), Haddad et al. (2014), and Streit et al. (2015).

Some studies use biomarkers and, in particular, cortisol as a steroid hormone that responds to stress in order to measure objective wellbeing benefits of urban green spaces.[7] Thompson et al. (2012) collected cortisol levels derived from multiple-saliva sampling of 25 subjects aged 35–55 in a highly deprived area (72 per cent of the respondents were unemployed) in Dundee, UK, over a period of four weeks. The authors then related mean cortisol levels to the percentage of green space (including parks, woodlands, scrub, and other natural environments) in census area statistic wards of subjects (which are similar to post code areas). They find a significant, negative association between cortisol secretion and green space, which also holds for self-reported measures of stress (using the Perceived Stress Scale) and mental illbeing (using the Short-Form Warwick and Edinburgh Mental Wellbeing Scale). In a follow-up study of 106 subjects from the same area, the authors show that there are significant gender differences in stress patterns by levels of green space, with less green space yielding higher levels of stress in women (Roe et al., 2013). Note that, when measuring cortisol (which has been shown to be a rather short-term measure of stress), timing of measurement and individual differences matter (Miller et al., 2007). Studies investigating the natural environment more generally include, for example, Ulrich et al. (1991), Hartig et al. (2003), and Park et al. (2010).

Besides cortisol, biomarkers with a potential to show objective wellbeing benefits of urban green spaces include pro-inflammatory and anti-inflammatory cytokines, which are immune proteins involved in inflammatory response. In severe cases of mental illbeing such as depression, the inflammatory response system of the human body has been shown to be activated (Dowlati et al., 2010; Miller and Raison, 2016), yielding an increase in pro-inflammatory cytokines (for example, cytokines IL-1β and IL-6) and a decrease in anti-inflammatory ones (for example, cytokine IL-10, interferon IFN-γ, and chemokine IL-8). It is imaginable that heterogeneous impacts of urban green spaces by socio-economic status (Mitchell and Popham, 2008) are mirrored by heterogeneous impacts on mental wellbeing: individuals

---

7 For an account of how self-reported measures of subjective wellbeing relate to objective measures such as biomarkers, see Kung et al. (2019).

with lower mental wellbeing at the outset, or outright mental illbeing, might benefit more from urban greenery than others, which may then be reflected in differential immune response. Studies on the relationship between brain imagery, biomarkers, and urban green spaces are still in their infancy.

Notwithstanding issues of sample size, measurement, and interpretation, using brain imagery and biomarkers as objective outcomes for wellbeing may meaningfully complement self-reported life satisfaction used by traditional methods in three ways: first, they may shed light on potential transmission mechanisms. Second, they may help validate self-reported measures and reduce concerns about construct validity. Finally, they may help verify impacts on self-reported measures, reducing remaining concerns about self-report bias. In the context of the UK, the UK Biobank may be a promising source for outcomes in the area of biomarkers.

10.2.3   Innovations in measuring prices

Rental prices played only a minor role in our study, which valued urban green spaces monetarily using wellbeing data. Rather than using them as an outcome as in hedonic-pricing regressions, we selectively controlled for rental prices in our life-satisfaction regressions to reduce concerns about endogeneity resulting from omitted variables (rental prices may explain self-selection of residents into particular urban areas with more or less green). Controlling for rental prices, however, may not only reduce concerns about endogeneity but may also matter for monetisation: to the extent that (positive) impacts of urban green spaces have already been internalised in (higher) rental prices (which depends on the degree of housing market perfection), controlling for rental prices in our life-satisfaction regressions yields the residual impact of urban green spaces on wellbeing net of what has already been internalised. The total monetary value of urban green spaces is then composed of the monetised wellbeing impact plus the monetised rental price impact, implying that, eventually, wellbeing and hedonic price data have to be used complementarily in order to arrive at the true monetary valuation of urban green spaces.

The SOEP includes data on actual and hypothetical rental prices. The latter are obtained by asking house owners (who, by definition, do not pay any rent) to convert their house prices into hypothetical rental prices (which, of course, may be subject to measurement error and bias).[8] When selectively controlling for rental prices in our life-satisfaction regressions (in order to account for self-selection of residents and elicit the residual wellbeing impact), we create an index that combines both actual and hypothetical rental prices. This approach, however, is less than perfect: besides measurement error and bias when converting (current) house prices into hypothetical rental prices, it comingles house owners with renters, two very different groups of residents. Additionally, there are concerns about using self-reported measures of rental prices, which are – besides recorded only annually

---

8 The SOEP does not include house prices.

– often quickly estimated, introducing measurement error and thus endogeneity in a right-hand-side variable.

Web-scraping of real estate prices

Innovations in measuring prices, in particular the use of big data from web-scraping, can alleviate some of these concerns. The basic idea behind web-scraping is to program a short routine (for example, using Python) that downloads a single page (the input file) from a web site, searches (parses) that page for relevant information (for example, using Python LXML), and, when found, saves the extracted information in a newly created file (the output file). This is often done repeatedly in a loop to save relevant information from many, similarly structured pages – as is the case, for example, with listings on online real estate market places such as Zillow. Web-scraped information from such online real estate market places typically includes, besides the actual purchase and rental prices of dwellings, the timestamps of their listing and their approximate location, often in terms of street name, city, and postal code, allowing us to merge data on real estate prices with data on households or data on urban green spaces based on (quite approximate) geographical identifiers. Web-scraping also works for dwelling and amenity characteristics associated with a listed dwelling, and can therefore provide insights into the relevant structure of a neighbourhood.[9]

The advantage of web-scraped real estate prices is, arguably, that they come in much higher frequency and much more accurately reflect the true characteristics of real estate markets in a given geographical area, alleviating some of the concerns of traditional, annual self-reported measures, which are often prone to measurement error and bias. Concerns that online market places capture only a selected, non-representative sample of dwellings are probably over-rated nowadays, as listing dwellings online has become somewhat common practice. A disadvantage is that web-scraped information on real estate prices and characteristics can hardly be allocated to a single respondent in survey data but only to the (close-by) area in which a respondent lives. This, however, is often sufficiently accurate to make web-scraping of real estate prices at least an appropriate complement to self-reported measures.

10.2.4   Data on urban green spaces

Data on urban green spaces in our study come from the European Urban Atlas (EUA), a comparative study of land use in major European cities published by the European Environment Agency (2011). Based on satellite imagery, in this data set, urban areas greater than 0.25 hectares are allocated exclusively to well-defined categories of urban land use. Compared to data on land *cover*, data on land *use* are preferable as they provide information on actually observable patterns of usage,

---

9 Web-scrapers can be easily programmed, and there are many tutorials online. See Neves (2018), for example.

implying that, for example, what is classified as a park is actually used as one. This is accomplished by adding another layer of human verification after a machine-based allocation into the different predefined categories of urban land use.

Note that, at the time of writing our study, the EUA included only a single cross-section (that is, 2006), implying that urban land use in our estimation sample changes only for respondents who move – a feature we are exploiting in our empirical strategy. At the same time, however, this introduces measurement error in our right-hand-side variable, and thus endogeneity. Arguably, endogeneity resulting from measurement error in the variable of interest is small in our case, given that areas such as parks and urban green spaces are rather persistent over time. Recently, a new wave (that is, 2012) has become available which allows constructing a pseudo-panel of urban land use, and thus implementing an alternative approach. We will turn to this issue in more detail when discussing our empirical strategy.

Our variable of interest is urban green spaces, defined as land for predominantly recreational use, including parks, castle parks, suburban natural areas used as parks, gardens, and zoos. Although quite a heterogeneous category, these are two dominant features of urban green spaces that stand out: they have predominantly recreational value and they are publicly accessible, and thus public goods. The EUA provides data in the form of shapefiles, which allows calculating the exact coverage of urban green spaces as a measure of availability in a pre-defined treatment radius around each household. We choose a treatment radius of 1,000 metres, and define coverage of urban green spaces in terms of hectares within the $(1,000 \times 1,000 \times \pi)$ / 10,000 hectare area around each household (Figure 10.1). Moreover, as a measure of reachability, we calculate the Euclidean distance in 100 metres between each household and the nearest urban green space. Finally, besides urban green spaces, we also calculate the coverages and distances of vacant land, forests, and water areas as controls in our regressions.

10.2.5   Innovations in measuring fragmentation of urban green spaces

Relating the amount of urban green spaces around households, or the distance between urban green spaces and households, to the wellbeing of household members is a fairly straightforward approach that has been replicated many times in the literature. It gives an answer to the basic question of whether more green is associated with more wellbeing. It does, however, give no answer to the question of how this green is to be arranged and structured around households for positive wellbeing impacts to manifest themselves, arguably an important question from an urban development and planning perspective. It also matters from a purely academic point of view: the way urban green spaces are arranged and structured points towards the specific transmission channels of impacts, for example, social interaction or cognitive restoration.

Take 5 hectares of urban green space, for example: these could be arranged all in one patch, yielding a continuous area, or scattered across many patches, yielding a

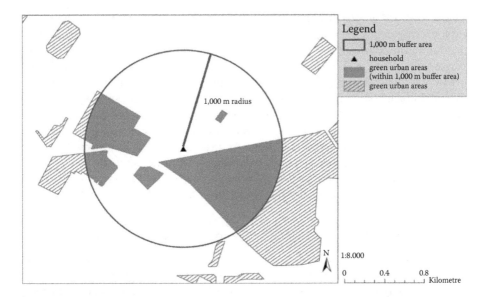

Source: Krekel et al. (2016).

Figure 10.1   Definition of coverage in hectares of urban green space around household

discontinuous area, with some patches potentially being closer to each other and others more distant. Moreover, patches could be structured in different ways: some could be small, others could be large; some could be round, others could be edgy. Finally, if urban green space is scattered across many patches and less uniformly integrated with its surroundings, it could interact in different ways with other types of urban land use such as, for example, water areas in its vicinity or with the landscape overall. Our study design gives no answer to this question: traditional measures such as coverages (either as total area covered or as a percentage of landscape) and distances are invariant to aspects of fragmentation.

There exist various geographical fragmentation measures that could be used to shed light on the question of how urban green spaces should be arranged and structured to maximise wellbeing impacts in their surroundings. When it comes to their arrangement, the number of patches in the landscape and the patch density (the number of patches in the landscape divided by the total landscape area) might matter for wellbeing. Likewise, the mean patch size and the largest patch index (the area of the largest patch in the landscape divided by the total landscape area) might be relevant. When it comes to structure, typical fragmentation measures include the total edge (the total length of all border segments of urban green spaces with other types of urban land use) and the edge density (the total length of all border segments divided by the total landscape area). Common measures of overall land-scape fragmentation, and hence interaction of urban green spaces with other types of urban land use, include, for example, Simpson's diversity index or Shannon's evenness index.

To our knowledge, there exists only one study to date – Bertram et al. (2020) – that explores fragmentation of urban green spaces. Further applying these various fragmentation measures, therefore, seems promising, although computationally cumbersome: it requires the exact geographical coordinates of both households and urban green spaces, and each fragmentation measure must be calculated separately for each household. Although possible with SOEP and EUA, with about 11,000 households per year, calculations take time. Note that, due to satellite imagery resolution, the EUA captures only objects with a size equal to or greater than 0.25 hectares, neglecting smaller objects. As a result, potentially scattered, smaller patches of urban green spaces are not captured *per se*, implying that – to the extent that such scattered, smaller patches of urban green spaces matter for wellbeing – estimates in our study can be interpreted as lower bounds.

10.2.6   Innovations in measuring quality of urban green spaces

Studying the arrangement and structure of urban green spaces is, arguably, a simple way to explore a particular dimension of their quality, made easy by the fact that their exact geographical coordinates are available as shapefiles. Apart from their shapes, however, data sets such as the EUA provide no information on the quality of urban green spaces, with quality defined here as the difference in wellbeing benefits that different urban green spaces yield, keeping quantity constant.[10] Urban green spaces might differ substantially in terms of design (for example, they may combine green areas with water bodies, trees, or flower beds) and infrastructure (for example, they may incorporate pavements, benches, or lighting at night). To our knowledge, there exists no study to date that explores the quality of urban green spaces (most likely due to data limitations), even though it is quite imaginable that different qualities may have different wellbeing benefits or even disbenefits: a large green space that is perceived as unmanaged and that lacks lighting at night, for example, might easily stir fear of crime and actually reduce wellbeing (Kuo et al., 1998). It is important to note that effects estimated in our study and in other studies in the literature, therefore, reflect the wellbeing benefits of the *average* green space. From an urban development and planning perspective, however, it is important to know exactly which elements, or qualities, of urban green spaces yield which wellbeing benefits.

Crowdsourced imagery

Fortunately, novel data and methods can overcome some of these issues. Innovations in measuring quality of urban green spaces, in particular the use of big data from crowdsourced imagery such as Geograph, Google Street View, and Mappiness, combined with novel machine learning algorithms to better understand their qual-

---

10 The difference in wellbeing benefits that the same urban green space yields for different people relates to heterogeneous effects, which is an entirely different question. There is an established literature which shows that urban green spaces have different effects on different people. For example, men (Richardson and Mitchell, 2010), older people (Maas et al., 2006), and low-income households (Mitchell and Popham, 2008) have been shown to benefit relatively more from urban green spaces in their surroundings.

ity, can shed light on exactly which elements of urban green spaces matter for well-being.[11] Geograph Worldwide, which is run by a not-for-profit company in the UK, is an online depository for photographs with the explicit aim to collect, publish, organise, and preserve representative images and associated information for every square kilometre of Great Britain, Ireland, and the Isle of Man (Geograph, 2019a).[12] Contributors, who can be any user (there are currently about 13,000 users), are encouraged to upload their photos (there are currently about 5 million photos) to the depository, which are then made freely available to the general public (users retain their copyright). Google Street View is even more promising, relying on automated photographs from Street View vehicles rather than crowdsourcing: after registering online to obtain a key and a signature, its Street View Static API can be used to download a static photograph taken from a Street View vehicle for a particular location, under a pre-specified compass heading of the camera, horizontal field of view, pitch angle, and zoom (Google, 2019a). Unlike Geograph, however, Google Street View is not free: given a monthly download volume of up to 100,000 static photographs, 1,000 shots cost USD 7.00 (Google, 2019b). Finally, Mappiness, which we already know from its innovative experience-sampling of wellbeing, in its latest version includes a function that asks app users when located outdoors to take a photo of what lies straight ahead of them, and then add that photograph to a public map.

Of course, crowdsourced imagery may induce selection issues. In terms of Mappiness, and to a lesser extent Geograph, these pertain to what is actually photographed: although Mappiness prompts app users to take a picture of what lies straight ahead of them, users may not follow that instruction, and, if so, only for certain motives. Moreover, in the case of both Mappiness and Geograph, the exact location of users may not be random but related to scenery or amenities around them, making certain, picturesque motives more likely than others, and thereby potentially biasing the quality of surroundings upwards. In the case of urban green spaces, this could mean that (parts of) green spaces with higher quality (and thus potentially higher wellbeing benefits) are more likely to be sampled. Google Street View is more objective (simply because everything around a Street View vehicle is captured) but limited to areas that are accessible by car. Nevertheless, even though selection issues exist, the tendency for more and more crowdsourced imagery to become available over time also means that selection issues become less and less. Taken together, big data from crowdsourced imagery such as Geograph, Google Street View, and Mappiness therefore provide a growingly viable way to measure hitherto non-measurable quality aspects.

Seresinhe et al. (2015) exploit big data from Data Science Lab's ScenicOrNot – a web site that crowdsources ratings of scenic beauty (currently, there are about 1.5 million ratings) for georeferenced photographs from Geograph – to study the relationship between scenic beauty and health. The authors find that lower values

---

11 For a review of using big data to value urban environments more generally, see Glaeser et al. (2018).
12 There is now also a depository available for Germany (Geograph, 2019b).

of scenic beauty are associated with significantly lower values of self-reported health over 1-kilometre grid squares in the Census for England and Wales. This result holds across urban, suburban, and rural areas even when controlling for a wide range of socio-economic indicators. Importantly, the authors show that scenic beauty rather than the sheer presence of green spaces matters for self-reported health, pointing towards the importance of quality rather than quantity of urban green and, potentially, towards important interactions between urban green and other types of land use such as, for example, forests or water bodies. Seresinhe et al. (2019) replicate this finding for self-reported measures of wellbeing rather than health, using data from the photo module of Mappiness. Another interesting study is Saiz et al. (2018): the authors relate the upload frequency of georeferenced photographs on Flickr and Panoramio – two online photo-sharing web sites – to the beauty ratings of 1,000 buildings across the US originating from an independent beauty survey. They find that the upload frequency of photos of buildings is highly predictive of their beauty ratings, thus validating the use of localised user-generated image uploads on photo-sharing web sites to measure the aesthetic appeal of the urban environment.

Machine learning

Often, however, big data from crowdsourced imagery by themselves are not enough: they need to be combined with novel methods to make use of the amount of information that exists and to extract the type of information that is of interest. In the case of quality of urban green spaces, this involves, in principle, three steps: first, each image needs to be allocated a value for quality, based on certain pre-defined characteristics. This may be a single (discrete or continuous) index or a count value of certain elements within the image, such as infrastructure. Given the sheer number of images, this can hardly be accomplished by humans but calls for novel methods in the area of machine-based allocation. Second, once a value for quality has been allocated to each image, one or more images need to be allocated to each patch of urban green space (the exact geographical location of which could, for example, be obtained from the EUA). Finally, once one or more images have been allocated to each patch, values for quality have to be aggregated, yielding an aggregate value for the quality of the respective patch of urban green space. Optionally, a weighting during aggregation could be applied to lend relatively more importance to certain quality characteristics.

While steps two and three are straightforward, step one is more complex: here, machine learning in the area of computer vision, and in particular deep learning algorithms such as convolutional neural networks (CNN), can help allocate a value for quality, based on certain pre-defined characteristics. A convolutional neural network perceives an image as, for example, a three-dimensional object as opposed to a one-dimensional canvas, with each dimension – referred to as *input channel* – pertaining to a colour (red, green, and blue). To process the image, the algorithm scans each input channel by running a smaller layer – the *convolutional layer* or *kernel* – over it, yielding reduced input channels or *kernel channels*, and, when these are combined, a one-dimensional *convoluted feature output*. After pooling and flattening the output into a column vector, it is then fed forward into a neural network which is able to distinguish between features (for example, edges, contours, or colours), classifying them by comparing values in the column vector with pre-defined ones. Neural networks can, via back-propagation, be trained to become better at classifying over time, starting with low-level evolving towards high-level features.

Seresinhe et al. (2017), using images from ScenicOrNot, apply the Places365 CNN model (trained on the Places2 database) to extract probabilities of place categories such as mountains or valleys combined with the Places205 AlexNet CNN (trained on the Scene UNderstanding attribute database) to extract probabilities of place characteristics such as trees or flowers. The authors find that place categories like canals or gardens in urban settings are associated with significantly higher scenic beauty, while man-made structures like highways or parking lots are associated with significantly lower beauty (the exception being man-made historical structures). Importantly, large areas of green spaces such as grass or sports fields are perceived as less scenic, most likely due to their flat grass structures. Law et al. (2018a), using images from both Google Street View and ScenicOrNot, study the relationship between street frontages, house prices, and scenic beauty, showing that active frontages (that is, frontages containing windows or doors) as opposed to blank frontages (frontages containing walls, fences, or garages) are associated with significantly higher scenic beauty and (presumably as a result) house prices (about 4 per cent). The authors employ the original Street-Frontage-Net (SFN) CNN to classify street frontages as either active or blank combined with a modified version trained on ScenicOrNot images. In a similar setting, Law et al. (2018b) use street images from Google Street View and aerial images from Bing to augment hedonic-pricing regressions for property prices in London.

Such novel methods in the area of machine learning have already made significant contributions to the field, showing, for example, that urban green spaces by themselves are not necessarily associated with higher wellbeing, but that quality and perceived scenic beauty matter for wellbeing benefits. Given rapid advances in machine learning, these methods are likely to substantially change the field in the future. This is especially true when it comes to identifying more fine-grained elements of the quality of urban green spaces.

Satellite imagery on chlorophyll activity

Other innovations in measuring the quality of urban green spaces exploit their biological features: for Europe, for example, satellite imagery on chlorophyll activity – an integral feature of greenery – can be obtained from the World Data Center for Remote Sensing of the Atmosphere (WDC-RSAT) and, in particular, the Medium Resolution Imaging Spectrometer (MERIS), which is part of the core instrument payload of the European Space Agency's environmental research satellite ENVISAT-1 (WDC-RSAT, 2019a, 2019b). ENVISAT-1 flies on a sun-synchronous orbit at a mean altitude of about 800 kilometres, with an orbit time of 101 minutes and a repeat cycle of 35 days (European Space Agency, 2019). MERIS, which allows for global coverage of the Earth in three days, is an imaging spectrometre measuring solar radiation reflected by the Earth in 15 visible-near infrared spectral bands from about 412.5 to 900 nanometres, with a spatial sampling between 0.26 and 0.39 kilometres (depending on the angle of the satellite relative to the Earth's surface). Chlorophyll activity can be sensed in a centre wavelength bandwidth range from 442.5 ± 10 to 681.25 ± 7.5 nanometres.

Satellite imagery on chlorophyll activity is aggregated in the so-called AVHRR Compatible Normalized Difference Vegetation Index (NDVI) derived from MERIS data (Figure 10.2). AVHRR stands for Advanced Very High Resolution Radiometer, and refers to a type of imaging spectrometre typically installed on US satellites that operates on broader spectral channels than MERIS (hence the necessity to transform the index to make data obtained from both spectrometres compatible). The NDVI is a continuous, maximum value, composite index which is available for Europe on a daily, ten-day, and monthly basis (WDC-RSAT,

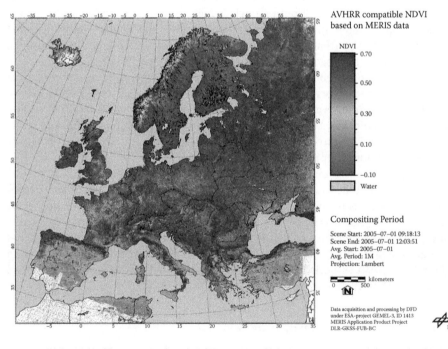

Note: NDVI as monthly composite for July 2005. Ocean and lake areas are presented in grey; clouds are masked out as bad values (white).

Source: WDC-RSAT (2019b).

Figure 10.2   AVHRR compatible Normalized Difference Vegetation Index derived from MERIS data (NDVI)

2019c). It can be downloaded from the EOWEB GeoPortal (2019), the web portal for interactive access to the DLR (German Aerospace Center) Earth observation data holdings.

Although satellite imagery on chlorophyll activity is certainly a very specific type of data on quality, pertaining mostly to (parts of) ecosystem services of urban green spaces, it can also shed light on important mechanisms through which wellbeing benefits of greenery may come about. One of the advantages of this type of data is that it is, arguably, exogenous: for individuals already residing in the vicinity of urban green spaces, short-term meteorologically induced changes in chlorophyll activity should not be related to moving behaviour due to surroundings. By using this type of data in combination with an appropriate empirical strategy, one can, therefore, get closer to causality than with conventional data sources.

10.3   Empirical methods

To estimate the effect of urban green spaces on residential wellbeing, in our study we estimate a linear regression model. More specifically, we regress the life satisfaction of household members on the coverage in hectares of urban green spaces in a 1-kilometre radius around households, alongside a rich set of controls as well as city and individual fixed effects. Note that our data on residential wellbeing include repeated measurements, whereas our data on urban green spaces include only one measurement, implying that, by including individual fixed effects in our regression model, effects are identified by residents who move (as for others, fixed effects and variables of interest are perfectly collinear).

Although we show that most residents who move state they are moving for reasons primarily *not* related to their surroundings, reducing concerns about self-selection of residents into areas with higher or lower coverages of urban green spaces, this approach has several issues. The most obvious is that moving can be seen as a two-stage process: although residents may be moving for reasons primarily not related to their surroundings, once they move in a first stage they may – in a second stage – also optimise their surroundings at their destination (when moving anyway). Unfortunately, there is little we can do about this, as the SOEP does not ask respondents about secondary moving reasons. Fortunately, however, there are new developments in terms of data that allow researchers to overcome issues of reverse causality more convincingly in the future.

10.3.1   Time-variation in urban green spaces

Recently, the 2012 wave of the EUA was released, allowing researchers to estimate the effect of *changes* in urban green spaces over time on the wellbeing of residents *who do not move*. To the extent that changes in urban green spaces are *exogenous* – that is, not directly related to the wellbeing of residents (for example, through a reform that affects the presence of urban green spaces without affecting the wellbeing of residents indirectly in other ways) – identified effects on *stayers* can be interpreted as causal.

The European Environment Agency (EEA) provides three interesting datasets: first, it provides land use maps for over 300 large urban zones and their surroundings (defined as urban areas with equal to or greater than 100,000 inhabitants) for the 2006 reference year in EU27 (used in our study). Second, it provides land use maps for over 800 *functional urban areas* and their surroundings (defined as urban areas with equal to or greater than 50,000 inhabitants) for the 2012 reference year in EEA39.[13] As definitions of different types of land use have remained constant over time, both reference years can be used to calculate changes in coverages of urban green spaces over time. Finally, it provides a street tree change layer capturing changes in tree canopy along streets in selected functional urban areas, which is interesting in itself (European Environment Agency, 2018).

Time-variation in urban green spaces brings us one step closer to causality. Yet, two issues remain: land use is rather persistent over short periods of time, implying that time-variation in urban green spaces between 2006 and 2012 is likely to pick up considerable noise and measurement error. Most importantly, however, time-variation by itself does not solve reverse causality: what is ultimately needed is an instrument or exogenous variation that changes the coverage of urban green spaces around households without simultaneously affecting the wellbeing of household members. This calls for experimental or quasi-experimental approaches.

10.3.2   Field experiments and quasi-experiments

There are a few field experiments that leverage exogenous variations in urban green spaces. Most were conducted in Philadelphia, Pennsylvania, USA, which had a pioneering vacant lot greening programme. It involved removing trash, grading the land, planting new grass and some trees, installing a low wooden perimeter fence, and performing regular monthly maintenance. Branas et al. (2011) study the causal effect of vacant lot greening on crime and health outcomes, exploiting parts of this programme in which 4,436 vacant lots totalling over 725,000 square metres were greened during the period 1999 to 2008. The authors employ a difference-in-differences design, comparing treated (that is, greened) vacant lots over time with a randomly chosen number of control lots from a pool of eligible, vacant lots. They find that greening has a significant, positive effect on residents' self-reported stress and exercise in selected sections of the city while, at the same time, reducing violent crime and vandalism.[14] Respondents living around newly greened vacant lots also report perceiving their environment as safer (Garvin et al., 2013), and property prices tend to increase post-treatment (Heckert and Mennis, 2012). South et al.

---

13 Functional urban areas are territorial and functional units in which people live, work, access amenities, and interact socially. They are spatially determined based on commuting flows rather than administrative boundaries.

14 Kondo et al. (2016) confirm the crime-reducing effects of vacant lot greening at the example of the Youngstown Neighborhood Development Corporation's Lots of Green programme.

(2018) exploit the same programme and a similar study design during the period 2011 to 2014, studying the mental health of 342 community-dwelling adults, measured in terms of the Kessler-6 Psychological Distress Scale and its sub-components. The authors allocate 541 vacant lots to be treated during the study period into three groups: a greening intervention, a trash clean-up intervention, and no intervention. They find that, 18 months post-treatment, greening reduces poor mental health relative to no intervention, driven by reductions in feelings of worthlessness and depression (especially for households living below the poverty line). Interestingly, the trash clean-up intervention had no significant impact, pointing towards the importance of particular, intrinsic quality aspects of greenery for human health. Unfortunately, none of the authors studied the wellbeing impacts of vacant lot greening more directly while failing to report costs, which renders cost-benefit or cost-effectiveness analyses difficult. It is quite likely, however, that health benefits and benefits from reductions in health inequalities outweigh costs of vacant lot greening.

Field experiments like these clearly demonstrate the value in collaborating with local developers and planners to gauge random, exogenous variations in urban green spaces and overcome issues of reverse causality. To the extent that such collaborations are not possible, however, quasi-experiments may be a feasible alternative. Urban developments not directly related to creating greenery – such as the decommissioning of inner-city airports (for example, Berlin-Tempelhof), borders (for example, the Berlin Wall), or the potential abolishment of green belts – could be used to estimate causal effects of urban green spaces on residential wellbeing. To our knowledge, there exists no study exploiting such developments to date.

References

Adler, M. D., P. Dolan, and G. Kavetsos, "Would you choose to be happy? Tradeoffs between happiness and the other dimensions of life in a large population survey," *Journal of Economic Behavior & Organization*, 139, 60–73, 2017.

Ambrey, C., and C. Fleming, "Public greenspace and life satisfaction in urban Australia," *Urban Studies*, 51(6), 1290–1321, 2014.

Bateman, I. J., B. H. Day, A. P. Jones, and S. Jude, "Reducing gain–loss asymmetry: A virtual reality choice experiment valuing land use change," *Journal of Environmental Economics and Management*, 58(1), 106–118, 2009.

Bellet, C., and P. Frijters, "Big data and well-being," in: Helliwell, J., R. Layard, and J. Sachs (eds), *World Happiness Report*, New York: Sustainable Development Solutions Network, 2019.

Benjamin, D. J., O. Heffetz, M. S. Kimball, and A. Rees-Jones, "What do you think would make you happier? What do you think you would choose?", *American Economic Review*, 102(5), 2083–2110, 2012.

Benjamin, D. J., O. Heffetz, M. S. Kimball, and A. Rees-Jones, "Can marginal rates of substitution be inferred from happiness data? Evidence from residency choices," *American Economic Review*, 104(11), 3498–3528, 2014.

Bertram, C., and K. Rehdanz, "The role of urban green space for human well-being," *Ecological Economics*, 120, 139–152, 2015.

Bertram, C., J. Goebel, C. Krekel, and K. Rehdanz, "Urban land use fragmentation and human well-being," *Kiel Working Paper*, 2147, 2020.

Branas, C., R. A. Cheney, J. M. MacDonald, V. W. Tam, T. D. Jackson, and T. R. Ten Have, "A difference-in-differences analysis of health, safety, and greening vacant urban space," *American Journal of Epidemiology*, 174(11), 1296–1306, 2011.

Carson, R. T., and J. J. Louviere, "A Common Nomenclature for Stated Preference Elicitation Approaches," *Environmental and Resource Economics*, 49(4), 539–559, 2011.

Clark, A. E., S. Flèche, R. Layard, N. Powdthavee, and G. Ward, *The Origins of Happiness: The Science of Well-Being Over the Life Course*, Princeton, NJ: Princeton University Press, 2018.

Czembrowski, P., and J. Kronenberg, "Hedonic pricing and different urban green space types and sizes: Insights into the discussion on valuing ecosystem services," *Landscape and Urban Planning*, 146, 11–19, 2016.

Diener, E., E. M. Suh, R. E. Lucas, and H. L. Smith, "Subjective well-being: Three decades of progress," *Psychological Bulletin*, 125, 276–302, 1999.

Dolan, P., *Happiness by Design: Finding Pleasure and Purpose in Everyday Life*, London: Penguin, 2014.

Dolan, P., and G. Kavetsos, "Happy talk: Mode of administration effects on subjective well-being," *Journal of Happiness Studies*, 17(3), 1273–1291, 2016.

Dolan, P., and R. Metcalfe, "Measuring subjective wellbeing: Recommendations on measures for use by national governments," *Journal of Social Policy*, 41(2), 409–427, 2012.

Dowlati, Y., N. Herrmann, W. Swardfager, H. Liu, L. Sham, E. K. Reim, and K. L. Lanctot, "A meta-analysis of cytokines in major depression," *Biological Psychiatry*, 67, 446–457, 2010.

EOWEB GeoPortal, *EOWEB GeoPortal*, Online: http://geoservice.dlr.de/egp/, last accessed 15 April 2019, 2019.

European Environment Agency, *Mapping Guide for a European Urban Atlas*, Brussels: European Environment Agency, 2011.

European Environment Agency, *Copernicus Land Monitoring Service: Urban Atlas*, Online: http://www.eea.europa.eu/data-and-maps/data/copernicus-land-monitoring-service-urban-atlas, last accessed 16 April 2019, 2018.

European Space Agency, *Envisat: Earth Online*, Online: http://earth.esa.int/web/guest/missions/esa-operational-eo-missions/envisat, last accessed 14 April 2019, 2019.

Garvin, E. C., C. C. Cannuscio, and C. C. Branas, "Greening vacant lots to reduce violent crime: a randomised controlled trial," *Injury Prevention*, 19, 198–203, 2013.

Geograph, *Geograph Worldwide*, Online: http://www.geograph.org, last accessed 10 April 2019, 2019a.

Geograph, *Geograph Deutschland*, Online: http://geo-en.hlipp.de, last accessed 10 April 2019, 2019b.

Gibbons, S., S. Mourato, and G. M. Resende, "The amenity value of English nature: A hedonic price approach," *Environmental and Resource Economics*, 57(2), 175–196, 2014.

Glaeser, E. L., S. D. Kominers, M. Luca, and N. Naik, "Big data and big cities: The promises and limitations of improved measures of urban life," *Economic Inquiry*, 56(1), 114–137, 2018.

Google, *Developer Guide, Street View Static API*, Online: http://developers.google.com/maps/documentation/streetview/intro, last accessed 10 April 2019, 2019a.

Google, *Street View Static API, Usage and Billing*, Online: http://developers.google.com/maps/documentation/streetview/usage-and-billing, last accessed 10 April 2019, 2019b.

Haddad, L., A. Schaefer, F. Streit, F. Lederbogen, O. Grimm, S. Wuest, M. Deuschle, P. Kirsch, H. Tost, and A. Meyer-Lindenberg, "Brain structure correlates of urban upbringing, an environmental risk factor for schizophrenia," *Schizophrenia Bulletin*, 41(1), 115–122, 2014.

Hartig, T., G. W. Evans, L. D. Jammer, D. S. Davis, and T. Gaerling, "Tracking restoration in natural and urban field settings," *Journal of Environmental Psychology*, 23(2), 109–123, 2003.

Heckert, M., and J. Mennis, "The economic impact of greening urban vacant land: A spatial difference-in-differences analysis," *Environment and Planning A*, 44, 3010–3027, 2012.

Kahneman, D., B. L. Frederickson, C. A. Schreiber, and D. A. Redelmeier, "When more pain is preferred to less: Adding a better end," *Psychological Science*, 4(6), 401–405, 1993.

Kahneman, D., P. P. Wakker, and R. Sarin, "Back to Bentham? Explorations of experienced utility," *Quarterly Journal of Economics*, 112(2), 375–405, 1997.

Kavetsos, G., M. Dimitriadou, and P. Dolan, "Measuring happiness: Context matters," *Applied Economics Letters*, 21(5), 308–311, 2014.

Kondo, M., B. Hohl, S. Han, and C. Branas, "Effects of greening and community reuse of vacant lots on crime," *Urban Studies*, 53(15), 3279–3295, 2016.

Kong, F., H. Yin, and N. Nakagoshi, "Using GIS and landscape metrics in the hedonic price modeling of the amenity value of urban green space: A case study in Jinan City, China," *Landscape and Urban Planning*, 79(3–4), 240–252, 2007.

Krekel, C., and R. Odermatt, "Behavioural spatial economics: Utility misprediction in locational choices and spatial sorting," *mimeo*, 2019.

Krekel, C., and A. Zerrahn, "Does the presence of wind turbines have negative externalities for people in their surroundings? Evidence from well-being data," *Journal of Environmental Economics and Management*, 82, 221–238, 2017.

Krekel, C., J. Kolbe, and H. Wuestemann, "The greener, the happier? The effect of urban land use on residential well-being," *Ecological Economics*, 121, 117–127, 2016.

Kuehn, S., S. Duezel, P. Eibich, C. Krekel, H. Wuestemann, J. Kolbe, J. Martensson, J. Goebel, J. Gallinat, G. G. Wagner, and U. Lindenberger, "In search of features that constitute an 'enriched environment' in humans: Associations between geographical properties and brain structure," *Nature: Scientific Reports*, 7(11920), 1–8, 2017.

Kung, C., D. Johnston, and M. Shields, "Validating reports of poor subjective wellbeing against objective biomarkers," *mimeo*, 2019.

Kuo, F. E., M. Bacaicoa, and W. C. Sullivan, "Transforming inner-city landscapes: Trees, sense of safety, and preference," *Environment and Behavior*, 30(1), 28–59, 1998.

Law, S., C. I. Seresinhe, Y. Shen, and M. Gutierrez-Roig, "Street-frontage-net: Urban image classification using deep convolutional neural networks," *International Journal of Geographical Information Science*, 2018a.

Law, S., B. Paige, and C. Russell, "Take a look around: Using street view and satellite images to estimate house prices," *mimeo*, 2018b.

Lederbogen, F., P. Kirsch, L. Haddad, F. Streit, H. Tost, P. Schuch, S. Wuest, J. C. Pruessner, M. Rietschel, M. Deuschle, and A. Meyer-Lindenberg, "City living and urban upbringing affect neural social stress processing in humans," *Nature*, 474, 498–501, 2011.

Luechinger, S., "Valuing air quality using the life satisfaction approach," *Economic Journal*, 119(536), 482–515, 2009.

Maas, J., R. A. Verheij, P. P. Groenewegen, S. de Vries, and P. Spreeuwenberg, "Green space, urbanity, and health: How strong is the relation?," *Journal of Epidemiology and Community Health*, 60, 587–592, 2006.

MacKerron, G., and S. Mourato, "Happiness is greater in natural environments," *Global Environmental Change*, 23, 992–1000, 2013.

Mappiness, *Mappiness, the happiness mapping app*, Online: http://v1.mappiness.org.uk/, last accessed 24 March 2019, 2019a.

Mappiness, *Mappiness 2.0*, Online: http://www.mappinessapp.com/, last accessed 24 March 2019, 2019b.

Miller, A. H., and C. L. Raison, "The role of inflammation in depression: From evolutionary imperative to modern treatment target," *Nature Reviews Immunology*, 16(1), 22, 2016.

Miller, G. E., E. Chen, and E. S. Zhou, "If it goes up, must it come down? Chronic stress and the hypothalamic-pituitary-adrenocortical axis in humans," *Psychological Bulletin*, 133(1), 25–45, 2007.

Mitchell, R., and F. Popham, "Effect of exposure to natural environment on health inequalities: An observational population study," *Lancet*, 372(9650), 1655–1660, 2008.

Morancho, A. B., "A hedonic valuation of urban green areas," *Landscape and Urban Planning*, 66(1), 35–41, 2003.

Neves, F., "I was looking for a house, so I built a web scraper in Python!," Online: http://towardsdata science.com/looking-for-a-house-build-a-web-scraper-to-help-you-5ab25badc83e, last accessed 08 April 2019.

Park, B. J., Y. Tsunetsugu, T. Kasetani, T. Kagawa, and Y. Miyazaki, "The physiological effects of Shinrin-yoku (taking in the forest atmosphere or forest bathing): Evidence from field experiments in 24 forests across Japan," *Environmental Health and Preventive Medicine*, 15(18), 18–26, 2010.

Patterson, Z., J. M. Darbani, A. Rezaei, J. Zacharias, and A. Yazdizadeh, "Comparing text-only and virtual reality discrete choice experiments of neighbourhood choice," *Landscape and Urban Planning*, 157, 63–74, 2017.

Richardson, E. A., and R. Mitchell, "Gender differences in relationships between urban green space and health in the United Kingdom," *Social Science & Medicine*, 71(3), 568–575, 2010.

Roe, J. J., C. W. Thompson, P. A. Aspinall, M. J. Brewer, E. I. Duff, D. Miller, R. Mitchell, and A. Clow, "Green space and stress: Evidence from cortisol measures in deprived urban communities," *International Journal of Environmental Research and Public Health*, 10(9), 4086–4103, 2013.

Saiz, A., A. Salazar, and J. Bernard, "Crowdsourcing architectural beauty: Online photo frequency predicts building aesthetic ratings," *PLOS ONE*, 13(7), 2018.

Schwartz, N., F. Strack, D. Kommer, and D. Wagner, "Soccer, rooms, and the quality of your life: Mood effects on judgments of satisfaction with life in general and with specific domains," *European Journal of Social Psychology*, 17(1), 69–79, 1987.

Seresinhe, C. I., T. Preis, and H. S. Moat, "Quantifying the impact of scenic environments on health," *Nature: Scientific Reports*, 5, 16899, 2015.

Seresinhe, C. I., T. Preis, and H. S. Moat, "Using deep learning to quantify the beauty of outdoor places," *Royal Society Open Science*, 4(7), 2017.

Seresinhe, C. I., T. Preis, G. MacKerron, and H. S. Moat, "Happiness is greater in more scenic locations," *Nature: Scientific Reports*, 9(4498), 2019.

South, E. C., B. C. Hohl, and M. C. Kondo, "Effect of greening vacant land on mental health of community-dwelling adults: A cluster randomized trial," *Journal of the American Medical Association*, 1(3), e180298, 2018.

Streit, F., L. Haddad, T. Paul, J. Frank, A. Schaefer, J. Nikitopoulos, C. Akdeniz, F. Lederbogen, J. Treutlein, S. Witt, A. Meyer-Lindenberg, M. Rietschel, P. Kirsch, and S. Wuest, "A functional variant in the neuropeptide S receptor 1 gene moderates the influence of urban upbringing on stress processing in the amygdala," *Stress*, 17(4), 352–361, 2015.

Thompson, C. W., J. Roe, P. Aspinall, R. Mitchell, A. Clow, and D. Miller, "More green space is linked to less stress in deprived communities: Evidence from salivary cortisol patterns," *Landscape and Urban Planning*, 105(3), 221–229, 2012.

Ulrich, R. S., R. F. Simons, B. D. Losito, E. Fiorito, M. A. Miles, and M. Zelson, "Stress recovery during exposure to natural and urban environments," *Journal of Environmental Psychology*, 11(3), 201–230, 1991.

Wagner, G. G., J. R. Frick, and J. Schupp, "The German Socio-Economic Panel Study (SOEP): Scope, evolution and enhancements," *Schmollers Jahrbuch*, 127(1), 139–170, 2007.

Wagner, G. G., J. Goebel, P. Krause, R. Pischner, and I. Sieber, "Das Sozio-oekonomische Panel (SOEP): Multidisziplinäres Haushaltspanel und Kohortenstudie für Deutschland – Eine Einführung (für neue Datennutzer) mit einem Ausblick (für erfahrene Anwender)," *AStA Wirtschafts- und Sozialstatistisches Archiv*, 2(4), 301–328, 2008.

Welsch, H., "Environmental welfare analysis: A life satisfaction approach," *Ecological Economics*, 62(3–4), 544–551, 2007.

Welsch, H., and J. Kühling, "Using happiness data for environmental valuation: Issues and applications," *Journal of Economic Surveys*, 23(2), 385–406, 2009.

Welsch, H., and S. Ferreira, "Environment, well-being, and experienced preference," *International Review of Environmental and Resource Economics*, 7, 205–238, 2013.

White, M. P., I. Alcock, B. W. Wheeler, and M. H. Depledge, "Would you be happier living in a greener urban area? A fixed-effects analysis of panel data," *Psychological Science*, 24(6), 920–928, 2013.

World Data Center for Remote Sensing of the Atmosphere (WDC-RSAT), *MERIS NDVI WDC-RSAT*, Online: http://wdc.dlr.de/data_products/SURFACE/ndvi_meris.php, last accessed 14 April 2019, 2019a.

World Data Center for Remote Sensing of the Atmosphere, *MERIS Sensor WDC-RSAT*, Online: http://wdc.dlr.de/data_products/SURFACE/ndvi_meris.php, last accessed 14 April 2019, 2019b.

World Data Center for Remote Sensing of the Atmosphere, *AVHRR Sensor WDC-RSAT*, Online: http://wdc.dlr.de/sensors/avhrr/, last accessed 15 April 2019, 2019c.

Zheng, S., J. Wang, C. Sun, X. Zhang, and M. E. Kahn, "Air pollution lowers Chinese urbanites' expressed happiness on social media," *Nature: Human Behaviour*, 3, 237–243, 2019.

11 Are household borrowing constraints bad for the environment? Theory and cross-country evidence

Dana C. Andersen

11.1 Introduction

Credit market imperfections are a pervasive feature in nearly all countries, particularly less developed countries (for a survey, see Browning and Lusardi, 1996). The result is an excess of demand, or rationing, of loanable funds, which prevents firms and households from financing investments (Stiglitz and Weiss, 1981; Aghion and Bolton, 1992; among many others). Investment in human capital, in particular, is affected by credit market imperfections as human capital cannot be collateralized (Hart and Moore, 1994).[1] Because human capital is an essential precursor to the development of clean (i.e., less polluting) industries, credit market imperfections can worsen environmental performance by orienting production towards more pollution-intensive production. Overcoming credit constraints is, therefore, crucial for achieving economic growth based on advancing human capital and knowledge, which is less environmentally damaging compared to economic growth based on physical-capital accumulation.

What links credit market imperfections (henceforth credit constraints) and environmental performance? Previous research on this question has focused on the effect of credit constraints on firm investment decisions as well as general-equilibrium effects such as the number and composition of firms in the industry, abstracting from factor endowments of the economy. Andersen (2016) develops a heterogeneous-firm general-equilibrium model, demonstrating that credit constraints generate three distinct effects that bear on environmental performance. First, credit constraints preclude investment in technology upgrading, including investments in pollution abatement technologies and, more generally, investments in process or product innovation, which would increase factor intensity and decrease output. Because constraining pollution abatement choices and increasing factor intensity (e.g., energy intensity) are generally associated with an increase in emissions intensity, but a decrease in output is associated with a decrease in

---

1 That households are affected by credit constraints, even in high-income countries, is empirically supported. For example, Grant (2007) estimates that nearly one-third of households in the US are credit constrained, and that credit constraints affect young households to an even larger extent.

emissions, the effect of credit constraints on firm-level environmental performance is ambiguous (technology-upgrading effect). Second, credit constraints result in an economy consisting of smaller but generally more pollution-intensive firms (selection effect). Third, credit constraints result in an economy consisting of more numerous firms (market-size effect).[2] Because the effects of credit constraints are confounding in nature, Andersen (2016) investigates the effect of credit market reforms on aggregate country-level air-pollution concentrations, finding that reducing credit constraints significantly improves environmental performance.

While technology choice is an abstract concept that encompasses all factors that bear on the mapping between inputs and outputs (including bad outputs, such as pollution), Andersen (2017) focuses in particular on the role of credit constraints on firm-level capital-asset investment decisions and their repercussions on environmental performance. Andersen (2017) argues that tangible assets (such as buildings and structures, equipment, and natural resources) can be pledged as collateral to overcome credit constraints, whereas intangible assets (such as human capital, research and development, and marketing) tend to be inalienable and therefore cannot be pledged as collateral. An insight of the incomplete contracts literature (Williamson, 1988; Hart and Moore, 1994) is that credit constraints can be overcome by investing in assets that can be pledged as collateral, implying that firms facing more acute credit constraints will invest more in tangible assets at the expense of intangible assets. This increase in the share of tangible assets in investment has repercussions for the environment as tangible assets are generally responsible for generating pollution emissions. Using measures of firm-level pollution emissions and creditworthiness, Andersen (2017) documents empirical evidence that credit constraints significantly increase pollution emissions. Moreover, as predicted, credit constraints distort the composition of assets towards tangible assets, and tangible assets are associated with increased pollution emissions.

The aforementioned studies abstract from (hold constant) factor endowments as well as structural change, and therefore are primarily suited to investigate within-country variation in pollution over the short run. Credit constraints can, however, have more profound effects on environmental performance by bearing on factor endowments and patterns of production in the long run. In particular, because investment in human capital is acutely affected by credit constraints (Hart and Moore, 1994), credit constraints promote industries employing physical capital more intensively and human capital less intensively.[3] Credit constraints thus

---

2 That credit constraints increase the number of firms in the economy might seem counterintuitive, but is explained by the fact that *reducing* credit constraints allows a subset of marginal firms to invest in a technology upgrade and expand their scale of production, thereby crowding out smaller competitors.

3 This is evidenced, indirectly, by significant variation in returns to education across countries (Psacharopoulos and Patrinos, 2004), including remarkably high returns in developing countries to programs alleviating credit constraints (e.g., conditional cash transfers). On the other hand, physical and financial capital can be collateralized much easier and can be concentrated within firms, thereby circumventing transaction costs associated with under-developed credit markets. As a result, the marginal product of capital displays very little variation across countries after accounting for all inputs (Caselli and Feyrer, 2006).

constrain human-capital-intensive industries – such as information technology, high-tech manufacturing, fiber optics, research institutions, universities, and so on – which are generally less pollution intensive than physical-capital intensive industries (Antweiler et al., 2001; Andersen, 2017).[4]

This chapter develops a simple theoretical model by extending the two-sector, general equilibrium framework used in the trade and the environment literature to include credit constraints that bear on human-capital investment decisions. That human-capital accumulation reduces pollution in a small open economy has been theoretically demonstrated in the trade and the environment literature (Copeland and Scott Taylor, 2004). The result follows from the familiar Rybczynski theorem of international trade. Because production of dirty goods is physical-capital intensive, whereas production of clean goods is human-capital intensive (Antweiler et al., 2001; Andersen, 2017), an increase in human capital draws resources from the dirty sectors, leading to a more than proportional expansion of output in clean sectors and an absolute decline in output in dirty sectors. Thus, for a constant pollution intensity (pollution per unit of dirty good produced), an increase in human capital reduces pollution via the *composition* effect (share of dirty goods in output). An increase in human capital might also engender an endogenous policy response leading to tighter environmental regulations whenever environmental quality is a normal good, thereby reducing pollution intensity via the *technique*. Thus, credit constraints increase pollution whenever they impinge on investment in human capital.

The main prediction of the model is supported for air pollutants sulfur dioxide (SO_2) and lead, using pollution measures from the World Health Organization's Automated Meteorological Information System (AMIS) for about 150 cities in 45 countries. Following the financial development and growth literature, I use private credit as a proxy for credit constraints, as well as variation in the legal rights of creditors against defaulting debtors (bankruptcy laws) and the presence of credit bureau registries (credit market reforms). The advantage of employing private credit as a measure of credit constraints is that it aggregates all of the various sources of credit constraints, such as imperfect information and contract enforcement, into a single-dimensional measure that is consistent across countries and over time. The drawback is that, to the extent that credit is unequally distributed, private credit might be an imperfect measure of the extent to which households face credit constraints. Another concern is that private credit is determined by both exogenous and endogenous factors, and endogenous variation is a potential source of bias in the estimates.[5] The latter drawback is the primary motivation for using narrowly defined credit-market reforms, which are arguably less subject to

---

4 The growth and the environment literature emphasizes human-capital accumulation (Antweiler et al., 2001) and "knowledge" accumulation (Aghion and Howitt, 1998) as clean inputs, which allow for sustainable growth, in contrast to physical capital accumulation, which necessarily increases pollution.

5 Whether variation in private credit is endogenous is model-specific and refers to the instance of correlation between private credit and the residuals of the regression. Endogeneity concerns are discussed in Section 11.3.

endogeneity concerns. The empirical results demonstrate that credit constraints increase air pollution using a reduced-form approach and both types of measures of credit constraints, and the results are robust with respect to additional control variables and various sensitivity checks.

More broadly, this chapter is related to two areas of research. First, the Environmental Kuznets Curve (EKC) literature posits that one explanation for a potential inverted U-shaped relationship between income per capita and environmental damage is that countries grow by physical capital accumulation in their early stages of development and by human capital accumulation, which is less damaging to the environment, in later stages. Second, several recent papers have considered the relationship between financial development and environmental performance, arguing that a reduction in financing costs may stimulate environmental projects. I briefly recount these studies and highlight the important points of departure.

The EKC literature is broadly focused on the reduced-form relationship between income per capita and environmental degradation, as well as uncovering the mechanisms linking the two variables. While the literature is generally skeptical of a simple, consistent inverted U-shaped relationship between income per capita and environmental degradation – both from a theoretical and empirical point of view (Copeland and Scott Taylor, 2004; Stern, 2004, among others) – the literature has spurred greater interest in understanding why economic growth might generate heterogeneous (non-constant) effects in terms of environmental damage. The primary explanations advanced for non-constant effects in general, and the EKC hypothesis in particular, are: (1) sources of growth, (2) income effects, (3) threshold effects, and (4) increasing returns to abatement.[6] This chapter is mostly related to sources of growth explanations, which postulate that structural change transforms the composition of output from resource- and pollution-intensive goods to human-capital-intensive goods. A precursor to this transformation is, therefore, overcoming credit constraints, especially for poor countries that lack sufficient savings to finance investments. Moreover, because developing countries typically have weak property rights, imperfect contract enforcement, unstable political institutions, and underdeveloped information systems, among other problems, credit markets typically perform poorly (Banerjee and Duflo, 2005). Thus, if economic growth translates into improved institutions, which in turn reduce credit market imperfections, then economic growth achieved by increased human-capital accumulation and greater human-capital intensive production might be relatively less environmentally damaging, or even reduce environmental degradation. The focus on credit constraints is however absent in the literature, and the predictions are not necessarily identical as countries with similar income may face dissimilar credit market imperfections.

---

6 For a survey of the literature, see Copeland and Scott Taylor (2004) or Stern (2004). Examples of papers by explanation are: (1) Grossman and Krueger (1995); (2) Lopez (1994); (3) Selden and Song (1994); Stokey (1998); and (4)
 Andreoni and Levinson (2001).

A limited number of recent studies have examined the effect of financial development on environmental performance (Dasgupta et al., 2001, 2006). Dasgupta et al. show that financial markets punish environmentally damaging firms by reducing firm value in a handful of low- and middle-income countries, suggesting that equity markets confer environmental benefits (at least in part). Tamazian et al. (2009) posit that financial development reduces financing costs, including the cost of investment in environmental projects, and find that financial development and CO_2 emissions are negatively related. Similarly, Tamazian and Rao (2010) show that financial development is especially important for local and state governments as many environmental projects are undertaken by the public sector. This chapter emphasizes that financial liberalization, however, might not improve environmental performance because credit constraints might impinge on investment in human capital. This conceptual distinction is brought to bear on the empirics as well – the aforementioned papers focus on financial liberalization and financial openness, whereas this chapter focuses on credit constraints, which are more relevant to financing investments in human capital. Finally, Lopez and Islam (2011) show that fiscal spending aimed at reducing market failures, including credit market imperfections, reduces pollution, which provides indirect evidence that credit market imperfections increase pollution.[7]

The remainder of this chapter consists of a conceptual model (Section 11.2), empirical model and results (Section 11.3), and conclusion (Section 11.4).

11.2   Conceptual model

The model demonstrates that credit constraints reduce investment in human capital, which in turn promotes production of dirty goods over clean goods, thereby increasing pollution. The result is demonstrated for both exogenous and endogenous environmental policy. The result is a consequence of credit market imperfections affecting investment in human capital, and that human-capital-intensive sectors entail less pollution than physical-capital-intensive sectors (Antweiler et al., 2001).

The exposition follows the framework developed by Copeland and Scott Taylor (2004). I consider a small open economy producing two final goods (a "clean" and a "dirty" good) with physical capital and human capital as primary factors. The dirty good uses pollution as a factor of production and is physical-capital intensive (pollution can also be considered a joint output under certain conditions), whereas the clean good does not use pollution as a factor of production and is human-capital intensive.

---

7 It is not possible to assess, however, whether the empirical relationship between fiscal spending and pollution is via reducing credit market imperfections or some other channel as their definition of market failures is quite broad.

11.2.1   Production

Consider a small open economy producing two goods, X and Y, which are produced with a constant returns to scale technology using two primary factors, physical and human capital (K and L). Good Y is treated as the numeraire and p denotes the price of good X. For simplicity, production of X entails pollution, but production of Y does not. I assume pollution reduces the utility of consumers, but does not affect production.

Production of good Y is

$$Y = H(K_y, L_y)$$

where H is increasing, linearly homogenous, and concave.

For analytical convenience, pollution is treated as an input in production of good X, rather than as a joint output. Production of good X is given by

$$X = Z^{\alpha} [F(K_x, L_x)]^{1-\alpha}, 0 < \alpha < 1$$

where $Z < F$ whenever firms undertake abatement and $Z = F$ whenever abatement does not occur. Thus, $Z \leq F$. F is increasing, linearly homogeneous, and concave.

Modeling pollution emissions as an additional factor of production is conventional in the environmental economics literature. The underlying assumption is that reducing emissions entails the diversion of productive inputs towards abatement activities, thereby reducing the availability of inputs to production of the final consumption good. Incorporating abatement activities as implicit in the production process follows under certain assumptions regarding the abatement and production technologies. (See Cropper and Oates, 1992, for a discussion of the assumptions generating the result.) The conventional model has been criticized for two primary reasons that limit the applicability of the results. First, treating pollution as an input in the production process is inconsistent with the input–output framework used for national economic accounts (Leontief, 1970; Muller et al., 2011; among many others). Second, it has been criticized on the basis of incompatibility with materials balance (or conservation laws of mass and energy) (Pethig, 2006; Krysiak and Krysiak, 2003).

Because the primary aim of this chapter is to develop a simple theoretical model that yields testable reduced-form predictions, I keep the model intentionally simple, despite the above limitations.[8] While future research might employ an environmental input–output analysis that explicitly accounts for material flows of raw materials as inputs and emissions as outputs, the specific predictions of the model are

---

8 Pethig (2006: 186) highlights that "fully regarding the materials-balance principle in theoretical analysis comes at the cost of enormous additional complexity which tends to prevent the derivation of informative results."

likely to be unchanged as long as human-capital-intensive sectors entail less mate-rial requirements than physical-capital-intensive sectors. Moreover, the approach employed here would be consistent with the balance of materials principle as long as either (i) human-capital-intensive sectors employ less materials in production or (ii) emissions generated from physical-capital-intensive sectors require more intensive use of traditional inputs to convert into "abatement residuals" (Pethig, 2006).

The government taxes pollution or issues an equivalent number of pollution per-mits. Assuming some abatement is undertaken, perfect competition implies that the pollution intensity of the dirty sector is given by

$$e \equiv \frac{z}{x} = \frac{\alpha p}{\tau} < 1$$

where τ is the price of pollution permits.

Full employment of primary factors (that is, $K_y + K_x = K$ and $L_y + L_x = L$) implies that output can be expressed in terms of aggregate factor endowments and prices:

$$x = x(p, \tau, K, L) \ and \ y = y(p, \tau, K, L)$$

Moreover, perfect competition implies that national income can be expressed as the maximum value function:

$$G(p, K, L, z) = \max_{x,y} \{px + y : (x, y) \in T(K, L, z)\}$$

where T represents the feasible technology set.

11.2.2   Producer-consumers

Suppose the economy admits a representative producer-consumer with prefer-ences over consumption goods and environmental quality. Utility is homothetic and strongly separable in consumption and the environment. Without loss of gen-erality, suppose the price of good X is also normalized to unity. Indirect utility is given by

$$V(I, z) = v(I) - h(z)$$

where I represents real disposable income. As conventional, I assume that $v' > 0$, $v'' < 0$, $h' > 0$, and $h'' > 0$.

The representative agent lives for two periods. In period 0, she borrows in order to invest in human capital (schooling) and to purchase consumption goods. In period 1, she produces the two final goods using human capital determined in the previous period and a fixed supply of physical capital purchased on a spot market. Further, she repays the loan with interest and consumes her remaining income. Lifetime utility is therefore given by

$$W = v(I_0) + \rho(v(I_1) - h(z))$$

where $0 < \rho < 1$ is the discount factor. I assume all generations inherent in an exogenous level of pollution in period 0, which does not affect equilibrium choices due to strong separability of preferences. The representative agent therefore faces the following set of budget constraints:

$$I_0 = B - qL$$

$$I_1 = G(K, L, z) - (1 + r)B$$

where B represents the net asset position at the end of period 0 (borrowing), q represents the cost of investing in human capital (inverse of productivity of investment), r represents the interest rate, and G is real national income.

11.2.3 Credit constraints

The representative agent faces a borrowing constraint such that her net asset position in period 0 cannot exceed a fixed fraction of the present value income. That is,

$$B \leq \theta \frac{G(K, L, z)}{1 + r}$$

Maximization with respect to borrowing therefore implies

$$\frac{\partial v}{\partial I_0} = \rho \frac{\partial v}{\partial I_1} (1 + r) + \lambda_B$$

where $\lambda_B \geq 0$ is the shadow value of borrowed assets. In comparison, the optimal unconstrained ($\lambda_B = 0$) borrowing satisfies

$$\frac{\partial v}{\partial \tilde{I}_0} = \rho \frac{\partial v}{\partial \tilde{I}_1} (1 + r)$$

where tilde represents the unconstrained optimal. It is straightforward to show that $\lambda_B > 0$ implies $I_0/I_1 < \tilde{I}_0/\tilde{I}_1$. That is, the ratio of disposable income in period 0 to period 1 is less for credit-constrained individuals. To derive sharp results for the effect of credit constraints on investment in human capital, additional structure is required.

11.2.4 Producer-consumer assumptions

A1: The credit constraint is binding: $\lambda_B > 0$.

A2: The elasticity of marginal utility with respect to income is greater than unity: $-\frac{v''}{v'} I \geq 1$.

Assumption A1 is necessary for credit constraints to be binding, and assumption A2 is generally supported by empirical evidence (Layard et al., 2008). I assume that the representative agent treats factor prices and the credit constraint as exogenous (investing in human capital does not relax her credit constraint).

Because the credit constraint is binding, we can substitute $B = \theta G/(1+r)$ and solve for the optimal credit-constrained investment in human capital directly. Thus, the first order condition for an interior solution is given by

$$q\frac{\partial v}{\partial I_0} = \frac{\partial v}{\partial I_1}(1-\theta)w$$

where the wage rate of human capital is the first derivative of the national income function with respect to human capital $w = G_L$.

Result 1: *Investment in human capital is decreasing to the extent that households are credit constrained.*

Proof: Using the envelope theorem implies:

$$\frac{dL}{d\theta} = \frac{-q\dfrac{\partial^2 v}{\partial I_0^2}\dfrac{G}{1+r} + \rho w\left[-I_1\dfrac{\partial^2 v}{\partial I_1^2} - \dfrac{\partial v}{\partial I_1}\right]}{\mathcal{H}} > 0$$

where $\mathcal{H} > 0$ by the second order condition.

Result 1 follows from concavity of indirect utility and assumption A2. Thus, Result 1 implies $L \equiv L(\theta)$ is an increasing function of θ.

11.2.5   Pollution with exogenous environmental policy

In this section, I consider the effect of credit constraints on pollution via investment in human capital holding environmental policy constant. That is, I assume that environmental policy does not endogenously change in response to changes in credit constraints (that is, $\tau = \bar{\tau}$). While this is a useful benchmark, optimal environmental policy is generally dependent on credit constraints, and the subsequent section accounts for an endogenous environmental policy response. Because environmental policy is exogenous, pollution can be decomposed into the so-called "scale" and "composition" effects according to the following expression:

$$z = \bar{e}GS$$

where G is real national income (scale effect), and $S = x/G$ is the income share of industries producing good X (composition effect). Because the price of pollution permits is constant the emission intensity is also a fixed parameter, $\bar{e}$. Thus, a percentage change in pollution can be represented as

$$\hat{z} = \hat{G} + \hat{S}$$

where $\hat{z} = \frac{dz}{z}$ and so on. The following assumption drives the main result.

Production assumption A3: Sector X is capital-intensive relative to sector $Y = K_x/L_x > K_y/L_y$.

Again, assumption A3 is strongly supported by empirical evidence (Antweiler et al., 2001).

Result 2: *Under an exogenous environmental policy, pollution is decreasing in human capital and therefore increasing to the extent that households are credit constrained.*

Proof: By the Rybczynski theorem, an increase in human capital stimulates the human-capital-intensive sector, drawing factors from the dirty sector to the clean sector. That is,

$$\hat{z} = \in_{xL}\hat{L} < 0$$

where $\in_{xL} < 0$ is the elasticity of output of good X with respect to human capital.

Using that $\hat{G} = s_L \hat{L} + s_z \hat{z}$, where s_L represents the labor's share of national income and s_z represents pollution's share, the reduced-form relationship between pollution and income is given by

$$\hat{z} = \frac{\in_{xL}}{s_L + s_z \in_{xL}} \hat{G}$$

where the term $s_L + s_z \in_{xL}$ represents the elasticity of national income with respect to human capital, which is positive. That is, an increase in human capital decreases pollution and thus decreases income, but the net effect of an increase in human capital is strictly positive.

11.2.6   Pollution with endogenous environmental policy

In this section, I consider the effect of credit constraints, allowing for an endogenous policy response. That is, I assume that environmental policy is chosen to maximize utility and thus is adjusted in response to changes in credit constraints. A well-known result in the environmental economics literature (Lopez, 1994) is that marginal national income from an increase in pollution should equal the marginal rate of substitution between pollution and income (that is, marginal damages in terms of income). That is,

$$G_z = MD(p, I, z)$$

where $MD = h'/v'$. Moreover, perfect competition implies that aggregate pollution satisfies $\tau = G_z$.

Result 3: *Under an endogenous environmental policy, pollution is decreasing in human capital and therefore increasing in the extent that households are credit constrained.*

Proof: Using the envelope theorem implies

$$\frac{dz}{dL} = \frac{G_{zl} - MD_I G_L}{MD_I G_z + MD_z - G_{zz}} < 0$$

where subscript denotes partial derivatives. The denominator is positive by the second order condition.[9] The first term in the numerator represents the marginal change in the price of pollution permits with respect to human capital, that is, $G_{zl} = \frac{\partial \tau}{\partial L}$. Recall an increase in human capital diverts resource from the dirty sector by the Rybczynski theorem, which implies that the demand for pollution permits falls. The downward shift in the demand for pollution permits implies that the optimal price of pollution permits falls, $G_{zl} < 0$. Concavity of utility with respect to income and convexity with respect to pollution implies $MD_I > 0$ and $G_L = w > 0$. Thus, the numerator is strictly negative.

While Section 11.2.5 analyzed the effect of credit constraints on pollution under exogenous environmental policy and Section 11.2.6 analyzed the effect under fully endogenous environmental policy, empirically it is likely that the effect is somewhere between these two cases, at least in the short run. The reason is that environmental policy is likely to be persistent and it might take several years to adjust from one equilibrium to another. The two scenarios are therefore useful to bound the true effect of credit constraints, and to highlight that the magnitude of the long-run effect is likely to be larger than the short-run effect.

11.3   Empirical analysis

11.3.1   Empirical model

Results 1–3 motivate the empirical analysis. Result 1 demonstrates that credit constraints reduce investment in human capital. Results 2 and 3 demonstrate that human capital is negatively related to pollution, given exogenous and endogenous policy responses, respectively. Pollution is therefore given by

$$z = z(L(\theta), K)$$

where θ represents credit constraints, L is human capital, and K is physical capital. Results 1–3 imply that

$$\frac{dz}{d\theta} = \frac{\partial z}{\partial L}\frac{dL}{d\theta} < 0$$

---

9   This can be easily verified. MD_I is positive since $v'' < 0$ and similarly MD_z is positive since $h'' > 0$. Finally, concavity of the national income with respect to factor inputs is a standard result for income functions.

Recall that an increase in θ represents a relaxation of the borrowing constraint. Thus, a negative relationship implies that credit constraints increase pollution. The expression above implies that credit constraints affect pollution only via investment in human capital. The empirical analysis, however, adopts a more general framework, allowing credit constraints to affect pollution via various other channels besides human capital. Two reasons motivate this generalization. First, conventional measures of human capital, which are based on the average educational attainment of the adult population, are only partial measures of human capital. For example, the quality of education, as well as the health of the population, is also an important factor of human capital. Credit constraints might therefore be related to unobservable components of human capital, which in turn affect pollution. In other words, the effect of unobservable components of human capital might be reflected in the effect of credit constraints on pollution. Second, credit constraints might influence pollution through various other channels besides human capital. Examples include credit constraints affecting consumption choices, such as investment in durable goods. Thus, I do not rule out the possibility of a partial effect of credit constraints on pollution, which might be positive or negative. That is:

$$\frac{dz}{d\theta} = \frac{\partial z}{\partial \theta} + \frac{\partial z}{\partial L}\frac{dL}{d\theta}$$

Thus the following linear estimation model is employed:

1. $\ln z_{ijt} = \zeta \ln \theta_{jt} + \psi \ln L_{jt} + \chi'_{ijt}\Gamma + v_{ij} + \eta_t + \varepsilon_{ijt}$

where i indexes pollution site station, j indexes country, and t indexes year. The parameters ζ and ψ represent constant elasticities. The variable z_{ijt} is pollution concentration (SO_2 and lead) at site i, in country j, at time t; θ_{jt} is credit constraints in country j at time t; χ'_{ijt} is a vector of controls at site i, in country j, at time t; v_{ij} is a site-specific effect (random or fixed); η_t is a common year effect (dummy); and ε_{ijt} is a random error component.

Specification 1 isolates the impact of credit constraints on pollution for a given level of human capital, and the impact of human capital on pollution for given levels of credit constraints. Because credit constraints impinge on investment in human capital (Lochner and Monge-Naranjo, 2011), a negative relationship between human capital and pollution (ψ) suggests that reducing credit constraints reduces pollution via investment in human capital. A negative partial effect of reducing credit constraints on pollution (ζ) therefore indicates that the total effect of reducing credit constraints on pollution is negative. The subsequent sections demonstrate that, in fact, the partial effect of reducing credit constraints is negative.

While the objective of the theoretical and empirical analyses is to isolate the effects of credit constraints – both directly via (i) changes in human capital and in turn the composition of production, and indirectly via (ii) changes in environmental regulations and in turn the composition of production and the intensity of emissions within industries – there are certainly many other factors relevant to human capital accumulation, sectoral composition, and environmental regulations. For example, human capital depends not only on the incentives and constraints facing households but also on public investment in human capital, including the supply of education, job training, and health insurance and services. Governments also play a role in shaping patterns of production by encouraging, sometimes to a significant degree, certain industries over others. For example, many countries have pursued, with varying degrees of success, economic development based on promoting industries in which they have a comparative advantage (export-led growth). Policies bearing on the composition of production range from subsidies and tax advantages to specific industries (e.g., agriculture and natural resources) to investment in research and development and important infrastructure (e.g., medicines and communications). While the model and empirics do not directly grapple with these issues, the general insights of this chapter have broader policy implications, which are highlighted in the Conclusion.

11.3.2   Data

This section discusses the primary variables used. See Appendix Table 11A.1 for a complete list of sources and brief descriptions.

11.3.2.1   Credit constraints

Two complementary approaches are used to investigate the impact of credit constraints on the environment. First, private credit is used as a proxy for credit constraints. Private credit is the value of deposit money banks credit to the private sector.[10] This measure includes credit to the private sector, as opposed to credit to governments, public enterprises, and central banks. While private credit does not directly measure credit constraints, several studies have interpreted private credit as a measure of financial intermediary development, including the mitigation of information and transaction costs and credit constraints. For example, private credit is a standard indicator in the financial development and growth literature, and several studies have demonstrated that countries with higher levels of private credit experience faster economic growth and reduced poverty (Beck et al., 2000, 2009). The data are from Beck et al. (2009) and are maintained by the World Bank for the years 1960 to 2010 for almost all country-years with air pollution data.

Second, following the theoretical literature on credit constraints, proxies for the "power" of creditors and informational asymmetries are used. Theories of credit constraints advance two main explanations. First, lenders will be reluctant to lend to potential borrowers whenever their power to force repayment is circumscribed (Townsend, 1979; Aghion and Bolton, 1992; Hart and Moore, 1994).[11] The legal rights of creditors are an indicator variable indicating whether "secured creditors

---

10 The results are nearly identical using private credit from both deposit money banks and non-financial institutions.

11 The cited studies are the pioneering theoretical contributions. The literature is quite large and there are many more studies, both empirical and theoretical.

are able to seize their collateral after the petition for reorganization is approved" (Djankov et al., 2007: 302). These bankruptcy laws were originally investigated by La Porta et al. (1997, 1998), and were significantly expanded and updated by Djankov et al. (2007). Credit registries provide information on a borrower's credit history and current indebtedness to lenders. Jappelli and Pagano (2002) show that credit registries are important determinants of credit availability. Because the value of credit agencies increases over time as additional years of credit histories are amassed and trust is consolidated, the number of years elapsed since the establishment of a nation's credit agency is employed as a proxy variable. The number of years squared is also used to reflect diminishing marginal value over time.

11.3.2.2 Air pollution

Because the theoretical model is applicable to production-generated pollution, I focus on pollution emanating from production rather than pollution emanating from consumption. Lopez et al. (2011) show that among air pollutants with consistent data (sulfur dioxide, lead, ozone, volatile organic compounds, and carbon monoxide), sulfur dioxide (SO_2) and lead are the main air pollutants generated from production sources.[12] The majority of SO_2 and lead pollution is generated as a by-product of electricity generation and industrial processes.

Data for air pollution (SO_2 and lead) are from the World Health Organization's Automated Meteorological Information System (WHO-AMIS), which is provided by the US Environmental Protection Agency (EPA). This data set has been used extensively in the literature, and provides the most consistent measures of air pollution across countries and time. The data span from 1986 to 1999, and include 44 countries and 321 sites for SO_2 and 36 countries and 154 sites for lead. See Table 11A.2 for the list of countries included.

11.3.2.3 Additional covariates

This chapter follows Lopez and Islam (2011) for choosing the remaining proxy variables. Investment as a percentage of GDP is used as a proxy for physical capital, household consumption per capita for the income effect, GDP per land area for the scale effect, and an index of trade policy openness for the price index. Because there is no consistent data for the price of pollution, several indices of political institutions are used as proxies, including an index of democracy (Polity IV database) and regime stability (number of years since last regime change). GDP per capita growth controls for the capacity of institutions to adapt to a growing economy. Additional controls are discussed in the sensitivity analysis.

While the estimates of the additional covariates are interesting in their own right, the primary purpose of their inclusion is to isolate the effect of credit constraints on

---

12 Lopez et al. (2011) calculate the share of pollution emanating from (1) production, (2) consumption, or (3) both. The break-down for SO_2 is 80%, 2%, and 18%, whereas lead is 56%, 0%, and 44%.

the environment by accounting for potential confounding factors. Due to concerns regarding measurement error of the proxies, reverse causality, and omitted variables, the estimates of the covariates are likely to contain at least some degree of bias. The scale effect is likely to be particularly biased as a consequence of GDP reflecting both the production of goods and the economic value of economic activity aimed at mitigating or coping with environmental damages. For example, if a 1 percent increase in the production of goods leads to a 1 percent increase in pollution, then the true scale effect is unit elastic. However, the 1 percent increase in pollution will generally spur economic activity aimed at mitigating pollution damages, such as increased spending on medical services, environmental remediation, and so on. As a consequence, because these mitigation activities are counted in GDP, the empirical estimate of the scale effect will be less than the true scale effect.

11.3.2.4   Summary statistics

Table 11A.3 presents the summary statistics for the main variables of interest, and Table 11A.4 presents the mean values for all variables by private credit quartile.[13] For example, the first column represents the mean values for all variables with private credit less than the first quartile of the distribution. The values for private credit represent the mean of the quartile (not the quartile cut-offs). From Table 11A.4, air pollution and human capital are increasing in private credit from the lowest quartile to the second quartile and then monotonically decreasing to the highest quartile.

Creditor Rights is a dummy variable indicating whether creditors can legally seize their collateral, and Credit Bureau is the number of years since the establishment of a credit bureau registry. For the lowest private credit quartile, 28 percent of countries have creditor rights, whereas 69 percent of countries have creditor rights for the highest quartile. Similarly, credit bureau appears to be strongly related to private credit. Among the countries in the sample, seven do not have credit bureau registries at any point during span of the sample. Finally, private credit appears to be positively related to GDP per capita and positively related to the quality of political institutions.

11.3.3   Results

The baseline empirical specification is estimated using Ordinary Least Squares (OLS), Random Site Effects (RSE), and Fixed Site Effects (FSE) for SO_2 and lead. RSE and FSE control for unobservable site characteristics (random and fixed effects).

Tables 11A.5 and 11A.6 present the coefficient estimates for the dependent variables lead and SO_2 concentration, respectively. Specifications (1)–(3) use private credit as variation in credit constraints, whereas specification (4) uses proxies for

---

13 Quartile refers to blocks of 25% of the data.

credit constraints. As mentioned, the proxy variables include an indicator variable for whether creditors are permitted to seize their collateral after bankruptcy (Creditor Rights) and the number of years elapsed since the establishment of a credit bureau registry (Credit Bureau).

Recall the number of sites measuring lead is significantly smaller than the number of sites measuring SO_2, and the samples are not strictly nested. The R-squared is commensurate with previous studies, demonstrating that the goodness-of-fit is satisfactory in all specifications. The R-squared appears higher for the lead model, which might be due to a number of factors. The RSE over identification test casts doubt on the random effects orthogonality assumptions; thus, FSE results are perhaps more reliable.

As predicted by the model, the estimates for human capital are negative and significant at conventional significance levels, with the exception of the OLS specifications. Due to unobservable characteristics across both countries and sites, OLS estimates are likely to suffer from severe bias. The human capital estimates for lead are all significant at the 1 percent level, with the exception of one specification which is significant at the 5 percent level. Moreover, the human capital estimates for SO_2 are all significant at the 1 percent level. The estimates for human capital in the FSE specification range between -1.6 and -3.1 for lead, and between -0.7 and -0.9 for SO_2 concentration.

Using specification (3), the interpretation of the FSE estimates for human capital imply that an increase in the human capital index by 1 unit reduces lead and SO_2 pollution concentrations by 160 and 70 percent, respectively. Moreover, an increase in human capital by one standard deviation reduces lead and SO_2 pollution concentrations by approximately 0.54 and 0.22 standard deviations at the mean. The estimates therefore indicate that human capital is an important determinant of air pollution, both in terms of statistical significance and quantitative magnitude.

Similarly, the estimates for private credit are negative and significant at all conventional significance levels, with the exception of the OLS estimates and the RSE estimates for SO_2 concentration. Specification (3) implies that a 10 percent increase in private credit reduces lead and SO_2 concentrations by 6.8 and 2.4 percent, respectively. Moreover, an increase in private credit by one standard deviation reduces lead and SO_2 pollution concentration by approximately 1.38 and 0.49 standard deviations at the mean, respectively. Thus, the estimates indicate that private credit is an important determinant of air pollution.

The estimates for creditor rights are mostly insignificant, whereas the estimates for credit bureau are negative and significant at all significance levels. The squared term is positive, as expected from decreasing marginal value over time, but only significant in one specification. That creditor rights is insignificant can be interpreted in a number of ways. One interpretation is that credit constraints are not, in fact, determined by the particular bankruptcy laws considered. Another interpretation is that bankruptcy laws are relevant to credit constraints only insofar as credit constraints impinge on investment in human capital. In other words, the impact of credit constraints on pollution is only via investment in human capital. Thus, credit constraints do not influence pollution after controlling for the level of human capital.

The estimates of the remaining variables are mostly consistent with the literature, but very few are significant after controlling for fixed effects. The estimates for GDP to land size (proxy for the scale effect) in the FSE specifications are mostly positive and significant as expected, although one is negative and several are insignificant. The estimates for household consumption (proxy for income effect) are positive and significant in several specifications, contrary to expectations.[14] The political economy variables indicate that greater democracy and stability are associated with less pollution; however, the relationship is not particularly robust. The remaining variables do not appear to be significant or have contradictory signs.

11.3.3.1   Seemingly unrelated regressions (SURE)

While the model can be estimated equation-by-equation for lead and SO_2, the estimates are in general not as efficient when the error terms are correlated, which suggests employing seemingly unrelated regression equation (SURE) estimations. Because the number of site-year observations with both lead and SO_2 data are limited, the efficiency gained from employing SURE may not outweigh the efficiency loss due to restricting the sample. This sample restriction might also exacerbate selection bias.

Table 11A.7 presents the estimates using SURE. Because each equation contains exactly the same set of regressors, the coefficients should not change from the equation-by-equation estimates. Similar to the equation-by-equation estimations, all of the estimates for private credit and credit constraint proxies are negative and significant at the 1 percent level, with the exception of one estimate, which is significant at the 5 percent level. The estimates for human capital, especially for SO_2, are significantly larger using SURE, which is purely a consequence of selection bias, whereas the estimates for private credit are relatively unchanged.

11.3.4   Sensitivity analysis

While the FSE estimations control for time-invariant unobservable site characteristics, the presence of time-varying omitted variables could bias the estimated coefficients. To mitigate omitted variable bias, this chapter employs a procedure referred to as added controls. The added controls approach (Altonji et al., 2005) employs several sets of additional control variables in turn to reduce the possibility of omitted variable bias. The controls chosen need not be directly related to the

---

14 Lopez and Islam (2011) also find a positive income effect.

dependent variable, but should be correlated with omitted variables. An increase in the goodness-of-fit of the model with added controls, while maintaining consistent estimates of the variables of interest, reduces the likelihood of bias due to omitted variables.

Because inequality exacerbates credit market imperfections (Aghion et al., 1999), heterogeneous effects are explored by income GINI coefficients.[15] This serves as both a robustness check and as a further avenue of exploration. Finally, I employ iteratively reweighted least squares (IRWLS) to mitigate the influence of outliers.

11.3.4.1   *Added controls*

Several studies find that political institutions (Deacon, 2009), financial development (Tamazian et al., 2009), and demography and income (Copeland and Scott Taylor, 2004) are related to pollution, either as a consequence of promoting economic development or the provision of environmental services.[16] The added controls sensitivity analysis introduces a set of control variables for each of the aforementioned determinants in turn.

The variables included in the political institutions controls (*Governance*) include a nation's Polity score, which is a standard measure of governance ranging from -10 (most autocratic) to $+10$ (most democratic) and a dummy for proportional representation. Foreign direct investment (FDI) and deposit bank assets (*Finance*) are associated with economic performance in general and investment in particular, but are not directly related to credit constraints. Finally, GDP per capita (additional proxy for income), life expectancy at birth, population, and urbanization rates (*Demography and Income*) are likely correlated with household characteristics, such as environmental and consumption preferences, which affect pollution emanating from consumption rather than pollution emanating from production.

Table 11A.8 reports the estimates for private credit using the baseline FSE specification and added sets of controls.[17] Note that adding additional controls reduces the number of observations due to missing variables, which might exacerbate selection bias. In all specifications, the added controls increase the goodness-of-fit (adjusted R-squared), although only modestly.[18] The estimates for human capital are negative and significant at conventional significance levels (ranging between 1 percent and 10 percent significance levels). The estimates for private credit are negative and

---

15 Aghion et al. (1999) survey the literature on inequality and growth. One possible explanation, among many, for the result is that human-capital formation depends on fixed factors, and therefore exhibits diminishing returns.

16 Demography and income are related to the EKC literature, which was discussed in the introduction. Copeland and Scott Taylor (2004) provides a survey of the literature.

17 The results are similar using the proxies for credit constraints (not reported). The sensitivity analysis employs the identical set of controls as the FSE specification reported in Tables 11A.5 and 11A.6.

18 The adjusted R^2 without added controls varies across specifications because the estimations are performed only on the observations without missing data for the added controls. Thus, the comparison of the adjusted R^2 is for identical samples.

significant at the 1 percent significance level, except in one specification, which is significant at the 10 percent significance level.

11.3.4.2   Further robustness checks

Table 11A.9 reports estimates using IRWLS and exploring heterogeneous effects. IRWLS mitigates the influence of outliers using a maximum likelihood estimator for a general linear model. The estimates for human capital and credit are significant at conventional significance levels. Next, private credit is interacted with a dummy for sites in countries with income GINI coefficients above the median in 1980, which estimates the elasticity of pollution for sites in countries with income inequality above and below the median.[19] The estimated elasticities for private credit for SO_2 and lead concentrations in countries with income inequality below the median are -0.27 and -0.29, whereas the elasticity for countries with income inequality above the median are -0.39 and -0.94, respectively. The SO_2 estimate for countries with income inequality above the median is significant at all conventional significance levels but it is not significantly different from the estimate for countries with income inequality below the median. The lead estimate for countries above the median is significant at all significance levels, and is significantly different from the coefficient estimate for countries below the median. Thus, the impact of private credit on pollution is more than double in countries with higher income inequality for lead concentration.

11.4   Conclusion

In this chapter, a simple theoretical model is developed wherein credit constraints impinge on investment in human capital, which in turn orients production towards sectors employing pollution more intensively. Moreover, the effect of credit constraints on the environment is reinforced by endogenous environmental policies, which offset the reduction in human capital by devoting fewer resources to abatement. Thus credit constraints increase pollution emissions, with potentially larger long-run effects.

The main insight of the model is explored using production-generated air pollution concentrations (SO_2 and lead concentration), measured at over 250 sites across both low- and high-income countries. The results suggest that credit constraints increase pollution via investment in human capital as well as other channels. These results pass a battery of sensitivity analysis using a rich set of added controls, seemingly unrelated equation estimations, and various other sensitivity checks.

It should be highlighted that no one piece of evidence should be interpreted as definitive evidence of a causal relationship between credit constraints and

---

19 If a nation's income GINI coefficient is unavailable in 1980, the first available year is used. Most countries do not have annual data for this variable (it is typically calculated from census data); thus, the effect of income inequality cannot be identified in models employing fixed effects.

environmental performance. In contrast to previous studies that abstract from factor endowments, estimating the relationship between credit constraints and factor endowments, and in turn environmental performance, is admittedly more ambitious and difficult to tackle. The aim of this chapter is both to build on previous theoretical and empirical work on credit constraints and the environment and to provide suggestive evidence of a more far-reaching role of credit constraints in shaping long-run environmental performance.

This chapter points to several new directions for future research. First, the model was kept intentionally simple for tractability and to focus attention on the key issues. Future research might embed these issues into a more general framework, such as an environmental input–output model that explicitly accounts for material flows of raw materials. Moreover, to enrich the policy insights of the analysis, the model might consider a broader set of policy instruments, such as public investment in education (e.g., schooling) to overcome household credit constraints, or policies aimed at promoting the development of human-capital-intensive (or green) industries (e.g., differential corporate tax rates or R&D subsidies).

Second, on the empirical side, there remain several areas with significant room for improvement. The empirical analysis employed proxies of credit constraints, which are consistent measures of credit constraints available across countries and over time. Future research might overcome concerns regarding endogeneity and measurement error by exploiting policy changes that narrowly focused on reducing credit constraints for financing investments in human capital, such as variation in student-loan eligibility or generosity. Moreover, future research might attempt to unpack the reduced-form relationship between credit constraints and the environment by investigating the relationship between factor endowments and structural change, and the relationship between structural change and the environment. Moreover, extending the theoretical model along the lines described above and estimating the model's structural parameters would permit uncovering these intermediate relationships, as well as providing a basis for doing counterfactual policy analysis.

I conclude this chapter by highlighting several important implications of the results. If credit constraints are important determinants of environmental quality, then it is possible that reducing credit market imperfections promotes both economic development and reduced environmental degradation. A crucial caveat is that reforms must overcome credit market imperfections affecting investment in human capital, which are typically more difficult to overcome. Increasing capital inflows through financial market liberalization might have the opposite effect on the environment if the majority of households are unable to access credit. While this chapter does not directly grapple with broader policy instruments that might overcome some of the distortions associated with credit constraints, the findings suggest that policies aimed at promoting human capital or the development of human-capital-intensive industries might be effective at promoting development in a way that is less environmentally damaging than development based on physical capital accumulation.

References

Aghion, Philippe and Patrick Bolton (1992), An incomplete contracts approach to financial contracting. *Review of Economic Studies*, 59(3):473–494.

Aghion, Philippe and Peter Howitt (1998), *Endogenous Growth Theory*. Cambridge, MA: MIT Press.

Aghion, Philippe, Eve Caroli, and Cecilia Garcia-Penalosa (1999), Inequality and economic growth: the perspective of the new growth theories. *Journal of Economic Literature*, 37(4):1615–1660.

Andersen, Dana C. (2016), Credit constraints, technology upgrading, and the environment. *Journal of the Association of Environmental and Resource Economists* 3(2):283–319.

Andersen, Dana C. (2017), Do credit constraints favor dirty production? Theory and plant-level evidence. *Journal of Environmental Economics and Management* 84(C):189–208.

Andreoni, James and Arik Levinson (2001), The simple analytics of the environmental Kuznets curve. *Journal of Public Economics*, 80(2):269–286.

Antweiler, Werner, Brian R. Copeland, and Scott M. Taylor (2001), Is free trade good for the environment? *American Economic Review*, 91(4):877–908.

Banerjee, Abhijit and Esther Duflo (2005), Growth theory through the lens of development, in Philippe Aghion and Steven Durlauf (eds), *Handbook of Economic Growth*, vol. 1. Amsterdam: Elsevier, pp. 473–552.

Beck, Thorsten, Ross Levine, and Norman Loayza (2000), Finance and the sources of growth. *Journal of Financial Economics*, 58:261–300.

Beck, Thorsten, Asli Demirgüç-Kunt, and Ross Levine (2009), *Financial Institutions and Markets across Countries and over Time: Data and Analysis*. Washington, DC: World Bank.

Browning, Martin and Annamaria Lusardi (1996), Household saving: micro theories and micro facts. *Journal of Economic Literature*, 34(4):1797–1855.

Caselli, Francesco and James Feyrer (2006), The marginal product of capital. Paper presented at 7th Jacques Polak Annual Research Conference.

Copeland, Brian R. and M. Scott Taylor (2004), Trade, growth, and the environment. *Journal of Economic Literature*, 42(1):7–71.

Cropper, Maureen L. and Wallace E. Oates (1992), Environmental economics: a survey. *Journal of Economic Literature*, 30(2):675–740.

Dasgupta, Susmita, Benoit Laplante, and Nlandu Mamingi (2001), Pollution and capital markets in developing countries. *Journal of Environmental Economics and Management*, 42(3):310–335.

Dasgupta, Susmita, Jong Ho Hong, Benoit Laplante, and Nlandu Mamingi (2006), Disclosure of environmental violations and stock market in the Republic of Korea. *Ecological Economics*, 58(4):759–777.

Djankov, Simeon, Caralee McLiesh, and Andrei Shleifer (2007), Private credit in 129 countries. *Journal of Financial Economics*, 84(2):299–329.

Grant, Charles (2007), Estimating credit constraints among US households. *Oxford Economic Papers*, 59(4):583–605.

Grossman, Gene M. and Alan B. Krueger (1995), Economic growth and the environment. *Quarterly Journal of Economics*, 110(2):353–377.

Hall, Robert E. and Charles I. Jones (1999), Why do some countries produce so much more output per worker than others? *Quarterly Journal of Economics*, 114(1):83–116.

Hart, Oliver and John Moore (1994), A theory of debt based on the inalienability of human capital. *Quarterly Journal of Economics*, 109(4):841–879.

Jappelli, Tullio and Marco Pagano (2002), Information sharing, lending and defaults: cross-country evidence. *Journal of Banking & Finance*, 26(10):2017–2045.

Krysiak, Frank and Daniela Krysiak (2003), Production, consumption, and general equilibrium with physical constraints. *Journal of Environmental Economics and Management*, 46(3):513–538.

La Porta, Rafael, Florencio Lopez-de Silanes, Andrei Shleifer, and Robert Vishny (1997), Legal determinants of external finance. *Journal of Finance*, 52(3):1131–1150.

La Porta, Rafael, Florencio Lopez-de Silanes, Andrei Shleifer, and Robert W. Vishny (1998), Law and finance. *Journal of Political Economy*, 106(6):1113–1155.

Layard, R., G. Mayraz, and S. Nickell (2008), The marginal utility of income. *Journal of Public Economics*, 92(8–9):1846–1857.

Lochner, Lance and Alexander Monge-Naranjo (2011), The nature of credit constraints and human capital. *American Economic Review*, 101(6):2487–2529.

Lopez, Ramon (1994), The environment as a factor of production: the effects of economic growth and trade liberalization. *Journal of Environmental Economics and Management*, 27(2):163–184.

Lopez, Ramon, Gregmar I. Galinato, and Asif Islam (2011), Fiscal spending and the environment: Theory and empirics. *Journal of Environmental Economics and Management*, 62(2):180–198.

Pethig, Rüdiger (2006), Non-linear production, abatement, pollution and materials balance reconsidered. *Journal of Environmental Economics and Management*, 51(2):185–204.

Psacharopoulos, George and Harry Anthony Patrinos (2004), Returns to investment in education: a further update. *Education Economics*, 12(2):111–134.

Selden, Thomas M. and Daqing Song (1994), Environmental Quality and development: is there a Kuznets curve for air pollution emissions? *Journal of Environmental Economics and Management*, 27(2):147–162.

Stern, David I. (2004), The rise and fall of the environmental Kuznets curve. *World Development*, 32(8):1419–1439.

Stiglitz, Joseph E. and Andrew Weiss (1981), Credit rationing in markets with imperfect information. *American Economic Review*, 71(3):393–410.

Stokey, Nancy L. (1998), Are there limits to growth? *International Economic Review*, 39(1):1–31.

Tamazian, Artur and B. Bhaskara Rao (2010), Do economic, financial and institutional developments matter for environmental degradation? Evidence from transitional economies. *Energy Economics*, 32(1):137–145.

Tamazian, Artur, Juan Piñeiro Chousa, and Krishna Chaitanya Vadlamannati (2009), Does higher economic and financial development lead to environmental degradation? Evidence from BRIC countries. *Energy Policy*, 37(1):246–253.

Townsend, Robert M. (1979), Optimal contracts and competitive markets with costly state verification. *Journal of Economic Theory*, 21(2):265–293.

Williamson, Oliver E. (1988), Corporate finance and corporate governance. *Journal of Finance*, 43(3):567–591.

Appendix

Table 11A.1   Variable descriptions and sources

Variable	Description	Available	Source
SO$_2$	Sulfur dioxide concentration, micrograms per cubic meter	1986–1999	WHO-AMIS
Lead	Lead, micrograms per cubic meter	1986–1999	WHO-AMIS
Human Capital	Human Capital Index (methodology by Hall and Jones, 1999)	1960–2010	Barro and Lee (2010)
Credit	National private credit by deposit money banks	1960–2010	Beck and Demirgüç-Kunt (2012)
Investment	Gross capital formation	1950–2010	Penn World Tables (2012)
Government Consumption	Share of government consumption expenditures	1950–2010	Penn World Tables (2012)
Household Consumption	Market value of all final goods and services purchased by households and imputed rents	1960–2010	World Bank, World Development Indicators (WDI)
Growth GDP	Real GDP per capita growth in 2005 $	1960–2010	WDI
Ratio GDP to Land Area	Ratio of GDP per capita to land area (km^2)	1960–2010	WDI
Openness Index	Exports + imports as percentage of GDP	1950–2010	Penn World Tables
Index of Democracy	Index composed of competitiveness of political participation, openness, and competitiveness of executive recruitment, and constraints on chief executive (additive 11-point scale 0–10) (DEMOC)	1800–2010	Polity IV (2010) (www.system-icpeace.org/inscr)
Regime Stability	Number of years since most recent regime change or end of transition period defined by lack of stable political institutions	1800–2010	Polity IV
Polity Score	Composite index of DEMOC and Index of Autocracy (subtracting autocracy score from democracy score), ranging from +10 (strongly democratic) to −10 (strongly autocratic) (POLITY2)	1800–2010	Polity IV
Proportional Representation	Indicator variable for proportional representation	1975–2010	World Bank Database of Political Institutions (2009)
Tax Receipts	Total government tax revenue	1960–2010	WDI

Table 11A.1   (continued)

Variable	Description	Available	Source
Foreign Direct Investment	Net inflows of foreign direct investment	1960–2010	WDI
Primary School Completion Rate	Primary completion rate, total (% of relevant age group)	1960–2010	WDI
Life Expectancy	Life expectancy at birth, total (years)	1960–2010	WDI
Population	Total population	1960–2010	WDI
Urbanization Rate	Percentage of population living in urban areas	1960–2010	WDI
Site Characteristics	Dummy variables indicating site is located in city center, commercial, industrial, residential, or other	1986–1999	WHO-AMIS
Creditor Rights	Indicator variable indicating whether laws permit secured creditors to seize their collateral after bankruptcy	1978–2003	Djankov et al. (2007)
Credit Bureau	Number of years elapsed since establishment of private credit bureau registry	1978–2003	Djankov et al. (2007)

Table 11A.2   Countries in SO_2 and lead estimations (and # observations)

SO$_2$				Lead			
Argentina	29	Japan	57	Argentina	8	Japan	54
Australia	43	Korea, Rep.	100	Australia	55	Korea, Rep.	40
Austria	36	Kuwait	18	Belarus	7	Kuwait	11
Belgium	46	Latvia	55	Belgium	8	Latvia	35
Brazil	101	Lithuania	153	Bulgaria	78	Lithuania	39
Bulgaria	78	Mexico	161	Canada	41	Mexico	72
Canada	44	New Zealand	27	China	39	New Zealand	39
Chile	15	Peru	4	Costa Rica	15	Nicaragua	3
China	344	Philippines	20	Croatia	35	Panama	9
Colombia	12	Portugal	18	Denmark	6	Peru	4
Costa Rica	5	Romania	32	Ecuador	3	Portugal	14
Croatia	42	South Africa	55	El Salvador	15	Romania	12
Cuba	8	Spain	58	Finland	27	South Africa	18
Denmark	6	Sweden	2	France	11	Switzerland	19
Ecuador	47	Switzerland	28	Germany	92	Thailand	21
Estonia	3	Thailand	7	Guatemala	24	United Kingdom	34
Finland	32	Turkey	99	Honduras	18	United States	22
France	148	United Kingdom	124	India	68	Venezuela, RB	30
Germany	247	United States	26				
Greece	38	Uruguay	5				
Hungary	58	Venezuela, RB	4				
India	279						

Table 11A.3   Summary statistics: main variables

Variable	Mean	S.D.	Min	Q$_1$	Median	Q$_3$	Max
SO$_2$	37	43	0	12	23	43	430
Lead	0.25	0.37	0.00	0.06	0.13	0.28	3.84
Credit (per capita)	8,608	17,287	7	767	2,113	8,585	117,381
Human Capital	2.4	0.5	1.5	2.0	2.5	2.8	3.5
Creditor Rights (dummy)	0.47	0.50	0.00	0.00	0.00	1.00	1.00
Credit Bureau (years)	15.2	23.7	0.0	0.0	1.0	22.0	99.0

Table 11A.4   Summary statistics by credit quartile: all variables by mean

Credit Quartile	Q_1	Q_2	Q_3	Q_4	Average
SO_2 (micrograms/meter)	35	57	33	23	37
Lead (micrograms/meter)	0.16	0.51	0.21	0.12	0.24
Credit (per capita)	283	1,292	4,426	29,212	8,608
Human Capital	2.53	2.03	2.43	2.67	2.42
Creditor Rights (dummy)	0.28	0.38	0.52	0.69	0.46
Credit Bureau (years)	0.2	9.8	21.0	30.4	15.2
GDP (per capita)	728	3,571	12,222	22,198	9,561
Investment (% GDP)	23.4	20.9	21.9	22.6	22.2
Government Consumption (% GDP)	13.5	8.9	7.2	7.1	9.3
Household Consumption (per capita)	458	2,197	7,240	13,119	5,737
Growth GDP	5.9	3.7	3.2	2.2	3.7
GDP to Area (thousands)	90	196	1,306	4,617	1,523
Openness Index	30	39	46	41	39
Index of Democracy	6.1	5.8	7.2	9.8	7.1
Regime Stability	33	12	47	53	35
Polity Score	4.2	5.3	8.6	9.8	6.7
Proportional Representation	0.96	0.98	0.82	0.57	0.82
Tax Receipts (% GDP)	9.3	12.8	15.1	17.2	12.9
Foreign Direct Investment	1.1	2.5	1.5	1.2	1.6
Deposit Bank Assets (% GDP)	41	40	69	126	68
Primary School Completion Rate	92	94	98	97	95
Life Expectancy	64	70	74	77	71
Population (millions)	741	184	40	70	260
Urbanization Rate	69	53	62	77	65
Income GNI	34	47	45	32	42

Table 11A.5   Lead estimates using Ordinary Least Squares (OLS), Random Site Effects (RSE), and Fixed Site Effects (FSE)

	(1) OLS	(2) RSE	(3) FSE	(4) FSE
Human Capital	−0.214	−0.823***	−1.600**	−3.082***
	(0.182)	(0.294)	(0.646)	(0.699)
Credit	−0.148***	−0.270***	−0.683***	
	(0.039)	(0.053)	(0.090)	
Creditor Rights				0.089
				(0.129)
Credit Bureau				−0.141***
				(0.021)
Credit Bureau (squared)				0.002***
				(0.000)
Investment	−0.209*	0.332**	−0.482**	−0.460**
	(0.119)	(0.160)	(0.205)	(0.188)
Government Consumption	−1.368***	−0.292	−0.418	−0.101
	(0.151)	(0.215)	(0.323)	(0.187)
Household Consumption	−0.348***	0.297*	2.187***	2.062***
	(0.095)	(0.156)	(0.719)	(0.670)
GDP growth	−0.008	0.012	−0.018**	−0.004
	(0.012)	(0.007)	(0.008)	(0.007)
GDP to Area	0.111**	0.077	1.242**	−0.129
	(0.046)	(0.097)	(0.621)	(0.643)
Openness Index	0.011***	−0.000	−0.010*	−0.001
	(0.003)	(0.003)	(0.005)	(0.003)
Democracy Index	−0.013***	−0.001	0.004	0.003
	(0.003)	(0.002)	(0.003)	(0.003)
Regime Stability	−0.002*	−0.003*	−0.011***	−0.007*
	(0.001)	(0.002)	(0.004)	(0.004)
R^2	0.444	0.555	0.597	0.551
Observations	692	692	692	759
Number of sites	133	133	133	136
Sargan-Hansen Test (p-value)	–	0.000	–	–

Note: All estimations include year dummies, and OLS includes site-specific characteristics (dummies for city center, commercial, industrial, residential, or other). All prices in 2005 US$. Human capital methodology by Hall and Jones (1999). Credit is private credit by deposit money banks. Creditor Rights is a dummy variable indicating whether creditors are permitted to seize their collateral after bankruptcy. Credit Bureau is the number of years elapsed since the establishment of a private credit bureau registry. Human Capital, Credit, Creditor Rights, Credit Bureau, Investment, and Government Consumption are lagged one year. All variables are in log form, except Growth GDP, Openness Index, and all institutional indices. Standard errors in parentheses (*** $p<0.01$, ** $p<0.05$, * $p<0.1$).

Table 11A.6 SO_2 estimates using Ordinary Least Squares (OLS), Random Site Effects (RSE), and Fixed Site Effects (FSE)

	(1) OLS	(2) RSE	(3) FSE	(4) FSE
Human Capital	0.038	−0.528***	−0.655***	−0.943***
	(0.099)	(0.140)	(0.243)	(0.258)
Credit	0.102***	−0.032	−0.242***	
	(0.028)	(0.029)	(0.053)	
Creditor Rights				−0.049
				(0.055)
Credit Bureau				−0.059***
				(0.010)
Credit Bureau²				0.000
				(0.000)
Investment	−0.195	0.341***	0.130	0.068
	(0.121)	(0.086)	(0.117)	(0.092)
Government Consumption	−0.637***	−0.206**	−0.050	0.118
	(0.073)	(0.096)	(0.129)	(0.094)
Household Consumption	−0.211***	0.031	−0.011	0.813***
	(0.038)	(0.065)	(0.318)	(0.313)
GDP growth	0.017**	0.018***	0.007	0.010***
	(0.008)	(0.003)	(0.004)	(0.004)
GDP to Area	0.019	0.053	0.737***	−0.545*
	(0.019)	(0.050)	(0.254)	(0.282)
Openness Index	−0.001	−0.004	−0.001	0.005***
	(0.002)	(0.002)	(0.003)	(0.002)
Democracy Index	−0.015***	−0.003*	−0.001	−0.002
	(0.004)	(0.001)	(0.002)	(0.001)
Regime Stability	−0.003***	−0.001	−0.000	−0.001
	(0.001)	(0.001)	(0.002)	(0.002)
R^2	0.233	0.221	0.208	0.223
Observations	1,831	1,831	1,831	2,071
Number of sites	293	293	293	294
Sargan-Hansen Test (p-value)	–	0.000	–	–

Note: All estimations include year dummies and OLS includes site-specific characteristics (dummies for city center, commercial, industrial, residential, or other). All prices in 2005 US$. Human capital methodology by Hall and Jones (1999). Credit is private credit by deposit money banks. Creditor Rights is a dummy variable indicating whether creditors are permitted to seize their collateral after bankruptcy. Credit Bureau is the number of years elapsed since the establishment of a private credit bureau registry. Human Capital, Credit, Creditor Rights, Credit Bureau, Investment, and Government Consumption are lagged one year. All variables are in log form, except Growth GDP, Openness Index, and all institutional indices. Standard errors in parentheses (*** $p<0.01$, ** $p<0.05$, * $p<0.1$).

Table 11A.7 Seemingly unrelated estimation (SURE) of SO_2 and lead

	(SURE I)		(SURE II)	
Variables	SO_2	Lead	SO_2	Lead
Human Capital	−4.412***	−2.196***	−3.467***	−2.241***
	(0.711)	(0.746)	(0.698)	(0.759)
Credit	−0.184**	−0.775***		
	(0.087)	(0.091)		
Creditor Rights			−0.104	0.006
			(0.106)	(0.115)
Credit Bureau			−0.042**	−0.136***
			(0.017)	(0.019)
Investment	−0.069	−0.465**	−0.114	−0.576***
	(0.199)	(0.209)	(0.171)	(0.186)
Government Consumption	−1.004***	−0.539*	0.008	−0.411**
	(0.272)	(0.286)	(0.154)	(0.168)
Household Consumption	1.074	1.140	1.536***	2.777***
	(0.735)	(0.771)	(0.594)	(0.646)
GDP growth	0.004	−0.022***	0.004	−0.004
	(0.007)	(0.007)	(0.006)	(0.007)
GDP to Area	0.546	3.037***	−0.687	−0.668
	(0.600)	(0.629)	(0.553)	(0.602)
Openness Index	−0.004	0.004	0.005*	0.002
	(0.005)	(0.005)	(0.002)	(0.003)
Democracy Index	−0.002	0.005**	−0.005**	0.004
	(0.002)	(0.002)	(0.002)	(0.002)
Regime Stability	−0.013***	−0.015***	−0.003	−0.013***
	(0.005)	(0.005)	(0.004)	(0.004)
R^2	0.922	0.933	0.910	0.912
Observations	468	468	532	532

Note: All estimations include year dummies and OLS includes site-specific characteristics (dummies for city center, commercial, industrial, residential, or other). All prices in 2005 US$. Human capital methodology by Hall and Jones (1999). Credit is private credit by deposit money banks. Creditor Rights is a dummy variable indicating whether creditors are permitted to seize their collateral after bankruptcy. Credit Bureau is the number of years elapsed since the establishment of a private credit bureau registry. Human Capital, Credit, Creditor Rights, Credit Bureau, Investment, and Government Consumption are lagged one year. All variables are in log form, except Growth GDP, Openness Index, and all institutional indices. Standard errors in parentheses (*** $p<0.01$, ** $p<0.05$, * $p<0.1$).

Table 11A.8   Robustness checks (added controls) using Fixed Site Effects (FSE)

Variable	(1) SO_2	(2) Lead	(3) SO_2	(4) Lead	(5) SO_2	(6) Lead
Human Capital	−0.431*	−2.636***	−0.693**	−2.937***	−0.497*	−1.801**
	(0.239)	(0.727)	(0.288)	(0.785)	(0.276)	(0.745)
Credit	−0.290***	−0.572***	−0.298***	−0.297***	−0.602***	(0.110)
	(0.054)	(0.109)	−0.247*	(0.134)	(0.054)	(0.065)
Governance						
Polity Score	−0.044***	−0.010				
	(0.013)	(0.023)				
Proportional	1.116***	−0.310				
Representation	(0.148)	(0.189)				
Finance						
Foreign Direct			0.007	0.059**		
Investment						
			(0.015)	(0.027)		
Deposit Assets			0.137	−0.509***		
			(0.088)	(0.183)		
Demography & Income						
GDP					−4.800***	4.712***
					(0.901)	(1.556)
Life Expectancy					−0.130***	0.061
					(0.029)	(0.072)
Population					−3.921**	2.932
					(1.609)	(2.553)
Urbanization Rate					−0.489***	−0.209
					(0.117)	(0.288)
Adjusted R^2	0.161	0.534	0.029	0.531	0.142	0.551
Adjusted R^2 (w/o added controls)	0.111	0.528	0.028	0.524	0.091	0.522
Observations	1,636	656	1,762	658	1,753	651
Number of sites	267	130	292	132	291	130

Note: All estimations include year dummies and OLS includes site-specific characteristics (dummies for city center, commercial, industrial, residential, or other). All prices in 2005 US$. Human capital methodology by Hall and Jones (1999). Credit is private credit by deposit money banks. Creditor Rights is a dummy variable indicating whether creditors are permitted to seize their collateral after bankruptcy. Credit Bureau is the number of years elapsed since the establishment of a private credit bureau registry. Human Capital, Credit, Creditor Rights, Credit Bureau, Investment, and Government Consumption are lagged one year. All variables are in log form, except Growth GDP, Openness Index, Primary School Completion Rate, Life Expectancy, and Urbanization Rate and all institutional indices. Standard errors in parentheses (*** $p<0.01$, ** $p<0.05$, * $p<0.1$).

Table 11A.9   Iteratively Reweighted Least Squares (IRWLS) and heterogeneous effects

	IRWLS		Heterogeneous Effects	
	(1)	(2)	(3)	(4)
	SO_2	Lead	SO_2	Lead
Human Capital	−0.331*	−0.947*	−0.632**	−0.975
	(0.196)	(0.488)	(0.296)	(0.796)
Credit	−0.472***	−0.752***	−0.267***	−0.289**
	(0.043)	(0.064)	(0.068)	(0.115)
Credit × High Income GINI			−0.122	−0.647***
			(0.080)	(0.151)
Investment	−0.204**	−0.800***	0.141	−0.332*
	(0.093)	(0.149)	(0.126)	(0.199)
Government Consumption	0.163	−0.676***	−0.182	−0.553*
	(0.103)	(0.233)	(0.148)	(0.327)
Household Consumption	0.624**	1.777***	0.211	1.541**
	(0.255)	(0.529)	(0.337)	(0.686)
GDP growth	−0.006	−0.025***	0.005	−0.011
	(0.003)	(0.006)	(0.004)	(0.008)
GDP to Area	0.870***	2.166***	0.732***	1.723***
	(0.203)	(0.451)	(0.271)	(0.601)
Openness Index	0.004**	−0.009**	−0.002	0.004
	(0.002)	(0.004)	(0.003)	(0.005)
Democracy Index	0.001	0.004**	−0.000	0.005**
	(0.001)	(0.002)	(0.002)	(0.002)
Regime Stability	−0.000	−0.010***	−0.001	−0.012***
	(0.001)	(0.003)	(0.002)	(0.004)
R^2	0.944	0.959	0.216	0.646
Observations	1,686	628	1,643	618
Number of sites			284	123

Note: All estimations include year dummies. All prices in 2005 US$. All estimations use identical controls as baseline model (omitted from table to save space). Credit is private credit by deposit money banks. Deposit Bank Assets is Deposit Bank Money Assets. Credit, Investment, and Government Consumption are lagged one year. All variables are in log form, except Growth GDP, Openness Index, Primary School Completion Rate, Life Expectancy, and Population Density and all institutional indices. Robust errors in parentheses (*** $p<0.01$, ** $p<0.05$, * $p<0.1$).

12 Manufacturing doubt: how firms exploit scientific uncertainty to shape regulation

Yann Bramoullé and Caroline Orset

12.1 Introduction

Some of today's most worrying collective issues are scientifically highly complex. Consider, for instance, cancer, climate change or bee colony collapse disorder. Regulations to address them have to be adopted under significant scientific uncertainty, and governments and regulatory agencies have increasingly relied on scientific expertise for help. The social responsibility of scientists has grown, as have the detrimental consequences of science's dysfunctions. Unfortunately, and perhaps unsurprisingly, firms, lobbies and special interest groups have proved adept at distorting science to affect regulations. Their main strategies include: hiring and funding dissenting scientists; producing and publicizing favorable scientific findings; ghostwriting; funding diversion research; conducting large-scale science-denying communication campaigns; and placing biased experts on advisory and regulatory panels. Despite elaborate efforts to conceal them, these underhanded practices are regularly exposed through whistleblowing, investigative journalism and court judgments. The forced release of confidential corporate documents as part of the 1998 Tobacco Master Settlement Agreement (MSA) was a particular eye-opener for many scientists. In a fascinating and disturbing account, Proctor (2011) describes how the tobacco industry systematically manufactured doubt about the negative impacts of smoking on health. The health and welfare implications are staggering. Since then, evidence has accumulated regarding the depth and breadth of doubt-manufacturing by industrial lobbies. Special interest groups have, for instance, deliberately altered and biased the scientific process on climate change (Oreskes and Conway, 2010), herbicide safety (Waldman et al., 2017), endocrine disruptors' toxicity (Horel, 2015; Nicolopoulou-Stamati et al., 2001) and food safety (Séverac, 2015; Vodeb, 2017). The whole field of biomedical research appears to be plagued by conflicts of interest (PLoS Medicine Editors, 2009). Yet, despite their prevalence and high welfare cost, these unscrupulous practices have been largely neglected by economists so far.

Our community should now fill this gap. The powerful analytical tools of economics need to be brought out and used to shed light on doubt-manufacturing, both theoretically and empirically. Among the issues and questions that need addressing are the following. What is the relationship between industry effort and the extent of scientific uncertainty? What are the mechanisms through which regulations ultimately depend on both scientific progress and industry miscommunication? Is the choice of the appropriate regulation affected by doubt-manufacturing? In Section 12.2, we present a simple theoretical framework introduced in Bramoullé and Orset (2018) that provides a useful starting point to consider these issues. In this model, the government is assumed to be benevolent but populist, and maximizes social welfare as perceived by citizens. The industry can produce costly reports showing that its activity is not harmful, and citizens are unaware of the industry's miscommunication. We characterize the industry's optimal miscommunication. We notably show that it depends on scientists' beliefs in a discontinuous, non-monotonous way, and that it is strongly affected by the kind of regulation implemented (tax versus command and control). These models and results only constitute a first step towards a systematic economic analysis of doubt-manufacturing, however. In Section 12.3, we propose a roadmap for future research on the topic, highlighting critical issues deserving more investigation.

12.2   Benchmark framework

12.2.1   The model

In this section we present a simple theoretical framework, first introduced in Bramoullé and Orset (2018), to analyze the interaction between scientific uncertainty, firms' miscommunication and public policies. We consider a society composed of four groups of agents: firms, scientists, citizens and the government. We assume that the firms are risk-neutral, and their economic activity generates pollution, $e>0$, such as greenhouse gas emissions, which may be harmful to health and to the environment. The impacts of the pollution and the extent of harm it might cause are uncertain. The scientists have prior beliefs, $p_0 \epsilon [0,1]$, that pollution is harmful. They can do research to reduce this uncertainty and update their beliefs, $p \epsilon [0,1]$. The firms may decide to produce costly reports to show that their activity is not harmful. The number of reports they produce, $m \geq 0$, represents their miscommunication effort. Both firms and scientists communicate about the economic activity's impacts. The citizens update their beliefs, $q(p,m) \epsilon [0,1]$, unaware that the firms are miscommunicating. This assumption is consistent with evidence on the concealment of adverse scientific results by the tobacco industry and by Monsanto, and with the tendency of industry-funded scientists to hide their source of funding (Bero, 2013; Proctor, 2011; Waldman et al., 2017). Finally, the government considers public opinion when determining the degree of regulation of the pollution generated by firms, $e^* \geq 0$. The timing of this model is described in Figure 12.1.

Scientists. We consider a Bayesian model of scientific progress. Scientists can do research to reduce their uncertainty on the effects of pollution. They have prior beliefs, p_0, that pollution is harmful. They can run n experiments to learn about the impact of pollution. We consider an exogenous number of experiments

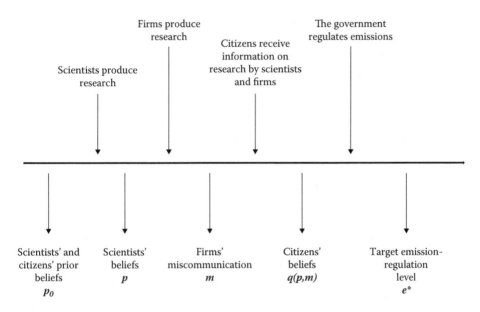

Figure 12.1   Timing of the model

here. Bramoullé and Orset (2018) further explore the implications of firms' miscommunication on endogenous research, and notably show that an independent funding agency, such as the National Science Foundation or the European Research Council, can help limit the negative impacts of doubt-manufacturing.

Each experiment provides a noisy signal on the true state of the world, and there is a probability $P \epsilon(1/2,1)$ of its findings being correct. Denote by k the number of experiments indicating that pollution is harmful. Applying Bayes' rule, we see that scientists' *ex-post* beliefs are equal to:

$$p = \frac{p_0 \binom{n}{k} P^k (1-p)^{n-k}}{p_0 \binom{n}{k} P^k (1-p)^{n-k} + (1-p_0) \binom{n}{k} P^{n-k}(1-p)^k}.$$

Let $\alpha = P/(1-P) > 1$ denote the relative accuracy of experimental findings. This yields:

$$p(p_0, k, n) = \frac{p_0 \alpha^k}{p_0 \alpha^k + (1-p_0)\alpha^{n-k}}.$$

This specification exhibits three properties:

(1)   If experiments are run in several stages, the final beliefs do not depend on their ordering.
(2)   The expectation of scientists' beliefs is equal to their prior beliefs.

(3)   As the number of experiments becomes arbitrarily large, scientific knowledge converges to the truth.

Firms. Firms' benefits from emitting emissions e are equal to $B(e) = be_0 e - \frac{1}{2} be^2$ with b, $e_0 > 0$. Emissions may generate damage. We assume that scientific uncertainty takes a binary form. Either pollution is harmful, and overall damage is equal to $D(e) = d_0 e + \frac{1}{2} de^2$ with d_0, $d \geq 0$, or pollution is not harmful and does not generate damage. We further assume that $d_0 < be_0$. The marginal benefit from the first unit of emission exceeds its marginal damage. At cost c, the industry can produce a report indicating that pollution is not harmful. We characterize the industry's miscommunication effort by the number of reports they produce, i.e., m.

Citizens. Citizens are unaware of the industry's involvement in biased research, and treat the information produced by the industry as independent scientific evidence. Thus, citizens do not distinguish between industry-generated information and scientific knowledge. Therefore, scientific knowledge, p, and industry communication, m, determine the citizens' belief, which is equal to:

$$q = \frac{p_0 \alpha^k}{p_0 \alpha^k + (1 - p_0) \alpha^{n-k+m}} = \frac{p}{p + (1-p) \alpha^m}.$$

This specification has two features:

(1)   The marginal impact of scientists' beliefs on citizens' beliefs is positive and increasing.
(2)   When scientists think that pollution is not likely to be harmful, the marginal impact of industry miscommunication on citizens' beliefs is decreasing in absolute value. On the other hand, when scientists think that pollution is likely to be harmful, miscommunication initially has an increasing marginal impact on citizens' beliefs in absolute value. These increasing returns capture a well-known property of Bayesian updating: extra information has the largest effect when the agent is most uncertain. In addition, the impact of extra information decreases as the agent becomes more certain.

Government. The government is benevolent and can be either *technocratic* when it maximizes the expected social welfare computed with up-to-date scientific knowledge: $W(p,e) = B(e) - pD(e)$ or *populist* when it maximizes social welfare as perceived by citizens: $W(q,e) = B(e) - qD(e)$. A technocratic government sets the emissions level to optimally balance social benefits and social costs as perceived by objective scientists. This means that $B'(e) = pD'(e)$, which yields:

$$e(p) = \frac{be_0 - pd_0}{b + pd}.$$

This corresponds to the first-best outcome. Note that e is decreasing and convex in scientific belief p.

A populist government sets the emissions level to optimally balance social benefits and social costs as perceived by potentially biased citizens. This means that $B'(e) = qD'(e)$, which yields:

$$e(q) = \frac{be_0 - qd_0}{b + qd}.$$

The level of regulation chosen by a populist government is then equal to $e(q)$. When citizens are less worried about the impacts of pollution than scientists, $q < p$ and $e(q) > e(p)$. A populist government then under-regulates with respect to the first best. This provides incentives for the industry to try to falsely reassure citizens on the effects of its activity.

12.2.2 Firms' optimal communication

In the absence of regulation, firms' benefits are maximized by emitting $e = e_0$, the "business as usual" level of pollution. However, the government can regulate firms' activity either by imposing a maximum level of emissions or through a tax on emissions. When the government is populist, the level of regulation depends on citizens' beliefs. This provides an incentive for firms to miscommunicate. We contrast the industry's optimal communication policy under command and control and under a tax on emissions.

Under command and control

Let $e(q) \leq e_0$ be the target level of regulated emissions. Under command and control, the government directly imposes this maximum level. The firm's objective is to maximize its payoff with respect to m:

$$\pi_c(m) = be_0 e(q(p, m)) - \frac{1}{2} be(q(p, m))^2 - cm.$$

Let us define:

(1) m_c^* as a solution to the problem of maximizing $\pi_c(m)$ over $[0, +\infty[$;
(2) $\bar{c}_c = \frac{4}{27} \ln(\alpha) \frac{b(d_0 + de_0)^2}{(b+d)^2}$ as a threshold cost for which the industry can produce a report indicating that pollution is not harmful;
(3) q_c^* as a target popular belief which verifies that $q_c^* = q(m_c^*, p)$;
(4) p_c^* as a threshold of scientists' belief such that $p_c^* > q_c^*$ and which verifies that $\varphi(p_c^*) = 0$ with $\varphi(p) = B(e(p)) - B(e(q_c^*)) + \frac{c}{\ln(\alpha)} [\ln(\frac{p}{1-p}) - \ln(\frac{q_c^*}{1-q_c^*})]$.

By maximizing $\pi_c(m)$ with respect to m, we obtain (see Bramoullé and Orset, 2018 for details):

(1)   When the cost c is higher than or equal to $\bar{c}_c$, it is too costly for firms to miscommunicate, meaning that $m_c^* = 0$.

(2)   On the other hand, when the cost c is lower than $\bar{c}_c$:

$$m_c^* = \begin{cases} 0 & \text{if } p \le q_c^* \\ \dfrac{1}{\ln(\alpha)}\left[\ln\left(\dfrac{p}{1-p}\right) - \ln\left(\dfrac{q_c^*}{1-q_c^*}\right)\right] & \text{if } q_c^* \le p \le p_c^* \\ 0 & \text{if } p_c^* \le p \end{cases}$$

The industry's optimal miscommunication policy varies over three domains. When the scientists' *ex-post* belief, p, is low and scientists believe that pollution is unlikely to be harmful, the benefits from miscommunication are too low and industry does not try to change citizens' beliefs. When scientists' *ex-post* belief takes intermediate values, and scientists are more uncertain about the effects of the pollution, the industry engages in miscommunication and targets a specific level of citizens' belief. As the scientists' *ex-post* belief increases, the target is unchanged and communication efforts first increase continuously. When the scientists' *ex-post* belief reaches a critical threshold, the costs of miscommunication become too high and the industry abruptly ceases its efforts. Optimal miscommunication is therefore non-monotonic and discontinuous in scientists' belief.

Under a tax on emissions

The government can tax emissions at rate t. Firms choose emissions to maximize $B(e) - te$, which yields $B'(e) = t$. The government then sets $t = B'(e^*) = b(e_0 - e^*)$. The firms' objective is to maximize the payoff with respect to m:

$$\pi_t(m) = \frac{1}{2}be(q(p, m))^2 - cm.$$

Let us define:

(1) m_t^* as a solution to the problem of maximizing $\pi_t(m)$ over $[0, +\infty[$;

(2) $\bar{p}_t$ as a threshold scientists' belief which verifies that $h(\bar{p}_t) = 0$ with $h(p) = b^2 e_0 - 2b(d_0 + e_0(b+d))p + (d_0(3b+d) + dbe_0)p^2$;

(3) $\bar{c}_t = ln(\alpha)b^2(d_0 + de_0)\dfrac{\bar{p}_t(1-\bar{p}_t)(be_0 - \bar{p}_t d_0)}{(b+\bar{p}_t d)^3}$ as a threshold cost for which the industry can produce a report indicating that pollution is not harmful;

(4) q_t^* as a target popular belief such that $\bar{p}_t > q_t^*$ which verifies that $q_t^* = q(m_t^*, p)$;

(5) $\bar{q}_t$ as a threshold popular belief such that $\bar{q}_t > \bar{p}_t$ which verifies that $g(\bar{q}_t) = g(q_t^*)$ with $g(q) = \dfrac{q(1-q)(be_0 - qd_0)}{(b+qd)^3}$.

(6) p_t^* as a threshold scientists' belief such that $p_t^* > q_t^*$ and which verifies that $\psi(p_t^*) = 0$ with $\psi(p) = \frac{1}{2}be(p)^2 - \frac{1}{2}be(q_t^*) + \frac{c}{\ln(\alpha)}[\ln(\frac{p}{1-p}) - \ln(\frac{q_t^*}{1-q_t^*})]$.

By maximizing $\pi_t(m)$ with respect to m, we obtain:

(1)   When cost c is higher than or equal to $\bar{c}_t$, it is too costly for the firms to communicate, meaning that $m_t^* = 0$.

(2) On the other hand, when cost c is lower than $\bar{c}_t$:

$$m^*_t = \begin{cases} 0 & \text{if } p \le q^*_t \\ \dfrac{1}{\ln(\alpha)}\left[\ln\left(\dfrac{p}{1-p}\right) - \ln\left(\dfrac{q^*_t}{1-q^*_t}\right)\right] & \text{if } q^*_t \le p \le p^*_t. \\ 0 & \text{if } p^*_t \le p \end{cases}$$

The industry's optimal miscommunication under a tax on emissions has a qualitatively similar shape to that under command and control. As scientists' belief increases, firms first do not communicate, then increase their effort in a monotonic way up to a threshold level of belief, above which they abruptly cease to miscommunicate. We then compare the levels of industry miscommunication quantitatively across the two kinds of environmental regulations.

We can show that if $be_0 \ge 2d_0 + de_0$, then marginal damages at zero are not too high and firms always miscommunicate more under a tax on emissions than under command and control. Observe that with both instruments, firms obtain lower profits because of the lower level of emissions: $B(e) < B(e_0)$. Under a tax on emissions, firms face an additional fiscal burden and have their profits further reduced by the amount of tax paid. This gives them an extra incentive to influence regulations as compared to under command and control.

Impact of the accuracy of experimental findings under command and control

An increase in the relative accuracy of experimental findings, α, has two countervailing effects:

(1) On the one hand, scientists converge more quickly towards the truth when the relative accuracy of experimental findings is higher. The variance in scientific beliefs tends to be higher when relative accuracy of experimental findings is higher; and, in the absence of industry miscommunication, this applies to citizens' beliefs as well.
(2) On the other hand, because citizens do not differentiate between information provided by the industry and by scientists, higher relative accuracy of experimental findings makes industry miscommunication more effective. Industry miscommunication thus emerges for higher communication costs and over a larger range of scientific beliefs. This runs counter to the first effect, and tends to slow the convergence of citizens' beliefs towards the truth.

12.2.3 Illustrations

Firms' miscommunication and citizens' beliefs

We represent in Figure 12.2 firms' miscommunication and citizens' beliefs under a tax on emissions and under command and control, for specific parameter values. Note that to calibrate or estimate this model, we would need to have access to quantitative data on firms' miscommunication. This kind of data is currently lacking and, as discussed below, we believe that collecting and assembling systematic data on firms' efforts at manufacturing doubt is an important direction for future research. Here, we choose parameter values for illustration and pedagogical purposes.

We set $b = 2$, $e_0 = 10$, $d_0 = 9.9$, and $d = 0.01$, implying that firms benefit from emitting emissions that are not too large in comparison to the damages, and suboptimal regulation may have large welfare costs. Note that these economic parameters could, in principle, be obtained from classical estimations of private benefits and social damages of pollution. We set $P = 0.64$, implying that experiments provide noisy signals on the true state of the world and scientists do not converge too quickly on the truth; and that $c = 4.3$, implying that the industry's miscommunication cost is neither too high nor too low. For these parameter values, we compute the thresholds: $\bar{c}_c \approx 4.31$, $q_c^* \approx 0.21$, $p_c^* \approx 0.99$ and $\bar{c}_t \approx 11.27$, $q_t^* \approx 0.08$, $p_t^* \approx 0.99$. We see, in particular, that the combination of a relatively low P and an intermediate c gives rise to relatively large miscommunication intervals.

While obtaining reliable estimates of experiments' accuracy and firms' miscommunication costs would require novel data and innovative empirical work, the presence of large miscommunication ranges appears to be a likely scenario.

We observe that citizens' beliefs remain at the target level q^* as long as the industry engages in miscommunication, returning to p when the industry ceases to miscommunicate.

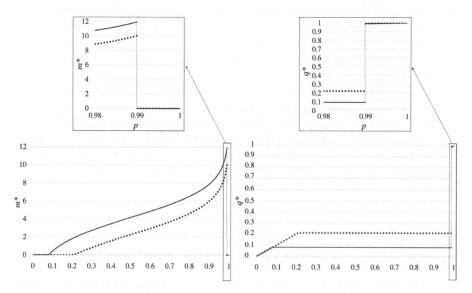

Figure 12.2   Firms' miscommunication and citizens' beliefs under tax on emissions (solid line) and under command and control (dotted line)

Impact of firms' miscommunication on welfare

In Figure 12.3, we depict the ratio of the level of welfare under the populist policy over the first-best level of welfare (technocratic policy), $W(p,e(q))/W(p,e(p))$, for the same parameter values as in Figure 12.2.

We see that relative welfare loss first increases with scientific belief, and hence with firms' miscommunication and the induced distortion in citizens' beliefs. When scientific belief becomes high enough, however, the industry stops miscommunicating and welfare returns to its first-best value. In addition, welfare losses are larger under a tax on emissions, due to the increased miscommunication.

12.2.4 Summary

Industry's miscommunication effort

(1) The industry's miscommunication effort is a non-monotonic and discontinuous function of scientific belief.

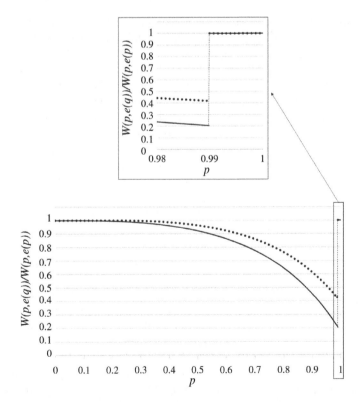

Figure 12.3 Welfare loss induced by firms' miscommunication under tax on emissions (solid line) and under command and control (dotted line)

(2)   As scientists become increasingly convinced that the activity is harmful, the industry first devotes more and more resources to falsely reassuring the citizens. When scientific belief reaches a critical threshold, however, countering the scientific consensus becomes too costly and the industry abruptly ceases its miscommunication.

(3)   (1) and (2) are robust to the type of instrument used (command and control or tax on emissions), but a natural condition leads to more industry miscommunication under a tax on emissions than under command and control.

Welfare

(1)   Welfare loss first increases as scientific belief increases; and when the industry stops miscommunicating, the welfare returns to its first-best value.

(2)   Welfare losses are greater under a tax on emissions than under command and control in circumstances where miscommunication is also greater.

12.3   Roadmap for future research

Much research is needed to better understand the determinants and impacts of doubt-manufacturing. This research should take at least three major directions. First, from a theoretical perspective, researchers should relax the simplifying assumptions made in the previous framework and should explore the causes and consequences of doubt-manufacturing in richer setups. We review below the few articles that have made some progress in this direction. Second, researchers should tackle these questions empirically and should confront the models, assumptions and results to data. To our knowledge, there is virtually no empirical economic literature on these issues, and filling this gap will require empirical skills and creativity. A third major direction of research is to derive the appropriate normative recommendations and public policy implications. What can be done, and at what level, to limit the negative impacts of doubt-manufacturing? What can the academic community, in particular, do to reduce or even eliminate, the conflicts of interests and unethical practices arising from special interests? These three directions of research are of course interrelated. Empirical facts should inform positive and normative theoretical explorations and theoretical developments should help guide the empirical analysis.

We next discuss the first direction of research in some detail. Doubt-manufacturing should be analyzed in frameworks involving: multiple periods, multiple lobbies and multiple lobbying strategies; richer models of belief formation and preferences concerning risk; and richer representations of science.

Dynamics. A natural step forward would be to consider a dynamic version of the static model presented in Section 12.2. Scientific progress and doubt-manufacturing naturally unfold over time, as pointed out, for instance, by Shapiro (2016: Introduction):

The Intergovernmental Panel on Climate Change [. . .] crystallized a scientific consensus that the climate is warming and that the cause is at least partly anthropogenic. The subsequent decade saw an explosion of activity by conservative think tanks and other organizations attempting to persuade the public that "the scientific evidence for global warming is highly uncertain."

Suppose, then, that scientists, firms, citizens and the government interact over multiple periods. Miscommunication by industry in one period will presumably have persistent effects on citizens' beliefs in later periods, and firms now account for the impact of their current actions on future regulations when choosing miscommunication efforts. A key question is how miscommunication affects regulatory trajectories and the central trade-off between commitment and flexibility. In contexts where scientific uncertainty may be resolved over time, is it better to act now and learn later, consistent with standard interpretations of the precautionary principle? Alternatively, is it better to learn first and act later, waiting for relative certainty before making costly sacrifices? Even with a single decision-maker, this question is complex and can be resolved in different ways, see e.g. Gollier et al. (2000). The presence of an industry willing and able to pervert the scientific process will extensively modify analysis of these intertemporal trade-offs.

An important point here is that, in practice, the precautionary principle has generally been subject to a wide range of interpretation. Industries have shown a remarkably consistent tendency to exploit the presence of scientific uncertainty to lobby for a "learn then act" approach, across widely differing contexts. More generally, note that optimal regulatory trajectories depend on the initial level of scientific uncertainty and on anticipated rates of future information arrival, and these different margins can be affected by doubt-manufacturing. A well-organized lobby could actively implement sophisticated strategies of scientific manipulation, aimed at minimizing discounted costs of regulation compliance. For instance, the lobby could drop the "learn then act" strategy as scientific evidence accumulates and regulation becomes unavoidable, in favor of strong regulatory commitment based on biased beliefs before scientific evidence becomes overwhelming. An industry may prefer several years of rigid but mild regulations to a period of no regulation followed by one of the strong regulations.

Lobbying. Another natural step forward would be to consider multiple lobbying groups as well as multiple forms of lobbying. In fact, several articles build on the literature on political economy and analyze how special interest groups compete to influence public opinion and regulation. Yu (2005) considers competition for political influence between an industrial and an environmental lobby through two channels: direct lobbying à la Grossman and Helpman (1994) and communication campaigns to influence voters' beliefs. He finds that direct and indirect lobbying efforts are complements, even though changes in the models' fundamentals can induce substitution between the two. In Baron (2005), two competing lobbies invest in finding evidence on the true state of nature, and then decide either to conceal this evidence or report it to the media. Evidence is either uninformative or fully informative. A bias towards regulation may arise in the presence of asymmetries between the lobbies. Sobbrio (2011) shows that competition among lobbies tends to generate noise and increase scientific uncertainty. Policy outcomes may be distorted even when voters are fully rational. In Shapiro (2016), a journalist reports on an unknown, policy-relevant state, and receives claims from two competing lobbies which are indistinguishable from facts. In equilibrium, voters can remain uninformed even when the journalist is perfectly informed.

The above analyses yield some interesting insights. In particular, competition among special interest groups generally increases uncertainty and slows down learning. However, these analyses also suffer from important shortcomings. Competition between lobbyists is a key driver of their results and outcomes; but they pay little or no attention to science, scientists and scientific progress, which are at best coarsely represented. Our view is that, although environmental lobbies too may engage in doubt-manufacturing, their relative lack of financial resources makes competition between them and industry a secondary force in doubt-manufacturing. Environmental efforts are simply dwarfed by industrial efforts to manipulate science. By contrast, science and scientific progress play a major role in resolving the uncertainty on the impacts of industrial activities, and hence should take center stage in the modeling. Bramoullé and Orset (2018) make progress in this direction by adopting a richer representation of science, where evidence can accumulate and bring scientists progressively closer to the truth, and by looking at the impact of doubt-manufacturing on research funding. However, much more could, and should, be done on this dimension. We discuss this in more detail below.

Even in the presence of a single lobby, an interesting question is how different lobbying strategies interact with doubt-manufacturing. In particular, are doubt-manufacturing and direct lobbying complementary or substitutes? We suspect that the results on firms' optimal communication would extend to a setup with multiple lobbying strategies, and that the sharp drop in communication effort would be accompanied by a sharp increase in direct lobbying. The possibility of science manipulation should further inform the debate on the regulation of political contributions. Limits to contributions, in particular, could in some circumstances lead to increased miscommunication and, possibly, to decreased welfare. Strategies used by firms to manufacture doubt could also directly contribute to other forms of lobbying. For instance, firms often employ biased scientists who play two roles: they produce biased research and can be placed as experts on advisory or regulatory panels. In the French context, for instance, the presence of biased experts with declared or undeclared conflicts of interest on administrative commissions seems to raise serious issues about the way regulations are adopted under scientific uncertainty (see Foucart, 2014 and Horel, 2015). These interactions and implications deserve further investigation.

Science. Science is a complex collective endeavor. In Bramoullé and Orset (2018), we focused our representation of the scientific process on the key question of the level of harm induced by economic activity, which is the relevant question for regulation.

In reality, science covers a wide variety of issues and questions. The different issues, fields and academic communities are in constant interaction, and what happens in one part of the scientific process may have deep repercussions on other parts. These interactions have been ruthlessly exploited by special interest groups in a way that is currently not clear to researchers. In particular, a richer representation of science needs to be developed to analyze a major doubt-manufacturing strategy: the funding of "distraction research". In many documented instances, firms have funded legitimate research which does not advance our knowledge on the consequences of their activities and distracts scientists' and citizens' attention from the issue. Distraction research can even generate macro biases in scientific advancement. For instance, the tobacco industry has been a major source of funding on the genetic causes of cancer (see Chapter 16 in Proctor, 2011). This is, of course, an important and legitimate question. The problem is that attention by the academic community is scarce; and this scarcity generates substitution effects in the specific questions analyzed by the academic community at some point in time. A deliberately induced focus on genetic explanations has thus postponed our understanding of the impact of environmental factors, such as smoking, on cancer. A more subtle, perverse effect of distraction research is that it helps establish industrial lobbies as genuine benefactors of scientific research. This ill-gained legitimacy, in turn, increases their ability to affect beliefs and regulations.

Beliefs. Another fundamental issue that deserves more research is how citizens, scientists and decision-makers form their beliefs. In Bramoullé and Orset (2018), citizens are Bayesian; and the only reason citizens' beliefs are incorrect is that the industry miscommunicates and that citizens are unaware of this miscommunication. In reality, the diffusion of scientific knowledge may be imperfect and lack of Bayesian rationality may be widespread. There is, in particular, expanding evidence that agents do not properly account for the sources of the information they receive when forming their beliefs, as explored in the literature on persuasion bias (DeMarzo et al., 2003) and correlation neglect (Levy and Razin, 2015). This is compounded by the important role played by information entrepreneurs such as journalists, media owners and internet influencers in the process of belief formation. For instance, Shapiro (2016) shows that the journalistic norm of "balanced" reporting prevents accurate reporting of the facts on climate change and contributes to the persistent public ignorance. Not taking sides when one side is objective and the other is biased may have strongly detrimental welfare consequences. Overall, the combination of behavioral biases and strategic manipulation of information may help explain the breadth and depth of misperceptions.

This raises important new questions. In particular, we suspect that lobbies are well aware of the main behavioral biases and the main mechanisms through which people form beliefs, and have gained experience in devising effective miscommunication strategies to best exploit these biases and mechanisms. Economic theorists are currently working hard to analyze Bayesian persuasion and the kinds of actions that can be taken to sway Bayesian decision-makers (Kamenica and Gentzkow, 2011). We believe an even greater research effort is needed to understand non-Bayesian persuasion, both theoretically and empirically, exploring how the beliefs of agents with behavioral biases can be influenced and what can be done to counter detrimental persuasion. Finally, note that citizens are risk-neutral in Bramoullé and Orset (2018). It would be interesting to introduce attitudes towards risk into the analysis. In reality, citizens are generally risk-averse and, in the presence of deep uncertainty on outcomes, they are likely averse to ambiguity (Mahmoudi and Pingle, 2018). How do risk-aversion and ambiguity-aversion affect firms' miscommunication?

Empirics. Applied economists should begin a systematic empirical investigation of doubt-manufacturing. An important part of this research effort will involve collecting relevant data in a shape that can be analyzed econometrically. The *Tobacco Documents*, for instance, constitute an extraordinary source of data on actual miscommunication practices. These are confidential corporate documents that were forcibly released as part of the 1998 Tobacco Master Settlement Agreement, and can be consulted at https://www.industrydocumentslibrary.ucsf.edu/tobacco/. Experimental tools developed by behavioral economists also have an important role to play here. In particular, economists should investigate belief formation experimentally in contexts where there is both scientific uncertainty and communication by special interest groups. More generally, economists should begin a systematic, quantitative investigation of critical issues including: the time lags often observed between when scientists reach a consensus on the need for regulation and when an effective public policy is implemented; people's persistent underestimation of the scientific consensus on climate change (Ding et al., 2011); sudden reversals in public opinion and in the official positions of special interest groups; and correlations between levels of scientific uncertainty, firms' communication efforts and actual regulations. For instance, an important qualitative report by the European Environment Agency (2013) shows that "false positives", where preventive actions undertaken due to early scientific warnings turn out to be unnecessary, are much less frequent than "false negatives", where no action is taken despite early warnings that are confirmed *ex-post*.

Normative implications. Doubt-manufacturing represents a deliberate distortion of the scientific process, with widespread negative consequences. The academic community is becoming increasingly aware of the threat this represents and, more generally, of the serious problems created by conflicts of interest. Early scandals, particularly in the medical sector, led to the adoption of disclosure rules by academic journals. These rules are now common, but do not appear to be very effective (Bero et al., 2005). Corporate-funded ghostwriting is still suspected of being a major problem in biomedical research (PloS Medicine Editors, 2009; Thacker, 2014). One difficulty is that academia seems generally ill-equipped to address systematic, deliberate wrong-doing. Historically, academia's governance has been greatly decentralized and has strongly relied on researchers' goodwill, objectivity and honesty. Sanctions are informal and essentially involve reputation. While this may be appropriate to deal with the occasional dishonest researcher, its effectiveness in countering doubt-manufacturing is less sure. We believe that an effective counter to doubt-manufacturing will require reflection on the academic system and institutional innovations.

How can academic journals better ensure that authors fully and truthfully disclose their conflicts of interest? How can the emergence of conflicts of interest be avoided in the first place? What can be done to reduce corporate ghostwriting and the use of dissident scientists to serve corporate interests? To address these issues, the scientific community will need to invent new and more effective sanctions, and to become much better at finding and exposing concealed conflicts of interest. This will likely require more whistleblowing, more scientific investigative journalism and an expansion of anonymous discussion sites like PubPeer. Even more difficult will be addressing the issues raised by distraction research. To conclude, scientists from all disciplines need to realize that scientific process is subject to systematic attacks by special interest groups, and should devote part of their formidable brainpower to finding and developing effective counters.

References

Baron, David P. 2005. Competing for the public through the news media, *Journal of Economics and Management Strategy*, 14(2), 339–376.

Bero, Lisa A. 2013. Tobacco industry manipulation of research, in *Late Lessons from Early Warnings: Science, Precaution, Innovation*. European Environment Agency (EEA) Report n. 1/2013. Copenhagen: EEA, p. 17.

Bero, Lisa A., Glantz, Stanton and M.K. Hong. 2005. The limits of competing interest disclosures, *Tobacco Control*, 14, 118–126.

Bramoullé, Yann and Caroline Orset. 2018. Manufacturing doubt, *Journal of Environmental Economics and Management*, 90, 119–133.

DeMarzo, Peter M., Vayanos, Dimitri and Jeffrey Zwiebel. 2003. Persuasion bias, social influence and unidimensional opinions, *Quarterly Journal of Economics*, 118(3), 909–968.

Ding, Ding, Maibach, Edward W., Zhao, Xiaoquan, Roser-Renouf, Connie and Anthony Leiserowitz. 2011. Support for climate policy and societal action are linked to perceptions about scientific agreement, *Nature Climate Change*, 1, 462–466.

European Environment Agency. 2013. *Late Lessons from Early Warnings: Science, Precaution, Innovation*. EEA Report n. 1/2013. Copenhagen: EEA.

Foucart, Stéphane. 2014. *La fabrique du mensonge: comment les industriels manipulent la science et nous mettent en danger*. Paris: Folio.

Gollier, Christian, Jullien, Bruno and Nicolas Treich. 2000. Scientific progress and irreversibility: an economic interpretation of the precautionary principle, *Journal of Public Economics*, 75, 229–253.

Grossman, Gene M. and Elhanan Helpman. 1994. Protection for sale, *American Economic Review*, 84(4), 833–850.

Horel, Stéphane. 2015. *Intoxication: perturbateurs endocriniens, lobbyistes et eurocrates: une bataille d'influence contre la santé*. Paris: Découverte.

Kamenic, Emir and Matthew Gentzkow. 2011. Bayesian persuasion, *American Economic Review*, 101, 2590–2615.

Levy, Gilat and Ronny Razin. 2015. Does polarisation of opinions lead to polarisation of platforms? The case of correlation neglect, *Quarterly Journal of Political Science*, 10(3), 321–355.

Mahmoudi, Mina and Mark Pingle. 2018. Bounded rationality, ambiguity, and choice, *Journal of Behavioral and Experimental Economics*, 75, 141–153.

Nicolopoulou-Stamati, Polyxeni, Hens, Luc and Vyvyan C. Howard. 2001. *Endocrine Disrupters: Environmental Health and Policies*. Dordrecht: Springer.

Oreskes, Naomi and Erik Conway. 2010. *Merchants of Doubt: How a Handful of Scientists Obscured the Truth on Issues from Tobacco Smoke to Global Warming*. New York: Bloomsbury.

PLoS Medicine Editors. 2009. Ghostwriting: the dirty little secret of medical publishing that just got bigger, *PLoS Medicine*, 6(9), e1000156.

Proctor, Robert N. 2011. *Golden Holocaust: Origins of the Cigarette Catastrophe and the Case for Abolition*. Berkeley and Los Angeles: University of California Press.

Séverac, Claire. 2015. *La guerre secrète contre les peoples*. Choisel: Elie et Mado.

Shapiro, Jesse M. 2016. Special interests and the media: theory and an application to climate change, *Journal of Public Economics*, 144, 91–108.

Sobbrio, Francesco. 2011. Indirect lobbying and media bias, *Quarterly Journal of Political Science*, 6(3–4), 235–274.

Thacker, Paul D. 2014. Consumers deserve to know who's funding health research, *Harvard Business Review*, 2 December.

Vodeb, Oliver. 2017. *Food Democracy: Critical Lessons in Food, Communication, Design and Art*. Bristol: Intellect.

Waldman, Peter, Stecker, Tiffany and Joel Rosenblatt. 2017. Monsanto was its own ghostwriter for some safety reviews, *Bloomberg Businessweek*, 9 August.

Yu, Zhihao. 2005. Environmental protection: a theory of direct and indirect competition for political influence, *Review of Economic Studies*, 72, 269–286.

13 Solution design through a stakeholder process as a new perspective for environmental economics with illustrations from Indian case studies

René Kemp and Shyama V. Ramani

13.1 Introduction

Environmental economics is concerned with the optimal allocation of resources in situations of pollution in which the costs of pollution reduction differ across polluters and where asymmetric emission-related benefits and environmental damage exist. Through calibrated models such as the DICE model of Nordhaus (1994) and theoretical models of the welfare properties of pollution taxes, tradeable permits and environmental regulation, it provides policy analysis.[1] It also draws upon related sub-disciplines like political economy (Oates and Portney, 2003) and game theory (Pavlova and de Zeeuw, 2012) to evaluate policy and collective action impacting the environment. Founded on economic theory and dominated by econometrics and mathematical models it blackboxes actual processes of change. In response, alternative approaches such as steady state economics and ecological footprint analysis have been developed outside environmental economics, under the names of Sustainability Economics and Ecological Economics. Here, the focus is on sustainability and co-evolution rather than efficiency and prices (van den Bergh, 2001). In this vein, the present chapter outlines an approach called 'solution design' as a model for co-designing sustainability transitions for contemporary societal challenges through systemic dialogue or consensus building.

Such an approach is relevant because national and regional governments are increasingly embracing the 'challenge' of harnessing knowledge and promoting innovation and engagement towards local and global priorities. We have a global development agenda in the form of 17 United Nations Sustainable Development Goals (SDGs) for 2030.[2] Similarly, the European Union (EU)'s Horizon 2020 project has identified 7 Grand Societal Challenges,[3] and international agencies like

---

1 Seminal publications are Weitzman's (1974) analysis of the superiority of price-based instruments and quantity-based instruments for different environmental damage functions and Milliman and Prince's (1989) analysis of the incentives for innovation in pollution control under different policy instruments.

2 https://www.undp.org/content/undp/en/home/sustainable-development-goals.html.

3 https://ec.europa.eu/programmes/horizon2020/en/h2020-section/societal-challenges.

US AID and the Bill and Melinda Gates Foundation are targeting specific Grand Development Challenges.[4] A common feature of these challenge-based initiatives is an 'all-hands-on-deck' approach soliciting diverse societal stakeholders to take an active part in sustainability transitions.

In connection with sustainable development, various scholars have employed the term 'transition'. In 1999, the Board on Sustainable Development of the US National Research Council published a book called *Our Common Journey: A Transition toward Sustainability* (NRC, 1999). In the same year, the Tellus Institute in Boston and the Stockholm Environment Institute published a report entitled *Great Transition* in which they offer various scenarios for a transition to a sustainable global society (Raskin et al., 1999). Both publications were followed by a book called *Sustainable Development: The Challenge of Transition* (Schmandt and Ward, 2000). In these works, the term transition is used as a general term for society-wide changes to more sustainable practices and technologies.

In the last 18 years a specialized literature developed in which the term transition is defined and used as a theoretical concept in 1) historical studies looking back at past transitions, and 2) deliberations about steering societies towards more sustainable systems of provision and associated practices. The focus is on transformative change (system innovation), drawing on a (co-evolutionary) socio-technical perspective. Seminal articles in the field are Rotmans et al. (2001), Berkhout et al. (2004), Geels and Schot (2007), Grin et al. (2010) and Smith et al. (2010). Good overviews of the field are offered by Markard et al. (2012) and Loorbach et al. (2017).

According to scholars working in this field, sustainability transitions are transformation processes to systems of production and consumption that are inherently more sustainable (e.g. a switch to renewables, a circular economy and forms of transport other than petrol cars and aviation). They involve system changes with attractive services for end-users; but the process by which they become attractive takes a long while and a great deal of cooperation and coordination among innovation actors. Two other conditions (besides the coordination of innovation activities) are winning over political support and more favourable framework conditions. Examples of sustainability transitions that occurred in the past are: the hygienic transition around 1900 (from cesspools or pit latrines to toilets and integrated sewer systems); and the waste management transition consisting of better waste management practices – such as sanitary waste landfilling, landfill prohibitions for various waste categories and mandatory separate collection of organic household waste (Geels and Kemp, 2007; Kemp and van Lente, 2011). For meeting the target of limiting global warming to 1.5°C and reducing air pollution we need transitions in energy and mobility; and for reducing resource use and waste we need to close material loops (a transition to a circular economy).

---

4 https://grandchallenges.org/initiatives.

Achieving these transitions is difficult because of: sunk cost advantages of existing technologies; infrastructure needs of new technologies; the need for new technologies to become cheaper and better adapted to user needs; institutional rigidities; and social structural behaviours (Kemp, 1994; Cowan and Gunby, 1996; Foxon, 2007; Seto et al., 2016; Lorek and Spangenberg, 2014).

Two ways to move to systems based on alternative technologies are: 1) to promote green technologies via subsidy policies and innovation policies; and 2) to discourage the use of non-sustainable technologies via pollution taxes, carbon taxes, regulations and nudges. Each of these policies has limits to their use, having to do with the costs and resistance.

In this chapter we propose a third way of working towards transitional change – through a design-based approach that starts from the needs and concerns of real people and organizations, and that explicitly deals with the associated systemic possibilities and constraints. We call this approach 'solution design' because of the explicit attention to matching possibilities with needs and proactive attention to negative side-effects. In solution design the needs of end-users and producers are being matched with possibilities for positive change through processes of social learning and guided evolution. The model is part of a tradition in design which aspires to drive system-level change (Press and Cooper, 2003; Murray et al., 2010; Bason, 2016; Irwin, 2015). Solution design combines design thinking with social science in a stakeholder process.

Solution design draws upon elements of four different streams of literature:

1. innovation studies, a multidisciplinary field comprising different approaches (for overviews, see Fagerberg et al., 2012 and Martin et al., 2012);
2. capacity development (Mytelka et al., 2012; Eade, 1997);
3. social learning in rural resource management (Röling and van der Fliert, 1994; Leeuwis and Pyburn, 2002); and
4. technology assessment and reflexive modernization (Grin et al., 2004; Voss et al., 2006; Bos et al., 2009; van Mierlo et al., 2010).

To those aspects a transition lens of system change is applied to construct frameworks involving innovation (Geels, 2005; Grin et al., 2010; Elzen and Wieczorek, 2005) at the meso-regime and meso-sectoral level as opposed to the traditional macroeconomic or micro-organizational settings (Steward, 2012). Solution design has a number of desirable features, which we illustrate through our discussion below of bollworm pest and the elimination of open defecation in India. Solution design takes care of a number of difficulties for any type of managed change.

First, the present work takes into consideration the complementarity between diverse kinds/sources of lock-ins (technological, institutional, infrastructural, behavioural, cultural, etc.) and the design of policy responses. Though these factors have been noted in the literature and their role in keeping back sustainability has been extensively studied, there are few frameworks that permit tracing their interrelationships in pushing or holding back sustainability transitions. To close this gap, we develop a policy tool focusing on six central elements that make up the 'SISTER' framework:

1. characterization of the *system* concerned;
2. *innovation* and new infrastructure for transition;
3. the *shared* learning or vision and skilling necessary for transition;
4. leveraging of appropriate *technologies* and capabilities required for transition;
5. *engagement* needed for successful implementation with cooperation from the systemic actors; and
6. necessary, sufficient and/or favourable conditions for *replication* of intervention.

In short, our SISTER framework facilitates understanding of past evolution and identification of the diverse types of investments required for a sustainability transition by considering these six sets of factors.

Second, the SISTER framework of solution design seeks to bring evidence of what works to policymakers, and seeks to prevent 'policy resistance' through a stakeholder process which aims to achieve buy-in to new socio-technical solutions. According to de Gooyert et al. (2016), 'policy resistance' is the tendency of a system to defeat the policies designed to improve it, and this is a persistent problem in sustainability transitions.

Third, the SISTER solution design addresses the critiques highlighted by Lachman (2013). In his survey of transition approaches, he points out the need for frameworks that can be applied to both developed and developing country contexts and asks for an expansion of the focus – to go beyond technological innovation by including non-technological innovations and other systemic features such as social norms, consumption patterns, etc.

Fourth, the SISTER framework responds to the call by Lorek and Spangenberg (2014) to integrate better in sustainability transition studies the role of non-governmental organizations (NGOs), social enterprises and civil society, which can stimulate and mobilise the forces necessary for institutional changes through bottom-up initiatives, networking and advocacy efforts.

The cases demonstrate the utility of a design-based stakeholder approach that addresses the real concerns of actors and the associated systemic possibilities and constraints for which we will present details at the end of the chapter, the remainder of which is organized as follows. Section 13.2 presents our theoretical framework for solution design (SISTER). This is followed in Section 13.3 by two case studies of innovation-based transitions for green development in India, namely genetically modified cotton and low-cost toilets. The first case comprises a transition in technology paradigms in the Indian cotton sector, from being a high pesticide using activity to a lower pesticide consuming one. The second refers to an enormous behavioural transition of at least 50 per cent of the Indian population from open defecation to the use of toilets, in a mission to lower environmental contamination and support human dignity. Section 13.4 presents a design-based approach called 'solution design' as a (policy) tool for stakeholder engagement, involving research, innovation and outreach activities for sustainability transitions. The research element could benefit from environmental economics. At present, the two perspectives are quite separate from each other, but this could change.

13.2   The SISTER framework for an innovation-oriented approach to sustainability transitions

In this section we offer a conceptual framework for evaluating market-led and government- and donor-based approaches for diffusing green technologies. The framework is applied to two cases of innovation as an organizational framework for describing experiences and making recommendations. The case studies highlight the many difficulties and failures in creating robust and affordable green solutions in developing countries. The sources for this are: relying too much on commercial solutions from industry; a public sector research and extension system in need of reform and boost; solution designs that did not consider second round effects of agro-ecological systems or sanitation; and clientelism and poor capabilities for good decision making in government. As mentioned above, the framework consists of six elements:

S – for the System of interaction, composed of actors and their relations
I – for Infrastructure, institutions and innovation
S – for Social learning and skilling
T – for Technology (new technology, technology redesign or better/new utilization of existing technology)
E – for the Engagement of technology promoters with users
R – for Replication through policies for diffusion, adapted to changing circumstances, dealing with negative side-effects.

The framework is actor-centred by involving economic actors local firms, foreign firms, private organizations), public agencies, consumers, universities and public labs, NGOs and state institutions. Nature is also part of it. By Nature, we mean the ecology or the 'natural environment' within which the economic actors carry out their activities. Nature is a non-human, non-strategic player in the innovation system that does not seek to maximize self-payoffs vis-à-vis the moves of other players. Instead, it responds with biophysical actions according to universal biophysical laws of the actions of economic players. While the play of economic actors can be predicted to a large extent by assuming that they are driven by maximization of self-interest, only the short-run responses of Nature can be forecast using the existing scientific knowledge base. The need for considering the interplay between natural environment and socio-economic change is the central feature

GMVs case actor system   Sanitation case actor system

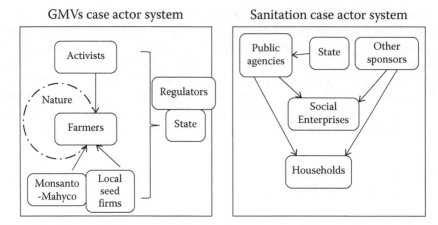

Figure 13.1   Examples of sectoral innovation systems

of social-ecological systems analysis, a field that started with the seminal publication by Berkes and Folke (1998) and whose evolution is described in Colding and Barthel (2019).

In Figure 13.1 important actors involved in the two cases of genetically modified plant varieties and sanitation are given. It shows that the actor systems are quite different from each other.

The actors are constrained by capabilities and resources, and operate under implicit and explicit rules in the form of established practices, laws, social norms, fashions, etc. at multiple levels that guide the relations and interactions among individuals, groups and organizations. Our perspective is mindful of the situated and actor-specific nature of knowledge, and assigns a positive role for policymakers and platforms of deliberation and action.

13.3   Illustrations of the application of solution designs: two case studies

13.3.1   Diffusion of genetically modified plant varieties (GMVs)[5]

The problem: In developing countries, poor farmers are burdened by an ever-pressing need to increase productivity, which often leads them to apply more chemicals such as fertilizers and pesticides. However, over time, this leads to substantial environmental degradation, which lowers soil fertility and ultimately productivity, as illustrated by the yellowing of the Green Revolution (Murgai et al., 2001; Larson et al., 2004). Finding a solution to this problem would clearly impact poverty, health and the environment.

---

5 This case study is drawn from prior works by Shyama Ramani listed in the references.

A systemic solution: To stem falling productivity the main types of solutions proposed have been knowledge generation on agro-ecological practices, better machinery, safer agrochemicals and higher-quality seeds. These have been traditionally produced by universities and public laboratories, and diffused by agricultural extension services and seed breeders. However, since the 1990s, agri-biotech multinationals (MNEs) like Monsanto, DuPont and Syngenta have introduced a radical innovation in the form of seeds derived from genetically modified plant varieties, or GMVs. With desirable traits such as pest resistance, GMVs lower the need for agrochemicals, and lessen soil and water contamination. Hence, they can also be considered a radical eco-innovation that can be at the base of a sustainability transition.

The stakeholder response: GMVs have triggered ideological clashes among innovators, MNEs and societal stakeholders worldwide (Bennett et al., 2013; Azadi and Ho, 2010). It is difficult, if not impossible, to ascertain with precision the medium- to long-term risks (or even benefits) from laboratory or field trial data because of genuine scientific uncertainty. Local actors question the legitimacy of the technology and its carriers, for seeds form the basis of sustenance of farmers and ultimately society. Further, policy and civil society representatives are concerned that the proprietary rights of GMVs are almost entirely in private hands.

The naysayer response: Apparently, 38 countries have simply banned GMVs in all their forms, in an extreme application of the precautionary principle that advocates taking preventative measures to tackle potential threats to society.[6] Indeed, while the precautionary principle is accepted in general worldwide, it is interpreted differently in different countries, leading to different outcomes vis-à-vis GMVs. The European stance to ban GMV cultivation is founded on a 'process-based' regulatory framework wherein the techniques used to create the innovation also determine the form of regulation, in contrast to a product-based regulatory framework, followed in the USA and Canada, which focuses only on the inherent risk of the final product.

The application of the precautionary principle is supported by studies confirming that diffusion of GMVs has led to genetic contamination of conventional plants and the emergence of super weeds with increased resistance to herbicides (Gilbert, 2013). For instance, Weaver and Morris (2005) explain that while such risks of genetic contamination are present with conventional varieties also, it is essentially the process of creating GMVs that increases the risk of unpredictable consequences. They point out that genetic modification is often to enable the targeted plants to produce proteins that they would not otherwise produce; but this creates a risk that the GMVs may also produce proteins that were not intended, and such effects may be manifested with a time lag longer than that required for safety tests.

---

6 https://sustainablepulse.com/2015/10/22/gm-crops-now-banned-in-36-countries-worldwide-sustainable-pulse-research/#.XKsRwtixXIU. There is no public agency document that has statistics on where GM crops are banned.

A GMV enthusiast – diffusion of Bt cotton in India: Genetically modified cotton is also referred to as Bt cotton because it contains the cry1Ac gene transferred from a bacterium called *Bacillus thuringiensis.* This gene is responsible for expressing a toxin that kills insect pests popularly known as bollworms, which feed on flowers, buds and leaves. Whenever a pest eats any part of a Bt plant variety it dies, thereby limiting losses in yields. By switching to Bt cotton hybrids, farmers have the possibility of reducing yield loss due to pest attack, lowering pesticide spraying and saving on labour costs. Thus, GM seeds like Bt cotton are an eco-innovation. Its popularity with farmers makes it the third most diffused GMV globally, after maize and soybean, with 24.1 million hectares devoted to it, and the top GMV in emerging countries.[7]

By the start of the 1990s Indian cotton yields were among the lowest in world, with high cost of cultivation, poor-quality seeds and poor fibre attributes of hybrids, which deteriorated rapidly with successive pickings. The consumption of pesticides in cotton cultivation was as high as 54 per cent of the total pesticide consumption in the country, reflecting the need for farmers to save the produce from pernicious bollworms. Such pesticide usage not only increased the burden on poor farmers but also severely damaged the environment (Raghuram, 2002). Thus, Bt cotton provided a potentially empowering and environmentally friendly solution.

Monsanto's Bt cotton varieties were available in the US market by 1995, but with foresight the company had reached out to emerging country targets even before it commercialized Bt cotton in the USA. By 1998, it had established the joint venture Mahyco Monsanto Biotech (India) company (MMB). By 2000, MMB obtained permission from the Department of Biotechnology to conduct large-scale trials in India. This was met with strong protests from activists, and the matter went to the Supreme Court. Then, in 2001 the Genetic Engineering Approval Committee (GEAC), which operates under the Ministry of Environment, received a complaint from Monsanto of industrial misconduct by a local seed firm whereby Bt cotton seeds had been diffused and planted at a time when its commercialization had not been approved in India. This was because a bollworm infestation had swept through the state of Gujarat but in some zones the cotton crop was unaffected, raising suspicions. Monsanto could not press charges against the local company as its Bt gene was not patent protected in India. Then agents of GEAC immediately threatened to burn the cotton fields grown with these seeds that were illegal as they had not yet been approved. However, as farmers hugged their plants and protested, nothing could be done except to make Bt cotton legal, by 2002. That said, as the head of the local firm was a former employee of Monsanto and no charges were finally pressed against him, there was speculation that this diffusion could have been intentional to demonstrate the value of Bt cotton to poor farmers, and gain their support.

---

7 http://www.isaaa.org/resources/publications/briefs/53/download/isaaa-brief-53-2017.pdf Table 35.

The Indian government tried to preserve environmental security initially by impos-ing a regulation that any Bt cotton field had to be surrounded by a belt of non-Bt cotton constituting at least 20 per cent of the total cultivated area to catch any pollen from the GMV field and contain contamination. However, for small farmers this was not economical, so they did not comply with the regulation (Jayarman, 2002). In response, given that the Indian regulatory bureaucracy did not have the wherewithal to allocate personnel for comprehensive monitoring and punishment of thousands of small farmers, it changed the regulation instead. Now, even plant-ing of refuges is voluntary.

Presently, there is a flourishing illegal markets for Bt cotton seeds, i.e. seeds which have not been validated by the Indian biosafety regulatory system before entering the market. Demand for illegal seeds is also high due to their confirmed ability to resist bollworm and their low price (Jayaraman, 2002). The market for unauthor-ized seeds is supported by the development of new varieties created by local farm-ing ingenuity and by informal social networks between farmers based on trust, though their quality is affirmed to be lower than that of the legal seeds (Morse et al., 2005).

There have been heavy policy swings. For instance, bowing to activists, the Indian Ministry of Environment and Forests initially imposed an indefinite moratorium on the commercialization of, Bt brinjal (aubergine), the first GM food crop to seek approval (in 2010). Then, in 2014 the newly elected government lifted the morato-rium, and approved field trials for GM mustard in 2016. But, due to protests, the moratorium was reinstated in 2017. Despite these controversies, there is still no institutional mechanism that allows for the participation and consensus building on GM policy through dialogue between all stakeholders, and farmer groups are notably absent in the discourse between activists (who claim to represent them) and the government (Kanaujia and Bhattacharya, 2017).

From this chequered history, it is possible to infer recommendations for achieving better outcomes. These are provided in Table 13.1. The reason for using the SISTER framework for structuring the recommendations is that it helps us to understand the value of the model for solution design offered in the next section.

What insights are provided by the GMV case study for environmental economists? First, environmental economics should create space for the possibility of irrecon-cilable controversy – when people disagree on values at stake and on means–ends relationships, and thus the knowledge for resolving the debate (Hoppe, 2011, Chapter 5). The greater the controversy surrounding a societal challenge, the greater the need for solution design (with many elements) rather than a solu-tion with focus on a single set of related instrument variables. Controversy refers to differences of opinion among stakeholders that can escalate into prolonged public disagreements, risk of misallocation of resources or costly investment in consensus building. To minimize controversy the Indian government had to make diverse concessions to different stakeholders; but to ensure farmer welfare and

Table 13.1   Recommendations to improve the impact of GMVs

SISTER Element	Remedial Measures
Innovation	Invest in R&D to develop new GMVs that do not contain Monsanto's genes in public sector laboratories
Systemic learning capabilities	Invest in training the agricultural research service to transfer science-based information on possible implications of GMVs in the long run along with short-term benefits
Technology	Invest in training farmer groups on the usefulness of appropriate agro-ecological practices for GMV cultivation, and especially the need for refuges as a safety net against widespread contamination and development of super weeds
Engagement	Make regulation clear and accountable; engage in systemic dialogue with all stakeholders, especially giving farmer groups a voice
Replication	Use a strategy for wider diffusion that is attentive to all of the above points in terms of catch-up on innovation capabilities, education of farmers, systemic dialogue and enforcement of regulation have to be addressed, otherwise controversy will continue to prevail

long-term environmental security, specially directed investments are necessary in education, research and institutional reform. Thus, in solution design optimal allocation of resources *ex ante* and calibrated models have no meaning as designs are an exploration of stakeholder pathways and associated outcomes. However, impact analysis remains important and should be undertaken periodically to fine-tune the pathway.

Second, the greater the complexity, the greater the need for a solution design process through which a multitude of possibilities are investigated for different socio-technical and biophysical contexts. There are many definitions of complexity: in our case, greater complexity means less control for any economic actor, including the state, to control systemic outcomes. For example, the Indian government could not prevent Monsanto from commercializing, even though entry was through the back door. Similarly, it would be very costly for any government to monitor thousands of farmers for compliance. It has to therefore ensure welfare through strengthening farmers' knowledge and the innovative capabilities of public laboratories. Again, detailed modelling for optimal allocation of resources for planned transitions works in systems in which the actions of economic actors are controlled through enforcement of regulation combined with incentives. Otherwise, solution designs tackling the shortcomings of the systemic outcomes and their associated externalities have to be called in. We now turn to the second case: strategies to eliminate open defecation in India.

13.3.2   Eliminating open defecation (OD) in India through diffusion of low-cost toilets[8]

Problem: At the start of the millennium, 51 per cent of the global population had no access to a functioning toilet; this now stands at 39 per cent, with about 2.4 billion people still lacking access to sanitation. Excreta-related diseases refer to infections by pathogens that are present and thrive in excreta. Excreta-related infections trigger illnesses that range from relatively innocuous diarrhoea to life-threatening diseases or debilitating states. Among communicable excreta-related diseases, as of 2016, diarrhoeal diseases were the number two cause of deaths in lower middle-income countries (911,451 per year among communicable diseases) and the number one cause in low-income countries (383,400 per year).[9] Even in 2016, disability-adjusted life years (DALYs) due to diarrhoeal diseases ranked second in low-income countries and fourth in lower middle-income countries.[10] Finally, lack of sanitation also keeps women under threat of harassment, violence and rape, and forces millions of girls in developing countries to abandon education at puberty (UNHR, 2011).

Solution: Starting from the premise that any product is an innovation for a potential user who currently has no access to one, toilets are akin to an innovation for households that never used them before. Moreover, even though an artefact such as a low-cost toilet is associated with a simple technology, it costs at least ten times more than a cheap mobile phone, and additional efforts are required to make users 'accept' it and change their behaviour away from open defecation. Thus, it is not an enticing sector for firms, and the mantle of toilet diffusion falls on social entrepreneurs and the state. Here, we summarize the efforts of the latter.

In most developing countries, national sanitation drives have evolved to be one of the following four types.

Type 1 – Free/subsidized provision in top-down programmes: Initially, the state diffused sanitation via state-funded national programmes. These purely top-down initiatives provided toilets as a merit good to households on the assumption that availability will lead to usage. Such programmes were for the most part major failures due to lack of demand from people who did not see the need or feel the desire for sanitation, and badly constructed toilets by public agencies.

Type 2 – Demand/Community-Led Total Sanitation (CLTS): In the late 1990s, development consultant Kamal Kar proposed a novel pathway to eliminate OD that came to be called the Community-Led Total Sanitation (CLTS) approach (Kar and Chambers, 2008). It was revolutionary in the sense that it moved away from

---

8 This section is based on Shyama V. Ramani's prior work on sanitation both as a researcher and practitioner for about 14 years (see References). It also includes her writing in academic blogs.

9 http://www.who.int/healthinfo/global_burden_disease/en/.

10 https://www.who.int/healthinfo/global_burden_disease/estimates/en/index1.html.

the provision of subsidies to incentivize toilet construction, and instead proposed community-level discussions as a more effective policy instrument for behavioural change. CLTS involved triggering repugnance and shame through self-appraisal of OD. Under this approach, communities are facilitated to conduct their own analysis of the impact of OD on health, and take action to become open defecation free.

As a people-centric approach grounded in participatory development, CLTS is supposed to give quick results at low cost. Hygiene behaviour is expected to improve through improved knowledge and awareness of health- and environment-related issues. International bodies like the World Bank's Water and Sanitation Programme (WSP), Plan International, UNICEF, WaterAid, the UN's Water Supply and Sanitation Collaborative Council (WSSCC), World Vision, etc. enthusiastically took to the Handbook and have promoted CLTS worldwide, encouraging governments to make it a cornerstone of their national policy.

Type 3 – Community-Led Total Sanitation (CLTS) with government subsidy: A comparative study of CLTS and pure subsidy schemes found that community motivation alone did not increase hygienic latrine ownership, and neither did supply-side interventions. However, a combination of the two worked best, and encouraged investment in toilets even among unsubsidized neighbours (Guiteras et al., 2015). At the same time, in contrast to large-scale infrastructure-focused initiatives, NGO-led programmes focus more on building trust and good will with the beneficiaries first, and hence the likelihood of success of sanitation interventions increases with their participation (Carrad et al., 2009). For instance, in Bangladesh micro-finance institutions facilitated the usage of subsidies for toilet construction, and NGOs created awareness on the benefits of hygiene behaviour so that the toilets were fully used (Hadi, 2000). Despite the enormous organizational and institutional diversity in sanitation delivery platforms, governments and particularly local authorities play a central role worldwide, and public funding is an irreplaceable condition for success (Castro, 2012).

Type 4 – Consortium-led sanitation drives: Under the present global agenda, SDG6 has created business opportunities for private actors to contribute to sanitation coverage. However, large firms, which are the typical partners of the state, are not active in the low-cost sanitation sector and have no business interests in contributing to sanitation coverage. Therefore, the private actors to tackle major necessities are mainly social enterprises operating in novel consortia involving public agencies, large firms and international bodies. Different consortia could drive sanitation differently and, when done properly, also better.

13.3.3   What is the end result?

Public and private investment: There has been huge investment in building toilets and creating awareness and motivation through education by national governments and international agencies. Governments are sponsoring the development of a private market for sanitation in a variety of ways with non-profits, self-help groups, women's organizations, village councils and municipalities. Private firms that are active in the Water, Sanitation and Hygiene (WASH) sector consist of two types. Category 1 comprises companies whose main line of activity (i.e. production, distribution, retail, other services, etc.) is in WASH – such as Unilever, PepsiCo, CocaCola and Carlsberg. Category 2 consists of firms outside the WASH sector that sponsor projects as part of their corporate social responsibility (CSR) programmes. The drivers of CSR engagement in WASH sectors are: new market creation, building brand equity, strengthening employee engagement and/or mitigation of societal risks.

Money also is being spent on innovation. Since 2010, the Bill and Melinda Gates Foundation has allocated $200 million to bring out sanitation innovations, and it intends to invest $200 million to achieve the 2030 target of zero open defecation to achieve a market value of $6 billion (Tang, 2018). In India, premiere engineering institutions such as the Indian Institute of Technology (IIT) regularly come out with new models, and entrepreneurs regularly showcase innovations related to sanitation.

Adoption of toilets: From the supply side, there is a major problem of dissemination of good-quality toilets by all kinds of sponsors – the state, international agencies and private firms. Thousands of toilets lie abandoned in India (and in Africa), either never used or abandoned after short use due to poor construction quality or inappropriate technology design. Low-quality toilets can have systemic impact. When a toilet's superstructure begins to deteriorate or the toilet stops working well, problems can emerge. For example, if a family cannot afford or does not want to invest in repairs, or if there is no local agency to repair toilets (which is often the case), foul odours and leaks may begin. This, in turn, creates negative perceptions about toilets, which may trigger a bandwagon effect such that the whole community ultimately returns to open defecation (Ramani and SadreGhazi, 2014).

Impact on environment and health: The commonly diffused models are a single or double pit latrine, and septic-tank based toilets. However, when pits or septic tanks are made incorrectly, or put too close to one another (double pits) or too close to a water source, or when the bottom of the pit is not sufficiently above groundwater level, the use of toilets can contaminate groundwater sources. The contamination following sanitation drives and negative impacts on health has been noted (Graham and Polizzotto, 2013; Pujari et al., 2012) but so far not resolved. Masonry is one element of the problem. Usually, sponsors run one-week programmes to teach masonry for toilet construction as it is assumed that this skill can be acquired in a week, which is almost always never the case. In addition, illiterate rural masons are often intimidated even by such formal training. They usually learn their craft by doing, or through apprenticeships leading to a learning trajectory that is slow, shaky and tacit – meaning that two people with the same skill set may execute a project differently.

Impact on women and human dignity: While the CLTS has been hailed and promoted in many projects and countries, it has not had the desired impact in others.
Women, despite having a high demand for safe toilet facilities, continue to practise
unsafe sanitation because of gender-based power dynamics at the household level
influencing toilet adoption and use that policy is unable to address (Khanna and
Das, 2016). WASH interventions in schools have not prioritised menstrual hygiene,
thus exposing girls and the entire school community to health-related hazards
(Ndlovu and Bhala, 2016). Strategies of shaming to promote toilets have created
a problem of their own. In 2017, it was reported that some unscrupulous officials
in some Indian states (e.g. Rajasthan and Madhya Pradesh) were photographing
women defecating as a shaming strategy. A male activist who protested in Rajasthan
was lynched, according to eyewitnesses (Ramani, 2017).

Despite some successes, it remains a major challenge to diffuse quality and safe
sanitation in developing countries. As for the first case, we use the experiences
to make recommendations for better strategies of diffusion and innovation
(Table 13.2).

What insights follow from the case study of the Indian national programme for
universal sanitation coverage, as a typical, government-led project in a developing
country, for environmental economists?

First, the greater the number of objectives to fulfil, the greater is the need for a
solution design. Worldwide, governments are grappling with achieving the triple
bottom line – a combination of economic development, environmental sustainability and social inclusion (Sachs, 2012). For instance, to improve the health status
of citizens, universal sanitation coverage is necessary. To achieve this as quickly as
possible with available resources, the Indian government is sponsoring the building
of millions of pit latrines, many of which will be contaminating water sources and
soil in a decade's time. Furthermore, many of the targeted beneficiaries are not
interested in adopting toilets, especially the ecologically safe ones. Thus, to tackle
these multiple problems, they should be implementing a solution design which
can be improved as proposed in the recommendations. Scientific evidence has an
important role to play in this. Measurements of contamination by households and
by public programmes would be most useful to convince all stakeholders to go for
a slower and safer process of universal sanitation coverage. The implications of different technology designs for contamination would also be a good area for solution
exploration.

Second, the greater the agency problem in projects, the greater the potential for
solution design. In developing countries, increasingly public–private consortia
are being sought to attain national missions, and small and medium-sized social
enterprises (SMEs) are playing a greater role. However, consortia are racked by
incomplete information about one another's capabilities and intentions. Long-term
impact is jointly determined by the true intentions of the partners, their capabilities
and the nature of contextual challenges. Therefore, solution designs (rather than

Table 13.2   Recommendations to improve the impact of sanitation drives

SISTER Element	Remedial Measures
Innovation	Invest in user-friendly alternatives to pit latrines (improve on urine diverting dry toilets)
	Invest in toilet seats that can be fitted over rural pan squat toilets
	Invest in creation of community toilets that can produce energy from human waste
	Create good models to run clean community toilets as a sustainable business
Infrastructure	Better-quality toilets: the challenge is to diffuse not just any toilet but a high-quality, long-lasting, non-contaminating product that minimizes water and soil pollution and promotes sustained use. This will require the sanitation subsystem (i.e. the part under the toilet seat/slab) and its waste-processing technology design to be adapted to the geophysical features of the targeted zone, taking into account soil type, rainfall, water table, water availability, wind velocity and slope.
Social learning and skilling	Invest in training masons to build safe toilets, and monitor them to test if they have assimilated the knowledge
	Create certification of skills so that quality can be signalled clearly
	Invest in training all in the supply chain on the dangers of building unsafe and unsustainable sanitation
	Create material for teaching about sanitation and hygiene behaviour that is localized and respectful of the challenges of the poor
Technology	Ensure that the type of toilet built is fit for the environment and, in the case of pit latrines, ensure that the base of the pit is at least 3 metres above the water source even during the rainy season
Engagement	Limit the implementation of shaming strategies to developing community-level awareness and motivation so that individuals are not targeted and harassed
Replication	Only toilets suitable for use should be disseminated; this requires toilet expertise, (biophysical) knowledge of the context of application and proper training of masons

pre-designated solutions) are required to incentivize different partners in different ways for high-quality, sustained social impact. Again, monitoring systems, impact analysis and sustainability audits vis-à-vis the environment are necessary to avoid good results that are, alas, short-lived. These are issues that have been studied by environmental economists. Agent-based modelling may be used to good effect here.

Third, environmental economists have developed sophisticated methods of evaluating willingness to pay. Application of these methods, combined with scientific evidence on the long-term costs of contamination by pit latrines and negative externalities to the environment caused by OD, would be useful to accelerate the process of safe universal sanitation coverage. Sharing of costs by households and not placing the entire responsibility on providers would be welfare enhancing.

13.4   A model of solution design based on the SISTER framework

In this section we present an approach called 'solution design' as a policy tool to address contemporary societal challenges with extensive stakeholder outreach for consensus building. The tool is based on the negative experiences with market-led approaches and push strategies of donors and governments. The model of solution design, which is based on the SISTER framework elements outlined in Section 13.2, is mindful of the situated and actor-specific knowledge, needs and concerns; recognizes complexity, is attentive to the possibility of unexpected results in innovation-based change; and assigns a positive role for policymakers and social research. For ease of exposition, we present the model as a step plan.

The first step consists of system analysis in terms of the problem at hand and the need for multifunctional solutions that address multiple issues (including cultural issues of gender and inequality). In this step, the state has a special responsibility in making sure that systemic solutions are being investigated through integrated thinking and for enquiring into root causes of problems. An analysis of the sources of lock-in to suboptimal practices is part of the analysis. Let this step be given by 'S' for system analysis. The system analysis element in the stakeholder process of solution design is important for helping participants to define the main system imperfections and their interrelationships, and hence to recognize complexity, multi-causality and unexpected results. In addition to this, it helps participants question assumptions about trade-offs, interests and roles instead of taking them as given (van Mierlo et al., 2010; Bos et al., 2009).

The second step consists of programmes for developing adequate technologies and innovations, alongside adequate testing of these. The technologies should make best use of local and non-local knowledge and capabilities.

Third, based on the deliberations in steps 1 and 2, a plan is constructed for implementation of solutions selected for use. This involves soliciting a variety of engagements (E) from economic actors for the generation, diffusion and adoption of the technology and innovation elements of the solution design. There is systemic learning (S) and responses by the economic actors based on this.

Fourth, a solution-based transition is initiated through the use of promotion strategies and policies to limit negative effects. For making good policies, the recommendations of Rodrik (2014) for green industrial policy are particularly useful. According to him, policy action should be grounded in deep knowledge about innovation possibilities and the factors that keep the exploitation of those possibilities back. For this, he attributes positive value to deliberation councils, supplier

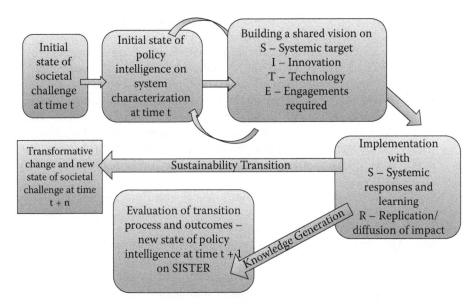

Figure 13.2   An innovation-based solution design framework

development forums, search networks, regional collaborative innovation centres, investment advisory councils, sectoral round-tables and private–public venture funds. Policies for use are based on identified barriers, which are ascertained in discussions with experts and business. Another important task is to adapt the policies on the basis of policy impact analysis and policy evaluation. For safeguarding the public interest and obtaining buy-in, policy agencies should be publicly accountable as to their failures and successes. Without all of this, we easily get policy failure.

With implementation, there is systemic learning (S) and responses from systemic actors. This leads to a refinement of the solution design elements SISTER. Solution design thus is based on a reflexive, iterative process. A visualization of the solution design model based on the SISTER framework is given in Figure 13.2.

The solution design model uses features of the opportunities-to-impact R&D cycle of van de Fliert and Braun (2002), consisting of three steps to be undertaken in an iterative, cyclical manner:

1.   Research and development: an iterative and synergistic set of co-creative processes is conducted to:
   •   identify needs and opportunities
   •   generate new information and innovations through basic and/or applied research
   •   consolidate these with existing practice
   •   translate them into learning objectives, activities and models for enhanced systemic performance.

2. Extension and implementation to targeted stakeholders: the learning models developed are passed on to and implemented by extension organizations, through which the innovations are shared with larger groups of targeted stakeholders. They test and evaluate the information and innovations, internalize (or reject) them in their practices and share them with fellow users, which should finally lead to impact at the individual and community levels.
3. Monitoring and evaluation: a reflective mechanism is set in place where each step of the cycle is reviewed and adjusted, and appropriateness of outputs from research and development activities is measured by quality of processes, effects and impacts occurring during extension and implementation.

Among the different actors, the state has a special role in making sure that solution designs take into account interests of systemic actors, and especially those of the needy and vulnerable who lack organization and resources. Through networks of public agencies, the state may intervene in the form of funding special R&D projects, funding extension programmes (or undertaking them themselves) and safeguarding the public interest through regulation and the use of standards. To be able to do so, they have to engage in capacity building inside and outside the state. A solution design serves the goal of orienting government agencies towards actions to address the societal challenge.

13.5   Conclusions

In this chapter, we outlined a model of solution design for sustainability problems of bad sanitation and waste management. Solution design is a design-based approach that starts from the needs and concerns of real people (which are ascertained) with proactive attention to negative side-effects. Solution design combines design thinking with social science in a stakeholder process. The model is relevant for developing countries and developed countries; but the focus in this chapter is on developing countries, where we illustrate the need for solution design for the cases of bollworm pest and the elimination of open defecation in India.

What is the relevance of the solution design approach for environmental economists? In our mind, environmental economists can play a useful role in solution design in three ways. First, they can incorporate in their welfare analysis the welfare gains and disbenefits (costs in economic terms) of particular technology options because of differences in the context of application (biophysical differences, but also differences related to people aspects of capabilities and institutions and incentives under which people make choices). Agent-based models in a heterogeneous fitness landscape appears a particularly fruitful avenue for understanding actor-based interdependencies and differences. Second, in their interactions with policymakers (direct or indirect), they can advocate policy prescriptions in an economic, informed way. The solution design approach merits attention from scholars of environmental economics because system change pathways not only require coalitions but also helpful policy frameworks that tilt the playing field in the right direction so that environmentally and socially advantageous change can take place in a sustained way. The experience with action research may also allow them to become action researchers themselves (like us), allowing them to act as change agents. Third, they may want to pay more attention to controversies that are not conducive to a rational problem-solving approach, but call for interest accommodation and dialogue (Hoppe, 2011). In our assessment, evolutionary economics is better equipped to deal with issues of complexity than with controversy. Collaboration with other social science disciplines and ecological scientists helps deal with such aspects.

To sum up, to address the grand societal challenges of today we need to create innovations and arrangements around which to gain legitimacy from the concerned societal stakeholders. Inventions sprouting from research laboratories have a role to play, but the main challenge lies in finding suitable socio-technical solutions for use. Markets do not necessarily generate the best solutions, and government policies may inadequately consider risks of particular products and local needs. Knowledge of what works and what does not obtained from trials and early diffusion offers useful feedback for policy. Integrating these elements in environmental economics will improve the relevance of the analysis through a better treatment of innovation and people/agency aspects of change. For a good understanding of systemic evolution and solution designs, knowledge of local contexts, culture, history and institutions is important.

References

Azadi, H., & Ho, P. (2010). Genetically modified and organic crops in developing countries: a review of options for food security. *Biotechnology Advances*, 28(1): 160–168.

Bason, C. (2016). *Design for Policy*. London: Taylor & Francis.

Bennett, A. B., Chi-Ham, C., Barrows, G., Sexton, S., & Zilberman, D. (2013). Agricultural biotechnology: economics, environment, ethics, and the future. *Annual Review of Environment and Resources*, 38: 249–279.

Berkes, F., & Folke, C. (eds) (1998). *Linking Social and Ecological Systems: Management Practices and Social Mechanisms for Building Resilience*. Cambridge: Cambridge University Press.

Berkhout, F., Smith, A., & Stirling, A. (2004). Technological regimes, transition contexts and the environment, in B. Elzen, F. Geels and K. Green (eds), *System Innovation and the Transition to Sustainability: Theory, Evidence and Policy*. Cheltenham, UK and Northampton, MA, USA: Edward Elgar Publishing, pp. 48–75.

Bos, A. P., Groot Koerkamp, P., Gosselink, J. M. J., & Bokma, S. (2009). Reflexive interactive design and its application in a project on sustainable dairy systems. *Outlook on Agriculture*, 38(2): 137–145.

Carrard, N., Pedi, D., Willetts, J., & Powell, B. (2009). Non-government organisation engagement in the sanitation sector: opportunities to maximise benefits. *Water Science and Technology*, 60: 3109–3119.

Castro, J. E. (2012). *Water and Sanitation Services: Public Policy and Management*. London: Earthscan.

Colding, J., & Barthel, S. (2019). Exploring the social-ecological systems discourse 20 years later. *Ecology and Society*, 24(1): 2. https://doi.org/10.5751/ES-10598-240102.

Cowan, R., & Gunby, P. (1996). Sprayed to death: path dependence, lock-in and pest control strategies. *Economic Journal*, 106(436): 521–542.

de Gooyert, V., Rouwette, E. A. J. A., van Kranenburg, H. L., Freeman, R. E., & van Breen, H. J. (2016). Sustainability transition dynamics: towards overcoming policy resistance. *Technological Forecasting and Social Change*, 111: 135–145.

Eade, D. (1997). *Capacity-Building: An Approach to People-Centred Development*. Oxford: Oxfam.

Elzen. B., & Wieczorek, A. (2005). Transitions towards sustainability through system innovation. *Technological Forecasting and Social Change*, 72: 651–661.

Fagerberg, J., Fosaas, M., & Sapprasert, K. (2012). Innovation: exploring the knowledge base. *Research Policy*, 41(7): 1132–1153.

Foxon, T. J. (2007). Technological lock-in and the role of innovation. In G. Atkinson, S. Dietz, & E. Neumayer (eds.), *Handbook of Sustainable Development*. Cheltenham, UK and Northampton, MA, USA: Edward Elgar Publishing, pp. 140–152.

Geels, F. W., & Kemp, R. (2007). Dynamics in socio-technical systems: typology of change processes and contrasting case studies. *Technology in Society*, 29(4): 441–455.

Geels, F. W., & Schot, J. (2007). Typology of sociotechnical transition pathways. *Research Policy*, 36: 399–417.

Geels, F. (2005). Co-evolution of technology and society: the transition in water supply and personal hygiene in the Netherlands (1850–1930) – a case study in multi-level perspective. *Technology in Society*, 27(3): 363– 97.

Gilbert, N. (2013). A hard look at GM crops. *Nature*, 497: 24–26.

Graham, J. P., & Polizzotto, M. L. (2013). Pit latrines and their impacts on groundwater quality: a systematic review. *Environmental Health Perspectives*, 121(5): 521–530.

Grin, J., Felix, F., Bos, B., & Spoelstra, S. (2004). Practices for reflexive design: lessons from a Dutch programme on sustainable agriculture. *International Journal of Foresight and Innovation Policy*, 1(1–2): 126–149.

Grin, J., Rotmans, J., & Schot, J. (eds) (2010). *Transitions to Sustainable Development: New Directions in the Study of Long Term Transformative Change*. New York: Routledge.

Guiteras, R., Levinsohn, J., & Mobarak, A. M. (2015). Encouraging sanitation investment in the developing world: a cluster-randomized trial. *Science*, 348(6237): 903–906.

Hadi, A. (2000). A participatory approach to sanitation: experience of Bangladeshi NGOs. *Health Policy and Planning*, 15(3): 332–337.

Hoppe, R. (2011). *The Governance of Problems: Puzzling, Powering, Participation*. Bristol: Policy Press.

Irwin, T. (2015). Transition design: a proposal for a new area of design practice, study, and research. *Design and Culture*, 7(2): 229–246.

Jayaraman, K. S. (2002). India approves GM cotton. *Nature Biotechnology*, 20: 415.

Kanaujia, A., & Bhattacharya, S. (2017). The genetically modified (GM) crop debate in India: a critical introspection. Paper for 15th Globalics Conference. Athens, Greece, 9–11 October.

Kar, K., & Chambers, R. (2008). *Handbook on Community-Led Total Sanitation*. Brighton: Institute of Development Studies (IDS).

Khanna, T., & Das, M. (2016). Why gender matters in the solution towards safe sanitation? Reflections from rural India. *Global Public Health*, 11(10): 1185–1201.

Kemp, R. (1994). Technology and the transition to environmental sustainability. *Futures*, 26: 1023–1046.

Kemp, R., & van Lente, H. (2011). The dual challenge of sustainability transitions. *Environmental Innovation and Societal Transitions*, 1(1): 121–124.

Kemp, R., & Never, B. (2016). Green transition, industrial policy, and economic development. *Oxford Review of Economic Policy*, 33(1): 66–84. https://doi.org/10.1093/oxrep/grw037.

Lachman, D. A. (2012). A survey and review of approaches to study transitions. *Energy Policy*, 58: 269–276.

Larson, D., Jones, E., & Pannu, R. R. S. (2004). Instability in Indian agriculture: a challenge to the green revolution technology. *Food Policy*, 29: 257–273.

Leeuwis, C., & Pyburn, R. (eds) (2002). *Wheelbarrows Full Of Frogs: Social Learning In Rural Resource Management*. Assen: Van Gorcum.

Loorbach, D., Frantzeskaki, N., & Avelino, F. (2017). Sustainability transitions research: transforming science and practice for societal change. *Annual Review of Environmental Resources*, 42: 599–626.

Lorek, S., & Spangenberg, J. H. (2014). Sustainable consumption within a sustainable economy: beyond green growth and green economies. *Journal of Cleaner Production*, 63: 33–44.

Markard, J., Raven, R., & Truffer, B. (2012). Sustainability transitions: an emerging field of research and its prospects. *Research Policy*, 41(6): 955–967.

Martin, B. R., Nightingale, P., & Yegros-Yegros, A. (2012). Science and technology studies: exploring the knowledge base. *Research Policy*, 41(7): 1182–1204.

Milliman, S. R., & Prince, R. (1989). Firm incentives to promote technical change in pollution control. *Journal of Environmental Economics and Management*, 17: 247–265.

Morse, S., Bennett, R., & Ismael, Y. (2005). Comparing the performance of official and unofficial genetically modified cotton in India. *AgBioForum*, 8(1): 1–6.

Murgai, R., Ali, M., & Byerlee, D. (2001). Productivity growth and sustainability in post-green revolution agriculture: the case of the Indian and Pakistan Punjabs. *World Bank Research Observer*, 16(2): 199–218.

Murray, R., Caulier-Grice, J., & Mulgan, G. (2010). *The Open Book of Social Innovation: Ways to Design, Develop and Grow Social Innovation*. London: National Endowment for Science, Technology and the Arts (NESTA).

Mytelka, L., Aguayo, F., Boyle, G., Breukers, S., de Scheemaker, G., Abdel Gelil, I., Kemp, R., Monkelbaan, J., Rossini, C., Watson, J., & Wolson, R. (2012). Policies for capacity development, in T. B. Johansson, A. Patwardhan, N. Nakicenovic & L. Gomez-Echeverri (eds), *Global Energy Assessment: Toward a Sustainable Future*. Cambridge: Cambridge University Press, pp. 1745–1802. doi:10.1017/CBO9780511793677.031.

National Research Council (1999). *Our Common Journey: A Transition toward Sustainability*. Washington, DC: National Academy Press.

Ndlovu, E., & Bhala, E. (2016). Menstrual hygiene – a salient hazard in rural schools: a case of Masvingo district of Zimbabwe. *Jàmbá: Journal of Disaster Risk Studies*, 8(2): 1–8.

Nordhaus, W. D. (1994). *Managing the Global Commons: The Economics of Climate Change*. Cambridge, MA: MIT Press.

Oates, W. E., & Portney, P. R. (2003). The political economy of environmental policy, in K. G. Mäler & J. R. Vincent (eds), *Handbook of Environmental Economics*, vol. 1. Amsterdam: Elsevier, pp. 325–354.

Pavlova, Y., & de Zeeuw, A. (2012). Asymmetries in international environmental agreements. *Environment and Development Economics*, 18: 51–68.

Press, M., & Cooper, R. (2003). *The Design Experience: The Role of Design and Designers in the Twenty-First Century*. Aldershot: Ashgate.

Pujari, P. R., Padmakar, C., Labhasetwar, P. K., Mahore, P., & Ganguly, A. (2012). Assessment of the impact of on-site sanitation systems on groundwater pollution in two diverse geological settings: a case study from India. *Environmental Monitoring and Assessment*, 184(1): 251–263.

Raghuram, N. (2002). India joins the GM club. *Trends in Plant Science*, 7(7): 322–323.

Ramani, S. V. (2017). Would the Mahatma approve? On nudging vs. lynching (to use toilets) in India. UNU-MERIT, 2 October. https://www.merit.unu.edu/would-the-mahatma-approve-on-nudging-vs-lynching-to-use-toilets-in-india.

Ramani, S. V. (2019). On consortium driven sanitation interventions to end open defecation: insights from an Indian village study. *Innovation and Development*, 1–17. https://doi.org/10.1080/2157930X.2019.1580934.

Ramani, S. V., & SadreGhazi, S. (2014). Where is the toilet please? The sanitation sectoral innovation system in Rural India, in S. V. Ramani (ed.), *Innovation in India*. New Delhi: Cambridge University Press.

Ramani, S. V., & Thutupalli, A. (2015). Emergence of controversy in technology transitions: green revolution and Bt cotton in India. *Technological Forecasting and Social Change*, 100: 198–212.

Ramani, S. V., SadreGhazi, S., & Duysters, G. (2012). On the diffusion of toilets as bottom of the pyramid innovation: lessons from sanitation entrepreneurs. *Technological Forecasting and Social Change*, 79(4): 676–687.

Ramani, S. V., SadreGhazi, S., & Gupta, S. (2017). Catalysing innovation for social impact: the role of social enterprises in the Indian sanitation sector. *Technological Forecasting and Social Change*, 121: 216–227.

Ramani, S. V., Thutupalli, A., & Urias, E. (2017). High-value hi-tech product introduction in emerging countries: the role and construction of legitimacy. *Qualitative Market Research: An International Journal*, 20(2): 208–225.

Raskin, P., Banur, T., Gallopin, G., Gutman, P., & Hammond, A. (1999). *Great Transition: The Promise and Lure of the Times Ahead*. Boston, MA: Tellus Institute and Stockholm Environment Institute.

Rodrik, D. (2014). Green industrial policy. *Oxford Review of Economic Policy*, 30(3): 469–491.

Röling, N., & van de Fliert, E. (1994). Transforming extension for sustainable agriculture: the case of integrated pest management in Indonesia. *Agriculture and Human Values*, 11(2–3): 96–108.

Rotmans, J., Kemp, R., & van Asselt, M. (2001). More evolution than revolution: transition management in public policy. *Foresight*, 3(1): 15–31.

Sachs, J. D. (2012). From millennium development goals to sustainable development goals. *The Lancet*, 379: 2206–2211.

Schmandt, J., & Ward, C. H. (eds) (2000). *Sustainable DEVELOPMENT: The Challenge of Transition*. Cambridge: Cambridge University Press.

Seto, K. C., Davis, S. J., Mitchell, R. B., Stokes, E. C., Unruh, G., & Ürge-Vorsatz, D. (2016). Carbon lock-in: types, causes, and policy implications, *Annual Review of Environment and Resources*, 41(1): 425–452.

Smith, A., Voß, J.-P., & Grin, J. (2010). Innovation studies and sustainability transitions: the allure of the multi-level perspective and its challenges. *Research Policy*, 39(4): 435–448.

Steward, F. (2012). Transformative innovation policy to meet the challenge of climate change: socio-technical networks aligned with consumption and end-use as new transition arenas for a low-carbon society or green economy. *Technology Analysis and Strategic Management*, 24(4): 331–343.

Tang, D. (2018). Bill Gates puts up $400m for safer sanitation, *The Times*, 7 November. https://www.thetimes.co.uk/article/bill-gates-puts-up-400m-for-safer-sanitation-l7mm6kd8m.

UNHR (2011). Women and girls and their right to sanitation. https://www.ohchr.org/EN/NewsEvents/Pages/Womenandgirlsrighttosanitation.aspx.

Van de Fliert, E. & Braun, A. R. (2002). Conceptualizing integrative, farmer participatory research for sustainable agriculture: from opportunities to impact. *Agriculture and Human Values*, 19(1): 25–38.

Van den Bergh, J. C. J. M. (2001). Ecological economics: themes, approaches, and differences with environmental economics. *Regional Environmental Change*, 2: 13–23.

van Mierlo, B. C., Regeer, B., van Amstel, M., Arkesteijn, M. C. M., Beekman, V., Bunders, J. F. G., de Cock Buning, T., Elzen, B., Hoes, A. C., & Leeuwis, C. (2010). *Reflexive Monitoring in Action: A Guide for Monitoring System Innovation Projects*. Wageningen/Amsterdam: Communication and Innovation Studies, WUR/Athena Institute.

Voss, J.-P., Bauknecht, D., & Kemp, R. (eds) (2006). *Reflexive Governance for Sustainable Development*. Cheltenham, UK and Northampton, MA, USA: Edward Elgar Publishing.

Weaver, S. A. and Morris, M. C. (2005). Risks associated with genetic modification: an annotated bibliography of peer reviewed natural science publications. *Journal of Agricultural and Environmental Ethics*, 18(2): 157–189.

Weitzman, M. (1974). Prices versus quantities. *Review of Economic Studies*, 41: 477–491.

14 Optimizing the reversal of life: a coevolutionary response

Jalel Sager and Richard B. Norgaard

14.1 Background

We are on a great ship now in Arctic waters, still heading north ever faster. A few smaller icebergs have been struck and the damaged portions of the ship have been sealed off. The ship's officers intermittently announce over the public address system that changing course would threaten the ship's great voyage, maybe even damage the fine engines. Few of us grasp many details of the great voyage, why we must continually accelerate, or the engines that power us, but our belief in them holds strong. The ship, of grand and robust construction, is powered by fossil fuels. And, without power, the great voyage would end. The grand ship cannot simply transform into multiple sailboats. And so, the voyage continues on with most passengers, save those in steerage lost in the damaged portions, still little affected, and the rich still thoroughly enjoying the cruise. The menace of ice grows. The lives of those in steerage are further threatened by the breakdown of the ship's ventilation and water purification systems. Yet the ship continues onward with pianists still playing in multiple ballrooms.

We, even some traveling in steerage, believe in the mythology of the great voyage, the magnanimity of the ship, and the necessity of fossil fuels. The ship has carried us through many seas and rough waters, outlasting ships of Soviet design. We know the power of its great engines. The power of the ship assures our voyage and our beliefs in destiny. Other complex societies have collapsed, as Joseph Tainter (1988) has so well documented, yet dire facts do not get through our consciousness of perpetual progress in the great accelerating voyage to somewhere.

In the last few decades, passenger-scientists have come to grasp the larger significance of how fossil fuels came to be and their use to power the ship. The great voyage relies on consuming the fossil biomass from the earlier plant life that put the right amount of oxygen in Earth's atmosphere while setting Earth's thermostat to an appropriate level. Burning fossil fuels is reversing the very processes that made lives of diverse species we know, including humans, possible. We have many explanations for why, in the face of potential catastrophe, modern society has been in denial (Norgaard 2011). Geological scientists are debating diligently over whether the Anthropocene is an actual geologic era. Economists dither boldly over whether carbon taxes or cap and trade are best. Either way, economists have been optimizing the reversal of life against supposed benefits of the great voyage. They use values derived from market behavior generated along the delusional voyage to date. Questioning the purpose and destination of the great voyage, and calling for reversing it and valuing the miracle of life, has only been a position of a few so-called pessimists. Optimists implicitly deny the larger science of Earth's history. In this closing chapter we present a coevolutionary framing, complemented by the importance of public economistic beliefs we call economism, to elaborate humanity's predicament.[1] Though not optimistic, we write and carry on life because we are hopeful.[2]

14.2   Framing reality

Over the next half century, global society faces a significant probability of economic breakdown, human suffering, and the loss of a supportive environment due to climate change (IPCC 2018, Weitzman 2009).

The coevolutionary framework (Norgaard 1994) highlights the "mechanical" feedbacks and the coevolutionary processes of selection among the components of values, knowledge, technology, social organization, and the environment. Each component is affecting each of the other components, yet all are tightly interlocked. In this framework there are no clear divides between nature and society, between knowledge and values, or between technology and social organization. Coevolutionary systems change, but there are no guideposts other than the maintenance of diversity in each component to assure ongoing coevolution, to determine progress. We augment the coevolutionary framework specifically with a fossil fuel component to highlight the climate crisis.

We also work with the idea of "economism." A few scholars have used this term to emphasize how the dominance of economic thinking as part of modernity's knowledge system has brought about today's social and environmental crises. As economic thinking became clustered around neoliberalism, the dominance of assumptions about individualism, materialism, and perfectly informed actors has had consequences (Kwak 2016). Our economism includes these concerns while emphasizing the need of the public to hold beliefs that sustain the system (Knight 1932, 448–49). The current economic system was constructed around publicly held economistic beliefs in the efficacy and ethics of markets, the importance of individualism and material consumption, as well as the belief that progress, indeed modern salvation, comes through GDP growth. Much like money is fundamentally a belief system, it is necessary for the public to hold economistic beliefs to maintain and promote the economy we have (Goodchild 2009). The susceptibility of the

---

1 This chapter previews some of the key themes of a book Norgaard is writing on American economism and draws on Norgaard et al. (2016), Norgaard (2019), and Goddard et al. (2019).

2 Jalel Sager became a first-time father during the process of writing this chapter.

public to these beliefs allows economists to continue espousing their logic with its limited form and assumptions for policy decisions. Indeed, due to their coevolution through time, economic reality increasingly reflects economism. The beliefs keep the ship on course in the great voyage to somewhere. Economism is fundamentally religious; it has replaced earlier Christian beliefs (Lehmann 2016) and it became syncretic with Protestantism to form prosperity gospel, the largest expansion of followers in the history of Christendom (Cox 1995 and 2016).

We provide the following: 1) a stylized diagram of mutually interacting major elements of society and the "environment" or natural world, duly respecting all the complications that phrase entails; and 2) a narrative about how fossil-fuel-driven late capitalism is very much informed not only by the interaction between technology and resources, but also by mutual influence between fossil fuel exploitation and the very structure of our society and nature of our value systems (Malm 2016). Fossil technologies and their nuclear cousins also afford great economic and military power, key factors in global politics and economics too. These organizational forms and values have, in turn, progressively left much of the world, and especially the United States, following something like a religion of markets.

Our essential point is that global society cannot continue to have the organizational and technological structures, continue along its course, and have the same supporting economism that we currently have without also consuming fossil fuels. We would not hold the values we do today without our technology and organizational structures that coevolved around fossil fuels. Yet, likewise, we would not have the fossil technology and organizational structures we have without the supporting beliefs that have coevolved with and maintained them until now. Figure 14.1 highlights how key interrelationships have coevolved into a tightly interlocked system. This is why it is so very hard for us to transition to a non-fossil future. Coevolution explains how the system has coevolved to be dependent on energetically dense chemical compounds accumulated through past life.

An obvious example of coevolutionary interlock is the focus on maintaining cars as part of a non-fossil future. Our attachment to cars springs not only from their convenience in getting us around, but also very much through how fossil fuels and cars have shaped our economic geography (areal social organization) to our values of individual freedom and the mythology of the "open road." Simply substituting a bus for a car, perhaps a good societal choice, ignores the larger context of the technology—its mutual selection with other key technologies and features of economy and society, including evolved senses of need (values). But we have also become accustomed to strawberries from California, asparagus from Peru, or tulips from the Netherlands. How we value things has coevolved with comparative advantages in a globalized economy. Pulling on one string reveals a net of relationships. These relationships are lines of selection, importantly, and in societies that are based on cars or fossil fuels will select against substitutions that do not fit political (organizational) or cultural (values) choices. Those who propose climate solutions will be more effective if their solutions recognize and work with this.

Going beyond our personal interdependence with automobiles, global politics and national defense are also interconnected with fossil fuels. The ability to project and the need to project national power are tightly interconnected with fossil-based energy and a growing economy. The transition to renewable energy equates to a unilateral reduction in power, something most world leaders are not willing to risk. In an unstable world—where security is not a given or where rival factions compete for supremacy and domination, with threats of invasion and energy expropriation looming—the need for protection, or at least a sense of protection, presents a true problem for climate change mitigation and adaptation. While the US government may produce a serious report occasionally on the national security threats posed by a warming world, the daily sense of urgency seems to be still focused on the large, energy-intensive, and technologically advanced rivals for global superpower status—the United States, China, Europe, and Russia—and their proxy battles being fought around the world.

And yet coevolution is also about change. This gives us hope. Yes, coevolution explains tight interlock; but it also explains a process of change. Furthermore, in ecological systems change sometimes occurs rapidly (Gould 1988). Interlock and change are oppositional in mechanistic frameworks, each blocking the other. But they are integral to a coevolutionary framework. Moreover, in ecology, a viable ecosystem, albeit initially less complex, re-emerges after rapid change. Some species exit the ecosystem, perhaps to become extinct. This would be comparable to particular current aspects of technology, social organization, values, and knowledge being lost, at least on a global scale. As we transition out of fossil fuels, hopefully rapidly but not too disastrously, some aspects of social organization, technologies, knowledge, and values that coevolved with fossil fuels will collapse, and new aspects of these components will emerge and become more important as in ecological systems. Coevolutionary foresight—acknowledging and working with coevolution-

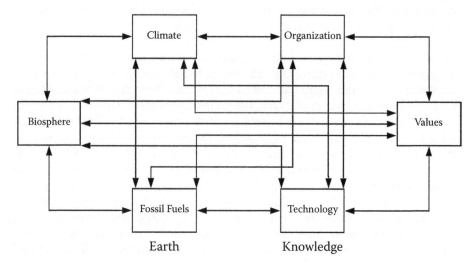

Figure 14.1 Coevolution between society and the environment

ary processes—may help smooth the processes of loss and re-emergence and help make them more equitable.

The multiple feedbacks illustrated in this representation in Figure 14.1 suggest why effective actions to mitigate and adapt to climate change have been so slow in being implemented. Effective changes must be aimed at the full range of feedbacks supporting fossil fuel use. Coal first, then oil and natural gas have interacted over several centuries with human technology in such a significant manner that the interactions between natural resources and technologies are likely the most salient driver of the human story. But all the feedbacks in Figure 14.1 are important. Cheap power and thereby transportation and industry, including the industrialization of agriculture, have facilitated the global expansion of capitalism as well as opening up wholly new markets. Information processing and communication technologies have also expanded and opened up markets, facilitated the management of larger and larger corporate bureaucracies, while also opening up global communication channels that facilitate nongovernmental organizations (NGOs), and through them weak global corporate accountability. Replacing the fossil fuel economy will entail restructuring a multitude of interacting elements.[3]

Looking at Figure 14.1 as merely mechanical interconnections, a massive substitution of renewable energy sources is a difficult proposition, not only from an energetic point of view but also because it threatens the role fossil energy has played as a major driver of the system and corporate and economic growth. The philosophy of laissez-faire capitalism, the animating spirit of economism, has become the strongest prophylactic against taking major climate action. Even getting "the price right" so the "market can work" involves such a host of government interventions and system interactions—enforcing political action on the part of governments, market creation on the part of financial authorities, tax or quota-setting on the part of economists—so as to make the exercise somewhat absurd, let alone ineffective. Yet our faith in markets and mechanistic understanding of the system demands that this is how we reduce carbon, by arguing over its proper price and the price of the biosphere as well, until, perhaps, Chicago reaches 100°F in February. Viewing Figure 14.1 as a representation of coevolutionary processes, we see that it looks more susceptible to change.

To date, most of us have warring intuitions: on one hand, we sense that global changes severely threaten the biosphere and endanger the continuity of human life; and, on the other, we have faith that the existing system will find a solution, perhaps a simple technological silver bullet, soon enough on its own. The vast majority of us, certainly those who do not directly work with nature, have been separated from many of the impacts of climate change. Somewhere else there may have been flooding, or drought, or fire; yes, ice sheets are melting, but these have been simply news events, albeit disturbing. We expressed surprise at especially strong rainfalls,

---

3 This is the coevolutionary analog to the old Einstein quote, that "problems cannot be solved on the level of thinking in which they were created."

powerful hurricanes, or heatwaves—but it did not last. Yet this is changing. Sea level rise, eroding coastlines, floods, droughts, and the rapid increase in wildfires and other extreme events are affecting rich and poor alike. In the American West, from where we write, electrical grid systems are being shut down to prevent fires. The future is now.

Disparities in income and wealth have become a very important feature of late capitalism. The ownership and control of fossil resources, of course, tends to be concentrated among the rich. Social power tends to be concentrated among those who consume the most. Powerful social-economic coalitions with large claims on fossil resources also tend to be among the most militarily strong groups, both within and between nations.

The world is currently organized around both economic globalization and competing national units with rival military forces. There is an emergent layer of world governance struggling to be born—with elements such as the United Nations and the International Court of Justice, the laws of international waters, and so on—which has not reached the point of creating an enforceable global peace. In fact, our greatest, most enforced global superstructure of laws likely remains the global trade system. All of these elements are under strain from neo-nationalist forces that wish to reaffirm the strength of the national level of organization reached by global society and undermine the emergent international level.

Meanwhile, it is the interaction of the fossil fuel technology elements with the organizational structure that has laid the groundwork for this new, contested layer of organization. From an energetic, structuralist point of view, declining energy productivity and resources would likely weaken the international level of organization—slowing trade, transport, development of new markets, etc. Put more concretely, if it was coal that allowed the British to create a globe-spanning empire, and the control of oil that allowed the emergence of the US-led international order from 1945, it is not clear what resource will drive the next level of integration, given the stumbles and perils of nuclear energy. There is some recent evidence of the dissolution of the latter order.

14.3   Possible directions

Here we are left with the overarching question of what, then, can and should be done. How can our economy and its supporting economism be reformed? What would a modern Martin Luther nail to the church door? How would he even find the door of a church given the dispersion of economic dogma in academic departments, reserve banks, and think-tanks? How can "economism" become "biospherism" or something of the like?

We might posit that destruction or disruption of our global system of organization is not desirable to the majority of the world's people. Yet we need to accept that the organizations and values we built on the back of a fossil expansion may not be up to the task of solving our climate problems. They were built for sustaining growth and managing rivalries in the global system—yet they are also the best infrastructure we have for solving the climate problem as a planet rather than a devolving set of regions and states.

Some of the central tenets of economism must be challenged—for example that gross inequality is merely a regrettable by-product of the system and not a threat to global stability. Change will be smoother if we face the essential institutions within our social organization, constructed around economistic beliefs, that cleave between those who live luxuriously and those in poverty. Acknowledging the differences in opportunities by class is essential for realistic, and thereby effective, solutions. From the divergence of political economy into economics in the early twentieth century, power and class have been hidden behind a wall of partial equilibrium marginal formalism in the most important temples of the discipline. The reformation is underway, with researchers such as Thomas Piketty and Emmanuel Saez and others, along with the winners of the 2019 Bank of Sweden Prize in Economic Sciences in Memory of Alfred Nobel (the Nobel Prize): Abhijit Banerjee, Esther Duflo, and Michael Kremer for their efforts to put complex empirical evidence before simple dogma. But there is still much bridging to do. Our earlier and still underlying values have been under assault by economism—from what is admittedly and proudly a "value-free" environment, where once stood the discipline of moral philosophy—and it will take much work and clear thought, also bravery, to reclaim them.

This problem of an economism inappropriate to reality, along with the energy issue, is the most vexing. Both energy and economic distribution invoke the gods that provide and protect. They force many people to give up, voluntarily, a measure of protection or provision. It is difficult to get around this fact—as it is to get around the fact that for most people, especially the most powerful, the planet's life and climate are abstract and only tangential to daily urban life. Finally, we have to give some thought to the idea that our philosophies, our -isms, often lag behind our "is"—they change after our fundamental material realities and relationships.

Assuming this is true, and that we as individuals all have to put one shoulder to the wheel, that society does in fact respond to many individuals acting in concert; assuming this is all true, an extension of the coevolution model suggests we have to move on three fronts at once to help society adjust to climate change and internal social strain:

1. We must focus scientific and technical advance on changing the dominant Resources–Technology–Organization interaction;
2. We must work in the Values arena on the all-important ideologies of economism—begin separating people from its more pernicious dogma via modern communications methods (long philosophical books seem to have less hold these days); and

3.   We must expose by whatever means necessary the Climate and Life aspects of the Biosphere side of the equation to the public—visibility does not mean simply telling everyone that everything is dying. We do not yet have good methods for creating deep connections between urbanites and the Climate–Life world besides natural television or expensive vacations; we need mass cultural events of a different scope and power.

It has happened before, in the lives of societies, that old beliefs, after much death and destruction, have been traded for new ones more suited to the times. No matter what, humans in aggregate require security that they will be provided for and protected. Any movement that does not satisfy these needs will be selected against, sooner or later. To persist as a global society we must reunite this sense of security with values that sanctify the gracious gifts of the natural world, and the moral gifts we have received as a species.

References

Cox, Harvey. 1995. *Fire from Heaven: The Rise of Pentecostal Spirituality and the Reshaping of Religion in the Twenty-First Century*. Addison-Wesley. Reading, MA.

Cox, Harvey. 2016. *The Market as God*. Harvard University Press. Cambridge, MA.

Goddard, Jessica J., Giorgos Kallis, and Richard B. Norgaard. 2019. Keeping Multiple Antennae Up: Coevolutionary Foundations for Methodological Pluralism. *Ecological Economics* **165**: 1–9.

Goodchild, Philip. 2009. *Theology of Money*. Duke University Press. Durham, NC.

Gould, Stephen Jay. 1988. *Time's Arrow, Time's Cycles: Myth and Metaphor in the Discovery of Geological Time*. Harvard University Press. Cambridge, MA.

Intergovernmental Panel on Climate Change. 2018. *Global Warming of 1.5°C: A Special Report*. https://www.ipcc.ch/sr15/

Knight, F. H. 1932. The Newer Economics and the Control of Economic Activity. *Journal of Political Economy* **40**(4): 433–476.

Kwak, James. 2016. *Economism: Bad Economics and the Rise of Inequality*. Pantheon. New York.

Lehmann, Chris. 2016. *The Money Cult: Capitalism, Christianity, and the Unmaking of the American Dream*. Melvin House. New York.

Malm, Andreas. 2016. *Fossil Capital: The Rise of Steam Power and the Roots of Global Warming*. Verso. London.

Norgaard, Kari M. 2011. Climate Denial: Emotions, Psychology, Culture, and Political Economy. In John S. Dryzek, Richard B. Norgaard, and David Schlosberg (eds). *The Oxford Handbook of Climate Change and Society*. Oxford University Press. Oxford.

Norgaard, Richard B. 1994. *Development Betrayed: The End of Progress and a Coevolutionary Revisioning of the Future*. Routledge. London.

Norgaard, Richard. B. 2019. Economism and the Econocene: A Coevolutionary Interpretation. *Real-World Economics Review* **87**: 114–131.

Norgaard, Richard B., Jessica J. Goddard, and Jalel Sager. 2016. Economics, Economism, and Ecological Crisis. In Mary Evelyn Tucker, John Grim, and Willis Jenkins (eds). *The Routledge Handbook on Religion and Ecology*. Routledge. London (pp. 402–411).

Tainter, Joseph A. 1988. *The Collapse of Complex Societies*. Cambridge University Press. Cambridge.

Weitzman, Martin. 2009. On Modelling and Interpreting the Economics of Catastrophic Climate Change. *Review of Economics and Statistics* **91**(1): 1–19.

Index